PLATO'S *REPUBLIC*

PLATO'S *REPUBLIC*

A Dialogue in 16 Chapters

ALAIN BADIOU

Translated by Susan Spitzer and
Introduction by Kenneth Reinhard

Columbia University Press
New York

Columbia University Press
Publishers Since 1893
New York   Chichester, West Sussex
cup.columbia.edu
First published in French as *La République de Platon* © Librairie Arthème Fayard, 2012
This translation copyright © Polity Press 2012

Library of Congress Cataloging-in-Publication Data
Badiou, Alain.
    [République de Platon. English]
Plato's Republic : a dialogue in 16 chapters / Alain Badiou ; translated by Susan Spitzer ;
introduction by Kenneth Reinhard.
        p.   cm.
Includes bibiographical references and index.
ISBN 978-0-231-16016-2 (cloth : alk paper) — ISBN 978-0-231-50065-4 (ebook)
1.   Plato. Republic. I.   Title.

JC71.P6B2813   2012
321'.07—dc23
                                                                    2012014207

Printed and bound in Great Britain by the MPG Books Group

∞ Columbia University Press books are printed in permanent and durable acid-free
paper.

c 10 9 8 7 6 5 4 3 2 1

CONTENTS

The numbers and letters in parentheses after each chapter title (e.g. 327a) refer to a division of the text into sections, each usually about ten lines long. Although this division owes its existence solely to ancient methods of editing and paginating manuscripts, it has become the traditional one, enabling readers to find their place not only in the Greek text but also in the available translations, which include such indications in the text – something I have not done.

CONTENTS

INTRODUCTION

Badiou's Sublime Translation of the *Republic*

Kenneth Reinhard

Alain Badiou stands, virtually alone among major philosophers at the beginning of the twenty-first century, as a self-proclaimed Platonist, the champion of what he calls a "Platonism of the multiple."[1] In an intellectual genealogy that few contemporary thinkers would share, there are, for Badiou, "only three crucial philosophers": Descartes, Hegel, and above all, Plato.[2] In a 1994 interview, Badiou describes his privileging of Plato as a kind of "coquetry," but he insists it is a *serious* coquetry.[3] There is no doubt something contrarian in flirting with Platonism today, when modern philosophy and critical theory have generally agreed in denouncing it as idealism, essentialism, logocentrism, or even proto-fascism; but Badiou's relationship with Plato is more love affair than idle dalliance – provocative, perhaps, but also a passionate attachment whose implications for his thinking continue to unfold. As in the legend of the gateway to Plato's Academy, which was reputed to bear the warning "let no one ignorant of geometry enter," the approach to Badiou's thinking requires a rigorous and transformative engagement with Plato's mathematical imperative, the only mast strong enough to resist the siren call of sophistry. Plato is, for Badiou, the first philosopher *tout court* precisely insofar as he is the first to establish philosophy's ontological foundation in mathematics, on the one hand, and its necessarily antagonistic relationship with sophistry, on the other. Moreover, it is from Plato that Badiou derives his articulation of truth into four fields or sets of "procedures," which are distinct from philosophy but are its conditions: science, politics, art, and love.[4]

For Badiou, Plato is the first warrior in the eternal battle of philosophy against sophistry, of truth against opinion, and the progenitor of the living idea of communism. If, as Badiou argues, sophistry is "a system that creates a dissymmetry of power through the general equivalence of opinions," we might say that philosophy uses the dissymmetry of opinions and truths to create a general equivalence or availability of power.[5] There is no place for truth in sophistic debates, where it will inevitably be suspected of authoritarianism. Truth cannot be produced through the exchange of opinions, and in the *Republic* the arch-sophist Thrasymachus is not convinced by Socrates' arguments but merely "reduced to silence." Truth is already there, embodied in the subjective position represented by Socrates, and Plato's dialogues, above all the *Republic*, will explore and articulate its consequences.

An unorthodox reading of Plato has been central to Badiou's thinking, at least since his early book, *The Concept of Model*, which originated as a lecture in Althusser's seminar, just days before the great events in Paris of May 1968. Badiou's 1988 work, *Being and Event*, opens with a strongly unconventional reading of Plato's *Parmenides* as a theory of "inconsistent multiplicity," irreducible to the ontology of the One and the Many, an argument he expands in "The Question of Being Today," published in the 1998 *Briefings on Existence*. Badiou's 1989–90 seminar on Plato's *Republic* examines the relationship between the philosophical concept of Truth and the four truth procedures; and Badiou comments extensively on Plato and mathematical "Platonism" in numerous essays throughout the '90s.[6] Plato is a recurrent touchstone in Badiou's 2006 *Logics of Worlds*; and its 2009 companion, *Second Manifesto for Philosophy*, culminates with a chapter on the "Platonic Idea." In recent years Badiou has devoted three major interconnected projects to Plato: the three years of seminars (2007–2010) entitled "For Today – Plato!"[7]; a forthcoming screenplay on *The Life of Plato*; and the translation – or, as he calls it at times, "hypertranslation" – into French of Plato's *Republic* – translated here into living American English by Susan Spitzer.

If a certain critique of Plato begins already with Aristotle, the twentieth century was pervasively anti-Platonic. Many otherwise disparate schools of thought agree in their rejection of what they call "Platonism." In the opening session of his 2007 seminar on Plato (as well as in numerous essays and talks), Badiou describes six major forms of modern anti-Platonism:

1 the vitalist anti-Platonism of Nietzsche, Bergson, and Deleuze, who see Plato as the theorist of an unchanging ideal realm of perfect being, hostile to the living reality of becoming. Plato,

according to Nietzsche (perhaps the most pre-eminent among modern anti-Platonists), is the first "priest," the first to turn life against itself, and thus one source of the metaphysical "disease" of which we must still be cured;

2 the analytic anti-Platonism of Russell, the later Wittgenstein, and Carnap, who associate Plato with the belief in supersensible mathematical objects;

3 Marxist anti-Platonism, for which Plato is the origin of the notorious sensible/intelligible opposition, hence the source of idealism and the beginning of the history of ideology. Badiou frequently refers to this mode of anti-Platonism by citing the dictionary of philosophy commissioned by Stalin, where Plato is defined as "ideologue of the slave owners";

4 the existentialist anti-Platonism of Kierkegaard and Sartre, who see Plato as subordinating the singularity of existence and the creative negativity of non-being to eternal essences and to the stasis of being;

5 Heideggerian anti-Platonism, according to which Plato obscures Being itself (and thus the ontological difference between Being and beings) by submitting it to the representational idea. For Heidegger, Plato flattens the originary Greek account of truth as *aletheia*, "unconcealing," into one of knowledge as correspondence;

6 the anti-Platonism of political philosophy, which regards Plato's politics as "totalitarian," as closing off the free circulation of opinions in order to assert a rigid politics, which tolerates no dissent. Exemplary here is Karl Popper's attack on Plato in *The Open Society and Its Enemies*, but Badiou also includes the more "noble" example of Hannah Arendt.

Badiou argues that each of these anti-Platonisms accuses Plato of ignoring a key element that they consider to be the very kernel of the real: for the vitalists, "becoming"; for analytic philosophy, "language"; for Marxists, "concrete social relations"; for the existentialists, "negativity"; for the Heideggerians, "thinking" as distinct from mere "knowledge"; and for political philosophy, "democracy" itself. But these objections to Plato are inconsistent with each other and do not add up to a coherent attack or to a counter-position beyond their shared anti-Platonism. The two notable exceptions to this general agreement that Plato fails to address the real, both emerging from the Maoism of the sixties, are what Badiou calls the "mystical Platonism" of Guy Lardreau and Christian Jambet and Badiou's own mathematical Platonism. Mathematical Platonism, according to Badiou, is a subjective construction that begins with the thesis that there is something incommensurable about all existing measures, something similar to the irrational relation between a diagonal and the sides of a square. But, unlike the exponents of mystical Platonism, Badiou insists that it is incumbent on us to *determine* this non-relation, to construct a new measure for the immeasurable; and in the extended work along this process, Plato will be our guide.

The fact that two out of Badiou's three current projects on Plato are themselves works of art indicates the special position Plato has among Badiou's primary influences or "masters": for him, Plato is the great philosopher of the Idea, of course, but he is also a powerful literary artist in his dialogues – and, according to legend, the author of several tragedies in his youth.[8] It has frequently been pointed out that, despite Plato's rather extreme criticisms of mimetic poetry and theater in the *Republic*, that work itself is clearly one of great poetic and dramatic art. Badiou's translation of the *Republic* emphasizes and enhances these literary qualities by refashioning Plato's sketchy interlocutors – for the most part bobble-headed yes-men who barely interrupt the relentless stream of Socratic discourse – into richly imagined characters, remarkably alive, complicated, and passionate.[9] Badiou's theatricalization of the *Republic* also involves the redistribution of comments from Socrates to his interlocutors, so that what in Plato is a series of statements in Badiou becomes more dialogic, more representative of conflicting desires. And, while Socrates and his young disciples discuss the most serious questions of truth, justice, and communism, the mood of their discourse shifts rapidly from excitement to boredom, from melancholia to elation, from hilarity to frustration, and from petty rivalry to earnest collaboration. It is as if the austere situation of a play by Beckett were inhabited by characters by Brecht. At one point in Badiou's translation Socrates remarks: "I had a calling to become a comic actor [. . .] but I preferred the theater of philosophy." Something similar could be said about Badiou, who began his career as a novelist and later became a playwright. Moreover, Badiou's literary works are often based on a certain kind of "translation." His six plays (two tragedies, *The Red Scarf* and *Incident at Antioch*, and the four *Ahmed* comedies) imitate dramas by Aristophanes, Molière, and Claudel, transposing elements of character and plot into novel situations and liberally sampling fragments and at times entire passages of text. Although Badiou's translation of the *Republic* is the most sustained presentation to date of his philosophical relationship with Plato, it should also be considered a central part of his literary or dramatic *oeuvre* – a sort of "Platonic

Variations" or "Incident at Piraeus." Some readers may be scandalized by the liberties Badiou takes in his translation: his systematic modifications of certain terms (e.g. "the gods" is translated as "the Other"), his occasional elimination of entire passages (e.g. Plato's notorious argument for euthanasia, or much of the discussion of the family), his pervasive anachronistic references (e.g. to AIDS, iPods, or Euros), and his frequent expansion of brief comments into lengthy discourses. Badiou's language (and Susan Spitzer's translation) is colloquial, colorful, and at times rather gritty: Socrates and his interlocutors speak like Europeans or Americans of today or of the recent past, and their cultural references are both classical and contemporary; they move easily between Homer and Pessoa, Heraclitus and Deleuze, Aeschylus and Pirandello.

It would clearly be a mistake to read Badiou's translation as if it were a scholarly edition, to be judged in terms established by the long history of translations of Plato. But it would be no less wrong to accuse Badiou of not having translated the *Republic* faithfully – or, at least, that would be to misunderstand Badiou's intention here, which is indeed, above all, fidelity to Plato. For Badiou, however, fidelity is not a matter of custodial conservation; nor is it the unattainable ideal of an inevitably corrupting process (*traduttore, traditore*). For Badiou, fidelity is the subjective disposition that results from the decision in the wake of an event to participate in the construction of a truth. To be faithful is to follow the consequences of such an event – the sudden emergence of a void or excess in a world that previously seemed complete – wherever they may lead. In this sense, Badiou's translation of the *Republic* is faithful to the event that "Plato" names – the origin of philosophy itself in its antagonism to sophistry and rivalry with poetry – more than it is to Plato's text as a historical document. It so happens that Badiou's translation is *also* largely faithful to the text of the *Republic*, with an ear closely attuned to Greek philology and form – but translational fidelity here is an act of *participation* rather than one of re-presentation or linguistic reinscription: Badiou's *Republic* participates in the ideas of Plato's *Republic* – above all, the idea of the "Idea" – and his fidelity to Plato's text is conditioned by his fidelity to Plato's ideas.

Etymologically, a "translation" is something that is carried or transposed from one language or locus to another; by calling this book, as he has done at times, a *hyper*translation, Badiou suggests that it goes above and beyond the usual assumptions about the work of translation, taking its text to what we might call a sublime – *hypselos* (ὑψηλός) – place of new topological proximities, unmappable according to the conventional metrics of history and geography. The hyper-space opened up by Badiou's translation is a realm of ideas, but it is no heavenly empyrean; Badiou's *Republic* is neither a philosophical purification nor a literary modernization of Plato in the sense of being an attempt to reduce historical distance for the sake of making an ancient text more familiar, a part of our world. On the contrary, Badiou's "hyper"translation *sublimates* Plato's text, in Lacan's sense of sublimation as "the elevation of an object to the status of a Thing," which is precisely to *de*-familiarize it, to bring out its strangeness – at least from the perspective of current opinion about Plato and Platonism.[10] In his 2010 seminar on Plato Badiou describes sublimation as a mode of subjective estrangement: "If he [the subject] may occasionally be a creator, it's not because he is adapted to the world in which he lives, but on the contrary because he is *not*, and because he has had to follow the paths of *sublimation*." In Freudian terms, received opinion about Plato's *Republic* corresponds to the adaptive inertia of the dialectic of the pleasure and reality princi-ples, which assures that our understanding follows paths we have previously traversed, and which yield moderate but reliable satisfac-tions – such as the clichés of "Platonism" that we take delight both in repeating and in denouncing. Many of our commonplaces about Plato and Platonism, according to Badiou, are confections propa-gated by Aristotle, by the so-called "Neoplatonic" philosophers, by Christianity, and by the various modes of modern "anti-Platonism" we have briefly discussed. Badiou's hypertranslation sublimates Plato out of that frequently gauzy history of ideas by dramatizing him as the philosopher who asks us to leave the cave of opinion, the comfort zone of "what most people think," and to participate in the collective construction of some truths from the new perspective that such an exit affords. In this sense, Badiou's hypertranslation lifts the *Republic* out of the cave of "Platonism" precisely through its fidelity to the Platonic idea, to that which, we might say, to continue our Lacanian terminology, is "in Plato more than Plato." At the very conclusion of his seminar of April 14, 2010, Badiou describes his translational fidelity to Plato in theatrical, indeed operatic terms: "at the end of Richard Wagner's *Die Walküre*, Brünnhilde, the disobedient daugh-ter, defends herself by arguing that her goal was merely to realize Wotan's initial intentions, and it ends with her being pardoned by Wotan. And similarly, I hope to be pardoned by Plato."

In his seminar of March 10, 2010, Badiou describes the four key operations or transformations that he employs in his translation of the *Republic*: formal restructuration, universalization, conceptual displacement, and contemporaneity. The conventional organization of the *Republic* into ten books is of course post-Platonic, and *formal restructuration* first of all involves a new division of Plato's text into sixteen chapters (plus Prologue and Epilogue) that reflect Badiou's account of their central concerns and distinctions. So, for example, his Chapters 6 and 7 on "Objective Justice" and "Subjective Justice" include what in conventional editions are the end of Book 3 and the whole of Book 4. This reorganization, however, is not merely for the sake of distinguishing the text's thematic elements, but it acts as a kind of *repunctuation* of the discourse, in the manner in which a Lacanian psychoanalyst might intervene in an analysand's discourse by adding or removing a comma or a period that transforms its meaning, or by unexpectedly cutting the session itself short, in order to draw attention to the sudden emergence of a new way of understanding its significance. Badiou's chapter break here, between chapters 6 and 7, asserts that subjective justice is not continuous with objective justice but distinct, an entirely different (and finally more pressing) matter. So, near the end of the anthropological discussion of objective justice in the state in Chapter 6, Socrates remarks that they "haven't made an iota of progress" toward the true meaning of justice; and the discussion of subjective justice (both individual and collective) in Chapter 7 opens with a suddenly urgent Socrates, "oddly on edge," pressing the interlocutors not to "waste any time" in their pursuit of the matter. If the discussion of subjective justice would seem to be the "theory" that should retroactively explain the earlier anthropological account, the chapter break before it resists such an implication, or at least it leaves it up to the reader to decide what kind of connection should be drawn between the two sections. And, as Badiou points out in his Plato seminar, this kind of restructuration emphasizes the *Republic*'s theatricality as a series of scenes that demand our active participation in the process of its unfolding.

Badiou describes the process of *universalization* by citing director Antoine Vitez's famous imperative "theater must be elitist for everyone." Whereas philosophy is apparently reserved for a select group of "guardians" of the state in the *Republic*, for Badiou this restriction is not essential to Plato's thinking, but merely a function of his historical situation and of his tendency to suture philosophical ideas to their political conditions. Indeed, the philosophical temperament is aristocratic, "exceptional," but Badiou insists that there is nothing to prevent it from being a *universal* exception, open in principle to all. The constant proponent of universalization in Badiou's translation, always pushing Socrates to extend his arguments to "all people without exception," is Amantha – Badiou's feminization of the character Adeimantus of Collytus, Plato's brother, and certainly his most conspicuous modification of Plato's text. Badiou also uses this technique of recasting a key male character as a woman in his play *The Incident at Antioch*, where the heroine, Paula, is in part a feminized version of Saint Paul. Amantha is an exceptionally vivid creation, one of the true delights of Badiou's text, and a character for whom Socrates (as well as Badiou) clearly has great love. To a certain extent, feminization is, for Badiou, a way of introducing what Hegel calls "the eternal irony of community" where it is missing; just as Paula questions the dialectics of state and revolution in *Incident*, so in Badiou's *Republic* Amantha has a much more critical role than Adeimantus has in Plato's. She frequently challenges Socrates, attacking any hint of sexism or other non-egalitarian views and questioning his reasoning when she thinks his arguments are unsound or inconsistent. She is a materialist, always quick to leap on Socrates when she suspects him of glossing over intellectual difficulties with evasive statements, or when her brother Glaucon has recourse to vague sociological, psychological, or anthropological categories. In Lacanian terms, we might say that Amantha is the hysteric to Socrates' master – and, just as every hysteric needs a master to criticize, so every master needs a hysteric to support his authority. But, despite the brilliance of Amantha's personality, the heat of her temper and the quickness of her thinking, Badiou does not use her merely to spice up the dialogue; nor does she represent just feminine "difference." In fact we could say that Amantha represents not so much the particular qualities of her gender as the *universality* of the *generic*: above all, she insists that Socrates remain true to the radical universalism and egalitarianism without exception of the communist idea, and for this reason her femininity is the mark of a refusal to mark differences.[11]

The translational process that Badiou calls *conceptual displacement* is meant to liberate Plato from the retroactive Aristotelian account of his so-called "dualisms." Against the common assumption that Plato draws a hard line between a realm of the "sensible" and a realm of the "intelligible," Badiou argued, already in his early book *The Concept of Model*, that Plato's account of "participation" implies that intelligible ideas are located *in* sensible things.[12] And in his recent seminar on Plato Badiou will argue for a similar displacement of the opposition between essence and existence, which is implied by the common rendering of *ousia* as "being" in translations of Plato and as "essence" in translations of Aristotle. So what does Plato mean by the word *ousia*? Badiou argues that we should understand it as Plato's version of the Parmenidean account of the indiscernibility of being and thinking: "*Ousia* designates that aspect of being which is identical to thinking [. . .] this point of indiscernibility between the particularity of the object and the universality of the thought of the object is exactly what Plato names the Idea." Hence Badiou will displace the concept of "essence" by translating *ousia* as "that which, of being, is exposed to thought."[13] Similarly, Badiou will displace the idea of "the Good" in Plato by translating the Greek τὸ ἀγαθόν ("the good") as "the truth," which would normally be the translation of the Greek τὸ ἀληθές. The displacement here is of the theological or moral sense that the modern concept of the Good brings with it: "Now the idea of the Good has no moral connotation. The idea of the Good involves thought's possibility of having an orientation, of having a *principle*. [. . .] The idea of the Good designates the orientation of thinking towards *ousia*." By shifting "the Good" to "the True," Badiou no doubt violates the letter of Plato's text, but he also thereby disengages the Good from the Neoplatonic and Christian opposition between good and evil in which it has long been mired, and thus he brings us closer to Plato's Idea.

Badiou's *contemporizations* of Plato in his translation are perhaps most conspicuous. But we should not understand the many references to elements of the contemporary world as an attempt to "modernize" Plato, to make him seem "relevant." The historical situation of Badiou's translation is intentionally vague: one moment Socrates might refer to Parmenides (whom he likes) or Aristotle (whom he dislikes) as contemporaries, and the next to Lacan or "old Hegel" as figures hovering in an indefinite past. Badiou's stated intention in his translation of the *Republic* is to remove it from the "discourse of the university," which has established Plato's text in its philological–historical context, but at the cost of embalming it as a relic of the past, to be studied and appreciated without living value. Paradoxically, such historicization tends to freeze the *Republic* in a certain atemporal moment, and Badiou's translation attempts, as he argues in his seminar of April 14, 2010, to *retemporalize* it, "to restore its true eternity, which is to be available for the present." This process of dislodging Plato from the confines of academia through translation also involves a certain degree of what Badiou calls "rectifying" Plato; it is not only modern philology that is constrained by its historicizing imperative, but Plato himself, who cannot fully exit from the cave of his particular situation. Indeed, in Badiou's translation, Socrates and his interlocutors criticize positions they regard as "vulgar Platonism," and Socrates even declares at one point: "taking advantage of the opportunity given me here by Badiou, I solemnly protest your brother Plato's interpretation of my thinking."

What for Plato was the struggle of philosophy and truth against sophistry and opinion is for Badiou the opposition of what he calls the "materialist dialectic" and "democratic materialism." What most people think today, as they more or less did in Plato's time, according to Badiou, is one version or another of democratic materialist ideology. In *Logics of Worlds*, Badiou describes democratic materialism as the belief that the world consists exclusively of "bodies," material entities, both animate and inanimate, and of "languages," the symbolic systems and cultural practices that structure bodies and organize their relationships in various contingent ways. If sophistry represents the cynical mode of democratic materialism, its more earnest (hence more ideologically dangerous) spokesman is Aristotle. Democratic materialism regards a human being as what we might call a *zoon doxastikon*, an "animal with opinions," essentially located in a body that is conditioned and inscribed by its exposure to various (inessential) linguistic systems and cultural practices. The coexistence of multiple symbolic systems is promoted by democratic materialism as an expression of its belief in their relative value and general equivalence; the only cultures that are not tolerated are those that are themselves deemed intolerant, because they regard their beliefs and practices as absolutely true or good. Democratic materialism rejects all transcendentalism and relegates spiritual and religious beliefs to the realm of local customs and practices, where they are honored – as long as they don't challenge the principle of universal equivalence or interfere with the free circulation of material goods and symbolic capital. Democratic materialism is deeply suspicious of uses of the word "truth" where it means anything other than logical consistency, representational correspondence, or scientific exactitude; any other sense of truth is dismissed as an attempt to dominate and hierarchize the fundamental equality of opinions. The implicit motto of democratic materialism is "live without any ideas; don't interrupt the circulation of opinions."

Kant famously combated dogmatic rationalism and its empiricist inversion by developing the "critical philosophy," in which knowledge of the world is always relative to a subject. The Kantian co-dependence of subject and object, however, itself became the new dogmatism that Quentin Meillassoux has called "correlationism" and that underlies the democratic materialism of today. The relativism that characterizes modern sophistry is based on the assumption that subject and object are contingently correlative, hence the most that any subject can claim is that something is true "in my experience" or "in my opinion."

It is Plato, according to Badiou, who first wages war against the democracy of opinions in classical Athens and insists that the only life worth living is one oriented by an idea and by our participation in a truth procedure. Hence Plato will be our guide for the critique of democratic materialism today and our inspiration for the "materialist dialectic" that Badiou will oppose to it. As a variety of materialism, the materialist dialectic agrees that there is nothing more than bodies and languages. Nevertheless, there are sometimes exceptions, bubbles of the earth, if you will, which fall out of the material relationships of bodies and languages and fundamentally transform them, allowing for the possibility of *truths*. Truths do not constitute some third type of thing, a spiritual or metaphysical entity, but are fully immanent to the world and composed of nothing more than bodies and languages. This does not mean, however, that truths are merely local, contingent, or transient. Truths are not part of the democracy of opinion concerning the essential animality of human life and the relativity of languages, and they cannot be adjudicated by the standards of representational correspondence, statistical probability, or majority rule. Truths, according to Badiou, are procedures that establish and expand new "generic sets" – groupings of elements not organized according to any shared objective predicates but merely by their subjective orientation around a common void. Human beings may collaborate in such "truth procedures," local experimental instantiations of universal, infinite, and eternal truths, and in so doing they participate in a subjectivity in excess of their corporeal and linguistic individuality.

Badiou describes three aspects of democratic materialist epistemology in his 2007–8 seminar on Plato: "analysis" (what are the structural conditions of the current situation?), "prediction" (in what direction will the current situation likely develop?), and "critique" (what are the contradictions underlying the current situation?). In contrast, the materialist dialectic argues that thought cannot be "analysis" of reality precisely because thinking, as participation in a truth procedure, is an *exception* to what is, an *interruption* of the laws and structures governing the possibilities of appearing in a particular world; ideas are neither descriptions of the world nor entities describable according to pre-existing conceptual categories. Moreover, thinking cannot be understood as "prediction" or as the calculation of probabilities, insofar as it is itself improbable and unpredictable, contingent on an "event" that cannot be foreseen and whose consequences cannot be merely extrapolated. Thinking involves chance, even luck, and demands risks that cannot be fully managed. Finally, thinking cannot be understood as "critique" insofar as it is not essentially negative (even if it involves negation) or dialectical (even if it makes use of dialectics), but positive, as the *affirmation* of a new possibility, previously unthought and for the most part still unthinkable according to the governing logic of the world. Critique may clear the ground for thinking, but it is only propaedeutic to thinking proper. According to Badiou, Plato's *Republic* is such an act of *thinking*: not simply analysis or critique of the existing Athenian democracy (although it implicitly includes both) or the utopian program for improving it, but thinking as the construction of an idea that, according to opinion, is inconceivable, or can only appear as "idealism." Thus, for Badiou, the *Republic* is an account of the production of a new *subjective disposition* that is based on the possibility of eternal and universal truths evidenced by mathematics and on the elaboration of the consequences of the decision to take up one or more of those truths.

But what does Badiou mean by truth? He clarifies this notion in his 2010 seminar on Plato, in terms of the Lacanian concepts of the real, the symbolic, and the imaginary. A truth is an infinite multiple (like all beings, according to Badiou); what distinguishes a truth from other infinite multiples, however, is its *genericity*, which means first of all that it is nearly indiscernible under the phenomenological structures of the particular world in which it occurs. According to the possibilities of description or predication available in that world, a truth does not exist. In this sense, a truth makes a "hole" in knowledge, since it is unrecognizable according to current categories of understanding. The *real* of a truth, Badiou argues, is the conjunction of its multiple generic being and its appearing in a world for a subject for whom that truth does indeed exist; hence we might say that the real of a truth is "anamorphic" in relation to what Heidegger calls the dominant "world picture," being only apparent through the radical reorientation provided by the subject's decision to be faithful to (that is, to pursue the possible consequences of) the trace left by an event. Moreover, the real of a truth is always "to come," insofar as that truth's generic being expands in unpredictable ways and its appearance in a world is only fragmentary, part of a subjective procedure that is always in process, as the "infinite promise" of truth. If the real of a truth is the sum of its being and appearing, the *symbolic* aspect of a truth is their *difference*: a truth is an exception to the rules of appearing, and as such "proves" those rules – that is, it demonstrates the normative operation of the existing symbolic order precisely by falling out of it, and at the same time it tests its limits by nevertheless appearing for the subject of that truth, who discerns the difference between its being and its appearing. Finally, there is an *imaginary* aspect of a truth – which is not to say "illusory" or unreal. The subject of a truth must evaluate the real of a truth in terms of its future perfect completion: how will the world appear once a truth procedure will have been followed to its end? The subject for whom a truth is both real and symbolic must *represent* (or imagine) the relationship between its fragmentary reality in the present and the symbolic system in which that truth will fully appear in the future. This "imaginary" function of a truth is its communicability, its possibility of being shared through something like a Kantian *sensus communis*: a truth is universal insofar as it excludes nobody on principle and potentially includes everybody, without exception.

Badiou demonstrates this tripartite structure of truth in the *Republic* in the relationship of myth, education, and collective life: the truth of Πολιτεία involves both symbolic *Bildung* and the "true lies" or imaginary constructions of utopian myth, so that the critique of the current situation can open the possibility of another world; but this education into the communist Idea depends on a transformation of the real – which, in the case of Plato just as today, involves the abolition of private property.

Yet, as Badiou points out in his seminar on Plato, "something is missing from Plato, and that's a doctrine of the event [. . .] what Plato lacks is a theory of opportunity, the favorable moment, a theory of chance" (January 23, 2008). But, although Plato does not have a fully developed theory of the event, Badiou finds suggestions of such a "chance" encounter at various points, and develops them. In a metaphor on education in Badiou's Chapter 10, Plato presents a sort of "parable of the sower," in which the fate of the seed depends upon the ground in which it is sown: with proper education, the universal philosophical temperament will thrive and grow; but, when this temperament is corrupted by the sophistry of politicians or by the media under the protection of the so-called "freedom of opinion," the good become not merely less good, but fully bad, active supporters of the general confusion. In Allan Bloom's translation of Plato, Socrates suggests that avoiding such an outcome is difficult, rare, and depends on something like divine intervention:

> if the nature we set down for the philosopher chances on a suitable course of learning, it will necessarily grow and come to every kind of

virtue; but if it isn't sown, planted, and nourished in what's suitable, it will come to all the opposite, unless one of the gods chances to assist it.[14]

If Plato might seem to be saying something along the lines of Heidegger's famous remark that "[p]hilosophy will not be able to bring about a direct change of the present state of the world [. . .] Only a god can still save us,"[15] Badiou understands the intervention of Plato's "gods" here quite differently.[16]

In Badiou's version, Amantha, in a flattering mood, replies to Socrates, "unless [. . .] it happens to encounter a teacher like you." But, for Badiou's Socrates, something more is required:

> No, that won't suffice! It still has to be seized by some event – a passionate love, a political uprising, an artistic upheaval, or what have you [. . .] No one has ever changed or will ever change, merely through moral lessons, a character that's been set in stone by prevailing opinion. Philosophy can only be effective if the political divine has intervened first, if some event interrupts the consensual routine [. . .] The unpredictable event, the emergence of a rallying cry and of a collective organization that couldn't have been foreseen in the ordinary confused babble of opinions and their so-called freedom. (Ch. 10, pp. 188–90)

For Badiou, education is not merely an activity of proper cultivation, to continue the horticultural metaphor; indeed it requires the *interruption* of "the consensual routine" of culture through the experience of an "event" and the subjective reorientation that it involves. If Badiou's translation cannot be taken to render Plato's literal meaning, it is nevertheless the result of considering Plato *as* an event, one that requires a kind of conversion, the break with received opinion, as much as the patient work of induction.

The use of an imaginary representation (or Midrash-like supplementation) to activate the relationship between the currently fragmentary real of a truth and its future complete symbolization evokes the mathematical procedure developed by Paul Cohen and known as "forcing," which has been a central idea in Badiou's work since the 1970s. In set theory, forcing is a means of generating new knowledge from within a current situation by, in a sense, wagering on the future perfect completion of a currently fragmentary truth. This knowledge depends on the addition of what the mathematician Thomas Jech calls "a sort of imaginary set" to a set-theoretical world or ground model, a *generic* set that, as of yet, we know only in part, and then on exploring the implications of its superaddition to the original world, which expands in unexpected new ways, depending on the promise that the partial knowledge (or "forcing conditions") that we now have will some day have been completed.

A truth procedure always takes place according to the protocols of one of philosophy's four "generic conditions" or modes of producing and expanding sets of indeterminately linked elements pertaining to an event.[17] Each of these procedures is taken up in the *Republic* in terms of its relation to philosophy: mathematics (as a science) is the preamble to philosophy, love is its mode of transmission, poetry is its seductive rival; but, above all, the central problem of the *Republic* will be the relationship – and distinction – between philosophy and politics. In Chapter 9 of Badiou's *Republic* there arises the question of the possibility of a practical implementation, in "empirical reality," of the "ideal model of the true political community" under discussion. Socrates resists the demand that he demonstrate how such an ideal could be fully realized, but he suggests two steps toward approaching such a demonstration. There is still the necessity for critique, first, to "show what's dysfunctional in countries that aren't run according to our [communist] principles"; second, to "uncover, case by case, a change that's trivial in itself but that would have the effect of reconfiguring the whole political community":

> Ideally, this change would concern only one point or two, at a pinch [. . .] above all, from the standpoint of the established order in which we'll isolate them, they should have no apparent importance. I'd even go so far as to say that, in the eyes of the state that we want to radically transform, the point to which the change would apply doesn't exist, as it were [. . .] What we need is a single, inexistent – albeit real – point, which, once it's been identified and spotlighted, will change everything and bring about the truth of the body politic. Yes! Let's change this one point bordering on nothingness and we'll be able to show that the whole of the state concerned will then completely change. (Ch. 9, p. 165)

This transformation of a single "inexistent" point and the exploration of a new generic set around this point, invisible from the outside but fully real and urgent from within, is a "translation" of the mathematical notion of *forcing* into political terms. Can we not also see Badiou's hypertranslation of Plato's *Republic* as itself such an act of forcing, meant to expand what is generic in Plato through the clarifying processes of subtraction and supplementation? Badiou's "generic translation" in this sense rectifies Plato, by insisting that truth is not just for the few, but for everyone. Badiou's "sublime" translation of Plato's *Republic* forces the set of guardian-philosophers to expand, this being the condition of participation in the eternal idea of communism. As Amantha never lets Socrates forget, the generic set of philosophers must come to include everyone in a universal exception without exception: "They must all be philosophers? [. . .] All without exception, said Socrates softly. Yes, without a single exception."

Notes

1 On Badiou's Platonism, see A. J. Bartlett's "Plato" (Bartlett, 2010) and *Badiou and Plato* (Bartlett, 2011); Justin Clemens' "Platonic Meditations" (Clemens, 2001); and Peter Hallward's comments on Badiou and Plato in his *Badiou: A Subject to Truth* (Hallward, 2003).

2 "In effect, I think there are only three crucial philosophers: Plato, Descartes and Hegel" (Badiou, 2009c, p. 529).

3 This remark is from an interview with Lauren Sedofsky, which was published in Alain Badiou's *Entretiens 1* (Badiou, 2011a, p. 177).

4 In *Logics of Worlds* Badiou writes: "The fact is that today – and on this point things haven't budged since Plato – we only know four types of truths: science (mathematics and physics), love, politics and the arts" (Badiou, 2009c, p. 71).

5 See Badiou's seminar on Plato of February 17, 2010 (which is available at http://www.entretemps.asso.fr/Badiou/09-10.htm).

6 See for example "Platonic Gesture," in Badiou's *Manifesto for Philosophy* (Badiou, 1999b); "Anti-Philosophy: Plato and Lacan," in his *Conditions* (Badiou, 2008a); Badiou's "Platon et/ou Aristote–Leibniz," in Panza and Salanskis (Badiou, 1995); and "The Question of Being Today" and "Platonism and Mathematical Ontology," in *Briefings on Existence* (Badiou, 2006a), the translation of his *Court traité d'ontologie transitoire* from 1998.

7 These seminars have not been published, but are available in redacted versions online (at http://www.entretemps.asso.fr/Badiou/seminaire.htm).

8 The other philosopher–dramatist whom Badiou especially admires is of course Sartre.

9 At one point in Badiou's translation, Glaucon becomes frustrated with Socrates' apparently tautological reasoning and refuses to follow him without question, as he does in Plato's text: "Am I supposed to say 'Yes, sure!' or 'Certainly!' [. . .] Have you read my brother Plato's write-ups of the dialogues? All the young people in them speak like that; they're all a bunch of yes-men."

10 Lacan, Seminar 7: "Thus, the most general formula that I can give you of sublimation is the following: it raises an object – and I don't mind the suggestion of a play on words in the term I use – to the dignity of the Thing" (Lacan, 1992, p. 112).

11 Let us recall that Badiou's symbol for the generic in *Being and Event* is ♀ (Badiou, 2005a, p. 356).

12 As Badiou indicates in a 2007 interview included in the English translation of *The Concept of Model*, "Platonism, in the end, is the knowledge of ideality. But this is also the knowledge that we have access to ideality only through that which participates in ideality. The great problem of Platonism is not really the distinction between the intelligible and the sensible, but the

understanding that sensible things participate in the intelligible" (Badiou, 2007b, p. 92).

13 See e.g. pp. 170, 208, 228, 230, 350, etc.

14 Plato, 1968, p. 171.

15 *Der Spiegel* interview with Martin Heidegger (Heidegger, 1976).

16 Badiou comments on Heidegger's remark in his essay "The Question of Being Today" (above, n. 6): "Can the One be unsealed from Being? [. . .] Can thought be saved without having to appeal to the prophecy of a return of the gods?" (p. 34). The response to this is of course, yes, and Plato will certainly be of more help in this project than Heidegger.

17 In Plato's case, that event was the living presence of Socrates – an inversion of Paul's relation to the living absence of Jesus. Hegel has noted the parallel between Socrates and Jesus, which, for him, is, however, based on death.

TRANSLATOR'S PREFACE

"Hypertranslation" is the word Alain Badiou has used, in *The Communist Hypothesis* and elsewhere, to describe his treatment of Plato's *Republic*. Not a "simple" translation into French of the Greek original, then, and still less a scholarly critique of it, Badiou's text transforms the *Republic* into something startlingly new by expanding, reducing, updating and dramatizing it, leavening it with humor and revitalizing its language with his own philosophical lexicon. Yet, for all the plasticity of the hypertranslation, its freewheeling appropriation of the sourcetext, it still remains an adaptation based firmly on his painstaking translation of Plato's language into modern French – as he reminds us in the Preface to this edition.

Such a hypertranslation inevitably problematizes the task of the translator, who must not lose sight of Plato's *Republic* even as it undergoes myriad transformations in its new French incarnation. Badiou may well have had something like this in mind when he remarked: "Imagine what a strange thing it must be to translate into English this sort of translation into French of a Greek text!" (Badiou, 2009b, p. 55). Working on the translation, I was reminded of a palimpsest, with one text, more ancient, underlying the other. In this case, however, the *scriptio inferior* – the inner text – far from being an entirely different text, was the very original, the sourcetext of my sourcetext, and perhaps the greatest work of philosophy ever written, at that. While my task was certainly facilitated by consulting other translations of the *Republic*, both in French and in English, the exercise often proved futile precisely to the extent that Badiou's work, albeit consistently faithful to the spirit of the *Republic*, nevertheless departs from it freely at every turn. The resulting English text might, then, be considered a sort of hyper-hypertranslation, at two degrees of separation from Plato – although not, it is hoped, from the truth, in the way in which the poets whom Socrates condemns are said to be at three degrees of separation from it.

Some brief comments, now, on a few features of the translation:

• *Colloquial speech* As is apparent from the first page of the Prologue, and perhaps especially there, the characters – and I stress the theatrical dimension of Badiou's text advisedly – speak much the way twenty-first century Americans do. The unquestionable youthfulness at the heart of Badiou's enterprise, owing to the vastly expanded roles of Socrates' young interlocutors Amantha and Glaucon, makes modern American speech an ideal vehicle for translation here. However much Socrates may play the starring role in the dialogue, it is clear that he is speaking not only *to* but *for* these young people, in whom he has the utmost confidence. By putting into their mouths – and, to a great extent, into Socrates' mouth as well – speech that sounds perfectly familiar to our ears, jaunty yet free of current slang for the most part, I hoped to convey the youthful quality that inheres in the work as a whole. Yet colloquial speech is balanced in the dialogue by highly sophisticated speech; it is their constant juxtaposition that is perhaps the most striking feature of the text.

• *"Dated" speech* There is a certain "dated" flavor that is more pronounced in the English translation than in the French original, owing to the use of one word in particular: "dear" (*cher*). The text is laden with phrases such as *mon cher maître, cher Socrate, ma chère fille*, and so forth. Such locutions, which are common in French even today, are as a rule omitted in English translations of modern texts, since they lend them an air of stuffiness. No great translation loss is incurred by eliminating them; and yet I decided to preserve them, because they seemed too integral to this particular text to be excised. *Cher*, in its various permutations in the dialogue, often conveys relationships between the characters in a way in which the neutral English "you" simply cannot, varying as it does from being deferential at times (Amantha and Glaucon vis-à-vis Socrates) to being affectionate (Socrates vis-à-vis his young interlocutors) to being ironic (Thrasymachus and Socrates mutually), with a few other subjective states in between. The inclusion of all these *dear*s risked making the dialogue sound a bit fusty; but – as Badiou's frequent evocations of the nearby Piraeus, of the patio of the harborside villa, of its columns, and so on remind us – this is, after all, supposed to be taking place in ancient Greece. In this way, too, retaining a certain old-fashioned formality in the otherwise contemporary American English of the conversation seemed to me justified.

• *Philosophical speech* As Badiou notes in his Preface, he renamed key concepts. Chief among these is the Idea of the Good, which has become the Idea of the True (*l'Idée du Vrai*). This might plausibly have been rendered as "The Idea of Truth," had Badiou not instructed me to maintain a clear distinction between *le vrai* and *la vérité*, a distinction he himself calls attention to in the dialogue. Glaucon's suggestion that it would greatly simplify matters just to call the Idea of the True "Truth" is followed by the line: "And yet, *said Socrates pensively. . .*" The teacher cannot quite relinquish his own terminology, however much it may strike Glaucon, and even perhaps the reader, as odd. (Incidentally, the word "teacher" is, itself, not quite a satisfactory rendering of the French word *maître*, which has connotations of "mentor" and "master" as well. "And yet" . . . we are forced to choose among them.) Overall, the philosophical terminology deployed in the text, its Lacanian resonances – "the Other" or the "big Other," the three "agencies" of the Subject, the "split Subject" – as well as the extensive vocabulary of being and appearing – "in its being," "being-in-truth," "that which of being is exposed to thought," and so on – are so many notes in a familiar Badiouian symphony. Finally, the long rhetorical periods in which Socrates and even Amantha and her brother occasionally indulge, with their intricate concatenation of clauses, showcase Badiou's verbal exuberance and his enduring love of classical language and literature. The description of the interrelationship between the three agencies of the Subject in Chapter 7 is a typical example of this.

• *Poetic speech* Where Plato cites a line or two from an ancient Greek author, Badiou might cite three, four, or more. And these extracts invariably appear in classical French alexandrine verse expressly composed for the purposes of his text. I quickly abandoned my initial efforts to reproduce these verses with existing rhymed English translations – the heroic couplets of Pope's *Iliad*, for example – when I realized how little these ultimately resembled the French. The constraints of rhyming, in both languages, certainly accounted for some of the lack of symmetry between them; but it was mainly the freedom of Badiou's adaptations, which veered wildly at times from the original, that precluded any use of existing translations. Reluctantly, then, I took it upon myself to match the French rhymes with English ones of my own, at the risk of "doing a number on old Badiou," as Socrates at one point claims Amantha has done on "old Homer." The text is, moreover, studded with farcical ditties, witty parodies, clever imitative odes of Badiou's own invention, again always rhymed, challenging me to come up with suitable approximations. The reader's indulgence is begged for these efforts, which I nevertheless hope will impart a little of the flavor of the ingenious originals.

• *Politically incorrect speech* There is a humorous moment in the dialogue when Socrates gets in a dig, as a linguistically conservative Frenchman might, at political correctness in speech. After mentioning, in a discussion on love of wisdom, a young person unable as yet to distinguish between what's important and what's not, he remarks: "Let's assume that *'he or she,' as the Anglophones say*, has no liking for theoretical knowledge" (my italics). In fact, Socrates in French virtually always uses *il* alone, which it would have been a serious error, in my opinion, to update as "he or she." I did occasionally use "they" or "them," as is standard now in English, when the reference clearly applied to both genders. For the most part, though, Socrates is politically incorrect in French and he remains so in English, as even the young people do. Amantha may take Socrates to task for his failure to include women in his examples, but her own speech, like his, is indifferent to political correctness of the Anglophone variety. However much a radical feminist project Socrates' "fifth system of government" may be, his speech in general often betrays a certain sexism, playful, no doubt, but pervasive in the text.

Thanks are due to a number of people for their help with this project. I am deeply grateful, first of all, to Alain Badiou, who not only granted me the privilege of translating this uniquely personal work of his, but patiently endured my relentless queries about it; and I am also grateful to Ken Reinhard for his unstinting friendship and wise counsel; to Maricarmen Rodríguez, the Spanish translator of the text, with whom I engaged in many spirited email discussions of major issues and obscure details; to Isabelle Vodoz, who read the entire manuscript, answering my questions with her typical perspicacity; to Joe Litvak, who generously helped me with some rhyming difficulties; and to Louise Burchill, Bruce Fink, Lynda Levy, and the members of the Southern California Literary Translators Association, for their assistance with various issues of translation and reference. Manuela Tecusan of Polity Press deserves special credit for her meticulous editing of the text and always thoughtful comments. My greatest debt of gratitude is to my husband, Patrick Coleman, without whose countless astute suggestions and constant loving encouragement this translation would not have been possible.

AUTHOR'S PREFACE TO THE ENGLISH EDITION

Alain Badiou

All French-language philosophers are aware of the difficulty involved in translating their texts into English. It is a severe test of the philosophical discourse's claim to universality.

To begin with, vocabulary presents an obstacle. One need only think of the concepts related to the French tradition's conception of subjectivity, starting with *sujet* and continuing with *conscience de*, *pour-soi*, *réflexivité*, and so on. Ontology fares just as poorly, if one considers the impracticality of translating into English the difference between *être* ("being") and *étant* ("a being," "beings") and the more general difficulty of turning verbs into nouns, of saying *le faire* ("the doing") or *le devenir* ("the becoming"), a practice that has become commonplace in French, following, it must be said, in the footsteps of Greek and German.

But syntax is of no help either. French tends toward abstractions owing to its rigid, invariable syntax, which ranks the sentence elements and the relationship between determiner and determined element in a well-nigh ceremonious order. It is an analytical language par excellence. English is much more flexible, much more free-ranging. Its prodigious wealth of adjectives and "ways of saying things" provides it with nuances of meaning to which French professes a lofty indifference. English is a descriptive language par excellence.

Just this difference alone between the two languages explains the radical opposition between Descartes' rationalistic, formal syntax, taken up by Rousseau, and the empirical, semi-skeptical tradition that began with Locke and came into its own with Hume.

That being the case, what can be said about the translation into English of a rendering into French of a Greek text? Especially when this French rendering aims to completely recontextualize the Greek text in such a way that its origins will be practically forgotten in the headlong rush of the most natural-sounding French possible, a French that embraces rather than translates the Greek text.

This amounts to saying that the work of Susan Spitzer and of those she consulted along the way for advice in bringing to fruition this English – or would it be more accurate to say American? – version of my *Plato's Republic* is truly a tour de force. There is much more creativity in it than in an ordinary translation since, for one thing, it involved a translation of a translation, and, for another, this twice removed "translation" had to re-produce a French-language re-creation intended for today's world. So it is important to appreciate the fact that Susan Spitzer has re-created in (American) English a re-creation of a text written in Greek more than two thousand years ago.

Knowing her as I do, I immediately thought she was up to the task. And so we worked on it almost simultaneously: week after week, she would receive the sections I had just finished writing. Little by little, an English version emerged at around the same time as the French text reached completion. Susan followed just a little behind me. Her creative inventions in English enhanced, and occasionally improved upon, the innovations in the French.

This is why I am now awarding her the title of co-author of the worldwide project of a *Plato's Republic* refashioned in the context of our world and addressed to one and all. It's not just capitalism that can boast of being modern and globalized. Plato can, too! And in English, the extremely important language of globalization, he owes it all to Susan Spitzer and her friends. We think *this* Plato is, and will be, a monkey wrench thrown in the machinery of Capital, a small contribution whose aim is to stop the juggernaut from crushing everything in its path. Because for hundreds of years now Plato has been saying, and will say again, I hope, in every language, that the order of thinking can triumph over the apparent law of things, that justice can triumph over the power of money – in a word, that communism, an old word whose utter newness the old philosopher will teach us, is possible.

An ancient book, then, that is now the bearer of unexpected good news.

PREFACE

How I Came to Write This Unclassifiable Book

This book took six years to complete.

Why? Why did I undertake this well-nigh obsessional project based on Plato? Because he is the one we need first and foremost today, for one reason in particular: he launched the idea that conducting our lives in the world assumes that some access to the absolute is available to us, not because a veridical God is looming over us (Descartes), nor because we ourselves are the historial figures of the becoming-subject of such an Absolute (both Hegel and Heidegger), but because the materiality of which we are composed participates – above and beyond individual corporeality and collective rhetoric – in the construction of eternal truths.

This notion of participation, which we know presents an enigma, allows us to go beyond the strictures of what I have called "democratic materialism": the contention that there are only individuals and communities, along with a few contracts negotiated between them, about which today's "philosophers" would have us expect nothing other than that they be fair. Since such "fairness" holds no interest for philosophers apart from the occasion it provides to note that it takes the form, and to an ever-increasing degree, of intolerable injustice in the world, we shall have to contend that, in addition to bodies and languages, there are eternal truths. We must be able to think that bodies and languages participate in time in the militant construction of this eternity. That is what Plato never stopped trying to make the deaf hear.

So I turned to the *Republic*, the Master's pivotal work, which is devoted precisely to the problem of justice, to show how powerfully it speaks to us today.

I began with my old copy of the Greek text, as reconstituted by Émile Chambry in the bilingual Budé collection (*Les Belles Lettres*,

1949), a copy on which I was already diligently working 54 years ago and which, as a result, is covered with a great many layers of annotations from a variety of different periods. I've actually been inspired by the *Republic* throughout the entire course of my philosophical adventures.

I've always found the division of the Greek text into ten books – a division that only made sense for the Alexandrian grammarians – to be absurd. So I've divided it up differently, according to what I think its real rhythm is, into a Prologue, sixteen chapters, and an Epilogue. The number of chapters varied while I was working on it, increasing from nine to sixteen for reasons of internal coherence. I ended up "treating" a total of eighteen sections.

I didn't treat them in order. Not at all. I began (in 2005) with the Prologue; next I went on to what ultimately became Chapter 16; then I wandered around, nearer the end at times, nearer the beginning at others, until, sometime around the winter of 2010/11, all I had left to condense was a sort of middle section, comprising Chapters 7 and 8, which are by no means the easiest or the funniest ones. I saved the hardest part for last.

What does "treating" the text mean?

I started out trying to understand it, all of it, in its own language. I was armed with my beloved study of Classics, including my previous readings of many passages; with the Bailly dictionary (Hachette, 16th edition, 1950); with Allard and Feuillâtre's grammar (Hachette, 1972 edition); and with three readily available French translations: Émile Chabry's, which I mentioned above, Léon Robin's (La Pléïade, 1950), and Robert Baccou's, published by Garnier Flammarion (1966). I set about it with single-minded determination; I didn't let anything slip by me; I wanted every sentence (and Plato sometimes writes memorably long and complicated sentences) to make sense to me. That initial effort was a one-on-one encounter between the text and myself. I didn't write a thing; I simply wanted the text to speak to me and not keep any sly secret hidden deep in its recesses.

Next, I would write whatever thoughts and sentences were afforded me by what I'd understood of the portion of the Greek text I considered I had mastered. The result, although never a forgetting of the original text, not even of its details, was nevertheless almost never a "translation" in the usual sense of the term. Plato was ever-present, although perhaps not a single one of his sentences was restored exactly as he wrote it. I would write this whole first version on the right-hand page of a big Canson sketchbook (I was to use 57 of these). This first draft had a huge number of crossings-out. Then, usually the next day,

I would revise this first attempt, as calmly as possible, and transcribe the revision onto the left-hand page of the sketchbook, opposite the first draft. Often I would depart one step further from the letter of the original text, but I maintain that such departures are a matter of greater philosophical fidelity to the text. This second handwritten version was then given to Isabelle Vodoz, who converted it into a computer file. She would note in red, in the typescript, anything that still seemed confusing or awkwardly phrased to her. When the file was sent to me, I would correct it on the basis of both her comments and my own criticisms. This gave rise to a third version of the text, which could be considered a final one – except, of course, for the final, final revision that was intended to unify the whole.

On a couple of rare occasions, I had to admit defeat. Here and there a few of the Greek sentences failed to inspire me. Scholars will no doubt spot them and use them to beef up the case against me in my trial for apostasy. The most serious of these capitulations occurs in Chapter 8, where an entire passage was purely and simply replaced by an improvisation of Socrates' that is of my own invention.

Gradually, in the very process of treating the text, certain more general techniques came to light that I would put to use and vary in the rest of the work. Here are a few examples of what I mean.

Introducing a female character Adeimantus became Amantha.

Complete freedom in the choice of references If an argument was better supported by a quotation from Freud than by an allusion to Hippocrates, I'd choose Freud, who would be assumed to be known to Socrates, which is not such a big deal.

Scientific updating The very astute remarks Plato makes on the basis of the theory of irrational numbers proved to be just as astute if it was algebraic topology that was being discussed.

Updating of the images The Cave of the famous myth is so like an enormous movie theater that it only takes describing that movie theater and having Plato's prisoners become spectator-prisoners of the contemporary sphere of media for it to be the same thing, only better.

An overview of History Why stick with the wars, revolutions, and tyrannical regimes of the Greek world when World War I, the Paris Commune, and Stalin are even more convincing examples?

Maintaining a true, heavily dramatized dialogue at all times What was the point of retaining Socrates' endless stream of fake questions, to which the young people, for pages on end, only respond with "yes," "of course," or "naturally"? A better solution would be either to accept for there to be a long, uninterrupted demonstrative speech or to give the interlocutors a share of the argument. It would also be better for Socrates' listeners to be recalcitrant at times. Socrates' argument against the poets is so stringent that even he himself, as can easily be sensed, wishes it weren't true. Let one of the young people hold her ground, let her say from beginning to end that she's unconvinced, and the inner split that poetry introduces into philosophy, a split that Plato already had a hunch about, will be clearly restored.

The reader will have no trouble discovering other such techniques.

Naturally, my own thinking and, more generally speaking, the contemporary philosophical context seep into my treatment of Plato's text, and probably all the more so when I'm unaware of it. I did, however, intentionally introduce, as it were axiomatically, notable changes in the "translation" of some fundamental concepts. Let me mention two of these decisions, which have far-reaching implications. I changed the famous "Idea of the Good" to the "Idea of the True," if not simply to "Truth." I also changed "soul" to "Subject." Thus, in my text, they'll speak of "a Subject's incorporation into a truth" rather than of "the soul's ascension toward the Good," and of "the three agencies of the Subject" rather than of "the three-part division of the soul." What's more, the famous three parts, which are often called "appetite," "spirit," and "reason," will be reprised, *qua* agencies, as "Desire," "Affect" and "Thought." I also gave myself permission to translate "God" as "the big Other," or even sometimes as "the Other" *tout court*.

At times, I deliberately proposed several different French words that accord with a single Greek word. Take, for instance, the formidable word *Politeia*, from which Plato's book borrows its traditional title. Translating it as "Republic" has no meaning today, if it ever had one. In my text I used at least five different words, depending on the context, in the various passages where I came up against *politeia*: "country," "state," "society," "city," and "system of government." To describe Plato's project itself, the "ideal City" he proposes, I used three different terms: "true system of government," "communism," and "fifth system of government." At other times I explicitly introduced a discussion, a hesitation, about what the appropriate word should be. Thus, in the long passage about tyranny and the tyrannical man, Socrates spontaneously uses the words from the Greek text ("tyranny," "tyrant"), while Amantha stubbornly insists that they use "fascism" and "fascist." In this way I hope to have succeeded in combining a constant proximity to the original text with a radical distancing from it, but a distancing on which the text, as it might function today, generously confers its legitimacy.

That, after all, is what it means for a text to be timeless.

CHARACTERS

SOCRATES
AMANTHA, Plato's sister
GLAUCON, Plato's brother
CEPHALUS, a rich old man from the Piraeus
POLEMARCHUS, a citizen of Athens
THRASYMACHUS, a renowned Sophist
CLEITOPHON, an admirer of Thrasymachus

PROLOGUE

The Conversation in the Villa on the Harbor (327a–336b)

*The day this whole tremendous affair began, Socrates was return-
ing from the harbor area, accompanied by Plato's youngest brother,
a guy by the name of Glaucon. They'd greeted the goddess of the
Northerners, those drunken sailors, with a kiss on either cheek and
had taken in the whole scene at the festival in her honor – the first one
ever! The local harbor residents' parade was awesome, incidentally.
And the Northerners' floats, overloaded with half-naked ladies, were
pretty cool, too.*

*Of all the countless guys named Polemarchus, the one who's the
son of Cephalus spotted the pair from a distance and sent a kid
running after them. "Wait for us!" yelled the young boy, tugging on
Socrates' jacket. "Where did you leave your master?" asked Socrates.
"He's running up behind you, wait for him!" "All right!" the guy
named Glaucon, Plato's younger brother, agreed. So who should
show up a few minutes later? A whole bunch of people, that's who!
Polemarchus, of course, the one who's the son of Cephalus, but
Niceratus, the one who's the son of Nicias, too, and lots of others,
who are the sons of lots of others, not to mention – I bet you'll never
guess! – Plato's sister, the beautiful Amantha. All these people were
coming from the festival, just like Socrates and Glaucon.*

*Polemarchus, the one who's, etc., then informed Socrates that,
alone against a whole group, he was no match for them, even if he
was backed up by the guy named Glaucon, however much he might
be Plato's brother. So he'd have to accept the pressing invitation
they'd all come to convey to him, to come for dinner in the stunning
harborside villa where Old Man Cephalus lived. Socrates objected
that, rather than start a hopeless fight, he could just as easily talk
things over with them calmly and convince the whole crew of them*

1

that he had good reasons for wanting to go home. Polemarchus coun-
tered that they'd all cover their ears and not listen to a word of his
seductive arguments.

It was right at this critical juncture that Plato's vivacious sister,
the aforementioned Amantha, who was seductive enough for two,
spoke up: "You may not be aware that tonight, as an extension of
the festivities in honor of the Northerners' shady goddess, the harbor
ship-owners are organizing a torch race on horseback. How about
that?! Huh?" "Holy smoke!" said Socrates, visibly taken with the
young lady's liveliness. "A relay race on horseback? You mean the
teams race on horseback and pass the torches to each other to win?"
"Exactly!" said Polemarchus-the-son-of, leaping into the breach of
Socrates's defenses. "And after the race the city council is throwing
a big all-night party. We're all going to go after dinner – everyone
and his brother will be there! There'll be tons of gorgeous girls, all of
Amantha's friends, and we'll shoot the breeze with them till dawn.
Come on! Let yourself go!"

Plato's younger brother, the guy named Glaucon, gave in right
away, and Socrates was secretly delighted to have to go along with
him, especially as part of a procession in which young Amantha was
literally glowing. And that was how the whole gang of them descended
upon Old Man Cephalus. Masses of people were already milling
around in the harborside villa. Lysias and Euthydemus were there,
and so were Euthydemus' sisters, escorted by Thrasymachus, the one
who was born in Chalcedon, and Charmantides, the one who was
born in Paeania, and the Cleitophon who's the son of Aristonymus,
too. And, naturally, Old Man Cephalus, looking much the worse
for wear, slumped against some cushions, with a wreath on his head
that was all askew because he'd just slaughtered a chicken out in the
courtyard as a sacrifice to the Northerners' dubious goddess.

They all took their seats respectfully in a circle around the likable
old codger. And no sooner had they done so than he admonished
Socrates:

–You certainly don't come out very often to this harbor suburb to
visit me, dear Socrates! Yet it would be "cool," as the young people
who follow you around everywhere say, if you did. If I still had the
strength to go into town easily you wouldn't have to come all the
way out here; I'd go and visit you. But, given the state of my legs,
you ought to come here more often. I must admit that, though I feel
that the pleasures of the body are gradually fading, at the same time I
feel that the pleasures of conversation are increasing. Wouldn't it be
possible for you, without necessarily having to leave those charming

2

young people, to come here often, as a friend, as a regular guest in this house?

Socrates politely shot back:

–Of course I can, dear Cephalus! Indeed, I'd like nothing better. It's always a pleasure to converse with venerable old men like you. As a matter of fact, I think we should ask them about the true nature of that last stretch of the road of life, on which they precede us, and which we, in our turn, will have to travel. Is the road rocky and difficult? Or smooth and easy? I'd be only too happy to ask your opinion, since you've reached that very time in life the poets speak of, the time they call "the threshold of old age." Is it a difficult time of life? Or, if not, how do you regard it?

–Well, you know, dear Socrates, I often go to meetings of the Senior Citizens' Circle, in a big building the city council put up south of the harbor. Naturally, we reminisce about the good old days. Nearly everyone my age gripes, consumed as they are by the memory of the pleasures of youth – sex, drinking, feasts, all that sort of thing. They resent the passage of time, as though they'd all lost huge fortunes. "Yes sir, life was good back then, but now, I'm telling you, it doesn't even deserve to be called life any more. . ." Some dwell on the indignities they endure at home: their young relatives take advantage of their old age; they're the constant butt of mockery and insolence. As a result, they all harp on the miseries that they say old age is to blame for. But I, for one, think they're not blaming the right cause; for, if it were really old age, I would feel its effects too, and so would everyone without exception who has reached the same age as myself. Yet I have personally met old people with a completely different attitude. The great poet Sophocles is a good example. I once happened to be around when a journalist who'd come to interview him asked him, rather rudely, I must say: "So, Sophocles, how's it going, sex-wise? Are you still able to make love to a woman?" The poet shut him up but good: "You hit the nail on the head, citizen!" he replied. "It's an amazing thing for me to be relieved of sexual desire, to be free at last from the clutches of a wild, raving master!" I was deeply impressed at the time by how perfect an answer that was, and even today the impact it had on me has not lessened at all. When old age comes, all that sex business is covered over with a sort of soothing freedom. Desires die down or even disappear altogether, and Sophocles' remark turns out to be absolutely true: we are indeed set free from a bunch of masters, all as insane as they are demanding. Ultimately, all these old people's complaints about their domestic tribulations have but one cause, which is not old age but the way people live. For those who

3

are both disciplined and open-minded, old age is not really tough. For those who are neither, youth and old age are equally awful.

As politeness requires us to go along with this sort of disquisition, and even to request more of the same, it was for the sole purpose of giving the old man the floor again that Socrates came out with a trite remark:

–When you say such wise and wonderful things, my dear Cephalus, I suspect your interlocutors disagree. They think it's easier to grow old when you're sitting on a pile of gold, and they attribute your peace of mind to the consolations of your wealth rather than to the generosity of your spirit. Aren't I right?

Cephalus took the bait and off he went again:

–Of course they don't believe me. I'm not saying that their criticism is worthless for all that, but it's less important than they think. I'm reminded of the marvelous story that's told about the Grand Admiral of the Fleet. One day a fellow from some godforsaken place in the North, from Seriphus, I think, was hurling insults at him. "You have no merit of your own," the guy, a raging republican, bellowed. "You yourself are just a little runt. You owe everything to Athens' power and to the dedication of its citizens!" Very calmly, the Grand Admiral of the Fleet then said to the maniac: "You're right, sir; if I were from Seriphus no one would know my name. But even if you were from Athens no one would know yours." We could take our cue from the Grand Admiral, to reply to the people who aren't rich and find old age hard to bear: "Of course, a reasonable man may find it hard to grow old with perfect equanimity if he also happens to be destitute; but, when it comes to an unreasonable man, even if he is rolling in money his old age will certainly not be any the less grim."

Socrates wanted to formalize this story about rich men's temperaments and said:

–Tell me, dear Cephalus, did you inherit your fortune or are you a self-made man?

–Neither. My grandfather, who was also a Cephalus, was a typical self-made man. He inherited a fortune comparable to my own and multiplied it five times over. My father, Lysanias, was a dyed-in-the-wool heir. In no time at all he divided by seven what had come to him from my grandfather, so that, by the time he died, there was a little less money left than I have now. As you can see, I've made it back to some extent, but not as much as all that. Being neither my grandfather nor my father, I'll settle for leaving my children not much more than I inherited from my father, nor any less. "A little more": that's my motto in all things.

4

–What prompted my question, *Socrates went on,* was that you don't strike me as someone who's overly fond of money. Now, that's often the case with people who didn't have to make their fortunes themselves: inheritors rather than self-made men. Self-made men are twice as devoted to money as people who inherit are. Like poets who love their own poems, or fathers their own children, money-makers take their money very seriously because it's their own creation – aside from the fact that, like everyone else, they value the comfort it affords. That's why these people are tiresome to be around: all they ever talk about is money.

–That, *said Cephalus,* is unfortunately the honest truth.

Socrates leaped at the opportunity he had opened up:

–But if people who talk about money all the time are so tiresome, what about money itself, then? Isn't it money, actually, that's insufferable? In your opinion, Cephalus, what's the greatest good that popular opinion perceives in the possession of an enormous fortune?

–I bet I'm practically the only one who appreciates it! Let's place ourselves at the moment when someone starts to seriously face the fact that he's going to die. He's then plagued by worries and fears about things he couldn't have cared less about before. He remembers the stories people tell about Hell, especially that punishment is meted out there for all the wrongs done here. Once, as a *bon vivant,* he used to scoff at such tales. But now, as a Subject, he wonders whether they might not be true. Eventually our man, enfeebled by old age and believing he's on the threshold of the hereafter, listens intently to all those fantastic stories. Tormented by suspicion and dread, he mentally reviews all the wrongs he may have done over the course of his life. If he finds a lot of them, then he wakes up with a start at night, as panic-stricken as a child who's had a nightmare, and his days are nothing but misery-filled anticipation. But if his soul-searching turns up no wrongdoing, well, then a pleasant feeling of hope comes over him, which the poet calls the "nurse to old age." You must remember, Socrates, those lines in which Pindar describes the man whose life was filled with justice and piety:

> Nurse to old age,
> From whom he's ne'er apart,
> Sweet hope who warms and soothes
> The mortal thinker's heart.[1]

Pindar is strikingly forceful and accurate here! It's with these lines in mind that I can reply without hesitation to the question you asked me: the wealth a man possesses is very beneficial – not in all cases, but for the man who is able to use it to do right. "Doing right" means never practicing deceit or deception, even unintentionally, and not being in debt to anyone – either to a man, to whom one might owe money, or to a god, to whom one might owe a sacrifice; in short, it means having no reason to dread leaving for the hereafter. It's obviously easier to do right when one possesses a fortune, and that's a huge advantage. Wealth has many others, as we know; but, if I examine them one by one, I can't see any that's more important for a completely reasonable man.

–What an admirable speech! *exclaimed Socrates*. But as regards this virtue of justice whose importance you emphasize, can we say that we've looked at the matter from every angle if we only take into account the two properties you accord it: in speech, truth, and in everyday life, returning to others what they've loaned you? The problem, I think, is that an action that's in keeping with these two properties may sometimes be just and sometimes unjust. Let me give you an example. Let's say someone borrowed some weapons from a friend who was of sound mind, but this friend later goes crazy and asks for the weapons back. Who would say that it's just to return them to him, or even to want to tell the whole truth and nothing but the truth at all costs to such a lunatic?

–Not I in any case! *said Cephalus*.

–So you can see that "telling the truth" and "returning what someone has loaned you" hardly constitute a definition of justice.

Polemarchus, who hadn't said a word till then, suddenly broke his silence:

–If the great poet Simonides[2] is to be trusted, that's, on the contrary, an excellent definition.

–I see that we're not out of the woods yet, *resumed old Cephalus*. But I'm afraid I'll have to leave the rest of the discussion to you. I still need to see to the sacrifice of a black goat.

–So Polemarchus is inheriting the fortune of your conversation! *joked Socrates*.

–Exactly! *said Cephalus with a smile.*

And he disappeared for good from the discussion, which would last – though the protagonists were far from suspecting as much – more than twenty hours!

–Well, *resumed Socrates, turning to Polemarchus,* you who have inherited the argument, tell us why you hold Simonides the poet's remarks about justice in such high regard.

–When Simonides says that it's just to give everyone his due, I think: yes, he's right.

−Oh, that Simonides! So wise and inspired! How can we not agree with him? That said, whatever can be the meaning of what he says about justice? Do you know, Polemarchus? I, at any rate, haven't the slightest idea. Clearly he's not saying – this was our counter-example a moment ago – that you should return the gun he loaned someone to a guy who's completely out of his mind and wants it back. Yet that's surely a thing that's owed him, isn't it?

−Yes.

−We'd agreed that, if someone loaned you that gun, it's not simply because its owner, who has gone stark raving mad, asks you for it back that you should return it to him. So Simonides, the wise poet, must mean something different from this when he says that justice consists in returning what's owed.

−He obviously has something else in mind. "To return" means that we should return to friends the tokens of friendship they give us. To friends one does good, never harm.

−My word, it's all clear now! A borrower who returns the money he borrowed from a lender is not really giving the lender back what's owed him if the borrower's returning it, like the lender's accepting it, are harmful to said lender, and if, moreover, lender and borrower are friends. Whew! Is that what you think Simonides' sentence means?

−Precisely.

−And even to our enemies should we return what, through an unfortunate twist of fate, we find ourselves owing them?

−Sure we should! What we owe them, we return to them! And what we owe an enemy, insofar as it's appropriate for an enemy, is . . . harm!

−It's as a true poet, apparently, that Simonides turned the definition of justice into a cryptic riddle. If I follow you, he was saying that it would be just to give everyone what's appropriate for them, which for some strange reason he called "what's due them."

−So then, *said Polemarchus, getting annoyed*, where's the problem?

−At this level of poetic ambiguity, only the big Other[3] can know for sure. Suppose the big Other asks the poet: "Simonides! To whom does the art[4] called 'medicine' give what's appropriate for him, or, to use your vocabulary, what's due him?" What would our poet respond?

−That's as easy as pie! He'd respond that medicine gives drugs, food and drink to bodies.

−What about the cook?

−The cook? What cook? *asked a panicky Polemarchus.*

7

–To whom does he give what's appropriate for him, or his "due," if you prefer, and what does such a gift consist of?

–The cook gives the appropriate seasonings to what's cooked.

Here Polemarchus was very pleased with himself. Moreover, Socrates congratulated him, saying:

–Excellent! And what about the art called "justice," then? What does it give, and to whom?

–If we bring justice into line with cooking and medicine, and if we're true to Simonides, we'll say: depending on whether it concerns friends or enemies, justice gives them either benefits or injuries.

–Now we're getting somewhere! It's crystal-clear. Simonides says justice is a matter of doing good to friends and harm to enemies. Fine, fine. . . But tell me: let's say some friends are in bad shape, and so are some enemies. Who's best able, when it comes to the sickness/health pair, to do good to the former and harm to the latter?

–That's a cinch! The doctor.

–And how about if both the friends and the enemies embark on a long sea crossing? Who can save them or drown them when there's a storm?

–No problem: the ship's captain.

–What about the just man? In what practical circumstances and on the basis of what activity is he best able to help his friends and harm his enemies?

–That's easy: in war. He'll defend the former and attack the latter.

–Dearest Polemarchus! If you're as fit as a fiddle, a doctor's of no use to you; if you're walking on dry land, you'll hardly need to have a lieutenant commander around. So, if I understand you correctly, "justice" and "the just man" are meaningless to people who aren't at war.

–Of course not! That's an absurd conclusion!

–So justice *is* useful in peacetime?

–Obviously.

–And so are farming, for providing good fruit, and shoemakers, for providing shoes. Then what about justice in peacetime? What use does it have? What does it enable you to get?

–It enables you to engage in, guarantee, and consolidate symbolic relationships.

–You mean agreements entered into with another person?

–Yes, contracts that have rules, which justice ensures respect for.

–Let's take a closer look at that. If you're playing chess, you place the pieces on the board in a certain order. That's a symbolic agreement, as you put it. As far as placing the pieces goes, who's the expert

– the just man or the professional player? Here's another example. Let's say you're building a house. To lay the bricks and stones properly, according to the rules, who's more useful, who's better? The just man or the bricklayer? Look, here's another one: the musician is certainly better than the just man at plucking the strings of a guitar according to the rules that govern chords. So, for what kinds of matters where a symbolic rule is involved is the just man a better associate than the chess player, the bricklayer, or the guitarist?

–I think it's for money matters.

–What sorts of money matters? If you're using money to buy a horse, for instance, the wise counselor, the man of useful symbols, will be the experienced rider; and if you're selling a boat, you're better off having a sailor as your associate than a just man who's clueless about such things. So I emphatically ask you again: in what kinds of matters where earning or spending money is involved will the just man be more useful than the others?

–I think it's when you want to get back the money you deposited or loaned, and to do it without incurring any loss.

–In a nutshell, it's when you don't intend to use the money and you're just letting it lie idle? Now *that*'s really interesting! Justice is useful precisely to the extent that the money is not being used. . .

–I'm afraid so.

–Let's pursue this promising direction. If you want to let a computer gather dust in your closet, justice is useful, but if you want to use it, the computer programmer's the useful one. If you need to keep a dusty old violin or a rusty shotgun up in a corner of the attic, that's when justice is essential! Because if you want to play a concerto or shoot a pheasant, you're better off with a violinist or a hunter.

–I don't quite see what you're getting at.

–Just this: if we follow the poet Simonides, whatever the practice involved, justice is useless when it comes to using things and useful when it comes to not using them.

–What a strange conclusion! What do *you* think, Polemarchus? *Amantha asked teasingly.*

Socrates hammered home the point.

–In essence, as far as both Simonides and you are concerned, justice is hardly very important. What good is something that's useful only to the extent that it's useless? But it gets even worse! You'd agree, I presume, that a professional boxer with a devastating punch can also block his opponent's blows, right? Or that someone who can ward off an STD is also someone who can infect his or her partner without their suspecting a thing?

9

–Come off it, Socrates! *whined Polemarchus.* You're losing it! What do syphilis or AIDS have to do with anything?

–Allow me one last example. Aren't someone who's a top-notch defender of an army in the field and someone who can steal the enemy's strategies and plans of action one and the same person?

–Yes, yes, of course! Your examples just keep repeating the same idea. . .

–. . . which is this: if someone's good at safeguarding things, then he must also be good at stealing.

–Isn't that self-evident?

–Could be, could be. . . But then, if the just man is good at safeguarding the money he's been given, he must also be good at stealing it.

–So *that*'s what the famous Socrates was getting at?

Socrates' and Polemarchus' duel then heated up. Glaucon and Amantha kept score.

–I'm afraid so! *retorted Socrates.* The just man, as you defined him, suddenly appears to us as a kind of thief. And I think you picked up this strange belief from Homer. Our national poet actually adores Odysseus' grandpa, the man called Autolycus. He relates with relish that when it came to stealing and lying, no one could touch him. I deduce from this that as far as Homer, Simonides, and you are concerned, dear Polemarchus, justice is the art of the thief. . .

–No way! Not at all! *Polemarchus interrupted him.*

–. . . provided that this art, *Socrates went on imperturbably,* helps one's friends and harms one's enemies. Stealing from one's enemies in order to give to one's friends – isn't that your definition of justice, or have I misunderstood?

–You're driving me crazy. I don't even know what I meant any more. But I won't give ground on one point: justice is a matter of helping one's friends and harming one's enemies.

–What do you call a friend, though? Someone who *seems* to be a great guy or someone who actually *is* a beautiful soul,[5] even if he doesn't seem like one? And I'd ask you the same question about enemies.

–We should love those we consider beautiful souls and hate scoundrels.

–But as you're very well aware, it happens that we make mistakes: sometimes we see beautiful souls where there are only scoundrels, and scoundrels where everyone's a decent person. So, in that case, it's the good people who are our enemies and the bad people who are our friends.

–Unfortunately, that does happen; that's a fact, *conceded Polemarchus.*

–Sticking with this same hypothesis, we see – if we accept Homer's, Simonides', and your definition – that it's just to help scoundrels and to harm beautiful souls. As beautiful souls are just and never do any wrong, we must conclude that, according to the three of you, it's just to harm those who are never unjust.

–What on earth are you talking about? Only a scoundrel could reason that way!

–So, it's the unjust whom it's just to harm, and the just whom it would be unjust not to help?

–Oh, that's more like it!

–But then, when someone's mistaken about the true nature of people, it may be just for that person to harm his friends, who happen to be scoundrels, and just to help his enemies, who are beautiful souls. Which is exactly the opposite of what we said Simonides meant.

Socrates, very pleased, turned to the young people: he'd scored a point, hadn't he? But Polemarchus stood up for himself.

–That fine argument proves only one thing, Socrates, namely that our definition of friends and enemies isn't correct. We said that a friend is someone who *seems* to be a beautiful soul. Instead we ought to say that a friend is someone who both *seems* to be and *is* a beautiful soul. Someone who seems to be one without really being one is not a friend but only the semblance of one. Being and appearing should be combined in the same way as far as enemies are concerned.

–Wonderful! The beautiful soul is thus the friend, and the scoundrel is the enemy. Therefore we'll have to change the definition of justice. It was: it is just to do good to a friend and harm to an enemy. In reality we ought to say: it is just to do good to a friend who's a beautiful soul and to harm an enemy who's a scoundrel.

–I think, *said Polemarchus, relieved by this apparent agreement,* that we've hit on the solution to the problem.

But Socrates added, with a wry smile:

–Not so fast! Just one more little question. Does a just man's nature give him the right to harm his neighbor, whatever he may be?

–Of course it does! You just said as much: we ought to harm all those scoundrels who are also our enemies.

–Regarding horses they say. . .

–Horses? *said a startled Polemarchus.* Why horses? No horse was ever anyone's evil enemy!

–. . . they say, *Socrates stubbornly persisted,* that if they're mistreated they never improve.

11

–Everyone knows that! Mistreating a horse makes him mean.

–And as for dogs. . .

–Dogs now! Good grief, we're looking for justice in a zoo!

–No, but I observe, I examine, I compare. If horses are mistreated, they get worse relative to the horse's proper virtue – which is to gallop straight ahead, fleetly carrying his rider, the rider's breastplate, his gaiters, his spear, and his pack. Needless to say, the horse's proper virtue is not the same as the dog's, not by a long shot. It's out of the question for a dog to carry a breastplated soldier and his gaiters. What remains true is that if a dog is mistreated, he'll become either fearful or ferocious, but in any case very bad relative to his proper virtue as a household pet – which, I repeat, is not a horse's. So it's true for both dogs and horses.

–What's true, Socrates? You're driving us crazy.

–The truth is that if they're mistreated, their proper virtue will be perverted. From horses and dogs to men, doesn't it follow logically? If the human species is mistreated, doesn't it become worse relative to its proper virtue?

–Oh, I get it! You're bringing in man by way of dogs! The conclusion seems fine to me. But the proper virtue of man still has to be determined. It's not like galloping or barking!

–But that's what I've been talking about right from the beginning of the evening! I contend that *the proper virtue of the human species is justice!* So it follows from my comparison that if human beings are mistreated they become more unjust than they were. It is therefore impossible for a just man to mistreat anyone.

–Wait a second! I'm missing something here – I don't see the logic of the argument.

–A musician, solely through the effect of his music, can't turn someone into a musical illiterate any more than a rider, through his equestrian skill alone, can make someone be totally ignorant about horses. So could we argue that a just man, solely through the effect of his justice, can make someone be more unjust than he was? Or, to cut to the chase, that it's the good people's virtue that breeds scoundrels? That's absurd, as much as it would be to argue that the effect of heat is to make things cold, or the effect of dryness to make things wet. No, it cannot be in the nature of a beautiful soul to harm anyone whatsoever. And since the just man is a beautiful soul, it's not in his nature to harm his friend, even if he were a scoundrel, nor indeed to harm anyone at all. That's an attribute of the unjust man, who for his part *is* a scoundrel.

A stunned Polemarchus surrendered, saying:

–I have to give up, I'm afraid. I can't compete with you.

Socrates then finished off his interlocutor:

–If anyone – even Simonides, even Homer – claims that justice amounts to giving everyone what's due him, and if his underlying thought is that the just man should harm his enemies and help his friends, we'll boldly argue that such remarks are unworthy of a wise man because, quite simply, they're untrue. The truth – it appeared to us in all its glory as the dialogue went on – is that it's never just to do harm. The fact that – from Simonides to Nietzsche, by way of Sade and many others – the opposite has been maintained will no longer intimidate us, you and me. Besides, far more than by the poets or thinkers, the maxim "it is just to harm one's enemies and to help one's friends" strikes me as something that could have been said by the Xerxeses, Alexanders, Hannibals, Napoleons, or Hitlers – that is, by all those in whom a sort of intoxication was caused, for a time, by the enormous scope of their power.

To which Polemarchus, won over, replied:

–You're rallying us to a whole worldview! I'm ready to do battle alongside you.

–In that case, let's begin at the beginning. If justice is not what the poets and tyrants claim it is, whatever can it be?

— 1 —

REDUCING THE SOPHIST TO SILENCE[1] (336b–357a)

A heavy silence had greeted Socrates' question. So Thrasymachus felt that his time to speak had come. Many times over the course of the discussion he'd been tormented by a burning desire to take part in it. But the people sitting around him had kept him from doing so because they wanted to follow the progression of the argument. This time, however, taking advantage of the confusion that had followed the return (oddly abrupt, it's true) to the original form of the question, Thrasymachus finally broke out of the silence they'd imposed on him and, flexing all his muscles, crouching like a wild beast about to bare its huge claws, he advanced on Socrates as if to tear him apart and devour him alive. Socrates and Polemarchus recoiled in terror. Once he'd reached the middle of the room, the monster glowered at the whole audience and began speaking in a voice to which the room's high ceiling, the French windows, the darkness that had fallen over the sailboats, indeed the whole world, seemed to lend a thunderous power:

–What pathetic hogwash Socrates has been subjecting us to for hours now! What's with all your kowtowing to each other and taking turns bombarding us with your stupid nonsense? If you[2] really want to know what justice is, Socrates, stop asking pointless questions and rubbing your hands in glee when you've refuted something one of your flustered sidekicks has managed to stammer out. Asking questions is easy, answering them less so. So tell us once and for all how *you* define justice. And don't come telling us that justice is anything but justice, that it's duty, expediency, advantage, profit, interest, and so on. Tell us precisely and clearly what you have to say. Because I won't be like all the bit players in your three-ring circus, I won't put up with all your hot air.

14

At these words, Socrates, feigning – or really feeling? – panicky astonishment, stared for a moment at Thrasymachus, the way you do when, on a snowy evening, you encounter a wolf who might lock his cruel eyes on you first, in which case you'll be struck dumb, or so the old country women say. Then he went on in a somewhat tremulous voice:

–Fortunately *I* saw *you* first tonight, you ferocious rhetorician! Otherwise I really might have lost my voice! But I still think I'll try to placate the wolf who pounced on our conversation as on a little lamb trembling in fear. . . Dear Thrasymachus! Don't be angry with us! If Polemarchus and I were completely wrong in the way we went about considering the problem, you know very well that it wasn't on purpose. Suppose we were searching for gold, like in a Western, with big cowboy hats on our heads and all that sort of thing. Can you really think that, with our feet in the water and our pans in our hands, we'd bother deferring to each other and saying "After you, pardner" and run the risk of not finding anything at all? Yet here we are searching for justice, which is a lot more important than some heap of gold nuggets, and you'd think us capable of playing nice with each other all the time instead of devoting the utmost seriousness to bringing its Idea to light. No way! That's simply not possible. The best hypothesis is that we're just plain incapable of finding what we're looking for. And in that case let me say to you and to all the clever people of your sort: instead of giving us a hard time, show us a little mercy.

After hearing this speech Thrasymachus let out a sardonic laugh that gave the whole audience the creeps.

–I was right, for Pete's sake! That's the famous Socratic irony[3] all right! I knew it, I told everyone around me: Socrates will never agree to answer. He'll be as ironic as can be and do anything he can to avoid having to answer a precise question. By Heracles! I told you so!

–That's because you're so clever, *Socrates said.* You set up your calculations with the utmost care. If you ask someone how to get the number twelve in a math problem, knowing you, you'll add: "Whatever you do, my friend, don't come telling me it's six times two, or four times three, or twenty-four divided by two, let alone that it's eleven plus one, or eight plus four or, as poor Kant wrote, seven plus five.[4] Spare me any such nonsense." You, at any rate, know perfectly well that with those kinds of prohibitions no one will be able to answer your question. But the other person can still ask *you* a few questions. For example: "What exactly is your aim, O most subtle Thrasymachus? That I shouldn't give you any of the answers you've forbidden me to give? But what if one, or even several, of them,

15

happen to be true? What's your hidden agenda then? That I should say something other than the truth?" How would you respond to this hypothetical interlocutor?

But Thrasymachus wasn't fazed and said:

–That's easy: What's that got to do with the question of justice? As usual, you're just switching horses as soon as you see that yours is going to lose the race.

–But there *is* a connection! My twelve and my justice are horses from the same stable. But, OK, let's assume that there's no connection. Do you imagine that if your interlocutor thinks there *is* one, he'll change the answer he thinks is right simply because you've forbidden it?

–Oh, for crying out loud! You want to do the very same thing! You want to define justice with one of the words I forbade you to use.

–Well, no wonder if I did. I'd just have to think, after giving it serious dialectical consideration, that it's the right word.

–All that stuff about duty, propriety, interest, advantage! *That's* the kind of junk you want to use to plug the leaky bucket of your argument? Confound it! If I can show you, first of all, that there's another answer you haven't even thought of and, second of all, that that answer blows to bits all the stupid things you've been kicking around, what sentence will you impose on yourself?

–The sentence that someone who doesn't know has to submit to: learning from someone who *does* know. That's the punishment I'll sentence myself to.

–Well, you'll be getting off lightly, *Thrasymachus said with a sneer.* In addition to having to learn, you'll have to fork over a big stack of dollars to me.

–I will when I have any, if I have any someday. . .

But Glaucon, a rich kid, didn't want the confrontation that was brewing to be put off on account of money.

–You have everything you need, Socrates, *he said.* And you, Thrasymachus, if it's money you're after, go ahead and say so! We'll all take up a collection for Socrates.

–Yeah, right! *hissed Thrasymachus.* So that Socrates can do his usual number on me: he never answers, the other person answers, he makes mincemeat of what the person says, he refutes him, and that's that!

–But, my dear friend, *said Socrates calmly,* how *can* I answer, given that, in the first place, I don't know, and, in the second place, all I ever do is say that the only thing I know is that I don't know, and, in the third place, even assuming that I *do* know and that I say

16

that I know, I would nevertheless keep quiet, since someone who's topnotch, namely you, has forbidden me beforehand to give any of the answers I deem appropriate to the question? You're the one who should speak, since in the first place you say you know, and in the second place you know what you say. Come on! Don't play hard to get! If you speak, you'll be doing me a favor, and you'll show that you don't look down on Glaucon's and his friends' desire to learn from the great Thrasymachus.

Glaucon and the others all chimed in and begged Thrasymachus to give in. It was plain that he wanted to, certain as he was of the applause that his devastating answer to the question of the day – "What is justice?" – would earn him. But for a moment longer he pretended to go on arguing that Socrates should be the one to answer. At last he gave up, remarking:

–This is the classic example of Socrates' "wisdom": he announces he has nothing to teach anyone, but when it comes to stealing other people's ideas, he's only too willing, and never says thank you!

–When you say I learn from others, *Socrates shot back,* you're perfectly right. But when you claim I never thank them, you're wrong. Naturally I don't pay for the lessons, because I don't have any dollars or euros or drachmas or yen. On the other hand, I'm very generous with praise. What's more, you'll soon find out how fervently I admire someone who speaks well – in fact, just as soon as you've answered my question, an answer that I have a hunch will surprise us all.

Thrasymachus then came forward, stood up very straight, and closed his eyes like the Pythia at Delphi, meditating. On the shade-filled patio the silence was deafening.

–Listen, listen very carefully. I say that justice is not and cannot be anything but the interest of the stronger.

He then fixed his withering gaze on Socrates. But the silence persisted, since Socrates, short and potbellied, his eyes big and round and his arms dangling at his sides, looked like a disappointed dog being offered a slice of pumpkin.

Thrasymachus was annoyed.

–So where's all this famous praise of yours? *he said.* You're as quiet as a mouse. You're such a sore loser, totally incapable of congratulating your opponent on his win. And you call yourself the wisest of men! Bravo!

–Forgive me, but first I have to be sure I understand you. Let's see. You say: "Justice is the interest of the stronger." What exactly does that statement mean? Take a bicycle racer, for example. Let's say he's the stronger party when it comes to biking up mountains. Let's say it's in his interest to dope himself by shooting EPO in his behind, so as to race even faster and to shatter all the records. You can't really mean, can you, that justice for *us* would be to inject ourselves relentlessly in the backside, since that's what's in the interest of the stronger?

–Oh, you're downright despicable, Socrates! You purposely misinterpret my words and plaster them onto some disgusting anecdote just to make me look like a fool.

–Not at all. I just think you need to clarify your splendid maxim. It's as hard and black as coal...

–Coal? What on earth are you talking about?

–. . . as the coal that diamonds are mined from. Let your maxim simmer a bit for us in the broth of its context, as our modern orators would say.

–All right, I see what you mean. You know that the constitutions of different countries can be monarchical, aristocratic, or democratic. Furthermore, in every country the government has a monopoly on force, specifically armed force. It can then be observed that every government makes laws favoring its own interest: democrats make democratic laws, aristocrats aristocratic laws, and so on. In short, governments, which have force at their command, declare whatever's in their own interest to be lawful and just. If a citizen disobeys, they punish him insofar as he has broken the law and acted unjustly. So that, dear friend, is what I say is invariably justice in every country: the interest of the government in power. And since that government has a monopoly on force, the conclusion that anyone who reasons correctly will draw from this is that justice is always and everywhere the same, namely what's in the interest of the stronger.

And, so saying, Thrasymachus cast a triumphant glance over the audience.

Socrates' face lit up:

–*Now* I understand what you meant!

But just as quickly it darkened:

–Unfortunately, I'm not at all sure that it's true. Right off the bat, someone hearing you might say *(and here Socrates impersonated a comic actor speaking with a nasal intonation)*: "Very odd! Very odd! And to be precise: very odd![5] Thrasymachus strictly forbade Socrates to say that justice is interest. But a couple of minutes later, what does he himself loudly proclaim? That justice is interest." Naturally I'd object to this guy with the stuffed nose: "Careful, sir, careful! He said interest, sure, but *of the stronger*."

–An insignificant detail! *snorted Thrasymachus.*

18

–Whether it's important or not isn't clear yet. But what *is* absolutely clear is that we need to examine whether it's really the truth that's coming out of your mouth, as naked and pure as a cherub.

–Would you get a load of this Socrates! *said a jubilant Thrasymachus, turning to face the audience.* He thinks I cough up angels!

–Let's put off examining your sputum till later. I'll grant you that what's just is in the interest of a Subject. Whether we should add "the stronger Subject" I'm not so sure, but we need to take a close look at that.

–Go ahead and look, Socrates, examine, consider, weigh, and quibble to your heart's content. We know what you're like!

–I thought I understood that, as far as you're concerned, it is just to obey the rulers of the state. Furthermore, you'd agree, I assume, that these rulers aren't infallible but do in fact make mistakes.

–Of course!

–Consequently, when they go about enacting laws, sometimes they get it right and sometimes they get it all wrong, don't they?

–You'd have to look long and hard to find a comment as banal and utterly uninteresting as that one.

–No doubt, no doubt. . . But if we follow your argument, we'll have to say that, for a ruler, to enact proper laws is to serve his own interest and to enact improper ones is to go against it. Right?

–That's self-evident.

–And to have to do what the rulers have decided, is that just, in your opinion?

–You sound like a broken record! Yes, yes, yes!

–So, if we adopt your definition of justice, we can conclude that it is just not only to do what's in the interest of the stronger, but also – and here's what's amazing – the opposite: what goes *against* the interest of the stronger.

–What on earth are you talking about?! *cried Thrasymachus.*

–The necessary implications of your definition. Let's slow down a bit. We'd agreed on one point, which you even considered a trivial one: when the rulers order their subjects to do this or that, even though it sometimes happens that these rulers are mistaken about what their own real interest is, it's still always just for the subjects to do exactly what the rulers order them to do. Yes or no?

–How many times do I have to tell you?! What a drag this is! Yes and yes.

–You therefore agreed that it's just to go against the interest of the rulers, hence of the stronger, when these rulers unintentionally order things to be done that are bad for them, since it's just – you said this

19

over and over – to do everything decreed by said rulers. It follows inexorably from this that it's just to do the exact opposite of what you say, since, in the case that concerns us here, to do what goes against the interest of the stronger is what the stronger orders the weaker to do.

The excitement this speech stirred up in the audience was enormous. Polemarchus awoke with a start, the pale Cleitophon turned red, Glaucon jumped up and down, and Amantha tugged nervously at her left ear. It was Polemarchus who took the plunge.

–I think Thrasymachus might as well close up shop and go home! *he exclaimed.*

–Yeah, sure, *muttered Cleitophon, who had become as pale as a ghost again.* Whatever Polemarchus says, Thrasymachus has got to do.

–But it was Thrasymachus himself who got tripped up on his own words! *Polemarchus retorted.* He agreed that the rulers sometimes order their subjects to do what's against the rulers' own interest and that it's just for the subjects to do so!

–Thrasymachus, *hissed Cleitophon, his face as white as plaster,* only posited *one* principle: it's just to do what the rulers order.

–Thrasymachus posited *two* principles, not just one, *an exasperated Polemarchus insisted.* First, that justice is what's in the interest of the stronger. And, second, that it's just to obey the rulers. Having thus upheld both a principle of interest and a principle of obedience, he had to admit that it sometimes happens that the stronger order the weaker, their subjects, to do what goes against the stronger's own interest. Hence it follows that justice is no more what's in the interest of the stronger than it is what goes *against* that interest.

–But, *shrieked Cleitophon, who had suddenly turned dark red again,* when Thrasymachus speaks of the interest of the stronger, it's a matter of a *subjective* phenomenon: what the stronger considers his own interest to be. That's what the weaker is obliged to do, and that, in Thrasymachus's opinion, is what is just.

–He didn't say anything of the kind, *muttered Polemarchus, upset.*

–It doesn't matter! *Socrates cut in.* If Thrasymachus now thinks something he didn't say earlier, let him tell us what he thinks. Or what he thinks he thinks. Come on, noble Thrasymachus, was that really your definition of justice: what the stronger *thinks* is in the interest of the stronger, regardless of the fact that, in reality, it may or may not be in his interest? May we say that that was the true meaning of what you said?

–Absolutely not! *Thrasymachus snapped back.* Would you ascribe the ridiculous notion to me that someone who makes a mistake is the stronger at the very moment when he's making a mistake?

–Well, yes, I really thought that that was what you were contending when you agreed that, since rulers aren't infallible, they're sometimes mistaken about what their own interest is.

–When it comes to rational argument, Socrates, you're nothing but a trickster. It's as though you were calling someone who makes a mistake about the cause of a patient's illness a "doctor" at the very moment he's making the mistake. Or someone who makes a serious mistake in his calculations a "mathematician" at the very moment he makes it. In my opinion,[6] when we say that a doctor makes a mistake or that a mathematician makes a mistake or that a grammarian makes a mistake, those are nothing but meaningless words. In my opinion, none of them can make a mistake, provided that his being, or rather his act, corresponds to the name we give him. And so, in my opinion once more, and to be precise – since Socrates is a stickler for precision – a craftsman, an expert, a creator, or an artist can never make a mistake when he acts in accordance with the predicate that defines him. In fact someone who makes a mistake does so only insofar as his knowledge has failed him, and therefore when he's stopped being the craftsman, expert, creator, or artist that we assumed he was. I conclude from this, in my opinion still, that none of those we call craftsman, scientist, or head of state can ever make a mistake insofar as one of these names applies to him, and this is so regardless of the fact that everyone stupidly says that the doctor "made a mistake" or the ruler "made a mistake." Please understand the answers I gave a moment ago in light of these commonsense remarks, Socrates. And, in order to be really perfectly precise, in my opinion absolutely perfectly precise, the hard and fast truth can be formulated in four steps. First, the head of state, *qua* head, cannot make a mistake. Second, insofar as he cannot make a mistake, he can decide what's best for himself. Third, that's what the subject, the person whom the ruler commands, must do – that and nothing else. And, fourth, we come back full circle to what I said at the outset, which, though Socrates pretended not to see as much, smashed all his claptrap to bits: justice consists in the fact that every practice is dictated by the interest of the stronger.

As though struck by the solemnity of the moment, Socrates nodded his head for quite a while. Then he said:

–In your opinion, still and always, I'm a trickster, am I? In your opinion, I questioned you the way I did in order to discredit you? Hmm? In your opinion?

–Of course! That's as plain as day! Everyone knows Socrates' dirty tricks! But, in my opinion, you're defeated before you even start. You can't hide your little game from me and, when you're up against someone like me, who sees right through it, you won't be able to overpower me in argument.

–I wouldn't even dream of trying, you venerable orator! However, to avoid giving me any pretext for my dirty tricks, could you tell us what you mean by the words "head of state" or "government," and also by the term "the stronger" in the famous maxim you just repeated: "Justice, which is what's in the interest of the head of state, who's the stronger, is what the subject, who's the weaker, must do"? Are you using these words and phrases in the precise sense they may have for us, or in a loose and general way? In your opinion, once more, is it a matter of speaking precisely or just "in a manner of speaking"?

–I'm speaking of the ruler and all that sort of thing in the strictest sense of the words, in my opinion. Go ahead and try to discredit me on all this, play the trickster. You won't be able to.

–In your opinion, would I be crazy enough to try to play the trickster vis-à-vis a Thrasymachus – in other words, to trim a charging lion's mane with a pair of little scissors?

–And yet that's what you just tried to do, you dumb barber!

–OK, let's drop the hairy metaphors. Let's get back to the problems at hand. What's the real aim of the doctor in the precise sense of the word, the doctor you were talking about a moment ago? To make money or to treat the sick? Answer only about the doctor whose activity is consistent with the generic term "doctor."

–To treat the sick, obviously!

–And what about an admiral? The admiral befitting his name, is he a commander of sailors or is he only an ordinary sailor himself?

–You're so annoying! He's a commander of sailors – there, I hope you're happy now.

–The fact that an admiral might happen to sail all by himself on an ordinary old boat is of no account as far as the designation "admiral of the fleet" is concerned and doesn't entail his being called an "ordinary sailor." Because it's not insofar as he sails one way or another that he's called "admiral," but rather by virtue of his skill and of the authority he has over the sailors. Right? In your personal opinion?

–Right. But you're wasting our time with all this naval crap.

–Anyway, it's clear that the doctor and the admiral each has his own particular interest. And the aim of each one's skill is to seek out and then provide each one with that interest. A skill considered in

22

itself obviously has no particular interest except to be as perfect as possible. So we can. . .

–Hold on! Not so fast! *Thrasymachus interrupted him.* What's all this business about the interest of a skill the only interest of which is the interest of someone who possesses that skill? I can see one of Socrates' typical dirty tricks coming on.

–Let me be crystal-clear. Suppose you asked me whether the body is self-sufficient or lacking something. I'd reply: "Sure it's lacking something! That's precisely why medical skill as we know it today was invented. The body is often in poor condition and can't get by on its own. Medical skill was developed and organized to serve the interests of the body." And, knowing trusty Thrasymachus, I'm sure he'll agree with my answer.

Thrasymachus sneered and blew his nose loudly.

–To agree with that sort of platitude any idiot would serve your purpose.

–So you agree, *said Socrates softly.* Now let's ask whether medical skill, in its turn, is in poor condition in the same way as the body. If so, it might need some other kind of skill to serve its interest and provide it with what it lacks. Do we need to go on? Do we need to grant that, for the same reasons, this second skill itself needs a third – and so on, *ad infinitum*? If this infinite regress seems odd, we can go back to the beginning and assume instead that medical skill itself sees to remedying its own defects. And the third possibility is that a skill requires neither a second skill nor itself to obtain what it lacks, given that, as a true skill, it has no deficiencies or flaws. In effect, we observe that a skill seeks only the interest of what it deals with, and, provided it's genuine, it remains faultless and flawless for as long as it remains, in the strict sense of the word "skill," entirely what it is. So there are three possibilities. Number one: to compensate for what it lacks, every "technique," which is sometimes how *techne* is translated – "professional skill" is a lot more precise, but clumsy – requires a technique of that technique, and so on *ad infinitum*. Number two: every technique is clearly a technique of itself and can therefore compensate for its own deficiencies. Number three: considered in and for itself, a technique lacks for nothing. My dear Thrasymachus, consider these three possibilities and tell us which one – in your opinion, of course – is the right one.

–In my opinion, it's the third one, without a doubt.

–Wonderful! So medicine isn't concerned with the interest of medicine but only with the interests of the body; the technique of horse training pays no heed to horse training but only to the horse.

A technique cares nothing about its own interest – it doesn't have one anyway – but only about the interest of its object, about what the skill that defines it deals with.

–All you're doing, in my opinion, is repeating my choice of the third hypothesis. Always the same old Socratic hot air!

–I'm doing it so that you won't accuse me of setting any traps for you. Here's my question: a skill gets the results it seeks from whatever it deals with, doesn't it? Otherwise it's not a skill, it's only the technique of nothing.

–Obviously! The "long detours" you go off on are so simple-minded!

–But anything that gets the results it expects from something is, in actual fact, what's in command of – or what exercises its authority over – that thing, isn't it?

Thrasymachus frowned, sensing a trap. But how could he avoid it? He decided to go for bravura:

– I for one don't think anyone can deny that.

–So a technique is in the position of a ruler, in other words of a commander, with respect to its object. Medicine rules the body; the admiral is the commander of the sailors. As far as sick bodies and sailors slaving away are concerned, doctors and admirals are the stronger parties. However – and you yourself admitted as much, without the slightest hesitation – they in no way serve their own interest but only the interest of the weaker, of whatever's ruled by them: the body, whose good health they desire, or the sailors, whom they want to see succeeding in sailing properly. So no technical skill either considers or prescribes what's in the interest of the stronger. Finally we see that no ruler, no government conceived of as a ruler either considers or prescribes what serves his (or its) own interest. On the contrary, a ruler prescribes what's in the interest of those he commands or rules and for whom he practices his skill. And it is with those people in mind – the subjects, the people who are ruled over, the sufferers, all of life's galley slaves – that a true master says what he says and does what he does.

At this, as they say in assembly sessions reports, "a ripple ran through the room." People smiled, whispered, looked either smug or dejected. Everyone was aware that a turning point had been reached in the debate: the definition of justice proposed by Thrasymachus had quite simply been changed into its opposite. They turned to look at him with pity and waited for a response from him, without really expecting that there would be one. When it did finally come, it caused great astonishment.

–Tell me, *asked Thrasymachus, his eyes suddenly twinkling gaily,* are you being properly supervised? Are your nanny and your tutor here with you?

–What do you mean? *said Socrates, visibly thrown off.* You should answer my question rather than talk such nonsense.

–It's just that, in my opinion, your nanny ought to do a better job of wiping your bottom if it's as shitty as your argument! And your tutor ought to teach you the difference between a sheep and a shepherd.

–What are you talking about? *an increasingly bewildered Socrates asked.*

–You seem to think that shepherds and cowherds are only interested in the well-being of the sheep and cattle, that it's only to please those sweet little sheep and great big bulls that they fatten them up and take care of them. That's ludicrous, my poor friend. The only reason they do so is so that their masters, the owners of these nice horned and woolly animals, can make a huge profit out of it. What should be said, then, about the people who are in power in a state? I'm talking about those who really wield the power. Do you think they're any different from the owners of herds or flocks? Are you so naïve as to think that they care about anything other than making a huge personal profit off the masses of their subjects? You think you're such an expert when it comes to questions about what is just and unjust, or justice and injustice, as you prefer, whereas in reality you don't know the first thing about any of it. You don't understand that "justice" and "what is just" designate *someone else*'s good: the interest, sure, but of this other person, the stronger party, the ruler. It follows, then, that what belongs to the subject or the servant is only, as my friend Jean-François Lyotard would say, the wrong done him.[7] "Injustice" means exactly the opposite. It's the name of an action that compels to obedience and servility people who are just and think that they must always act in accordance with moral laws. You're floundering around in the most abysmal ignorance regarding a host of empirical facts, such as the fact that subjects only act under the iron rule of the interest of the stronger and in so doing promote *his* happiness, in no way their own. What surprises me, actually, is your unbelievable naïveté. How can you not see that a just man, as compared with an unjust one, is the loser every time? Suppose, for instance, that the two of them start a business together and sign binding contracts with each another. Well, when the company's dissolved, you invariably see that the just man has lost his shirt in the venture and the unjust man has cleaned up. Or take the case of taxes and refunds. On the same amount of income, the just man always pays more taxes than the unjust man and doesn't get a dime back from the state, while the unjust man makes a mint. Now suppose that the just man and the unjust man are appointed as heads of some government office or other. First, what happens to the just man? At best – most of the time it's a lot worse – his private affairs, on the one hand, go down the tubes, since he can no longer devote the necessary time to them, and, on the other hand, inasmuch as he's just, he refuses to pilfer so much as a penny from the public till. The poor guy ends up being hated by his relatives and friends because – always on account of being just! – he categorically refuses to pull any strings for them so that they can rise rapidly through the ranks of the civil service. Now what happens to the unjust man? Exactly the opposite of these terrible things. Naturally I'm talking about the truly unjust man, the one who tramples on his underlings. He's the one to study if you want to gauge the enormous gap between all the wonderful things the unjust man enjoys in the secrecy of his private life and the abysmal poverty of the just man who lives in the full light of day. You'll have a perfect understanding of this gap if you turn your attention to perfect injustice, the sort that bestows the greatest happiness on the most dreadful scoundrels and plunges their victims, whose conscience won't allow them to become immoral in any way, into horrible, hopeless misery. This pure form of injustice is nothing other than tyranny. The tyrant's not stingy with his injustice! On the contrary, he appropriates other people's property on a grand scale, through force and cunning. He grabs everything in sight, making no distinction between public and private things any more than between sacred and profane ones. You'll notice that if some ordinary fellow fails to cover up a crime of that sort he's severely punished and thoroughly disgraced. Insults rain down on him, depending on what sort of vile deed he committed: Purveyor of human flesh! Heretic! Safecracker! Highway robber! Purse-snatcher! What a contrast with our tyrant, who has not only stolen his fellow citizens' property but has reduced them to slavery! Instead of showering him with insults, they call him a "happy man," or one "blessed by the gods." And it's not just his fellow citizens who suck up to him. It's all those who know the infamous acts of infamy that made him famous. Because the critics who criticize injustice aren't afraid of committing it, only of being subjected to it. Thus, dear Socrates, we've shown that injustice, when pushed to the necessary limits, is more powerful, inherently freer, and mightier than justice. As I said right from the start, justice is essentially the interest of the stronger. And the unjust man pays himself the interest from the capital he represents in his own person.

After dumping the huge bucket of his argument into the ears of the flabbergasted audience the way a firefighter dumps water on a fire, Thrasymachus thought he would leave to a hail of applause, as the undisputed champion of the rhetoricians' fight. But the audience didn't see it that way. They wanted to make him stay and explain more clearly the rational kernel of what he had just said. Socrates intervened, saying:

–Dear Thrasymachus! You virtuoso of fine phrases! You throw a gigantic argument at us and then all you can think about is taking off, without proving your position adequately or learning from everybody else whether things are really as you say or not. Do you think you were only dealing with some trivial matter? Come off it! You were attempting to define the rule of conduct for life as a whole, the imperative by which we can hope to live the most fruitful of lives.

–Do I seem like some country bumpkin who's unaware of the seriousness of what he's been talking about? *said Thrasymachus scornfully.*

–Well, you're doing a great job of *pretending* to be a country bumpkin, at any rate! Or else you couldn't care less about us, your audience. You don't give a damn about what might happen to us. Since we're ignorant about what you claim to know, our lives, when weighed on the scales of good and evil, might tip over to the wrong side. Come on, dear friend! Do a good turn! Impart your knowledge to us! It won't hurt you to do something good for all of us who are sitting here in a circle around you. To get you started, I'll tell you what I think. I'm going to be frank with you: you haven't convinced me. I don't believe that injustice benefits the Subject more than justice does, not even under the extreme conditions that you so brilliantly described for us: injustice has free rein, so to speak, and nothing stands in the way of the desires its evil actions spring from. Let's be perfectly clear, dear friend. We assume that an unjust man exists. We assume that he has the possibility of being unjust – an unlimited possibility – both covertly and by overt force. Well, I'm not in the least convinced that such a man will profit more from his injustice than he would have from the strictest observance of the principles of justice. And I don't think I'm the only one; I'm sure that others in this room share my belief. So convert us, O mighty rhetorician! Give us conclusive reasons for acknowledging that we're going wretchedly astray when we value justice more highly than injustice.

–How can I convince you, would you mind telling me? If my implacable reasoning was unsuccessful, I don't see what more I can

27

do. Unless I have to personally transfer my argument inside your brain!

–Oh no! Heaven forbid! Anything but that! To begin with, stick to your positions instead of misleading us, because you're always changing them without warning. Let me give you an example of that improper sort of change, which brings us back full circle, incidentally, to the start of our discussion. You first defined the doctor, as he really is, in the element of truth. But then, when it was a question of the shepherd, you didn't feel under any obligation to preserve the identity of the shepherd, who was also conceived of in his truth, logically, from start to finish. As your argument went on, the shepherd stopped being someone who tends to the well-being of his flock and instead became anything at all – a banquet guest who's only interested in feasting on couscous with lamb, or a speculator who sells tons of meat on the Stock Exchange without ever having set foot in a cowshed – anything but a shepherd! Yet the shepherd's technique is concerned with nothing but providing the best care to its own particular object, the flock. Because, as regards the strictly intrinsic determination of this technique's excellence, it is by its very nature obviously provided for, so long as its identity – to be the technique of tending flocks of sheep – remains the same.

–Which means, *Amantha interjected,* that it continues to merit its name.

–Precisely. For the same reasons, I thought that you and I were obliged to agree a little while ago that a given power, conceived of in its essence, considers only the welfare of the people under its care and over whom its authority is exercised. And that this was true of any power, whether it operates on the scale of the state or on the scale of the family.

–Whether it's public or private, *Glaucon added.*

–I'd say political or domestic instead, *Amantha corrected him.*

–Which leads me, *Socrates went on, his beady eyes fixed on Thrasymachus,* to ask you a question. Do you think that the people who rule states – and I mean those who are really the rulers, not puppet rulers, or figurehead presidents, or agents of capitalism, or people disguised as "representatives" – do so willingly?

–Oh, for Pete's sake! *exclaimed Thrasymachus.* I don't just think so, I *know* so.

–Knowledge is sacred. But knowledge, the lofty discipline of sociology, also teaches us that, when it comes to most government posts – under-secretaryships of this or that, cabinet posts, committees, commissions, bureaux, and agencies – nobody's willing to head them up for no pay. Inasmuch as they aren't going to personally profit from this little bit of power and they'll have to deal with the public, they demand a salary, and a very high one at that. So let's take a step back. Whenever one of the techniques is different from the others, don't we say that it's different because its own particular function is different from the others' functions?

–Wow! *said Amantha, turning to Thrasymachus.* Be careful you don't get lost in the maze of what's different from some other thing, because each of the other things is different from the other thing. . .

–My answer, *Thrasymachus declared, not without a certain pomposity,* is perfectly clear. It is indeed on account of its function that one technique differs from another.

–And each technique brings us a distinct and particular benefit, *Socrates continued.* When it comes to medicine, it's health; to piloting an airplane, it's speed and safety during the trip, and so on with all the others. Yes or no?

–Yes! I keep saying the same thing to you! Yes!

–And the technique. . . Oh, I really hate that translation of *techne*! I'll come up with a different one as the night goes on. Anyway, the technique whose former name used to be "mercenarism" and that, now that it's ubiquitous, is called "wage earning" has no specific function other than to bring in wages. Naturally, you'd never confuse a doctor with an airline pilot. If – and this is the rule that you, the stickler for precise language, are imposing on us – we have to define words with the utmost precision, we'd never call a ship's captain a "doctor" merely because the passengers, intoxicated by the sea air, are in great shape. So, I ask you, can we call any old form of wage earning "medicine" inasmuch as the wage earner feels better because he's received his pay?

–What are you getting at with all this balderdash? *grumbled Thrasymachus.*

–I'm getting to the fateful moment of my argument when all the different strands come together and everything becomes clear. Listen carefully to my question: are you going to equate medicine with wage earning by arguing that when the doctor cures people he earns a wage?

–That would be ludicrous.

–You acknowledged that each technique, considered in itself, brings us some benefit and that this benefit is a unique one, distinct from the one that another technique provides us. So if several different techniques bring us the same benefit, it's clear that that benefit derives from a common element that's added to the particular function of each of the techniques under consideration. Applying this principle is easy in the case at hand. When the practitioner of a given technique earns a wage, it's because he has added to the technique of which he's the expert that other, more general technique we called wage earning. But if he *doesn't* earn any wage, his technical performance is not nullified for all that. It's still what it is, and, in its being, it remains altogether external to the wage earned.

Thrasymachus sensed that the jaws of the argument were threatening to crush him. He put on an air of mock deference and said in an ironic tone of voice:

–If you say so, Socrates, then I'll say so, too.

–Then you'll have to accept the consequences. It's in fact now been established that no technique and no position of authority has its own interest as either its aim or its function. As I already said, a technique, if that's what we're dealing with, is only concerned with and prescribes what's in the interest of whatever its object and stakes are. And, if it's a position of authority, its aim is only the interest of the people under its authority. That's why I said a moment ago, my dear Thrasymachus, that no one, of his own free will, wanted to be in charge of anything, let alone commit to treating and resolving other people's troubles, without getting paid for it. For in that sort of situation the interest of the weaker, not of the stronger, has to be taken into consideration. The upshot is that everyone demands a wage for it. Of course they do! Someone who practices a technique efficiently and properly when taking care of a client is never concerned with or prescribes his *own* good. He only cares about what's best for the person he's working for, to whom he's nevertheless superior, since he's mastered a technique that the other person doesn't know a thing about. That's why, to remedy this apparent paradox – the superior one in the service of the inferior one – a very high wage almost always has to be given to the person who accepts a very senior position, a wage paid in cash or in the form of various honors. As for the person who obstinately refuses to accept such a position, he'll earn his wages in the form of a punishment.

Glaucon, noticing that a fed-up Thrasymachus was preparing to make a strategic get-away, felt duty-bound to put his own two cents in:

–Socrates! What exactly are you saying? I understand that the kind of wage corresponding to wage earning is different from the wage that's appropriate to techniques like medicine or ruling a great body like the state. But that a punishment – and of what sort? – should serve as wages for someone who turns down a position, and who therefore, since he renders no service, doesn't deserve any wages at all, is quite beyond me.

–Ask yourself what the wages of one of our best supporters, a really good philosopher, for instance, might be. Don't you know the reason why he'll sometimes resign himself to accepting an important position in government? Don't you know that, for him, careerism and greed are vices?

–Yes, so they are. But so what?

–You yourself, if memory serves, *Amantha interjected,* agreed to be president of the Council in Athens. It was around the time your beloved Alcibiades took a real beating at the Battle of Notion.[8] What wages did you receive?

–My dear girl, you're stirring up an extremely painful memory. Anyway, as you might expect, it wasn't a question of love either for power or for what it could earn me. At the height of the Cultural Revolution Mao Zedong issued the directive: "Get involved in state affairs."[9] When we obey that directive, we don't want to be treated either as wage earners who demand to get paid simply for performing their duties or as thieves who derive profits on the sly from doing so. Nor is it a question of going after honors, because we're not motivated by ambition. In fact, all of us – we philosophers of the new generation – think that willingly participating in the power of the existing state, without being obliged to do so by exceptional circumstances, is completely alien to our political principles. So it follows inexorably that the only thing that could compel us to participate would be the prospect of an inner punishment even harsher than the shame we'd feel about going after positions and remuneration. Now, in a situation of this sort, what might really be the most intolerable thing? It would be to be governed by scoundrels simply because we refused to accept power. The fear of such a punishment is the only reason why honorable people from time to time get involved at the highest level of state affairs. And it's clear that they do so neither out of personal interest nor for their own pleasure, but only because they think it's a necessary evil, given how impossible it is, when it comes to the challenges the state faces, to find better, or at least equally good, candidates for the posts they'll fill.

–Wait, wait! *Amantha cut in.* You're talking about the paradoxical involvement of decent people in a pretty corrupt state, where careerists, profiteers, and demagogues are usually running the show. But such dedication has never been of much use. I wonder how things would be in an ideal state, which was subject to principles of justice.

–If such a state were someday to exist, people would compete *not* to be in power, just as they do now to *be* in power.

–Negative elections! Incredible! *Glaucon snickered.*

–People would boast about having finally been elected *not* to have to fill any position, because the country, composed of free men and women and ruled by the principle of equality, would unanimously consider that a true leader is not concerned with his own interest but solely with the interest of the people as a whole. And the broad masses of citizens would find it more convenient and pleasant to trust their own personal fate to trustworthy people than to be personally entrusted themselves with the fate of enormous masses of people. So I cannot at all agree with Thrasymachus: justice is not and cannot be the interest of the stronger.

–But you haven't given us the *positive* counterpart of your refutation of the sophist, *grumbled Amantha.* What, in the final analysis, is justice?

–We'll see about that later. For the time being, there's a point that's been bothering me about what Thrasymachus said.

–You're going to switch horses again, I can tell, *said Amantha.*

–Let me just mention this point. Thrasymachus claims that the unjust man's life is much better than the just man's. What about you, Glaucon? Which life would you choose? Is there anything true about a hierarchy like that?

–Oh, come on! *said Amantha.* My kid brother knows only too well what you're hoping he'll say, so I'll say it for him: the just man's life is wonderful!

–Both of you, *insisted Socrates,* heard Thrasymachus go into detail about the incredible advantages of the unjust life, and you're still not convinced?

–I'd prefer to be positively convinced of the just man's superiority, *Amantha protested.* For the time being, I'll settle for not being convinced of the unjust man's superiority. We're stewing in negation.

–For once she's right, *Glaucon acknowledged.* Proving squarely that A is better than B is a different thing from proving that it's not true that B is better than A.

–All my compliments to the logician! *exclaimed Socrates.* But we need to choose a method. One way to proceed is by using enormous antitheses, speech versus speech. We set out all the benefits of justice at once, then Thrasymachus does the same for the benefits of injustice. We'll have to keep count of these benefits in each speech, or, in a nutshell, measure up what's been said on either side. And we'll need just people from outside to decide the dispute. The other way

32

of proceeding is to use the model we adopted at the beginning of the evening: through a close-fought game of questions and answers, we'll construct something both sides can agree to, and that way no outside third party will be necessary. We'll all be alternately the lawyers and the judges.

–That way's a lot better, *Glaucon agreed.*

Socrates then turned to Thrasymachus, who was partly reclining in an armchair with a glum look on his face and speaking only grudgingly, in that blasé tone of voice affected by people who have "seen it all," are "nobody's fool," and "have no more illusions."

–Come on now, Thrasymachus, buck up! Let's go back to the beginning. You maintain that, compared with perfect injustice, perfect justice is infinitely less advantageous.

–Yes, I do maintain that, *Thrasymachus said,* and I told you why.

–Let's see. You no doubt apply the pair of opposite predicates vice/virtue to the real pair justice/injustice. And I assume that, like everyone else, you attribute "virtue" to justice and "vice" to injustice.

Goaded by Socrates' assumption, Thrasymachus suddenly dropped his "weary skeptic" pose. He literally shrieked:

–You've got to be kidding! Are you trying to pull the old Socratic irony number on me again? Well, he who laughs last laughs best, sweetheart! I proved that injustice is universally advantageous to the unjust man, while justice is universally detrimental to the just man.

–So are you saying that justice is a vice?

–No, not exactly a vice, *Thrasymachus, quite pleased with himself, qualified.* It's more a matter of high-minded naïveté.

–So then, injustice, *Socrates pointed out,* is crassness.

–Not at all. It's a matter of accurate assessment of situations and of what can be gotten out of them.

At this Socrates showed signs of bewilderment. Scratching the back of his neck, he said:

–Your view, dear friend, is that the unjust are prudent people, who are thoroughly acquainted with the truth of situations?

–Yes, provided, of course, we're talking about those people who are able to enslave an entire city, or even a whole country. You seem to think I'm talking about mere pickpockets who swipe passengers' wallets in the subway. I'm not denying that petty crimes like that can be profitable, as long as you don't get caught. But it's not even worth talking about them if what we have in mind are the large-scale injustices of the tyrants I described for you a moment ago.

–I'm well aware of what you have in mind, *Socrates remarked.* But

33

every time you repeat such a thing in public I'm just as astonished as if I had never heard you hold forth before. So you rank injustice with virtue and wisdom, and justice with the opposite?

–Absolutely. And I'm thrilled that I've managed to astonish Socrates!

The aforementioned Socrates dreamily scratched the back of his neck again.

–I must admit, your position is suddenly a very tough proposition, *he said.* For the moment I don't see what can be objected to it. If you were to claim that injustice is very advantageous while conceding, as nearly everyone does, that it's a vice and loathsome, we could answer you on the grounds of conventional opinion. But it's clear that you'll argue that injustice is as noble and wonderful as it is advantageous. All the virtues we attribute to justice you'll attribute to injustice, which you've had the intellectual audacity to put on a par with virtue and wisdom.

–You've guessed perfectly the truths I base my arguments on.

–Well, *said Socrates softly,* but even so, we won't throw in the towel. We've got to go on arguing, at least as long as we're justified in assuming that you're saying what you really think. And I do think that you're not joking, you happy man, and that you're spontane-ously telling us the truth as you see it.

–Why should you give a shit – pardon my French – whether I'm saying what I "really" think or not? Just refute my explicit argument, if you can, which I doubt, and don't waste your time rummaging through the empty trashcans of what I "really" think. As if anyone "really" thought!

–You're right. I apologize for having really thought that you really thought. All the same, try to answer a few questions.

From that point on a real duel began, and not with blunted foils either. Amantha, Glaucon, Polemarchus, and all the rest of them kept score of the hits. Socrates struck the first blow.

–Tell me, Thrasymachus: does the just man, in your opinion, want to assert his superiority over another just man?

–No way! If he did have such an ambition, if he did want to crush one of his rivals in justice, he wouldn't be the well-bred, gullible fool that I said he was.

–Would he want a just action to enable him to get the better of other just men?

–Certainly not, for the same reason.

–But what about outdoing an unjust man, then? Would the just man have such a desire? And would he regard it as just or unjust?

34

–As big a nitwit as he is, the just man would think it just to outdo the unjust man all right, but he wouldn't be able to.

–Whether he's able to or not isn't our problem. I'm simply asking you, dearest friend, to clarify your thinking, which I'd summarize as follows: the just man doesn't consider that outdoing another just man is worthy of himself in the least, nor does he feel any desire to do so. However, he *does* have the desire to get the better of the unjust man, and he deems that desire to be entirely worthy of himself. Right?

–You're just repeating my answer.

–Well, I'm cautious. I'm taking one step at a time as I construct a thinking that you and I will be able to share. Let's turn to the unjust man now. Does he want to outdo the just man and to act in such a way as to overpower every just action?

–Obviously! The characteristic desire of the unjust man is to dominate the whole world.

–And so the unjust man will also want to outdo the unjust man and to overpower every other unjust action by his own action, so as to ensure his power over everything?

–No objection. You're getting on my nerves.

–So we agree on the just and the unjust man's relationship to people both like and unlike themselves.

–Uh-oh, *Glaucon piped up,* not so fast! The argument is starting to get convoluted. A little formalism wouldn't hurt.

–Be my guest, *said Socrates. You*'re the logician.

–OK, *said Glaucon, overjoyed at being able to slip in his formulas.* I call *J* the just man in general, and, if we have to distinguish between two different just men, we'll call them *J1* and *J2* respectively. I call the unjust man in general *U*, and, if we have to distinguish between two unjust men, we'll call them *U1* and *U2* respectively. For the relation "to outdo," I'll write the sign for a relation of inequality the way it's done in math. For example, $J > U$ means that the just man has the upper hand over the unjust man. It's just a simple notation, OK? It's not a truth for the time being. I'll write "equals," as in math, for the relation "does not outdo," or "is the same as, or identical to." For example, $J1 = J2$ means that two just men are the same. It's as simple as can be.

–But so what? *commented Amantha caustically.*

–So I can write where we stand very clearly with two formulas. With respect to the just man, we have: $[(J1 = J2)$ and $(J > U)]$. This formalizes the notion that, as concerns a just man, two just men won't have to outdo each other, but a just man *must* outdo an unjust man.

With respect to the unjust man, we have $[(U1 > U2)$ and $(U > J)]$: the unjust man must outdo both any other unjust man and any just man.

–All right, *said Amantha,* that's exactly what Thrasymachus and Socrates said. But what's the point?

–You'll see, *said Glaucon enigmatically,* you'll see. . .

–Anyway, *Socrates resumed,* we all now agree on both the form and the content. Let's turn to the real problems. According to you, most excellent Thrasymachus, the unjust man is knowledgeable and wise, while the just man is ignorant and stupid?

–I couldn't have put it better myself, *scoffed Thrasymachus.*

–So shall we say that the unjust man is like any man whose subjective determination is knowledge and wisdom?

–That's obvious. A man who has certain attributes is like anyone else who has them too, and he differs from anyone who doesn't have them! That's what the great Socrates has just discovered.

–What does the logician think? *asked Socrates, ignoring the sarcasm.*

Glaucon jumped at the chance to speak:

–If we let W stand for the wise and knowledgeable man, Thrasymachus' position, using the previous notations, can be expressed as: $U = W$.

–And of course, *said Socrates,* since the just man is ignorant and stupid, *dixit* Thrasymachus, he'll be like the perfectly stupid and totally ignorant man. In terms of logic, what does that give us?

–If we let I stand for the ignorant stupid man, *said Glaucon,* Thrasymachus' position can be expressed as $J = I$.

–Good! And now, let's talk about music and medicine.

–In short, *said Thrasymachus scornfully,* let's talk nonsense.

–No, these are just analogies. With respect to music, the musician is wise and knowledgeable, while the person who can't so much as read a note is neither one nor the other. Just as, when it comes to public health, the doctor is wise and knowledgeable and everyone else isn't.

–What's your point? *asked Thrasymachus, losing patience.*

–Do you think, my excellent friend, that when a musician tunes a piano, what he wants is to outdo another musician as regards tightening or loosening the strings? Or isn't it rather that he wants to achieve a result that any able musician will consider correct?

–There's only one correct position for each string, so your second hypothesis is the right one.

–On the other hand, our piano tuner will want to be better at it than just some ordinary guy who hardly knows what a piano is, won't he?

–I won't deny you the pleasure of seeing me agree with an inane remark like that.

–What does the logician have to say?

–If we let M stand for the musician in general, *said Glaucon, a tad pedantically,* H for someone who's hopeless at music, and M1 and M2 for two different musicians, we then get: $[(M1 = M2)$ and $(M > H)]$.

–That's a lot like the formulas for the just man! *remarked Amantha.*

–Let's not get ahead of. . . the music! *Socrates quipped.* It is, I think, just as obvious that the doctor's main concern, or at least his specifically medical one, won't be to outdo another doctor. His concern will be to cure his patient by making decisions that he discusses and shares with his colleagues. On the other hand, he'll outdo a guy who can't tell measles from a sunburn. Generally speaking, a person who's wise and knowledgeable in a given area – young Glaucon's W – wants to do as well as his peers and to outdo someone who knows nothing about the subject. Conversely, if someone who's neither wise nor knowledgeable is presumptuous enough to meddle obtrusively in things he knows nothing about, he'll say he's outdoing everyone – knowledgeable and ignorant people alike – since he's unable to tell them apart. What does the logician have to say about all this?

–If I use W again to stand for the wise and knowledgeable person, and if I use I to indicate "ignorant" and "stupid" – the pretentious person who knows nothing about the subject – I'll have the following in terms of formalizing their respective opinions:

$$\text{For } W1 \; [(W1 = W2) \text{ and } (W > I)]$$
$$\text{For } I1 \; [(I1 > I2) \text{ and } (I > W)]$$

–Exactly the same as you had for *J* and *U* a moment ago! *exclaimed Amantha.*

–Yes, that's so, *agreed Socrates.* You can compare the formulas, beloved Thrasymachus. You claimed that the unjust man was wise and knowledgeable, and therefore that Glaucon had to write $U = W$. And, needless to say, you also maintained that the just man, as the opposite of the unjust man, was neither knowledgeable nor wise but ignorant and stupid instead, which Glaucon suggested we express as $J = I$. But now, after our examples and the foregoing formulas, you can see that if the unjust man is wise and knowledgeable, which is expressed as W, he must think himself the equal of any other wise and knowledgeable person, hence of any unjust man, and he will only outdo someone who's ignorant and stupid, hence the just man. While, since the just man is ignorant and stupid, which is expressed as *I*, he'll have to want to outdo everyone. But a moment ago you vehemently stated – and Glaucon formalized your view – that exactly the opposite was true: it's the *unjust* man who, according to you, outdoes everyone.

–That's quite possible, *said Thrasymachus, feigning indifference.*

–What happened in the interim? Quite simply, you added two supplementary statements to what allowed you to conclude that the unjust man outdoes everyone: namely that the unjust man is wise and knowledgeable and that the just man is ignorant and stupid. As that leads you into the muddy waters of a contradiction, those additional statements will have to be abandoned. In reality the attributes have to be reversed: it's the just man who's wise and knowledgeable and the unjust man who's ignorant and stupid.

–We demonstrated by *reductio ad absurdum, Glaucon solemnly announced,* that we need to posit: $J = W$ and $U = I$.

–Do whatever you like, *said Thrasymachus.*

–You, too, have to take it as established, given the force of a proof whose every step you approved, that the just man abides in the truth of knowledge and the unjust man in the night of ignorance.

Thrasymachus conceded the point only with difficulty and very grudgingly. He was perspiring profusely even though the sea breeze, in the middle of the night, was cooling off the room. Those present even said they saw what no one would have ever thought it possible to see: Thrasymachus blushing!

But Socrates wanted to rub his nose in it.

–The fact that justice is wisdom and knowledge is now as true for you as it is for me. But there's another point that interests me. It was said by one of us, I don't know who, that injustice is stronger than justice, remember?

–I remember, *grumbled Thrasymachus.* But I don't like what you just said. Not a bit. And I'd have a lot to say about what you said, and even more about what you said *I* was supposed to be saying. However, if I speak, I know very well that you'll say that, instead of having a dialogue with you, all I'm doing is haranguing the crowd. My conclusion is perfectly clear, then: either you let me speak as I see fit, or else, if you're so enamored of your so-called "dialogues," go ahead! Ask questions! I'll act as though I were listening to some old woman telling old wives' tales: I'll just mutter "Fine!" absentmindedly and nod my head.

–Don't say "yes" with your head if you're convinced deep-down of "no"!

–I'll do whatever you like, since you won't let me speak. What more do you want?

–Nothing at all. Do whatever you feel like. *I'll* pose questions.

–Since you're imposing that on us, *sneered Thrasymachus,* pose away! Pose without pausing, and afterwards we'll take our repose.

–It's the same question as before, *Socrates went on patiently,* so that the discussion doesn't lose any of its coherence. What might justice really be, as compared with injustice? Someone, I'm not sure when, said that injustice was stronger than justice and opened up more possibilities in life than justice did. Now that we know that justice is wisdom and virtue, it's very easy to conclude that justice is the stronger, since injustice is merely ignorance. That's a point no one can ignore now. However, I have no desire to win the argument with something as simple as that but rather to consider things from a different angle. Would you be willing to say that in the past, in the present, and in the future there are states that have subjugated, are subjugating, and will subjugate other states unjustly and keep them under their heel, or attempt to do so, for a long time?

–Of course! And the best state, which means the one whose injustice is the most flagrant, will be better at it than any other.

–I know that's your position, *Socrates calmly replied.* But let's single out the following point: suppose one state becomes more powerful than another. Can it wield its dominance without having to have any recourse to a certain conception of justice? Or, like it or not, must a standard like that, however bogus it may be, come into play?

Thrasymachus nimbly avoided the trap of giving a clear-cut answer.

–If we start from the premise that you're imposing on us, namely that justice is wisdom and knowledge, any extended period of rule will require a kind of justice. But if, as I maintain, it's *injustice* that's wisdom and knowledge, then a rational and effective rule will require injustice, or even absolute injustice.

–At any rate I'm delighted, dear Thrasymachus, that you're not merely nodding your head yes or no. Your answers are perfectly courteous. That's proof to me that I'm not some rambling old woman.

–I'm only doing it to humor you.

–Well, humoring me's not such a bad idea! So humor me some more by continuing to answer my questions. In your opinion, can the success of a joint action, even a totally unjust one, be compatible with the unbridled reign of injustice within the group in question?

What I have in mind is a political party, an army, or even a gang of bandits or thieves, which are assumed to be involved in some unjust action.

–They certainly won't be able to pull off their crime if they spend all their time putting obstacles in each other's way.

–So, if they were to give up this internecine injustice, they'd have a better chance of success?

–Obviously, *said Thrasymachus glumly.*

–But why? Isn't it because injustice incites vicious rifts, hatreds, and feuds in every group, whereas a friendly meeting of minds and feelings flows from justice?

–All right, all right, Socrates! I don't want to argue with you anymore.

–You're too kind, dear friend. Just one more question. Wherever we look, we see that as soon as there's injustice, there's hatred. Whether you're free or a slave makes no difference: injustice leads to everyone hating everyone else. It's the triumph of the bitterest rifts and of the inability to do anything together. Even if only two people are involved, they'll be at odds with each other, they'll be mutual enemies, and they'll hate each other every bit as much as they hate just people. And, finally, if only one person's involved, most excellent Thrasymachus, will this feature of injustice remain just as invincible? Won't the person in question be at odds with himself?

–I have a feeling that that's how you'd like it to be.

–Your feeling is right. Wherever injustice takes root, whether in a city, a country, a party, an army, or any community whatsoever, it immediately renders the group in question incapable of acting, and it does so by exacerbating schisms and conflicts. Then it makes the group an enemy both of itself and of everyone opposed to it, since *they* persist in being just. Even if it's only in a single individual that injustice takes root, it will produce similar effects in him, since it's in its nature to do so. It will make him incapable of acting by reason of his inner split, and because it will be impossible for him to be of one mind with himself. In the end, he'll be as much his own bitter enemy as the enemy of everyone motivated by justice. But may I ask you one more question, you distinguished rhetorician?

–You may, just as much as you may not, *said Thrasymachus cryptically.*

–It's a very easy question: aren't the gods just?

–I'm guessing you hope they are.

–That's a good guess. It follows that the unjust man will also be the enemy of the gods, whose friend is the just man.

–Go on, feast on your own sweet arguments, Socrates. I sure as hell won't contradict you. Not when you've got all your groupies here.

–Come on then. You'll be giving me your share of treats by answering my questions. We've shown that just people appear on the world stage endowed with more wisdom, personal capabilities, and practical skills than unjust people, who are unable to join forces to do anything at all together. Some people claim that certain individuals, despite being patently unjust, have nonetheless managed to act expeditiously and successfully together. But "some people" couldn't be more wrong. Had these hypothetical individuals been *completely* unjust, they wouldn't have been able to keep from turning on one another, and their whole venture would have gone down the tubes. They obviously had a little bit of justice left, or enough, at any rate, not to attack one another at the very same time they were all attacking their enemies. It was this little surviving bit of justice that enabled them to act as they did. At the time when they embarked upon injustice, they were only half-corrupted by it, because people who are *wholly* wicked and practice injustice without the slightest vestige of justice are incapable of doing anything whatsoever. *That*'s how things really happen, not at all the way you said they did a moment ago. As for whether the just man's life is happier and better than the unjust man's, a question we'd promised ourselves we'd ask, we know the answer now, and even that this answer is self-evident, for it follows directly from everything we just said. Still, let's take a better look at it. It's not a mere rhetorical ploy that's at stake, but rather the very rule we must live by.

–If you want to take a better look at it, *said Thrasymachus,* just come closer.

–You strike me as being consumed with sarcasm, buddy. Tell me: in your opinion, do horses have a function of their own?

–Good old Socrates! OK, let's go for your horsey dialectic. Yes, horses have particular uses.

–And the function – regardless of whether it's a horse's, a young wild boar's, or a boa constrictor's – is what you can only do with that particular animal. Or at least what you can do best with it, right?

–Of course. But once you've finished your demonstration would you mind whispering to me what the functions of the young wild boar and the boa – whether constrictor or not – really are?

–You're making fun of my examples! OK, let me give you a different one. We can't see with anything but our eyes, or hear with anything but our ears. So those are their functions. And here's another: a vine stock could be pruned with a carving knife, a hatchet, or a long saw – right?

–I can picture you vividly! Socrates covered in sawdust, sawing the stock with his sibilant saw!

–But the best tool is a billhook expressly designed for pruning vines.

–You bet! As the poet said:

The billhook's your thing for pruning the vine:
Saw, hatchet, or knife? They're not worth your time!

–Quite the pastoral poet, this guy is! Anyway, pruning vines is the billhook's function.

–Yes, yes, yes, I say! I applaud you! You're amazing! Socrates the bilious philosopher of the billhook.

–I'll take your cheering to mean that you agree that a thing's function is what it alone can do, or what it does better than any other thing, at any rate. But something that has a function must also have a particular property of its own, owing to which the function exists. Thus the eyes and the ears each have a precise function – seeing and hearing – owing to the particular design of those organs, to the property that inheres in that design. If the organs had the opposite property. . .

–You mean blindness instead of the power of sight?

–What an organ's particular property or the defect opposed to that property may be is a matter of physiology and isn't our problem here. I'm simply asking you whether it's by means of their own particular property that existents make the function that's associated with them function properly, and whether it's when they work by means of the defect opposed to that property that the function malfunctions.

–You're using a bit of jargon there, *muttered Amantha.*

–But is it true or not? *said Socrates, losing his temper.*

–It's true for any existent that can be defined by its function, *Glaucon piped up.*

–This is the critical moment, when we've come back again to the road that will take us to the goal, *said Socrates not without a certain solemnity.* Isn't there a function particular to the Subject, which no other existent can perform and which is called "paying attention" or "applying principles," or "intending," and so forth? Could we ascribe these functions to anything other than a Subject? And aren't we obliged to say that they are particular to him? Isn't even the fact of living, in its most meaningful sense, a function particular to the Subject?

–Sure, whatever, *said Thrasymachus flippantly.*

–It therefore follows that the Subject has a particular property, a unique virtue, without which he would be unable to perform his functions.

–Let's admit that such a virtuous property does exist, *said Thrasymachus, bowing to him as he would to some minor provincial official.*

–Then you'll also have to accept the logical consequences of that first admission.

–Which are?

–A corrupt, reactive, or obscure Subject[10] is turned in the wrong direction or has only wicked intentions. By contrast, a faithful Subject, true to his own principles, can fulfill his obligations absolutely properly.

–I'll grant you all the moral tales you want.

–Didn't we agree by common consent that justice is the essential property of the Subject, his unique virtue, and that injustice is his chief vice?

–I only agreed to please you.

–That's as good a reason as any! And one from which a definite conclusion follows: the individual who participates in the becoming of a just Subject will have a life worthy of the name, and the unjust man will have a miserable life.

–There you go! Socrates' dialectic turns round and round, like a squirrel in a cage! Because your statement "the just man has a good life" is purely and simply the same view you had at the start. And you'd have us believe that it's the conclusion of your argument! But never mind, never mind.

–Someone whose life is a true life[11] is happy, and even blessed. Someone whose life is disgraceful is unhappy. So we've finally arrived at this crucial statement: the just man is happy, the unjust man is unhappy. Now, being unhappy is not advantageous, whereas being happy is. So I can finally state it categorically: it is not true, Professor Thrasymachus, that injustice is more advantageous than justice.

– Well, Professor Socrates can just go and party now till the sun comes up! And I, Thrasymachus, can just shut the hell up. I know how to keep quiet, my friends. You'll see what a virtuoso of rhetoric's silence is like. But that doesn't mean I agree.

With that, Thrasymachus pulled a chair over to the darkest corner of the room, sat down in it and closed his eyes. He was to stay absolutely still like that for a very long time. Socrates addressed his words to him without, however, looking at him:

–You're the co-champion of the sparring match, dear Thrasymachus. You answered my questions in an almost courteous manner and dropped your pretense of superiority and your leaden speeches. In my opinion, the intellectual feast wasn't very substantial. But that's my fault, not yours. I behaved like one of those gluttons who pounce on the dish that's just been served without having really savored the one before. At the very beginning we were seeking a reliable definition of justice. Before finding it, though, I rushed to investigate a related question about the predicates befitting justice: Is justice vice and ignorance, or is it wisdom and virtue? But then another question slipped in from the side: Is injustice more advantageous than justice? I instantly dropped the previous topic to deal with that minor one. The upshot of our whole dialogue is that I don't know anything, because, if I don't know what justice is, I know even less whether it deserves to be called virtue or not, let alone whether someone who's just is happy or unhappy.

Then, just like Thrasymachus, albeit on the other side of the room, Socrates sank into his armchair. He mopped his brow and said:

–Forgive me, you young people. It's late now and I'm exhausted. There have been oceans of words, and we don't know any more now than we did when we were walking half-drunk on the road back from Athens, after the harbor goddess' festival.

— 2 —

THE YOUNG PEOPLE'S PRESSING QUESTIONS (357a–368d)

After his spectacular victory – with Thrasymachus, reduced to silence, off sulking in his dark corner – Socrates thought he could rest on his laurels. Of course he'd conceded that, in the final analysis, he'd failed to define justice. But he'd prevented it from being equated with the rule of force. So he thought he was done with the discussion. He soon realized that it had been only a prelude, though, when young Glaucon, who was now proving to be even scrappier than his elder brother (nicknamed "Plato the Quibbler" in their little group), refused to accept the sophist's surrender and launched into a full-scale diatribe.

–Let's be serious, dear teacher. What's at stake in this intellectual sparring match is whether being just is in all circumstances better than being unjust. So you can't have it both ways: either you settle for appearances – acting as if you'd convinced us – or it's really to a *truth* that you want to win us over.

–To a truth, of course, *protested Socrates,* at least if I'm able to.

–Well, in that case you've got a long way to go! *said Glaucon, thrilled to be steering the dialogue.* You ought to start by classifying the different types of what you refer to indiscriminately as "the Good." I see at least three. First and foremost, there's the good that we seek not for its consequences but because we value it in its being. For example, enjoyment itself, and all those harmless pleasures from which nothing further results for the person experiencing them beyond the simple fact of enjoying them. Then there's the good that we love both for its own sake *and* for its consequences: for example thinking, seeing, being healthy, and so forth. We value goods of that sort for both those reasons. And finally there's a third sort of good: working out, for example, or recovering from an illness, the practice

45

of medicine itself or any other sort of activity that involves earning money. These goods we can naturally say are simultaneously unpleasant and beneficial for us. We desire them not for their own sake but solely for the wages they bring in or, more broadly speaking, for the consequences they bring about.

Socrates agreed with the classification, though not without asking the young man what his point was. So Glaucon asked him:

–Which category would you put justice in?

–In the finest of the three, the second! The category of goods that must be loved both for their own sake and for their consequences if we want to attain happiness.

–Well, you're not in the majority then, Socrates! Most people classify justice in the third category, goods that are of the intrinsically unpleasant kind but which we're nonetheless forced to pursue, either to earn a living or to defend our reputation against insidious opinions. Given what they're like in and of themselves, goods like these are to be avoided, so unpleasant are they.

–I'm well aware, *Socrates resumed,* that people have always and everywhere thought as much. Thrasymachus, moreover, kept harping on about it: "Let's praise injustice! Let's condemn justice!" But I go at my own pace. I only catch on to things quickly if they've been explained to me for a long time.

–So listen to me, then, *said Glaucon, who was delighted to be able to slip in another of his long speeches.* You might just agree. I think Thrasymachus, who was charmed like a snake by you, gave up a lot sooner than he needed to. To my mind, we haven't yet reached the point where the proof of either of the theses derives from true thought. I want to understand what justice and injustice are intrinsically and what their inherent natural effects are on a Subject in which they're assumed to be present. I don't give a damn about all that wages and side effects stuff. Here's my proposition, which I'm submitting for your approval, dear teacher. I'll sort of play Thrasymachus' role again and develop three points. The first point: a summary of the nature and origins of justice, or at least as it's regarded by prevailing opinion. The second point: to show how everyone who models their behavior on the idea of justice does so against their will, only under duress, and not at all because justice is a good. The third point: they're right to act as they do, because, according to them, the unjust man's life is infinitely better than the just man's.

Socrates seemed to become impatient at this and said:

–You're deluging us with lots of "according to prevailing opinion," "everyone who," and "according to them." But what do *you* think,

Glaucon? Philosophy's not like those "democratic" debates where everyone politely considers everyone else's opinions and yields to a majority of those present. *We* take the risk of truth.

–Socrates! *a horrified Glaucon exclaimed.* You know very well that I don't agree with Thrasymachus! But I have to admit that I'm troubled by this issue. On the one hand, the powerful arguments of Thrasymachus and hosts of mighty sophists behind him are still ringing in my ears, while on the other I have yet to hear anyone defend the idea that justice is better than injustice the way I'd like to hear it. I'd like justice to be lauded in and of itself, in terms of its own being, and I think you're the one, Socrates, who should do it. So I'm going to attempt to praise the unjust man's life, and after that I'll tell you how I'd like to hear you condemn injustice and praise justice. Is this plan OK with you?

–Absolutely! I can't think of any questions that deserve to be more urgently discussed than the ones you're putting to me. At any rate not for a Subject who thinks. . .

–And therefore is, *chuckled Amantha.*

–Very funny! *Glaucon remarked dryly, like someone who doesn't appreciate anachronistic jokes.* OK, you two, listen up. I'm going to take the bull by the horns. What is justice? Where does it come from?

Socrates, Amantha, and the other spectators of this battle of minds, sensing they were in for a humongous lecture, stretched out noisily and settled back on the cushions. But they didn't stand a chance of intimidating Glaucon.

–Almost everyone says that if things are allowed to run their natural course, doing an injustice is good, whereas suffering one is bad. It's even worse to suffer an injustice, however, than it's good to do one. The upshot of this disparity is that, as a result of seeing these countless injustices either done or suffered – something that people experience alternately, first actively then passively – those who lack the power either to avoid suffering them or to impose their will become convinced that the best solution is for all of them to sign a pact whereby no one will either commit or suffer injustice. That's the origin of the institution of laws and treaties. What the law commands is then declared to be "lawful" and "just." That, dear friends, is how justice arises, how it's structured: midway between the greatest good, which is to be able to do injustice without ever having to pay the penalty for it, and the most radical evil, which is to suffer injustice without being able to retaliate. As you can well imagine, this happy medium of justice hardly thrills anyone. In fact, no one loves justice the way a true good is loved. At the very most, it's respected only out

47

of weakness, incapable as we are of doing injustice. Because anyone who's capable of doing injustice and is a *real* man will take care not to sign any pact that prevents him from doing it! He'd have to be crazy to do so! So, there you have it: I've said everything there is to say about the intrinsic nature of justice and its natural origins, according to common opinion.

So now I've come to the critical question: is it only unwillingly, purely and simply because they lack the power to be unjust, that so many people obey the injunctions of justice? It would be best if I illustrated things for you by telling you a fable, a rational fiction of sorts. Let's give both the just and the unjust man the freedom to do exactly as they please, and then let's observe where each one's desire leads him. This way we'll catch the just man out in the act of committing injustice. Why? Because the natural inclination of the human animal, what he likes, is always to demand more than he has. He respects a norm of equality only when he is restrained by the force of law.

The thought experiment I have in mind is to give both the just and the unjust man the magic power of Gyges' ring. You all know the story. A few hundred years ago, a shepherd named Gyges was tending the King of Thule's[1] merino sheep. One day a great earthquake shook the field where the animals were grazing, an enormous crevice opened up, and Gyges, astonished but brave nonetheless, went down into the chasm. As the legend has it, he then came upon incomparable treasures, in the middle of which was an extraordinary hollow bronze horse with little windows in its sides. Gyges stuck his head into one of these openings and what did he see in the horse's belly? The corpse of a giant, totally naked except for a gold ring glittering on one of its fingers. Without another thought, Gyges stole the ring and fled. A few days later there was the monthly meeting of the shepherds, at which they prepared their report to the King of Thule on the state of the flocks and the merino wool stocks. Gyges was present, along with the others, with the ring on his finger. As usual, some incorrigible windbags were holding up the meeting and Gyges was bored stiff. Without giving it any thought, he twisted the bezel of the ring toward his palm. And lo and behold, he became invisible! Dumbfounded, he heard his colleagues sitting beside him talk about him as if he weren't there. He then twisted the bezel the other way, toward the outside of his hand, and bingo! He was visible again. He repeated the experiment a few more times: no doubt about it, the ring had magic powers. If you turned the bezel toward the inside, you were invisible, and if you turned it toward the outside, you were visible. So Gyges then contrived to get himself elected as the shepherds' delegate to the king and went to the palace. Doing whatever he pleased thanks to the magic ring, overtly at times and absolutely invisibly at others, he slept with the queen, who fell madly in love with him and became his accomplice. Together they set a trap for the king and killed him. Gyges the shepherd, armed with only his magic ring, seized power.

So now, here's our crucial experiment. We've got two rings like Gyges' and we put one on the just man's finger and the other on the unjust man's finger. We then note – it's as plain as day – that in neither case would anyone have such iron strength of will that he'd be able to abide strictly by justice and keep his hands off other people's property, when, with no risk at all, he could take whatever he wanted from the market, enter his neighbors' houses at night to rape whomever he felt like, murder the masters, and free the slaves – in short, behave like a god among men. As a result, it would be clear that there's no difference whatsoever between our two character types, the just man and the unjust man, both of whom pursue the exact same course in life; and I think we'd have conclusive proof of the issue we're concerned with here, namely that no one is just willingly, but only when they're forced to be. Being just is never regarded as something intrinsically worthwhile that enriches one's private life, since no sooner has someone realized that circumstances would allow him to be unjust than he becomes unjust. In fact, every human animal imagines injustice to be infinitely more advantageous to his own private interests than justice. And that's actually true, if we believe Thrasymachus and his crowd, whose arguments I'm currently drawing on for my own: if someone who possessed the powers of Gyges' ring couldn't bear to be unjust and didn't give free rein to his burning desire to take what belongs to others, he'd be regarded as a pathetic fool by everyone who knew about it. Naturally they'd sweetly sing his praises in public, but only in the hopes of fooling everyone else, so afraid would they be at the thought of suffering some terrible injustice themselves. So much for that aspect of the question.

Now let's turn to the decision about the quality of life of our two character types. The only way we'll be able to decide correctly about it is if we make them the extreme example of justice and the extreme example of injustice, respectively. Otherwise we won't understand a thing. How should this maximal difference between the two be effected? Regardless of whether it's the just man or the unjust man, let's not take away the slightest bit of his own particular characterization – justice in the one case, injustice in the other. Let's posit that each of them represents the perfect example of his type. Let the unjust man, for example, act like a skilled professional. An eminent physician or an excellent pilot knows exactly what their skill will enable them to do and what they won't be able to do. They'll either keep at a task or give it up, depending on whether the situation falls under the first case or the second. If they should happen to slip up, they know how to put things right. Similarly, the unjust man must be able to conceal as much as possible the injustices he constantly commits if he wants to be truly unjust. An unjust man who got caught would be a rank amateur! Because the highest degree of injustice is to seem just at the very moment when you're not. Let's give the perfectly unjust man this perfect form of injustice and not take away even the slightest bit of it. Let it be at the very moment he's most unjust that popular opinion bestows the title of World Champion of Justice on him. And if he should happen to go off course in his dirty dealings, let him be able to correct his mistakes. For instance, if one of his injustices is exposed and there is evidence to prove it, he'll be able to use his phony eloquence to persuade the crowd that he did no wrong and to turn them in his favor. Otherwise, if he has to fight it out, he'll come out on top thanks to his courage and strength, or thanks to his cronies and money if he has to bribe and silence his accusers. Next to this type of man, let's paint a picture of the just man, a man as simple as he is noble, the sort of man of whom Aeschylus says:

> 'Tis not seeming, but being, good that affords
> This man the true measure of all his rewards.[2]

So let's take away any appearance of virtue from him, because, if he seems to be just, the appearance of justice will bring him honors and rewards. It will then be impossible to know whether our man is the way he is because he's *really* just or he's that way merely in order to enjoy those honors and rewards. So that he may be absolutely different from the unjust man, let's exhibit him in his complete moral nakedness: nothing, except true justice! Let him – who's always innocent – appear as though he were guilty of the most heinous crimes, so that, when put to the test of pitiless public judgment and its terrible consequences, his inherent justice will be revealed in his not giving way on his desire.[3] Even though subjected to the torture of always appearing to be unjust while he's actually always just, our man will remain faithful to the death to his inner principles. In this way, our two character types, having reached the extremes of justice and injustice, will be clearly presented to our judgment and we'll be able to determine accurately which of the two is happier.

–My goodness! *exclaimed Socrates.* You're putting these two guys on display for us like a sculptor who'd burnish the bronze of his two most beautiful statues for an exhibition!

–I'm doing my best! *said Glaucon.* Given what our two guys – as you call them – are like, it's not too hard to predict what sort of life awaits each of them, and I'm going to give it a shot now. If I strike you as crass, dear Socrates, keep in mind that I'm merely the spokesman for everyone who thinks that, compared with injustice, justice – pardon the expression – isn't worth a rat's ass. All those people will say that everything to which the Marquis de Sade subjects his heroine, the virtuous, innocent, just Justine, will also befall the just man as we've described him. He'll be abducted, scourged, stretched on a rack, blinded by a hot iron, and after a thousand tortures he'll end his days impaled and confessing in his horrible agony that, as far as justice is concerned, it's better to want its appearance than its reality. That quote from Aeschylus – or so these proponents of injustice will say – could be applied more appropriately to the unjust man than to the just man, because it's the unjust man, they'll claim, who deals with what really exists, with real matters, rather than with living by appearances. He actually couldn't care less about the appearance of injustice; his desire is to be unjust. Like Amphiaraus in *The Seven against Thebes*:

> He wants not appearance but the quick of being,
> The harvest of his thought, from which spring all his plans.

As a certified expert in appearances, he seizes power in his country, waving the banner of a sham justice. He marries into whatever family he pleases. He gives his daughters in marriage to young men in high-level positions, and his sons marry wealthy heiresses. Every social group is open to him, for sex and scheming alike. Why? Because he has no qualms or compunction about being unjust. Armed with only this cynicism, he trounces his rivals as easily in the arena of sex as in political disputes. As a result, he gets richer with every passing day and is free to take care of his friends and to harm his enemies. He can also give powerful people, including the gods, all sorts of fabulous gifts, which is something the just man never can do. In this way, he wins the favor of those he needs in order to advance his career, even if they happen to be gods. In fact, it's quite likely that the gods themselves, having been bribed like this, will prefer him to the poor just man. So these, dear Socrates, are the arguments of the people who claim that the unjust man is destined for a much better life than the just man. You see how they even go so far as to maintain that this

51

superiority is indisputable in every case, regardless of whether it's men or the gods who are deciding about the worth of just and unjust men's lives.

Socrates was about to reply, but Amantha, her eyes shining, beat him to it.

–You can't really believe that this diatribe of my brother's settles the question, can you?

–Well, actually, yes! I was about to say that after a speech like that we might as well call it quits.

–Call it quits when the point to be discussed wasn't even broached?!

–OK, damn it! Let's give the famous proverb "Let brother stand by brother"[4] a feminine twist. Let's say it all together now: "Let sister help brother." If Glaucon's speech, despite its overwhelming length, omitted some crucial point, go for it, girl! Pull him out of the quagmire! As for me, the sheer mass of his words has knocked me over, floored me and rendered me quite incapable of coming to the aid of justice.

–Oh, that's a lot of baloney, dear teacher, and you should listen to what I have to say. We really do have an obligation to examine in their minutest detail the arguments opposed to the ones my brother just reeled off. Staunch supporters of justice, people who hate injustice with a passion, should come and give testimony under oath. Then we'll have a clearer idea of what my dear brother intended. Let's start with one very important point. Fathers and, more broadly speaking, those in charge of children's development are constantly telling them that they have to be just. But do they praise justice for its intrinsic excellence? Absolutely not. They couldn't care less about truth or morality; their sole criterion is life in society. The only thing that counts, as far as they're concerned, is the good reputation that boys and girls – especially girls – can get out of this so-called "justice." Volatile public opinion only has to decide that some guy or other is "just," and bingo! He immediately gets everyone's vote in an election, a good job, and an advantageous marriage. Everything Glaucon said about the advantages to be gained from having a reputation as an honorable, just person, whether warranted or not, is perfectly true. But the defense of opinions of this sort can go a lot further still. The gods themselves can be called upon to support them, on the basis of the good reputation a mortal has managed to enjoy in their eyes. The gods, it's said, reward the just man's righteousness with countless blessings. That's in fact the opinion of the good-natured Hesiod and his fellow-poet Homer. In *The Works and the Days* Hesiod says that, for the just, the gods have seen to it that the oaks

52

Bear acorns – that wonder! – at the top of the trees
And in the middle, honey, the product of bees.

And also, for the just, that their

Wool-bearing sheep are weighed down by their fleeces.

Moreover, according to Hesiod there are all sorts of other gifts like
these that the gods, via Nature, bestow on the just. His fellow-poet
Homer goes him one better – see Book 19 of the *Odyssey* – when he
compares the just man to

A god-fearing king, upholding the right,
For whom the dark earth bears wheat free from blight,
And luscious fruit comes from the laden trees
And lambs from the sheep and fish from the seas.

Musaeus[5] and his son shower the just with even more sensational
blessings from the gods. They imagine them seated around a banquet
table in Hades after they die, they toss garlands of flowers on their
heads and prepare a delicious feast in their honor. . . After which the
illustrious just are all constantly plastered, as if the fabulous reward
for virtue was eternal drunkenness. Other poets, when it comes to
the divine rewards garnered by the dead who've been saved by their
reputations, go positively all out. The just and faithful man, they say,
leaves behind him, in his own image, his children, his children's children, a whole never-ending posterity. I've noticed that the praises of
justice are always sung in this pompous style.

Now if we turn to the wicked and unjust, you should see how
the poets trash them! They make them slosh around in the revolting
sewers of the Underworld amid dog turds, skinned cats, and scraps
of rotting corpses. Or else they have to carry huge quantities of water
in a sieve for all eternity. And as for their life on earth – watch out!
If the Odes, Epodes and Electrodes of our Masters are to be believed,
the life of the unjust is scarcely any better than their death. Public
opinion abhors them, and everything my dear brother said about the
punishment meted out to just men whom public opinion mistakenly
regards as unjust, our poets, without changing an iota, make into the
fate of the *truly* unjust. It's this way, not otherwise, that they dole out
to justice and its opposite (let me express it in poetry the way they
do):

Luminous praise and censure black as coal
Falling straight down on the worth of their souls.

By Amantha, *Posthumous Works*, Volume 2.

–You really should. . . *Glaucon attempted to put in.*

–Wait, wait! I'm not done. I want to explore another idea about justice and injustice with you, dear Socrates. This particular idea you hear as much among people, over the course of a meal where the wine is flowing freely, as you do in the poets' high-flown utterances. All these folks sing mighty hymns together in praise of moderation and justice. Oh, how wonderful those virtues are! But before long you start to hear a few wrong notes in that enthusiastic chorus. Virtues are wonderful, OK, sure, no argument there. But you've got to admit that they're unpleasant, too. And a real hassle, you'd better believe. Vice and injustice, though, we should have the guts and honesty to admit, are very enjoyable, and easy to come by. After all, hardly anyone condemns them except conventional Opinion and the Law, that old kill-joy. And all of a sudden, the hymn to virtue changes key: the fashionable people and the poets all start singing, to an increasingly frenetic beat, that injustices are nearly always a lot more profitable. As a matter of fact, both among friends and at posh receptions, the singers in the chorus of the Good have themselves frequently indulged, in a disgusting albeit self-serving way, in praising rich crooks with plenty of access to powerful people and in badmouthing and looking down on nice guys, who are no doubt just but powerless and poor – the kind of guys the people at the top of the heap regard, if you'll pardon the expression, as shit – even if our Injustice rock singers secretly admit that these "pieces of shit" are morally superior to the crooks.

–Sister dear, *Glaucon ventured,* couldn't you. . .

–Stop interrupting me all the time, will you? There's one more thing I want to say. What's really mind-blowing is all these people's perception of the relationship between the gods and virtue. Take a really great guy, they say, or a super-nice girl. Well, there's a nine out of ten chance that the gods will dump a heap of trouble on them and that the crooks will be the ones who clean up in life. What's more, there are all these con artists, these scruffy prophets, besieging the big ocean-front mansions where all the rich crooks, as it happens, abound. The old codgers claim that, through a lot of sacrifices and magic tricks, they've managed to obtain special powers from the gods. For example, if one of these crooks, or one of his ancestors, committed some dreadful crime, the con artists can purify him of it for good: "You'll be home free, as far as that nasty business is concerned, in both this life and the next – if there *is* a next!" All it'll take are a few very convivial feasts paid for cash on the barrelhead directly to the grubby prophet. Or if some other guy, for reasons of business or sex, wants one of his rivals sidelined for a while, no problem: for a small fee the con artists will paralyze your enemy with phony spells and invisible chains. Note that nobody gives a damn about who's really just or unjust. These impostors all claim to have wrapped the gods around their little finger.

–Hey, hold on! Where are you going with this? *Glaucon cut in.* What do you. . .

–I've had it up to here with your interrupting me, *Amantha stubbornly went on.* I haven't mentioned the most important thing yet, which is that those con artists hide behind the authority of the poets.

–I'm not surprised! *exclaimed Socrates.*

–It's pretty surreal. For example they quote Hesiod, who crows about how easy it is to fall into vice:

> Vice in abundance is easy to get!
> The road there is smooth and very close by.
> But virtue takes effort, and tears, and sweat. . .

And I'd complete it in my own poetic vein:

> . . . Much more, by far, than a blink of your eye!

–Dear Amantha! *exclaimed Socrates.* You came up with a true decasyllable off the top of your head!

–And Homer! We call him, too, say the con artists, as a supporting witness for the theory that men can influence the gods. Take the *Iliad*, for example, when Phoenix is speaking to Achilles:

> The gods themselves have been known to relent.
> Fearing their wrath, guilty men then repent
> For sins and crimes, all the ways that they err.
> Libations, and vows, and due victims slain:
> The gods' angry hearts are soothed by these prayers
> And love men anew, their favor regained.

–My goodness, *said Socrates, smiling,* you did quite a number on old Homer![6]

–But Homer and Hesiod aren't the only ones. Our impostors also quote from a bunch of mysterious books by Musaeus and Orpheus, who they claim are the offspring of the Moon and the Muses. With all that stuff, they persuade not only individuals but sometimes entire states as well that you can be cleansed and purified of the most ghastly crimes, in both this life and the next, through ridiculous sacrifices and rituals. They call all this crap "initiations," which are supposed to

protect us from awful things in the hereafter. They go around shriek-
ing that if you haven't been initiated you're at risk of terrible torments. So just imagine, dear Socrates, what we young people, who are
just entering society, guided only by our own natural good character,
might think. No sooner have we arrived than our ears are bombarded
with all this talk and all these poems. We don't know anything, so
naturally we're curious about everything. Like bees gathering nectar,
we flit randomly from one rhetorical flower to another. And what
will we believe as a result of hearing all this gibberish about vice and
virtue, and the praises men and gods sing to them? What effect will all
this have on the Subjects we long to become? If we're able to deduce
from all this gobbledygook which path we should take to have the
best possible life, I'm telling you, Socrates, we young people will end
up concluding the way old Pindar did:

> To reach at last the lofty heights of life
> And live entrenched, no more to know strife,
> To Justice harsh must I devote my days
> Or seek instead deceitful, crooked ways?

–It's got to be pronounced "entrench-èd," or the meter will be off,
Socrates remarked.
–You're quibbling over details and not listening to me, Socrates! If
it's because I'm a woman, why don't you just say so and I'll leave.
–Oh, be quiet! *snapped Glaucon.* We *are* listening to you – you
can see very well that we are – and we haven't missed a single word
you've said.
–Well, anyway, that's the lesson we young people are taught everywhere we go. If I'm just without being able to *seem* as though I am,
I'll be in for a lot of trouble. If I'm unjust but have every appearance
of being just, I'll have an unbelievably divine life. So I say to myself:
since all the old sages are telling me, a young woman, that appearances trump truth every time, and that *they*'re the key to happiness,
I shouldn't think twice but just turn entirely in that direction. Slyer
than Reynard the fox in the fables, I'll draw an imaginary likeness of
justice all around myself, as a front or a façade.
–Sure, *interrupted Glaucon, eager to prove his good will as a lis-
tener,* but someone could say to you that if you're *really* a bad person
it's not easy to get away with it forever.
–And I'd reply: nothing worthwhile is easy. If we want to be happy,
we have no choice but to follow where these arguments lead. Still, it's
easier for several people to hide together: we'll organize a club for
promoting appearances and we'll all tell lies together. We all know

professors of duplicity who can teach us the orator's secrets and the lawyer's tricks of the trade. Once we're properly instructed, we'll use persuasion when it's possible to and force when it's not, and we'll come out on top without ever having to pay the penalty.

–But what about the gods? *Glaucon persisted.* It's impossible to escape their notice and just as hard to make them do our bidding.

–Well, what if these so-called gods simply didn't exist? Huh? Don't you think their non-existence would play quite a trick on justice?

–Yeah, *said Glaucon calmly,* but they may well exist. Would you take the chance that they didn't?

–Well, what if they *did* exist but couldn't care less about what people do? Which would be quite sensible of them, after all.

–OK, *said Glaucon even more calmly,* but what if they *do* care about human affairs? What will you do then?

–Let me tell you something. How do we know that the gods exist? Or rather, whom did we hear it from? Only from the myth-makers and the poets who've told their family histories. Yet, as I reminded you, these same myth-makers and poets say that you can easily appease the gods and make allies of them if you handle sacrifices, humble prayers and offerings properly. So you can't have it both ways: either you believe the poets about *both* points – point one, the gods exist; point two, their wrath toward men can be easily neutralized – or you don't believe them about *either* of the two points. Which means: point one, it's practically impossible to appease the gods; but, point two, they don't exist, so the matter's settled! So let's be unjust, and, to be on the safe side, devote a portion of what we get out of injustice to sacrifices and offerings.

–But by being just, *Glaucon calmly persisted,* you can be sure you don't have to worry about the gods. That's the simplest solution, after all.

–Yes, but it's a simplicity you pay for by having a lousy life! Because you give up the enormous rewards of injustice. If we're unjust, on the other hand, not only do we get those rewards, but with lots of prayers and offerings we can persuade the gods to disregard our transgressions and wicked acts and to spare us punishment altogether.

–But in the Underworld, *Glaucon pressed on without losing his cool,* we'll have to pay for the wrong we did in this world and we'll be punished – or, worse yet, the children of our children will be.

–Dear brother, try to reason like a free-thinker, like a real unbeliever, for once. Being initiated into mystery rites and about the gods of absolution can have a lot of influence over those tribunals in the Underworld. That, at any rate, is what we're told by powerful statesmen as well as by certain poets and prophets, those children of the gods who give us the signs of all reality.

–You ought to sum up your remarkable argument now, *said Socrates*. I've never heard you speak for so long; it's like you're competing with your brother's famous disquisitions. In light of all this, you should also clarify what you expect from me, Socrates. After all, I'm merely one of those "old sages" you were talking about, whom the younger generation simultaneously listens to and criticizes, wants both to follow and to repudiate.

–I will never ever repudiate you! But you mustn't let me down. . . It's a very simple question: What reasons are there for us, "us" the young, to prefer justice to the most cynical injustice, if all we have to do is conceal our wickedness under a veneer of respectability for both men and the gods to immediately let us go wherever our desires take us? Because that's really what we're being told, by popular opinion as much as by the leading lights of knowledge. The thought occurred to me, listening to them, that if someone were a really strong guy or very smart or extremely rich, or came from a jet-set background, you'd never be able to come up with any ploy or trick to persuade him to respect justice. And I mean *none*. I'd even say that if you yourself were to praise it he'd laugh in your face.

So in that case I can get something off my chest. Suppose there's some terrific guy – such as you, for example, Socrates – who can state outright that not a thing I've said holds water and who can convincingly prove, by the rules of strict logic, the superiority of justice. Well, I maintain that even this true sage will let go of all his anger and will feel infinitely forgiving toward the unjust, since he knows from experience that virtually no one is just willingly. Only those naturally guided by some godlike inner strength of being, or those who possess knowledge so superior that it's unique can steer clear of wrongdoing. Hardly anyone, in other words. In the world as it is, the only people who rant about injustice are cowards, the elderly, and invalids – in a nutshell, everyone who's too weak to commit it. It's so obvious! You only have to see how, of all those orators who get so worked up about injustice, the first one who's given the power to be unjust will instantly use it, and as much as he can! This brings us back full circle to our point of departure, to what prompted my brother and me, dear Socrates, to take part in this discussion that's keeping us awake. I had in mind a kind of petition that I'd have addressed to you, something along the lines of:

"O wonderful friend, dear Socrates, how is it that not a single one of you established defenders of justice – and this has been the case right from the heroes of old, a few of whose wise words have come down to us – has managed to condemn injustice and praise justice to the skies other than on some paltry grounds of reputation, fame or rewards? What justice and injustice are in and for themselves, in terms of their real power in the Subject where they reside as in their proper habitat, presenting no outward appearance, such that they go unnoticed by both men and the gods – this no one has adequately explained. As a result, no one has been able to prove by force of reason alone that, for the Subject imbued with them, injustice is the worst of evils and justice is not merely his highest good, but even his immanent Truth. And yet, if all of you – the established defenders of justice – had convinced us of that point right from the start and had drummed it into our heads when we were children, we wouldn't now have to be watching each other like hawks to make sure that none of us, being obsessed with opinion, commits an injustice. It would be up to each of us to be his own strict guardian, out of fear that the slightest injustice on our part might reveal that we were on intimate terms with the worst of evils."

That's what my petition would be, Socrates: that we might finally be protected from within from what corrupts us as Subjects. Everything else was only what some Thrasymachus or other, like the one who's pretending to be asleep over there, would say about justice and injustice, confusing the issue right from the start, in my opinion, with quibbles about the essential difference between the two.

–So what are you asking of me, dear Amantha, you who are so determined and clever, so pessimistic and resolute? What can I do for you?

–Let's not play games. If I went all out to defend conventional ideas, it was only because I was tormented by the desire to finally hear *you* – you, my Socrates – magnificently defend the opposite ones. Yes, my most fervent desire is for you not to be content with proving that justice is better than injustice; I want to hear a convincing description of the effects each of them produces, in a purely immanent way, on the Subject it seizes hold of. I want to understand the nature of these effects thoroughly, and I want the designation "Good" that's applied to the ones and "Evil" to the others to be justified. I want you to leave out any reference to other people's opinions and judgment, Socrates, which is something my brother Glaucon has already urged you to do. If you *don't* leave out those purely external references, if, as regards both justice and injustice, you confuse matters with opinions that are almost true, false-but-then-again-maybe-not, likely, uncertain, and the whole bit about appearances, I'm telling you flat out: I'll go around everywhere saying that it's not justice you're praising but only its appearance, and that it's not injustice you're disparaging but only its appearance. I'll spread a very bad impression of your work around, namely that you, too, actually advise the unjust man to conceal his injustice, that you *appear* to be opposed to Thrasymachus but that, "objectively," as Stalin put it at the time of the Moscow trials, you actually agree wholeheartedly with him. Because it all comes down to claiming that justice has no intrinsic worth, that in every case it's only advantageous to the stronger party, whereas if you practice injustice you always profit from it and it's only harmful to someone weaker than you are.

–Curses! *exclaimed Socrates.* You're going to pursue me in the streets like one of the Furies of philosophy! Equating me with Thrasymachus! What a horrible punishment!

–Shh! *said a startled Glaucon.* He's right over there – don't wake him up!

–It's your fault, too, *Amantha went on.* You taught us that justice was part of the realm of the Good. How many times did you assure us that it wasn't advantageous to the Subject merely on account of its consequences in society, but first and foremost in and of itself? For that reason you compared it – in keeping with your beloved method of concrete examples – to sight, hearing, intelligence, health, and all the goods that are justified by their own true nature, not by the play of opinions. So what we're expecting from you is for that damn miracle to finally occur: a praise of justice based on the positive effects that its unique nature has on the Subject who is its support; a condemnation of injustice based solely on the extensive damage it causes to that same Subject's becoming. As for material or societal benefits, opinions, good or bad reputation, throw all that stuff in the trash! Of course, given the pervasiveness of alienation and all the media propaganda, I'm not going to waste my outrage on some guy or other who's getting all choked up praising justice and condemning injustice as he sobs over its victims but who, as we can readily tell, has nothing in mind but his own reputation, comfort, security, and big executive salary. A guy like that is rotten to the core with complacency; he's absolutely convinced that the unsurpassable model of humanity, morality, and compassion is represented by the *petit bourgeois* of Western "democracies." He'll never understand the first thing about justice. That guy's had it, it's all over for him, forget about it! But *you*, Socrates, even if you were to order me to, I could never bear to see you compromise yourself for a single second with such a view of things. You've spent your whole life looking at the question of justice from every angle. On this critical night, merely proving to us that justice is superior to injustice is out of the question. You owe it to us and to yourself, only by examining the immanent effects of each one of them in the Subject, to establish that one is Good and the other Evil. Let me just add one more thing, so that everything's clear between us. Whether or not the subjective process of justice is outwardly visible to men or the gods is completely unimportant as far as the proof we're all expecting from you is concerned. And now I'll conclude: Down with opinion! Long live thought! Long live Socrates!

They all erupted into spontaneous applause, even Thrasymachus, who suddenly woke up, even Polemarchus, who was too drunk to get what was going on, even Glaucon, although he was jealous of his sister's brilliance and the obvious delight that her prose (too damn rambling, in his opinion) had sparked in Socrates' eyes. As soon as all the commotion died down, Socrates spoke up:

–Ah, youth! Youth rising eternally like the sun over the weary old world! You deserve to have a triumphal Ode written especially for you by Pindar and revised by Amantha, something like:

O Glaucon, Amantha, brighter by far's
Your noble line than the astral dome's stars!
So lofty your thoughts, acclaimed by our wine,
That the words to say them shock the Divine.[7]

They all burst out laughing, Socrates first and foremost. Then he continued:

– Yet it really *is* true that there's something divine about you young people, since, after speaking with such rare passion about the myriad advantages of injustice, you're still not convinced that it's better than justice, you really aren't. I'm basing my assumption about this "really" primarily on your actual behavior, on what I can see of your lives. If it were only a question of your arguments, I'd be wary! But I trust you. And the more I trust you, the more I sink into an aporia of sorts.

–Aha! *roared Thrasymachus to everyone's surprise.* There it is! Socratic aporia is back! Charge!

Thrasymachus rushed forward, lunged at Socrates, then collapsed and fell down, overcome once more by sheer exhaustion.

–Good old Thrasymachus is right. I'm consumed by an aporia. On the one hand, I don't know how to come to the aid of justice. I think I'm just not able to. One sign of this inability is that, at the end of the dispute with Thrasymachus a little while ago, I really thought I'd proved that justice is better than injustice. But I see that you young

61

people didn't think I was so great, since in your opinion everything has to be started over from scratch. But on the other hand I can't *not* come to the aid of justice. It would be like insulting my own life to stand idly by when justice is being vilified in my presence. So, should I give up? Not enter the fray? No – to both of those. Not while I still have breath in my body and the ability to speak. I've got to decide. The best solution would be to rush to the aid of justice to the best of my ability. But my abilities, I'm telling you, are only so–so. I'd be running the risk of total failure.

So then Glaucon, Amantha, Polemarchus – and Thrasymachus, who had revived again – all rallied around Socrates and begged him to try to find all the resources within himself for a triumphant demonstration concerning the nature of justice and injustice and the apprehension in truth of how they differ from each other.

But Socrates, as though he were all alone in the solitary night, said nothing more, withdrew, and vanished into himself.

–It's very late, *grumbled Thrasymachus,* dropping onto the tiled floor, arms outstretched, and starting to snore.

— 3 —

THE ORIGINS OF SOCIETY AND THE STATE (368d–376c)

In the deep blue night studded with lamplights, which had spread over all, in that sort of desert peopled by exhausted shadows where only a handful of observers – Amantha, Glaucon, Polemarchus, and Thrasymachus snoring away on the floor – had survived the dreary let-down in which parties always fizzle out, Socrates, badgered by his interlocutors to go on with the discussion, remained silent for quite a while. After all, the question "What is justice?" is of an overwhelmingly serious nature and, what's more, you need a very sure intellectual intuition to make sense of it. So the fact that these present-day young people were imploring him to guide them through this labyrinth affected Socrates deeply. But, put on the spot like this, he also felt a sort of discouragement. Was he himself even sure what a just man really was? Was he, when you came right down to it, a just man? Reclining in his armchair, he had been chewing all this over when he suddenly had an idea, which he immediately presented to his sparse audience.

–Since we're not really able to define the just man, let's try to proceed by analogy, or even, with any luck, by isomorphism.

–What's that? *Amantha asked.*

–If two things have exactly the same internal relations, the same structure, we say they're isomorphic. You can easily see the Greek roots: *iso-*, meaning "the same" or "equal," and *morphe*, meaning "form." Our two things are existentially different, but they have the same form.

–But what can possibly be isomorphic to the just man? *asked Glaucon.*

–Careful! It's not just isomorphism we're interested in. It's also intelligibility, legibility. The thing that's isomorphic to the just man must be easier to decipher, in terms of its structure, than the just man himself. Otherwise it's of no use.

—Yes, yes! *an enthusiastic Amantha exclaimed.* I think I've got a really great analogy. You show some very nearsighted people a text written in small letters on a small board that's at a great distance from them. They can't make it out at all. But among the nearsighted people there's a Socrates who informs them that the same text is written in big letters, very close by, on a big board. Now they can all make it out and they all applaud Socrates!

—Excellent, congratulations! *said Socrates with an ironic half-smile.* But all the same, we ought to add that your nearsighted Socrates is less nearsighted than the others.

—Why?

—Because if he was able to see that the text in big letters was the same as the one in small letters, it's because he could read the small letters. . . That's the whole problem, as a matter of fact. How can you demonstrate the isomorphism between two things if you can't make out anything about the structure of one of them? My method of isomorphisms is only an optical illusion, alas.

Glaucon and Amantha were bitterly disappointed and their faces fell. But then Socrates said:

—All right! But the eye also likes to be fooled! Let's see. If justice exists with respect to the individual, it also exists with respect to the community, the country, the political community, the state, or whatever you want to call it. Now, these collective entities are larger than isolated individuals, aren't they?

—Of course they are, *said Glaucon, perking up,* a lot larger!

—So, in this larger framework, justice may be easier to perceive. That's why we'll look into the state first and into the individual only later. The aim of our inquiry will be to find out what, in the formal structure of the smaller, is isomorphic to what we've observed in the larger. And we'll also have the history of countries to draw on as a resource. If we rationally examine how political communities originate, we'll be able by the same token to see how justice and injustice originate. By proceeding this way we can hope to find what we're looking for. So? Do you think it's worth a try? Think carefully! This is no small matter, trust me.

—My mind's made up! *said Amantha.* Let's have at it! Take no prisoners!

—Amantha's wishes are my commands, *said Socrates.* OK, I'll begin. Point number one: to explain how political communities come into being, I can see no other assumption to use than the fact that it's impossible for an individual to be self-sufficient. To survive, each of us needs a whole slew of things. One person seeks out another to satisfy a given need and then seeks out someone else to satisfy yet another need, and so on. The whole host of different needs brings into one place a whole host of people, all gathered together by the laws of association and mutual assistance. It's to this motley form of cohabitation that we give the name of country, political community, state, city-state, collective process, etc., depending on the context. Perhaps, temporarily, "society" is the most appropriate term, since we're doing sociology for the time being, dear friends, not philosophy!

Glaucon, a big fan of the social sciences, then chimed in:

–Since we're sociologizing, allow me to apply one of the great Marcel Mauss'[1] comments to the issue of universal communication: when gift is followed by counter-gift, each person assumes that the exchange is to his advantage. Shouldn't we therefore say that the basis of a political community, as we're rationally explaining its origins, is, quite simply, our needs? By "needs" I mean the basic essentials of survival: first and foremost food, the most critical of our needs, since the continuation of life depends on it; in the second place, shelter; and, in the third place, clothing and accessories such as shoes, scarves, gloves, hats, socks, caps, fasteners, belts, buttons, and so forth. The question, then, is how society – since you say that, at this point, that's the appropriate term – will be able to satisfy so many different demands.

–Your question, *said Socrates in a fatherly way,* already contains the answer. That's often the case with sociology. . . Production will have to be organized. One person will be a farmer, to grow food, another will be a builder, to build houses, and yet another will be a tailor, to make clothing. And for the accessories we'll need a good shoemaker. So our society will have at least four members! And what we'll call the division of labor can already come into play. It would be absurd for the farmer to use one quarter of his working time producing only the wheat necessary for his own personal survival, without being concerned about the other three people's survival, and to spend the other three quarters of his time building lopsided walls for his house, making clothes that are too tight for him, and stitching misshapen shoes. Meanwhile, the shoemaker, the tailor, and the builder would be knocking themselves out, each one on his own, trying to grow some inedible wheat on their ridiculously small plots of land. Far more rational – at least on the surface – is specialization. The farmer will spend all of his time producing excellent wheat, not just for himself but for the others as well, and he'll exchange this wheat for well-made shoes, a nice house, and clothes that fit well, which the shoemaker, the builder, and the tailor will have produced by devoting all of *their* time to it, too, for the benefit of society as a whole.

–But why do you say "on the surface"? *asked Amantha, who was one smart cookie.* Isn't the division of labor as rational as it seems?

–Ouch! *said Socrates with a smile.* I've been caught out! The division of labor undoubtedly explains the origin of real societies, but we'll see that it can't serve as a basis for the society of the future, the society that will be true to our idea of justice. In *that* society, everyone will have to be able to do everything, or just about.

–Fine, fine, *said the prosaic Glaucon.* But, for the time being, can we please just stick to the paths of reality? What should the social division of productive labor be based on?

–Underlying the division of labor, which has been in existence for several thousand years, there are two beliefs, which are as dubious as they are deeply ingrained. The first is that nature didn't give all people the same abilities. One person, it's said, is naturally good at one kind of work and another person is good at a different one. The second is that it's preferable for someone who has mastered a particular skill to devote himself to it full-time rather than spread himself thin, doing several different ones at the price of being less efficient at each of them. You can guess the obvious conclusion all by yourself.

–Well, *said Glaucon,* everything will work better, both quantitatively and qualitatively, if a person, in keeping with the natural order of abilities, does only one sort of job and sticks to that, regardless of what everyone else is doing or not doing.

–That's such a bleak vision of things! *said Amantha.*

–It's nevertheless the one that's prevailed throughout human history, right up until today, *Socrates shot back.*

–Yes, but that's merely a question of fact, of temporary necessity, which proves nothing as to the value of the method itself.

–True enough, *Socrates conceded,* and anyway I'm going to suggest something else. At any rate, what we can keep in mind, as far as this empirical – or historical – basis is concerned, is that a lot more people than we originally imagined will be needed to make up a social totality, even a rudimentary one. The farmer will have neither the time nor the ability to make a plow, any more than will the builder his trowel or his bricks, or the weaver and the shoemaker their wool, leather, and countless tools. So a blacksmith, a miner, a fitter, and lots of other skilled workers will have to be added to our little make-believe society. But we can't stop there. We'll need cattle-breeders and shepherds so that the farmer may have his plow pulled by an ox and the builder his cart pulled by sturdy good-natured mules. Not to mention that the shoemaker will want well-tanned hides for his leather. And the list goes on! The country's capital will have to import from else-where what it needs for its future development, so here come carriers and merchants. This early stage of commerce will have a boomerang effect on production, including agricultural production, because merchants can't go empty-handed to a country where they intend to buy what their own country needs. To buy, you have to sell; to import, you have to export. Hence the need to produce more wheat, wine, or goats than are required by our local needs. Hence an influx of new farmers, farmhands, shepherds, and cattle-breeders, who will obviously need to have housing and the necessary tools. Hence a new contingent of blacksmiths, builders, shoemakers, and other workers. On this basis commerce will thrive: there will be an influx of brokers, financiers, dealers, carriers, sales representatives, etc.

–Not to mention, *said Glaucon, thrilled by this staggering economic boom,* the ships that'll be needed for international trade, the shipbuilders, the sailors, the dockworkers, and so forth.

–Ah, yes, *said Socrates, smiling.* A slew of people, including for heavy labor: cargo handling, hauling, unloading, and so on. All those hefty guys who sell their labor day in and day out in exchange for money, for what's called a wage. That's why they make up the major-ity of wage earners. Note that in this way labor is bought, just as any other goods that are needed are bought. So we'll need a market and a currency that'll be the abstract symbol of everything circulating in the exchanges. Amantha! Are you asleep?

Amantha didn't respond. She was in fact asleep, with her head resting against the back of her chair and her arms dangling over the armrests. Apparently economics wasn't her cup of tea. Glaucon, on the other hand, was all fired up.

–But tell me, Socrates, *he said.* Let's say a farmer or a worker comes to sell a pair of oxen or some gardening tools in the market. But if there's no buyer interested in these goods, is he going to sit there in the marketplace for hours, or even for days, waiting for a customer to show up and neglecting his crops or his workshop? If that's the case, then sales transactions would conflict with what you said about the necessary continuity of working time.

–Good point! That's why we'll have to add to our primitive society all sorts of middlemen between the producers and the consum-ers. These people will spend all their time in the market or in trade bureaux, and their role will be both to exchange money for goods that are for sale and to exchange the goods purchased for money. In the meantime, the direct producer will go back to work. A distinction will have to be made between professional retailers, who spend all their time in the domestic markets and are money men, nothing more, and merchants, who take the risk of making long trips abroad and thus stimulate international trade.

–I think, *said Glaucon in conclusion,* that we've really covered every function and type of person required for a society to exist.

–Just about. So we can now return to the one thing that matters to us: where, in a primitive society like this, do justice and injustice come in?

–Oh, it's about time! *said Amantha, waking up fresh as a daisy.*

–I, for one, don't have a clue, *Glaucon admitted.* Justice? At such a rudimentary stage in the development of the forces of production? Maybe it exists in the exchanges that take place between the members of these little primitive communities?

–That's as good a guess as any. Let's examine the problem without getting discouraged. And first off, let's ask ourselves how people actually live in what you call "primitive communities," which Jean-Jacques Rousseau terms "the state of nature." Certainly, these "primitive" people produce wheat, wine, clothing, and shoes, and they build houses. Although they work naked and shoeless for the most part in summer, in winter they wear clothing and shoes appropriate to how cold it is.

–And what do these underdeveloped people eat? *Glaucon asked.*

–Flour, for the most part. Baked if it's barley, kneaded and dried if it's wheat flour. Oh, the flat cakes made by these so-called savages! Trust me, their culinary distinction is far superior to that of so many of our indigestible venison pâtés with port and ginger. And their rolls! All this is served on freshly cut reeds and bundles of clean leaves. The guests recline on couches made of yew branches and sprigs of myrtle. Old and young men alike feast, intermingled with the women and children. Crowned with garlands of flowers, they drink their sparkling wine and sing the praises of the Other. Their simple lives are thus woven together in happy harmony. And it's not out of greed or selfishness that they practice birth control, in line with what they can afford; it's so as never to run the risk of either extreme poverty or war.

Glaucon couldn't contain himself any longer.

–My God! *he exclaimed.* You've got these people attending a banquet with nothing but dry bread!

–Oh, a thousand pardons, you're right! I forgot the condiments. There's salt, of course, and olives, cheese, and onions. Then there are those boiled vegetables that are the daily fare of our farmers nowadays. We can even throw in a few desserts: figs, chickpeas, beans, and so on. Your "underdeveloped people" roast myrtle berries and acorns under the ashes, and they wash it all down with a glass of light-bodied wine. They thus live their lives in peace and Great Health.[2] They die at a ripe old age, murmuring: "Here we come, old age!" And they leave to their heirs a life in every way similar to their own.

Glaucon, truly furious, then said:

–Did you get us together for this late-night discussion to found a state of pigs? All we have to do now is get down on all fours and eat your acorns and boiled potatoes!

–But what else would you want to give these people? *Socrates calmly replied.* How else can their tranquil happiness be explained, except by how close they remained to their natural state, which they managed to preserve? Except by the decision they made not to deviate too far from the animal aspect of their lives?

–Well, you could at least have them lie on real beds, sit on real chairs around real tables, serve them meat for their meals and cream puffs for dessert. That would hardly be luxury yet!

–I see what you mean. It doesn't seem like a big deal, but it's actually a total change of method. It would no longer be chiefly a matter of studying the origins of society and the state, but rather what society and state become under conditions of abundance and the supposed delights of modern life. Well, maybe you're right. Your method may well allow us to understand at what precise moment and under what conditions justice and injustice emerge, as if naturally, in states. I maintain that the true political community is the one we've just described, which I depicted as the health itself of collective life. Now, if you're dead set on our examining a sick, feverish political community instead, fine, let's do it! I do in fact have the feeling that, as in your example, dear Glaucon, there are a lot of people for whom this kind of simple community, regardless of how natural it may be, wouldn't suffice any more than would the type of life that goes with it. They'll want to have beds, tables, all brand-new furnishings, meals prepared by three-star chefs, expensive perfumes, sexy call-girls, Baltic caviar, incense burning in silver pots, top-quality oriental pastry – in a nutshell, the full line of rare and superfluous products. In a world like that, it won't be the case that "the bare essentials" – the things you absolutely have to have – will mean houses, clothing, shoes, etc., no, because to these things they'll add painting, the motley assortment of objects that people put on display, gold, ivory, platinum, iridium, the whole gamut of precious materials.

–Oh, at last! We're finally in a civilized country! *said Glaucon approvingly.*

–But then we'll have to imagine the country in which we're establishing our theoretical fiction as being a lot bigger than we've done till now. Our perpetually healthy "primitive" society won't do. We'll have to fill it with a veritable throng of people who have no connection whatsoever with what's strictly necessary for communal life. For example, we'll have to have all sorts of hunters: rabbit, partridge, pheasant, deer, wild boar hunters, and so forth. And all sorts of imitators: those who use shapes and colors – painters – and those who use music and words – poets, composers, and all the people who run behind them: rhapsodists, crooners, rock, tango and rap groups, orchestra players, dancers, actors, distributors, producers, etc. And, in addition, the people running behind those who are already running behind the other ones: cosmetics manufacturers, and, last but not least, designers, makers of women's fashions, and – a breed that has developed only recently – makers of men's fashions. We'll have to create lots of jobs in the service industry, too: tutors who give private lessons in math or Ancient Greek to low-achieving kids, wet-nurses for babies whose stylish mothers don't want to ruin their breasts, piano teachers for pimply teenagers, chambermaids for luxury hotels, hairdressers for undoing chignons, not to mention master chefs and shellfish growers. But you can even throw in pigsty cleaners and that still won't be the end of it. It's endless, truth be told. In our original society, there was nothing like this, because people didn't have any use for it. But the way things stand now, we'll need all these people, and even – hey, I just thought of this – cattle galore, because the citizens of this type of society will have become meat-eaters. Which means, moreover, that with such a decadent diet we'll need. . . Amantha! Sleeping Beauty! What will we need?

–Doctors, *said Amantha gloomily.*

–Loads of doctors! And not just civil ones, military doctors, too, because the country, which till now was able to produce enough food for itself, will become too small and won't be able to feed a rapidly growing population. Hence the idea that it wouldn't be so bad to encroach on our neighbors' land. That way we'd have enough land for extensive farming and for livestock. If the neighbors in question overstep the bounds of basic necessity, just as we have done, and give in, just as we did, to the insatiable desire for possession, they'll come to the same conclusion we did: to encroach on their neighbor's land – *our* land. And where does this cross-border similarity of desires lead?

–To war, *said an increasingly gloomy Amantha.*

–Right, to war. . . A huge subject for philosophers, *said Socrates, thinking aloud.*

–Could you prove to us, *Amantha went on,* that the consequences of war are inevitably catastrophic, which is the pacifists' and non-violent resisters' thesis? Or should we instead think that there might be useful wars, even just wars, as many classical thinkers, but also most revolutionaries, have maintained? And then there's old Hegel, too, who thought that war is the obligatory dialectical moment of the subjective revelation of a nation. . . This issue has been bothering me for a long time now.

–The time's not yet ripe for drawing any conclusions about that. I just want to stress that we've found the origin of war to be in that terrible passion to acquire, that boundless desire to increase one's assets, whether financial (money and stocks), real estate (houses), furnishings (expensive objects), or property (land). Wherever this proprietary instinct takes hold of people's minds it's the source of the direst evils, both collective and private. Only, at this point, we're not in a position to propose, on indisputable grounds, a program for the abolition of private property. As you know, that's what's called communism, and we'll eventually get to it. But we've got to be methodical. We're only following the lines of force of the development of societies in order to understand at what precise point justice and injustice confront each other.

–So what do you conclude, then, from the emergence of wars? *asked a disappointed Amantha.*

–Quite simply, dear girl, that we have to expand our idea of the country again. Do we ever! Because we'll need an army on a war footing, prepared to defend both our old possessions and those we'll have recently seized by force, and to ruthlessly fight off any invaders.

–But aren't the members of this supposed political community capable of doing that themselves? *objected Glaucon.* They can take up arms, after all. A general mobilization can be declared.

–There you go falling into the ditch again instead of staying on the path the method prescribes for us. We all agreed – you like everybody else – that, at this stage in our inquiry into the origin of societies, the principle must remain a strict division of labor. According to the traditional view of things, a man – or a woman – cannot seriously master several different techniques. Now, doesn't everything connected with war define a technique? I have the feeling that, from down there at the bottom of your ditch, you're placing a much higher value on the shoemaker than on the soldier.

–Well, *said Amantha,* for once my dear brother's right. Making good shoes is certainly a lot more worthy of interest and a lot more important than killing your neighbor according to form.

–I couldn't care less about value judgments like that! *fumed Socrates.* In the context of the social division of labor, as it results for the time being from the whole real evolution of history, we said: the shoemaker cannot, and consequently must not. . .

–Well, how do you like that! *countered Amantha indignantly.* I'm not allowed any value judgments but *you*'re allowed a "one cannot, therefore one must not," as if the fact and the value were one and the same thing!

–That's right – in the context, which our method assumes, of the division of labor as a supposedly objective necessity! But only there! In this case, yes, we *do* have to say: the shoemaker must not be a weaver, a computer programmer, or a farmer. A shoemaker he is and a shoemaker he stays, in order to achieve perfection in the one profession that's his. Can the profession of soldier be excluded from that sort of consideration? To go off and fight a war, to master tactics and strategy, to use a weapon effectively, whatever it may be – anything from a dagger to a bazooka – to pilot a fighter plane, to destroy an enemy assault tank: is doing all that so much easier than mending the sole of a worn-out old shoe? Even to play jacks you have to start practicing when you're just a kid. Do you think that simply by virtue of taking down from your wall a shield and a sabre, or a rifle and a cartridge belt, you instantly become an extraordinary fighter who'll make the enemy take off like a rabbit as soon as he appears on the front lines? Really! You two are unbelievably presumptuous!

–Oh, don't get up on your high horse! *Amantha snapped.* You yourself don't believe for one second that that analogy between the shoemaker and the soldier can stand up to scrutiny. The soldier epitomizes a nation's subjectivity; he doesn't define a profession, except at the stage of decaying imperialism. Being a soldier is something required, something demanded of the individual by circumstances. We can perfectly well study what war requires of men outside the stupid context of the division of labor. It's been observed plenty of times that citizens who also happen to be mathematicians, peanut vendors, or machine-tool workers fight like lions against a fascist invader, and that's a lot more interesting than some stuff about shoes.

–Well, *said Socrates, staring in disbelief,* you're really letting me have it! What about you, dear Glaucon? What do *you* think?

–It seems to me, too, that we could study the features of a soldier without squeezing the inquiry into the narrow drawer of job classifications.

–Because to be a soldier, in a free country, *insisted Amantha,* is a militant principle. It's not a matter for sociologists. Let's not forget that our current intellectual business is the concept of justice, not the salary gap between shoemakers and cavalry colonels.

–OK, OK, *said Socrates, putting his hands up in mock surrender,* I give up. We're switching methods yet again. While waiting to get to the concept of justice, let's study the concept of soldier in and for itself, to speak like "old Hegel," as Amantha called him, I'm not really sure why. Let's begin at the beginning: the features, both objective and subjective, that must be cultivated in those – everyone, if we're adopting the communist hypothesis prematurely – who are forced by circumstances to become soldiers in order to guard the homeland.

–Right, *said Amantha,* to guard the homeland. We're excluding from our field of inquiry the will to conquest and plunder, the murderous rapacity. The soldier we're talking about is forced to become one in order to defend the justice that was established with great difficulty in his country. We're following in the footsteps of Jean Jaurès.[3] In his *The New Army*, every soldier is a citizen defending an Idea much more than a territory. Yes, let's call this type of soldier a "guardian." "Guardian" will be midway between "soldier" and "political militant."

–That's not bad, *opined Glaucon.* Let's do a phenomenology of the guardian.

–Since you young people are steering the discussion, go ahead and ask the first question. Fasten your seatbelts – here we go!

Glaucon stepped up to the plate.

–What are the features by which a good soldier can be recognized? *he asked.*

–A good guardian of justice, *Amantha corrected him.*

–Let's take a step back, *said Socrates imperturbably.* As big a step as possible: back to nature. Allow me to compare the human animal called up to fight a defensive war – our guardian, in other words – to those dogs that are called, as a matter of fact, "guard dogs." I think the guardian, like the dog, must have keen senses and be fast and strong: have keen senses, to detect where a threat may be lurking; be fast, to pursue it once it's been detected; and be strong, to fight it once it's been caught.

–I also think, *said Glaucon,* that, to fight well, it's not enough to be objectively strong; you've also got to be subjectively brave.

–Absolutely. Having keen senses and being fast, strong, and brave are at any rate precise goals as far as the training of a guardian is

73

concerned. But underlying all that, I think there's a sort of agency of the Subject, which we could call spirit, that's a blend of irascibility and bravery. We all know that there's something about anger that's indomitable and practically invincible. A Subject driven by the spirit I'm talking about knows no fear and could never imagine giving ground, not so much as an inch.

–I know a thing or two about that! *chuckled Amantha.* A little while ago I was pretty angry and *you* were the one, Socrates, who gave ground.

–Oh, but beware: "If the enemy advances, I retreat. But if the enemy halts, I counter-attack. And if he retreats, I pursue and destroy him."[4]

–Who said that?

–Mao. But let's sum up now! The objective qualities – physical and psychological – of our ideal guardian are keen senses, speed, strength, and courage. What makes a Subject of him is spirit, or, in other words, that potential for anger that keeps him from being a coward.

–The trouble with angry people, *objected Amantha,* is that they tend to be really aggressive when they encounter another person who's just like them. I get violently angry with other women all the time, just because I see that they're going to stand up to me. It's like guard dogs when they meet another guard dog on the street. You better watch out for all the biting! It's better to keep them muzzled.

–But we can't put muzzles on our guardians so that they won't bite each other, *Glaucon laughed.*

–We've got to resolve this dialectical problem, though, *Socrates interjected.* While they're ferocious toward enemies in the heat of battle, our guardians must nevertheless be perfectly civil toward our people in general, toward other guardians in particular, and even toward wounded enemy soldiers or ones who are taken prisoner. How can we foster a temperament that combines ferocity and civility, gentleness and toughness in our fellow citizens? If we accept the common idea that toughness and gentleness are mutually exclusive, we won't find a single acceptable guardian.

–We're at a dead end, *sighed Glaucon, who was actually quite tired.*

–No, we're not, not at all, you moron! *Amantha shot back.* Remember the comparison Socrates made, remember the dogs.

–Dogs? What dogs? *said a bewildered Glaucon.*

–A good guard dog can sense a threat, some evil intention or other, and will bare his teeth. But when it comes to anyone who's weak or familiar to him he's as affectionate and friendly as can be. Just look at the way those nice little doggies are with children, old people, family friends, peace-loving visitors! They roll over on their backs, they play up to them, they put up good-naturedly with having their ears pulled.

–That's what loving animals is all about. We know them so well! *said Socrates with a smile.* Yes, the dialectic of gentleness and toughness is a matter of knowing and recognizing. What counts is how sharply you can distinguish between something unfamiliar that endangers the collective process and something that promotes it. But that's not really the problem for me. It's that we've overlooked an essential feature of the guardians that nevertheless follows from Amantha's remark.

–Which one? *asked Glaucon, who'd been hoping they were done.*

–The dog Amantha's praising is actually a philosophical dog.

–What's a philosophical dog?

–A dog can distinguish between what's good, what's a threat, and what's harmless. It's this ability to recognize that determines whether it's his angry spirit – baring his teeth and attacking – that will be put into play or, on the contrary, his joyful spirit – capering around and asking to be petted. So the ideal guard dog subjects his subjective spirit to the idea of the Good. He's a perfect philosopher. He's not hungry for power but eager for knowledge.

–Whence the definition of the guardian: he's a good dog! *said Amantha in conclusion.*

–At any rate, like the guard dog, the true guardian aligns his inner dialectic – ferocity and civility – on the effects of a higher desire, the desire for knowledge. And, as the guardian epitomizes in his own particular features the society whose origins we've delineated, we know what every citizen of that society – since they're *all* called to be guardians – must try to be like: they must have keen senses and be fast, strong, brave, spirited, and a philosopher.

–That's some project! *Glaucon exclaimed enthusiastically.* It bears repeating: that's some project!

THE DISCIPLINES OF THE MIND

Literature and Music (376c–403c)

Socrates was rubbing his hands together, which, with him, was always a sign of deep satisfaction.

–My friends, *he said,* we've painted a remarkable portrait of the guardian, that is, of virtually everyone. But how on earth can someone like that be brought up and educated? How can the eternal child in him be tamed? It's a tough question. What's more, we might wonder whether giving an answer to it, assuming we're able to, will help us at all resolve the only real problem, the one we've been dealing with right from the start: What are the conditions under which justice and injustice emerge in the body politic? We need to focus on that so that we don't leave out any important argument, or waste our time asking totally pointless questions either.

At this, Amantha got upset and said:

–But how can the problem of political leadership not be connected to the ideas of the people who embody it, to what they know, to what they don't know, to what they love or loathe, and therefore to their childhood and education?

–Fine! Let's take the roundabout way then, however long it may be. Let's tell ourselves a beautiful story, worthy of the myths our poets relish. We have the ability, by virtue of reason alone, to define the future guardians' educational curriculum, that is – since everyone risks having to become a soldier – the ability to educate our youth.

–I love it when you're a storyteller! *laughed Amantha.*

–And a storyteller who's incapable of making anything up, I might add. Because how could one imagine a better education than the one that comes from the dawn of time: physical education for the body; scientific, artistic, and literary disciplines for the mind? And how could we reject the idea that you have to begin with the arts and letters? So we've got a ready-made beginning: What sort of literary and artistic education is appropriate for our future fellow citizens? You have the floor, Glaucon.

–Well, *said Glaucon bravely,* well. . . I don't have the slightest idea.

–All right, let's go about it methodically. In the arts and letters, as in the sciences, there are statements, propositions, arguments, narratives. Now, we know that there are two kinds of narratives: true ones and false ones. I maintain that both these kinds should enter into our educational curriculum. But priority should be given to the false ones.

–That's ludicrous! *said Amantha indignantly.* Teaching the future members of the political community, at the dawn of their life, only things that are false! Who are you trying to kid?

–What do you mean? That's exactly what we see all the time. The education of little children is begun by telling them stories, fables, isn't it? Yet those fables are nothing but lies, with a few odd truths mixed in.

–So what's to be done, then? *asked a bewildered Glaucon.*

–With all things, the beginning is the most important part. This rule applies particularly to the beginning of life, childhood. Isn't that the most propitious time to shape a given individual in the mold of the character type we want him to embody? So, if that's the case, is it reasonable to let children fall prey to any old myths made up by any old person? That would be tantamount to letting into their minds opinions that are precisely the opposite of the ones that, in our view, they should have when they grow up. So we should first and foremost supervise the storytellers. Those who make up good stories we should choose, and those who make up bad ones we should drop. Then we'll instruct nursemaids, mothers, fathers – if they want to get involved – that they should only tell their children the stories that have been selected, so that the children's minds might be molded by the murmur of fables even more than their bodies are by the fond touch of hands.

–But couldn't we ourselves, *Amantha put in,* write the new myths required by the education of children today?

–Your brother Plato wrote some really wonderful ones. But, for the time being, neither you nor I are poets. We're dealing with the origin of states, their nature, and their structure. For that reason, it's important for us to know which types of fables are suitable for poetic creativity in terms of its relationship with the education of the country's citizens. If need be, we might even declare our opposition to any use of clearly unsuitable types. But writing poetry's not our business.

–But isn't it heading down a very slippery slope, *Amantha*

continued, to presume to censure the poets while admitting that we ourselves are not poets in the least? And what will you ban, at the end of the day?

–The true lie. Purposeful and deliberately asserted falsehood is the enemy of the gods and men alike.

–But why the lie precisely?

–Because no one wants to be deceived, not even "accidentally on purpose,"[1] about vital matters in situations that are vital for them. There's nothing we fear more than being taken over inwardly that way by falsehood.

–I still don't quite get it, *Glaucon admitted.*

–Stop thinking that everything I utter is holy writ! What I'm saying is very simple: to be deceived, as a Subject, about the nature of things in themselves, to languish in such falsehood, not even to be aware of it, and thus to give shelter and protection to the false within ourselves is, once we finally become aware of it, the hardest thing for us to bear. Discovering our own errors causes us to hate deceit.

–Oh, I get it! I'll get it from now on!

–To be absolutely precise, what I called the "true lie" is in fact real ignorance: the ignorance of the deceived person just when he thinks he's inwardly becoming the Subject he's capable of being. The lie in speech merely imitates that real subjective affection and produces a derivative image of it, which is not exactly a pure lie. Only the "true lie," considered as a disorder of the Subject, incurs not only the gods' hatred but men's as well.

–OK, I understand it all now, thanks.

–The case of the lie in speech, that pale copy of the true lie, remains to be dealt with. There are some situations in which, unlike the true lie, the lie in speech doesn't deserve to be hated, such as when it's addressed to enemies, or to so-called friends whom a fit of madness or some extremely serious misunderstanding has incited to betray us or play some dirty trick on us. Lying words can, in those cases, act as a remedy to correct the suspicious intentions of such people. Another example, which we were discussing a little while ago, is that of myths. Since we don't know what the true circumstances were, inasmuch as they are lost in the mists of time, we can make up legends in which those circumstances are as much like their concealed truth as possible and thereby perform a useful service by lying.

–But fits of madness and ignorance are purely human affections, *objected Amantha.* There's nothing in what you're saying that would allow the *gods* to lie – or at least not if what we mean by "god" is the symbol of a humanity that has achieved its infinite perfection.

–You're absolutely right. "God," as I'm in the habit of saying, following Jacques Lacan, is just the nickname of the big Other – in other words, the repository of all the things worthy of being exalted in anyone you might chance to encounter. That being the case, we can say that no lying poet haunts the Divinity.

–Really? *said Glaucon, who was obsessed with the frivolous tales of sexual infidelity that mythology abounds in.* So there's nothing the gods can lie about?

–If God is the Other, the guarantor of all speech, absolutely nothing! *Amantha cut in sternly.*

–Whatever in a Subject is related to his spiritual, divine nature thus conceived is alien to lying, *added Socrates.* The only thing that can be called "God," that is to say, the pure essence of the Other – whether it exists or not is another story – is a symbolic being, perfectly simple and true in both word and deed, which neither changes itself into something else nor deceives others with trickery such as visions, misleading words, or fake signs. And that's the case regardless of whether you're awake or dreaming.

–You see! *commented Amantha to a crestfallen Glaucon.*

–Glaucon himself has to admit that when you tell stories or write poems that feature gods, it's illogical to have them change themselves, like common magicians, into something else, or to claim that they mislead us with lying words or shameful, rigged deeds. That's incidentally why, even though I admire Aeschylus, I can't approve of the passage in his tragedy *The Judgment of Arms* where Thetis says that Apollo, who was present at her wedding,

> Announced to me, smiling, the happy birth
> Of children belov'd, from all sickness free,
> The gods bestowing on me in my mirth
> The life I now curse as pure misery.
> Never a lie did I dream could proceed
> From the god's mouth, that Apollo divine,
> Who sang, at my wedding, a song so fine,
> Its promise so bright that, moved, I did heed.
> Yet Apollo – villain, low, vicious swine –
> Murdered my son. O most dastardly deed!

If a poet speaks that way about the gods or about the divine that is immanent in the Subject, we'll be angry! And we won't recommend his poem to the teachers in charge of instructing our citizens.

–Would you consider Kant to be right, then? *asked Glaucon.* Do you think that lying is evil, regardless of the context? Absolute evil? Would you inveigh, as he did, against Benjamin Constant, the defender of what Kant calls a "supposed right to tell a lie"?[2]

–I'm no advocate of formal moralism, not at all. I don't think it's possible to glorify lying, but I acknowledge that it can be empirically necessary to tell a lie.

–In what circumstances? Under what conditions? *Amantha asked sternly.*

–When an enemy's power requires us to use cunning and ploys. But, even then, the political leaders of the day must assume sole responsibility, which is still disgraceful, for the necessary lie. And they'll have to account for it in public once the danger is past. If, on the other hand, a private individual lies to the community for his own personal advantage, he'll be a lot more guilty in our eyes than a student who gives in to shame and hides from the gym teacher the fact that he has flat feet; or than a patient who's terrified in advance of the diagnosis the doctor may give him and "forgets" to tell him his most serious symptoms; or than a sailor who, to avoid having to work like a galley slave in the ship's hold, fails to tell the captain that the engines are overheating. As a rule, then, our young people will have to admit what they've done as soon as anyone asks them.

–You're right, *remarked Amantha,* but that's easier said than done.

–If one of our teachers catches anyone lying, be it

A boy eager to be a worker now,
A girl who's a sorceress in her dreams,
Someone who sees himself behind a plow,
Or even a poet in spring who schemes. . .

–The *Odyssey,* Book 17, *Amantha cut in,* but so transformed that it's barely recognizable![3]

–Bravo! *said Socrates, overjoyed.* Well, the teacher will tell the little liar off and publicly explain to him that any lie, endangering as it does the pact on which language is based, seriously undermines the political community.

–It's all clear now, as far as lying is concerned, *concluded Glaucon.* But what will we do about sobriety, self-restraint, reserve, prudent moderation, with all those rowdy teenage boys and those girls bursting with life?

–Well, will you listen to the wise old man! *Amantha said mockingly.*

–Oh, but he's right! It's not easy, *said Socrates.* We can extol the virtues of obeying orders, because we've understood the value of doing so, and of controlling violent urges – alcohol, drugs, sex, etc. – because they readily disrupt thought and action. Those are the imperatives of self-restraint for the guardians of the City. For once, we'll approve of Homer when he has Diomedes, speaking to Sthenelus, say:

Sit still, my friend, and obey my commands.

We'll also be satisfied with his description of the Greek army:

In silence the Greeks with courage forbore
Their generals' wrath and moved to the fore.

Amantha remarked:
–It sounds pretty Colonel Blimp-ish,[4] that description!
–It's obvious you've never fought in a war. Anyway, the very same Homer slips up when he has his hero, at the beginning of Book 9 of the *Odyssey*, say that there's nothing more splendid than

A table laden with bread and with meat
While poured in gold cups is a wine most sweet.

A ditty like that sure won't encourage boys and girls to stay sober!
–But there's something even worse than that! *exclaimed Glaucon.* It's in Book 14, I think, of the *Iliad*. Homer tells the story of Zeus, who's sitting there pensively all by himself while the other gods and men are sleeping and is suddenly overcome by such lust that he forgets whatever it was he was meditating about. Seeing Hera, who'd woken up, he doesn't even have the patience to go into her bedroom with her: he rips off her nightgown, throws her right down on the ground stark naked and enters her with no foreplay at all. As he's screwing her, he whispers that he's never desired her more, not even when they were young and they'd slept together "without their parents' knowledge."
–In Book 8 of the *Odyssey*, the story of Ares and Aphrodite, both of them totally naked, with chains thrown around them by Hephaestus when they were in the heat of the act, is pretty risqué, too, *Amantha added.*
–But still, *Socrates rectified,* Homer could also do justice to the endurance of a few illustrious men in the most difficult of circumstances. We should absolutely become imbued with verses such as:

Beating his chest, his heart he thus upbraids:
"Bear up, failing heart! This peril will fade!
Far worse you've endured, so be not afraid."

–The *Odyssey*, Book 20, right? *remarked Glaucon, happy to score a cultural point against his sister.* So what else is there, with respect to self-restraint?

81

–I'd like for us to talk a bit about corruption, *said Amantha,* about gifts, about wealth. Don't we have to put our militants on guard against all that sort of thing?

–Well, in that case we shouldn't agree with old Hesiod when he says:

> Swayed are they all by the lure of fine gifts.
> Young gods and old kings: none ever resists.

–OK, sure, *groaned Amantha.* But all this moral dissection of the old poets is kind of a drag. And, furthermore, you aren't saying a thing about the form, the rhythm, the images. We could be talking about a TV news show – it'd be no different.

–Fine, let's drop the moral subject matter of the stories, then, *Socrates conceded.* Let's talk about their style. That way we'll have linked the problem of the young guardians' education to both the content *and* the form of the literary works we'll be including in the curriculum.

–"Form," "style". . . What exactly does all that mean? *asked Glaucon, a little provocatively.*

–Let's begin with two basic facts. One: the speech of poets, when they're authors of stories, comes across as the narrative of what is happening, has happened, or will happen. Two: the style of the narrative can be indirect, direct – meaning mimetic – or a combination of the two.

–Oh, you've really lost me there, *Amantha declared.*

–Oh no! So you regard me as a ridiculous teacher? As a befuddled old pedant?

–Well, you can just get around it the way all bad teachers do: instead of explaining the general idea, you give a pretty stupid example, and that's that.

–I see you have a high opinion of my pedagogical abilities. Well, I'm going to do precisely what you suggested. I suppose you know the beginning of the *Iliad* by heart, when Chryses, Apollo's priest, asks Agamemnon to give him back his daughter. Agamemnon flies into a terrible rage and sends him packing. So then Chryses, humiliated, asks the god to give the Greeks a hard time. Take these two verses:

> The Greeks Chryses begged, their whole army and
> The Atreans, their chiefs, those in command.

You can see that the poet is not trying to make us think that the person speaking is anyone but himself. He relates Chryses' words like a witness who'd tell what he's seen or heard. That's indirect style.

But, in the verses that follow, the poet speaks as if he really *were* Chryses. He does indeed try to persuade us that it's not him, Homer, who's speaking but the old priest. And that's how Homer, by attributing the speech to a speaker who's supposedly someone other than the poet, wrote nearly all the stories of what happened in Troy and Ithaca. That's direct or mimetic style: Homer's like an actor playing the part of the father in verse.

–Don't these concepts still need to be clarified a little? *suggested Amantha.* What exactly characterizes a narrative?

–There is narrative when you relate objectively, from the outside, as it were, the words spoken by various people, as well as everything that happens in between these speeches.

–And what about imitation?

–If you express yourself as though you were saying other people's words yourself, you'll try to speak, as far as possible, the way in which everyone you introduce as going to speak is indeed supposed to speak, won't you?

–And that's what mimetic art is?

–Making yourself like someone else in tone of voice or manner: isn't that imitating the person you're trying to be like?

–Yeah, that's perfectly clear.

–So it follows that, even in their narratives, Homer and his successors all make use of mimesis. If the poet never disguised the fact that everything being said is his *own* speech, the poetic narrative would contain no imitation at all. But, just so you won't say again that you don't get it, I'm going to return to my favorite example, Book 1 of the *Iliad*. Homer there tells how Chryses implores the Greek kings to return his daughter to him for a ransom. If he'd gone on writing in indirect style, without disguising the fact that it's he, Homer, who's speaking and not Chryses, there wouldn't be the slightest imitation, there'd only be simple narrative. We'd get something like this – I'm disregarding meter because I'm not a poet. . .

–I'm not so sure about that, *Amantha interjected.* At any rate, your favorite disciple, my brother Plato, wrote tragedies. . .

–. . . that he burned!

–That's what *he* says. But has anyone looked under his mattress?! And you yourself often tell us splendid myths. Aren't you a sort of prose poet?

–You want a prose poet? I'll show you a prose poet! Here's what verses 22 to 42 of Book 1 of the *Iliad* would become if I had my way, put back into prose, and in indirect style:

"The priest came and prayed to the gods. He asked them to let the

Greeks capture Troy. Without getting slaughtered. Then he turned to the Greek kings. He begged them to return his daughter to him. For a hefty ransom. And out of consideration for the gods. He finished his speech. The Greeks were moved by it and won over. All except Agamemnon. Who got angry. And who told Chryses that his priestly trinkets wouldn't protect him. And who added that his daughter would grow old in Argos, of which he, the bearded king who comes forward,[5] was the king. And that in Argos his daughter would share her bed many times with the aforementioned bearded king. And Agamemnon concluded by telling Chryses, for the second time, to get the hell out. And to stop bugging the hell out of him. That is, if he wanted to get home in one piece, added Agamemnon, twirling his moustache. The old priest got the hell out without further ado. Lickety-split. But once out of the Greeks' sight he stopped. He got down on his knees under a palm tree and prayed to Apollo. He recited all the god's names and nicknames: my sweet little sun, my golden cheese, my adorable god of the roads. He asked him whether he'd liked the temples that his beloved priest, namely he, Chryses, had built for him. And whether he'd enjoyed the plump chickens, the fat oxen, and the smelly rams he'd sacrificed there for Him, the DSLS, the Dazzling Swollen Luminous Sphere. If the answer was "yes," said Chryses, then he, Chryses, was asking Apollo to pierce the Greek kings' potbellies with his flaming arrows. And thus to avenge through blood the tears that he, Chryses, had shed over the dire fate of his daughter."

And that, dear friends, is a narrative in an indirect, plain style, with no imitation.

–You can hardly call that – *and here Amantha made a face* – appealing. . .

–Could it be that you prefer the completely opposite style, the one that has only direct speech, because everything the poet says between two characters' speeches has been left out?

–You're talking about tragedy, *observed Glaucon.*

–You're right, and about comedy, too.

–It's all clear for me now, *Glaucon reassured himself.* I understood the distinctions you drew. Poetry and fiction can be entirely imitative, as is the case with comedies and tragedies, when the poet writes only in direct style.

–Except for the stage directions, *a suddenly pedantic Amantha remarked.*

–Yeah, OK, *retorted Glaucon, irritated once again by his sister.* The second possibility is that everything's in indirect style: the work is presented as a narrative written by the author. That's the case today with the "objective" or autobiographical novel, as it was in the past with dithyrambs or elegiac poetry. The third possibility is a combination of the other two, and that's the epic poem, as well as its ungrateful son, the great classical novel.

–Exactly. Now let's turn from description to prescription, from structure to rules. What will we tell writers they're allowed, from a political standpoint? Total freedom to imitate whatever they want, in the name of realism? Or a total ban on imitation, in the name of idealism and the authority of the glorious future? Or imitation only of models that are instructive, heroic, useful. . .

–In a nutshell, *Amantha added in a sarcastic tone,* nothing but "positive heroes."

–Right, *Glaucon agreed,* this all really comes down to the issue of a new revolutionary art, with one specific question as a result: do we officially authorize theater – tragedies and comedies – as the Greeks do? Do we forbid it, as the Christian Church did? Or do we keep a very close watch on it, as in the socialist states?

–Which executed Meyerhold,[6] the bastards! *said Amantha indignantly.*

–We can see, *said Socrates thoughtfully,* that it's a very difficult question. But wherever our rational argument, like the wind, takes us, that's where we should go.

–It seems to me, *said Amantha, anxious to defuse her anger,* that we need to return to the most general formulation of the problem. Is it or is it not important for the leaders, whoever they may be, to be experts in imitation? To be able to copy a model or, more broadly speaking, to reproduce reality?

–The problem, *said Socrates solemnly,* is that imitation leads to specialization. We saw the calamitous results of mechanical, slavish imitation when the Communist parties of the twentieth century took their inspiration from a single model: the Soviet Union, "the fatherland of socialism," with its Party that's always right and its glorious leader Stalin, "the little father of the people." In the sort of finitude inflicted on us by present circumstances, one and the same man cannot adequately imitate things that are too different from himself or too different from each other. The author of mimetic comedies can't write a tragedy effectively. Aristophanes isn't Sophocles, Molière isn't Racine, Feydeau isn't Ibsen. Even actors, those experts in imitation, can't play the whole gamut of human characters. The great Harlequins of the Commedia dell'arte, those cunning thieves and hearty gluttons, aren't good at playing great tragic princes broken down by fate.

85

–So what can we conclude from this? *asked a bewildered Glaucon.*

–We need to make a distinction between time periods. In the long run, our generic idea of Humanity and the collective effort required to realize its full potential will do away with all these limitations. Men, even if they're coarse fellows with a beard and a big potbelly, will be able to do virtuoso imitations of flirtatious young women with breathtaking cleavages, or of old women swearing at their husbands in colorfully vitriolic language. And the women will all be able to slip into the role of a big bully showing off at the bar in a café, bringing down the walls, and competing with the gods; or into the role of a jealous crybaby groveling at the feet of his unfaithful mistress. There's nothing surprising in that: under our system of government, depending on the circumstances and on the outcome of the lotteries, the shoemaker will also be a government minister, the baker woman an army officer, the bricklayer an architect, the supermarket check-out girl a secret agent or a diplomat. The whirl of constantly changing identities will be solidly grounded in societal roles!

–But when will this happen? Right away? Tomorrow? How do we go about it?

Socrates reflected, plainly at a loss for an answer. He drank a glass of dry white wine, was quiet for a moment, and then began again, as he often did, a bit off the topic.

–What should our leaders be? That is, what should all our country's citizens become, as soon as possible? Here's the definition I propose: they should be the artisans of the country's freedom.

–That's nice, *murmured Amantha,* "the artisans of the country's freedom."

–And with this artisanal work of active thought no imitating of anything whatsoever is involved, as a rule. Investigating, creating, and deciding are what's necessary. True politics precludes all representation; it's pure presentation. So, if any aspects of imitation are required, they can only be based on models from childhood, which support the virtues required by the inquiry among people, by the development of an orientation, and by the decision to put it into practice. We know what those virtues are: courage, self-restraint, concentration of thought, the disinterestedness of a free spirit. . . Indulging in the imitation – even ironic – of shameful behavior exposes the imitator to the risk of eventually becoming corrupted by the reality that the images he produces are inspired by. Naturally, an understanding of human madness and of how people can be despicable or cruel is necessary. But that doesn't require representing or imitating, let alone doing, everything that such human madness might dictate to the confused minds of our contemporaries.

–Your – temporary? – rejection of any purely mimetic language, at least in the political field, seems to me to suggest that, when it comes to the future leaders of our country, some very strictly defined forms will be required for what they might want to express or relate. And the situation will be quite different from the kind of "democratic," "anything goes" state of affairs we see today.

–That's right, my dear Glaucon. A sense of proportion will require the man or woman who has to give an account of an oral declaration or of an action to know when and how it is acceptable, or even requisite, to shift to direct style. Using imitation to give more persuasive force to what one has witnessed is necessary when it's a matter of actions whose truth can serve as an example – such as, let's say, new thoughts, daring acts undertaken in the name of clear principles, unprecedented forms of resistance to oppression and stupidity. People will think twice, on the other hand, before they imitate the indecisiveness, the weakness, or even the cowardice of a person subject to illness, the torments of a lover's jealousy, or the dangers of war. In those cases a clinical, indirect style is warranted. Why bother imitating those individual characters in which no Subject can ever come into being? Ultimately, if our future citizen has to report what he's seen, he'll make use of a hybrid narrative force. He'll combine imitation and plain narrative, direct and indirect style, in variable proportions, depending on what the subject is. Since truths are less common than ordinary shortcomings, however, indirect style, or plain narrative freely assumed as such, will prevail in conversation, and even more so in public speeches.

Glaucon then launched into one of those "syntheses" he had a knack for:

–In a nutshell, the more a guy who's not our type indulges in imitations, parodies, and pastiches, the more harshly we'll judge him. That's because, since he considers nothing unworthy of his eloquence, he won't hesitate to twist himself in knots and disguise his own voice in order to imitate anything or anyone. He'll make the sound of thunder by farting, of wind by whistling, of hail by clicking his tongue against the roof of his mouth, of every kind of engine by purring, of the oboe or clarinet by pinching his nostrils together, of axles and pulleys by grinding his teeth, and so on. He'll think it wonderful to bark, meow, bleat, moo, bray, etc. His entire art will be a virtuoso performance of imitations, in which only a few fragments of narrative will manage to find a place. He'll thus be at the opposite extreme of our way of speaking. Because what's necessary for us, who give priority to narration and indirect speech, is a simple kind of harmony, full of nuance, with a rhythm based on regularity, subtle accelerations, and short pauses. Bad eloquence, on the contrary, requires a whole baroque medley of rhythms, sounds, images, and rhetorical figures in order to give expression to its myriad imitations and, like a ventriloquist, voice all the human characters, all the animals, and even the morning breeze or the waves washing up on the sand in the evening when the tide comes in. In our country we'll reject such affectations and that eclectic baroque style. We'll be classical above all. We'll be satisfied with a plain narrative, which yields to imitation only when it's a matter of depicting virtue.

–And yet, *objected Socrates,* the hybrid, colorful style you're opposed to is pleasant and especially appealing to children, their teachers and, to tell the truth, the vast majority of people. You no doubt think that it doesn't accord with our conception of what is common or public, because in our country there will have to be subjective unity in the very variety of occupations. Certainly, in the society we're constructing, someone will be able to be a shoemaker as well as an airline pilot, a farmer as well as a Supreme Court justice, a colonel as well as a grocer. But it must be understood, of course, that the grocer won't *imitate* a colonel, since, when he's a colonel, that's what he really *is*. The possibility for this real diversity depends on the universal circulation of a shared thinking. Through the mediation of a common language, we acknowledge that no real-life diversity shall adversely affect the power of that thinking. If everyone is to be able to do everything that's open to human activity, there must be that fundamental simplicity of language that we already acknowledge in mathematics, which alone can allow us access to a unified thinking of the visible. For the thinking of what is, is not the imitation of its diversity but the always surprising grasp of the unity of its being. Hence the urgent need for a language as appropriate as possible to that unity.

–But then, *asked a worried Amantha,* what will we do about all those great poets who enchant us with their devious way of capturing, through the dizzying swirl of metaphors, all the infinitely varied and splendidly versatile beauty of the world we live in?

–If a poet of that type, who's adept at captivating us by constantly transforming language expressions, shows up on our country's doorstep, we'll give him a stirring public tribute. We won't hesitate to declare that he's a holy and miraculous being, a wizard of life. We'll anoint him with all the perfumes of Araby and crown him with laurels. And then we'll escort him back to the border, explaining to him that there are no men of his kind in our country and that there never can be any, because we've created a more sober, less obviously appealing kind of poetry, which is closer to prose, or even to mathematics, by adapting it to our overall project and to the type of education that goes along with it.

–That's all very well and good, *said Amantha,* but our country won't *have* any doorsteps or borders! You're well aware that its project is purely internationalist in scope. The proletariat has no country. A communist border agent would be a pathetic oxymoron!

–Which only proves, *Socrates shot back,* that what I was suggesting was an *image,* that I was speaking metaphorically. Trust me, this vision of the poet, banned from the city, will become famous!

–Oh, then *you're* the poet with the deceptive language and the enticing images!

–Well, *concluded Socrates,* I entrust you with the task of personally seeing to my deportation.

They all burst out laughing. Glaucon, though, remained focused on serious things.

–We've said hardly anything at all about music, and yet it's such an important thing for all young people.

–Let's start with the simplest things, *Socrates calmly resumed.* The basic components of a song are four in number: the lyrics, the melody, the harmony, and the rhythm. As for the lyrics, we'll require the same principles for them as we did for poetry. The melody must fit the lyrics. That's the tribute music pays to poetry. So that leaves harmony and rhythm. They're technical issues, which change rapidly, moreover, and are controversial. Should the harmony be tonal or atonal? The rhythms regular or irregular? And what about instrumental tones? Ancient, traditional, or modern instruments? Electroacoustical simulations? It all has to remain an open question. Artistic orientation can never be reduced to technique. What matters to me is pretty obvious: a musical style must be able to formalize situations involving a Subject by dialectically highlighting the new abilities it can demonstrate over and above the run-of-the-mill and clichés. We enjoy musics of personal emotion, but we also want there to be musics of courage. It's a very good thing for music to "imitate" the subjectivity of someone who has to overcome severe hardship, on his own or with the help of friends, and who does so tenaciously and without a lot of boasting about! These are the harmonies and rhythms we need, at any rate: those of courage and of endurance.

–In essence, *Glaucon recapped,* you're saying that, in a song, the excellence of the lyrics, melody, harmony, and rhythm comes from a sort of subjective simplicity. Not the simplicity of the fool or the ignorant person, but rather the sort of creative simplicity that targets, through a unique process of the mind, the true and the beautiful.

–The same principle, *Socrates added,* applies to all the arts. The opposition between subjective simplicity, which produces graceful actions and words, and the pretentious ugliness of attempts to impress the ignorant can be seen just as well in painting, in tapestry or embroidery, in architecture or design. In all these things moderation of expression is the rule, and whatever purports to take no account of it is regarded as vulgar, in terms of both its expression and its underlying subjective esthetics. Consequently, it's clear that the rules we're proposing, which aim at restricting the imitative or representational dimension of poetry and musical works, apply to the other arts as well. My insistence on speaking especially about poetry and music stems from the fact that beautiful melodies with a fast-paced rhythm and lavish orchestration affect a Subject's inner being more powerfully than anything else. As a result, if this kind of music is adapted to an education like ours, vice and ugliness will be hated right from childhood, even without reason having to come into play. And when the latter does make its voice heard, we'll enthusiastically and affectionately approve of its judgments, provided that true music has nurtured the strongest sensations of our early years.

Everyone was struck by Socrates' almost solemn tone. With his eyes closed and his face lacking all expression, he went on to say:

–When we began our studies, we didn't consider that we knew written signs satisfactorily until such time as we could recognize their letters – which are actually few in number – in all the combinations in which they occur, to the point where we could make them out everywhere, however large or small the groupings in which these letters are used. That's how you become a real reader, we thought. We could recognize signs from their reflection in water or in mirrors only if we had learned beforehand to know them as they really are. The science of images is identical to the science of the real whose image is the image.

–Where is he going with this? *muttered Amantha.*

–For the same reasons, I maintain that neither we ourselves nor the future guardians of our country will be real poet-musicians until we're able to distinguish the ideas of self-discipline, courage, high-mindedness, freedom of spirit, and all the virtues that are like the letters of a life worthy of the name. The guardians will have to be able to recognize these ideas, as well as the ideas of the vices with which the virtues are paired, in all the vital combinations in which they occur. They'll have to be able to perceive them or their images everywhere, whatever the circumstances, be they important or trivial, in which they're found. And they'll have to know that the science of ideas, that of the opposite ideas, and that of the images of all these things are really only one and the same science. Which means in particular that if a young woman or man combines an inner being imbued with a beautiful character and an outward appearance deriving from the same outstanding model, he or she will be, for those lucky enough to meet him or her, the most beautiful thing that can ever be seen. There's no doubt they'll be loved by poets, musicians, and all cultured people. If there's a real defect in this amalgamation, though, that love will fade, won't it?

–Well, the thing is, *stammered Glaucon, blushing,* if there's a serious *character* defect, it won't work. But a minor *physical* flaw doesn't always prevent love.

–Oh, *said Socrates, smiling,* I bet you know that from experience! You must have been in love with, or you're still in love with, a boy who's not exactly an Adonis. . . But you still won't say that being concerned exclusively with pleasure when it comes to love is a proof of moderation, will you?

–No, of course not, *said Glaucon rather miserably.* Pleasure can drive us mad as much as pain can.

–Pleasure can have something violent and excessive about it, can't it?

–Not all the time, but often enough.

–Can you give me an example of a pleasure that's at once greater and keener than sexual pleasure?

–There isn't any. Sex is a real frenzy of bodies.

–But shouldn't love, to the extent that it serves to pass on the learned forms of reason from one human being to another – from a teacher to his young disciple, for example – be a love that's oriented, on the model of that sober kind of music we were just talking about, by something whose very idea is beauty?

– Yes, I think so.

–This (so to speak) didactic love is called transference love by Freud, because it moves from the body to the Idea. It has to remain safe from madness and licentiousness. Between the old teacher and the young male or female disciple, who love each other with a true love that's gradually enveloped by the sharing of the Idea, it is indeed the body that's at issue, but not at all the incomparable pleasures of sex. Or rather these remain in the background, like a sort of invisible

91

energy from which thought draws the force to gain access to the sub-limity of the Idea. In the country whose Idea we're in the process of constructing, everyone will acknowledge that bodies are not alien to the becoming of the True. The taboo on sex won't go so far as to pro-hibit the didactic relationship from having a physical dimension. The practice of teaching involves the body and voice of the man or woman who teaches. Those you instruct must be loved, and the person who instructs you must be loved. It won't be considered scandalous for teachers, whatever their gender, to approach young people, to spend time with them, talk to them, kiss them, touch them. They'll be like fathers or mothers, whose aim is to pass on to their children the best thing in the world: the secret of a true life.

–But they won't have sex with their students, *Amantha said sharply.*

–Or at least if they do, *qualified Socrates, his beady eyes twinkling and laughing,* it will be in the context of a unique, long-lasting or even eternal passion, for which the teacher–student encounter will have merely furnished the opportunity.

–Oh, that famous opportunity, *interrupted Amantha,* that makes the thief.[7]

–Anyway, *said a satisfied Glaucon,* we've finished with literature and music now.

–And to do so, *Amantha remarked softly,* we needed nothing less than love.

They all remained silent for a moment. Outside, as the poet said, the night is ruled.[8]

— 5 —

THE DISCIPLINES OF THE BODY

Nutrition, Medicine, and Physical Education (403c–412c)

Amantha yawned loudly and said:
 – I'm afraid that, after literature and music, you're going to start talking about physical education now.
 –Well, of course! *said Glaucon.* How can working-class youth, who are always so quick to get into pointless fights, be disciplined if we don't get them interested in physical education?
 –Oh, it's all just about roosters, bulls, ganders, stallions, tomcats, hogs, rams, and billy-goats! *Amantha snapped back.* Stupid young males! But go on, go on, I'm listening.
 –I'd like to convince you about this, *said a conciliatory Socrates.* I agree with you that the naked, individuated body never requires educational thought. It's not possible for the body, however well trained it may be, to incite the individual whose life it sustains to dedicate himself to the True and thereby become a Subject. On the contrary, it's subjective incorporation into the True – the word "incorporation" deserves to be especially emphasized here – that affords the body the excellence it's capable of. So, after giving analytical thinking the care it requires, we'd do well to entrust it with the task of specifying what's best for the body, while we just content ourselves with providing the general headings so that we don't get bogged down in details – which I acknowledge can be tedious, dear Amantha, since I see you're already falling asleep.
 –I can see a first rule that's very important, *said Glaucon, as serious as could be.* It has to do with alcohol. Our militants, our guardians, our leaders, our soldiers – all of that means the same thing, namely, everyone – shouldn't get drunk. A guy who's guarding his sleeping fellow citizens should absolutely not be allowed to puke all over and stagger around with no idea where he is.

–It sure wouldn't be a good thing, *said Amantha,* if the guardians had to be guarded. . .

–But before you can think about drinking, you have to eat, *Socrates resumed.* In one respect, our militants can be compared to competitive athletes: they're likely to have to fight tough battles. So should we adopt the athletes' diet?

–Are you kidding?! *shrieked Glaucon.* Since they spend their whole life sleeping and training, they're most likely overfed; they shoot coke and other such crap, and they die young, foaming at the mouth, and no one dares to say why they do. Way to go, athletes!

–So we'll prescribe a simpler, more refined diet, because our young men and women will have to be ever-alert and able to see, hear, and identify anything unusual going on wherever they are. Even though being on active duty might subject them to frequent changes – the water they drink, the game they eat, the local customs, everything, when they're in the field, may be different from what they're used to – and even though they'll have to endure the desert sun and the snows of the Far North, they've got to stay in tip-top physical shape. So we can conclude from this that food, drink, and physical exercise must obey the same rules as those we identified for literary and musical culture: simplicity, moderation, and subtlety. War can show us the way here.

–War? Show us the way? What do you mean? exclaimed *an incredulous Amantha.*

–Well, let's read Homer again.

–I thought he was no good.

–He isn't, except when he's better than all the other poets combined. Remember what the heroes of the *Iliad* eat when they're in the field. Homer doesn't feed them fish – even though they're encamped by the sea – or boiled meat. The menu is always the same: grilled meat, salad, cheese. In addition to being light and healthily nutritious, a diet like that is easy for soldiers to stick to. All they have to do is light a wood fire and cook the meat over the embers. There's no need for carrying around those enormous cooking pots that are the bane of every army. Nor for mayonnaise or ketchup or other indigestible condiments. As for Sicilian lamb and French rabbit stews, our soldiers can do without them.

–Nor do I think, as far as moderation goes, *said Amantha, looking all innocent,* that it's absolutely necessary for them to spend their dollars on keeping a Ukrainian mistress with a mop of blonde hair and a shaved pussy.

–Oh, Amantha! *said Glaucon, blushing.*

–Never mind, never mind, *said Socrates with a smile.*

–Or to pig out, *Amantha went on,* the way I do on oriental pastries with honey.

–OK, never mind that either. . . The general principle is simple variety. In music, you have to know what the tonal, atonal, or serial possibilities and the regular oriental or non-retrogradable rhythms are, but not always combine them arbitrarily. Likewise, you can sensibly eat some of everything, but in moderation, and not always mix everything up together, the way the gluttonous Yankees always do, on a huge plate that you wolf down at top speed. Our motto will be: refinement, yes, obesity, no.

–The parallel can be extended still further, *said Glaucon.* Anarchic excess in the cultivation of the mind gives rise to collective disorientation. Anarchic excess in the care of the body gives rise to a proliferation of hypochondriacal disorders.

–That's true, *Socrates agreed.* And if disorientation and mental illnesses spread throughout a country, the only things that will flourish there, in terms of institutions, are law courts and hospitals. Even intelligent, healthy people make a beeline for them. The desperate need for doctors and lawyers is the surest sign of a defective, inferior public education system. That's why that need eventually affects every sector of society. Come to think of it, it's shameful, and it's conclusive proof of the lack of education, that what's right for oneself can only be determined by other people, who are thereby raised to the status of tyrants over our souls, since we're unable to decide for ourselves.

Socrates then got all worked up. His passionate tone took the audience aback.

–Shame on the man who not only spends the greater part of his life in court, as a defendant at times and as a plaintiff at others, but who also – and this is the height of vulgarity – sees nothing wrong with boasting that he's an expert when it comes to injustice! Shame on the man who gloats that he's able to insinuate himself into the sinuosities of sense and laughingly leap through legal loopholes, so adept is he at devious dealings that he can rapidly run rings around justice.[1] And all for such trivial, totally worthless stakes, because our man has no idea that true life is dependent on the beauty of its immanent truth and that there's no need for some indifferent old judge prattling and rambling on.

–Ye gods! *exclaimed Amantha.* What a diatribe!

–And I'd say the same, *Socrates went on,* about people who are always running to their doctor, and especially to their shrink. Sure,

sure, if you've been injured in an accident or you're laid up in bed with a high fever due to some disease that's going around, or if some abnormal chromosome is damaging your brain, you've got to seek medical attention. And anyone whose symbolic organization is being poisoned by a primal conflict that's getting in the way of his becoming-Subject is of course right to lie down on an analyst's couch. But very often, if you take a closer look at it, it's really a matter of our laziness, of a sort of gluttony concealing our lack of appetite for any truth, a depressive melancholy occasioned by our political cowardice, the neurotic helplessness into which we're plunged by our revolting acceptance of the world as it is. It's all this that obliges the ingenious descendants of Charcot, Freud, and Lacan to use the science of complicated names to classify our miasmic moods, the vapors of our sleepless nights: manic-depressive psychosis, anxiety neurosis, paranoia, hysteria, phobia, obsessional neurosis, abandonment syndrome, clinical depression, psychasthenia, and so on. Isn't that a scientific panorama of modern shame?

–Yeah, *said Glaucon,* those names alone peg us as the dreamers of a Night of the Living Dead.

–And just look at all those gore and slasher movies, *added Amantha,* with all the maniacs running around in them, symbolizing our fascination with everything that breaks human subjects down.

–Oh, to return to the days of Asclepius, even before Hippocrates! *exclaimed Socrates.* That simple, folksy medicine you find in Homer. . . In Book 11, I think it is, of the *Iliad,* Eurypylus is wounded and, to treat him, a woman gives him a remedy invented by Patrocles, Pramnian wine sprinkled with flour and grated cheese. Nowadays, we'd think a remedy of that sort would only make the fever worse. But in Homer everyone's delighted with it, even the patient!

–Socrates, *Amantha put in,* I have to take you to task! You're mixing everything up. In Homer's text it's Machaon who's given the wine with the cheese in it, not Eurypylus. True, in another passage, Patrocles does treat Eurypylus, but with crushed roots, not with floured wine.[2]

–It doesn't matter. I like that considerate, homespun kind of medicine.

–It's very nice, *joked Glaucon,* as long as you don't die from it.

–Modern nutrition science certainly has the advantage of being able to monitor the patient's objective progress step by step and to adapt his diet accordingly. But let's not forget the founder of this discipline, Herodicus of Megara. He was a big athlete. He'd become depressed and was constantly ill, so he invented that combination of physical exercise and plant-based medicine that's so in fashion today. You know those people in light-blue track suits who run along the streets huffing and puffing, decked out with gadgets designed to measure their blood pressure, respiration, perspiration, and heart rate. They drink certified pesticide-free spring water. They get down on their knees to salute the sunrise. They eat powdered poppy petals. Those are the descendants of our Herodicus.

–But what about Herodicus himself? *Glaucon inquired.* What happened to him?

–Before it debilitated his disciples, his diet and exercise regimen – this is poetic justice – tormented *him* for a long time. He was suffering, or so he thought, from a slow-growing, "special" cancer. In actual fact he was a cross between a melancholic and a sloth.[3] However much he may have combined walking on tiptoe, sleeping in broad daylight, a vegan diet heavy on dandelion salad with no oil, and mud poultices from the Indies, he still eventually died from his "special" cancer. While he was still young, he gave up everything in order to focus on treating himself. But throughout his long life he was constantly tormented by anxiety just because he hadn't taken the requisite number of steps on the tip of his toes or he'd inadvertently eaten a little slug in his dandelions, things of that sort.

–Wow! There's a totally health-conscious life and death for you! *remarked Amantha.*

–Herodicus didn't realize that what enables you to overcome melancholy is doing what you know you have to do, not for yourself but under the injunction of the Idea of the True.[4] Once you've been seized by that imperative, you realize how absurd it is to spend your whole life being sick and treating your illness. Any ordinary worker understands that, but rich people, whose supposed happiness everyone envies, are always holed up in private clinics.

–How do you explain such an odd thing? *asked Glaucon.*

–When a worker's sick, he asks the doctor to make him better – with antibiotics, anti-inflammatories, an operation if need be – and to give him a sick-leave certificate for the length of time his body's weakness will prevent him from handling a pickaxe on a construction site or from mechanically repeating his movements over and over on the assembly line, amid the racket of the boilerplates and steamrollers. Our worker won't put up with being on an endless soft diet accompanied by psychological and moral sermons, with showers all the time and group therapy sessions where people scream the primal scream of the newborn baby. As far as he's concerned, medicine is in a dialectical relationship with work, to which he has to return. He can see no point in a life spent treating night terrors or unexplainable paralyses, wearing a certified organic angora wool cap. So he tends to tell the doctor: "Don't take care of *me*, take care of my illness. You're here to make me better, not to take over my whole life. You should act in such a way that I won't need you anymore."

–And, *said Glaucon,* as a worker, he's certainly right.

–What do you mean, "as a worker"? Do you think rational medicine has to take the patient's social class into account?

–It's just that when a guy who lives off his investments gets sick, he doesn't think about having to go back to work.

–I don't think he thinks very much about anything at all! Not about the work he doesn't do or about any commitment he might have under the imperative of an Idea, something he strenuously avoids. We could obviously quote to him these lines, which were once quite well known:

When you're well-off and you don't have to work,
You must be a thinker, not just a jerk.[5]

–Who wrote that doggerel? *asked Amantha, appalled.*

–A guy who's totally forgotten now, someone named Phocylides.

–Besides, *said Glaucon,* you should try to think even if you're poor.

–*Especially* if you're poor, *Socrates corrected him.* But let's not get involved in a quarrel with Phocylides; we'd only be shouted down! It's very true, at any rate, that most wealthy people do not in the least believe that thinking and justice should take up any of their boundless free time. Instead, they're obsessed with treating in advance all the illnesses they might get and are freaked out as soon as they have an unexplained urge to scratch their leg.

–Absolutely right! *Glaucon excitedly exclaimed.* Pamper your body, get "in shape": that's the creed of the upper classes. They're always huffing and puffing away at their tennis game, doing push-ups on their desks, practicing their golf swing out on their patios, and getting their faces remodeled, like Frankenstein's creature, by the big-name plastic surgeons.

–They'd be better off studying philosophy, reading real books, learning poetry by heart, or reviewing the math they've forgotten since the days when they sweated over differential equations in order to pass the qualifying exams for getting into the "elite." And they'd be even better off inquiring discreetly and attentively into what the lives of the vast majority of their fellow citizens are like. This fetishism of the body, this obsession with health always stands in the way of the incorporation into truths, even the most innocuous ones.

Someone starts talking to you about philosophy and you wave them away, saying "I've got a headache"; or they talk about painting and you rattle off all your little bumps and bruises; and if they get around to serial music, well, then you start in on the whole saga of your bouts of diarrhea and lumbago.

–I've seen guys like that! *Amantha agreed.* I can't stand them!

–Neither could the legendary Asclepius. As a doctor, he only liked healthy people. An illness, he said, is only a temporary, localized exception to overall health. The patient, according to him, should live as much as possible the way he normally lived. If he had to give him medicine or operate without anesthesia on any of his organs, he did so swiftly and surely. Those, he said, are local actions in the general context of the Great Health. He'd read Nietzsche: life is speed. Nothing should be allowed to drag on. As far as he was concerned, death was the result of becoming unduly entrenched in illness. To some guy who objected to him that everyone dies eventually, he replied: "That's because, when you're old, you're worn down by the passage of time. So you value sleeping and being sick over being active and healthy." One day he said something that seemed absurd on the face of it but was actually very profound: "Death has nothing to do with the body, or illness, or anything like that. If it weren't for Time we would all be immortal."

–He was a philosopher of sorts.

–But a statesman, too! He developed a worldview that was suited to the military states of our ancestors. Remember, in Book 4 of the *Iliad*, when Pandarus wounds Menelaus? Everyone rushed over to him and

> With greedy mouths they sucked the wound he bore.
> They drank its blood infected and impure,
> Applied their soothing drugs the wound to cure.[6]

–Oh, Socrates! *Amanda reprimanded him.* What gobbledygook! That's not a real quote, it's a travesty! And, as is nearly always the case, your references are wrong. In Book 4, only Machaon does all that, not "all" the Greeks.

–My dear professor, please accept my deepest regrets for the mix-up. In any case, the truth is that, for Asclepius' disciples, restoring a warrior to health meant getting him back on his feet to fight again by using whatever means were most like his own natural powers. As for treating the hypochondriacal disorders of a rich old man of leisure, or devoting themselves to getting a young, stressed-out executive back in shape – thanks but no thanks.

–Wow, *said Glaucon admiringly,* that Asclepius sure was far-sighted.

–My dear boy, we're talking about *our* Asclepius, the Asclepius whom we'll make one of the icons of communist medicine. Not everyone agrees about him, though. Aeschylus, Euripides, and even old Pindar claim, for one thing, that Asclepius was the son of Apollo and, for another, that he one day undertook to treat a very old rich man who he knew was already clinically dead just because the family had paid him a huge sum of money beforehand. They even say that to punish him for his overweening greed, Zeus struck him with a thunderbolt.

At this, Glaucon's inner logician reasserted itself.

–That doesn't hold water, *he protested.* Given what we've said about the meaning of the gods, namely that they're the poetic names of the immanent authority of the True, we can't simultaneously agree with both Pindar's and the others' anecdotes. If Asclepius is Apollo's son, he can't be a crooked, dishonest doctor. And if he's a crooked, dishonest doctor, he can't be the son of a god.

–That's a perfect demonstration, *said Socrates delightedly.* Congratulations, my friend.

Amantha, who was beginning to get really bored, wanted everyone to get back to what she was most passionate about in all this – politics.

–This cult of Asclepius is all very well and good, *she said,* but a country under our system of government will need real doctors, won't it? And a real doctor has to have experience. He has to know the deepest secrets of corporeal well-being, sure, but also all the diseases, all the pathological states. If the only people he's ever "treated" are soldiers bursting with health, I wouldn't trust him.

–That occurred to me, too, *said Glaucon, jumping on the band-wagon.* What holds for judges has to hold for doctors. A good judge is someone who's seen it all, from the working-class kid who's arrested and roughed up just for smoking a joint outside his apartment building, to the high-society serial killer who's exposed only belatedly, and to all the other big- and small-time criminals in between. If all he's ever dealt with are naïve, frightened *petit bourgeois* types, he won't be worth much.

–It seems to me, *said Socrates after a moment's reflection,* that you're applying the same logical template to two very different problems. Let's start with doctors. The best ones are those who've been committed from a very early age to the scientific mastery of their art and also have had contact with the widest variety of bodies in poor health, including their own. It's very useful for them to have suffered

100

from many serious illnesses themselves and not to be like those people who are disgusted by the suffering of others because they themselves, to borrow Amantha's phrase, are "bursting with health." If it were doctors' bodies that treated the patients' bodies, doctors wouldn't be allowed to have a weak constitution and to constantly fall ill. But it's the doctors' *mental* faculties that treat the patients' bodies. And these mental faculties, which are related to the Subject, would be unfit to treat the body if they were suffering from some illness, not of the body but of the mind. Judges are a different case altogether. Let's temporarily define the judge as a Subject who purports to judge an individual's deeds. A Subject who, in his youth, only associated with immoral people and committed every conceivable crime with them has no chance of becoming capable of properly judging other people's criminal acts – unlike the doctor, who diagnoses his clients' illnesses on the basis of what he's learned from his own. If, as a future Subject, the judge must judge impartially, solely from the standpoint of his own good character, whatever appears before the rule of justice, he must have kept as far apart as possible from the ordinary forms of vice. Incidentally, that's why young men and women who are obviously of good character, like you, dear Amantha and Glaucon, have a sort of naïveté about them that makes them vulnerable to the wiles of unjust people: they don't have in themselves the affects that immoral people are typically motivated by. In fact, a good judge shouldn't be a young man. Only late in life, when he's on the verge of old age, has the knowledge of injustice come to him. He hasn't known it as an evil within himself personally but has studied it, over time, as an evil present in others. It's scientifically, not empirically, that he's developed his thinking about the true nature of that evil.

–You mean, *said Amantha, recapping,* that the perfect judge gets his knowledge from a sort of intellectual intuition that connects him to an external object, not from introspection based on his own personal experience?

–You put it a lot better than I did. Basically, the judge is an absolutely upright person. He possesses, so to speak, the integrity of the Subject he is to become. He provides a sharp contrast with that sort of wily, suspicious person who's been involved in a lot of shady dealings and who regards himself as particularly shrewd and experienced. When a guy like that consorts with people like himself, he's cagey and guarded, simply because he's acting according to models of behavior in himself that mirror those of his cohorts and accomplices. But when he comes up against mature people of experience and of proven integrity, this pseudo-clever guy's profound stupidity is immediately revealed. It's clear that he's suspicious for no good reason and that he hasn't got a clue as to what a solid character is, since he has no model for it in himself. That said, since he associates far more often with low-lifes than with decent people, he has a reputation for being a great connoisseur of real life rather than the perfect fool he actually is. We won't choose a person like that to fill the position of judge, at least not if the criterion for the position is a combination of wisdom and competence. We'll take the one we were talking about earlier, the person who partakes in the character proper to a Subject. Vice can never produce knowledge of both itself and virtue, whereas virtue, based as it is on a good natural character reinforced by education, can, over time, acquire true knowledge, of vice as well as of itself. It is therefore the virtuous man, not the immoral one, who acquires universal expertise.

–But what are the implications for our educational curriculum? *asked Glaucon worriedly.*

–You just have to declare that, in our country, medicine and the judicial system must conform to the model that we've just briefly presented. The outcome will be that the vast majority of people will see their physical and mental potential maximized. As for the rest – the chronically ill, the disabled, or the lazy or immoral people – we won't give up on them; on the contrary, we'll make every effort to help their bodies produce unfamiliar, useful movements and their minds, new insights. It'll take however much time it takes, but we'll never be stingy with time of that sort.[7]

–It sounds to me, *said Amantha, frowning,* like you're talking about a practice that has a bad reputation in Western democracies: the "re-education camps" that flourished in the socialist states during the twentieth century.

–I'm convinced that any kind of "camp" is a dreadful idea, or a pointless or criminal one. But how can we do without the idea of re-education? Given all the reactionary, purely conservative, or even totally worthless ideas the prevailing form of education today gives rise to, what else can we do but re-educate people?

–But what about the younger generation, then? *asked Glaucon.*

–They won't have to have anything to do with justice and judges if they're imbued with the kind of musical, literary, and poetic culture, at once simple and profound, that we've said will foster a life of enthusiasm and moderation. And couldn't we also say that a young man or woman who combines such a culture with appropriate physical exercise will in most cases have no need of medicine and doctors either?

102

–It's possible. But the whole problem is how to determine the right proportion of literary culture, on the one hand, and physical education, on the other.

–I'm afraid it's not easy. In my opinion, with physical education or anything that demands physical effort you have to aim at stimulating the type of energy that's particular to the Subject rather than be concerned about how strong the body is. Our ideal isn't the ordinary kind of athlete, who undergoes strenuous training and follows a special diet only in order to develop his brute strength. It's a matter of *subjective* fitness as far as we're concerned, not of bodily strength.

Socrates took a break. The night was black as ink and, as though wrapped in this cloak of darkness, Amantha lay down on the tile floor and fell right asleep. Sitting as still as ever in his chair, like an Egyptian god, Thrasymachus seemed to retreat into his own silence.

–Do you think, *ventured Glaucon,* that the aim of an education based on poetry and music, on the one hand, and on physical education, on the other, is to train the mind and body separately?

–Well, no. It's the individual's becoming-Subject that should be the objective of both disciplines. I'm sure you've noticed how hardcore athletes, the sort who work out on a daily basis in bodybuilding gyms, are brutal and coarse, and how music enthusiasts, the sort who listen to ballads every day, smoking their joints, are actually quite soft and over-sensitive.

–Yeah, I've noticed that, but what about it?

–Well, you could argue as follows. First, the athletes' brutality comes from an emotional energy which, if properly channeled, would become a fine sort of courage but when overstrained by constant working out is nothing but an amorphous kind of toughness. Second, the vapid mellowness of the enthusiast of poetry set to music comes from a contemplative nature conducive to philosophy, which, if properly channeled, would be calm and rigorous but, if too slack, deteriorates into an unacceptable kind of softness.

–So it's all a matter of the right proportions?

–Let's say: of moderation or of the proper balance between the disciplines. Because, remember, we said that our guardians, our communist citizens, had to combine real courage in the realm of the affects with a genuine philosophical nature in the realm of the intellect. The whole problem is how to harmonize the two, which will give the Subject steadfastness and self-restraint. If there's a conflict between them, however, the individual will turn out to be cowardly and brutal. And, if I may say so, you know the score!

–What do you mean? *asked Glaucon, taken aback.*

–I know some of your friends, girls and boys alike, *said Socrates,* who walk around night and day with earbuds stuck in their narrow ear canals like a funnel, so that the hypnotic drumbeat of their beloved songs can be poured into them. In so doing, I readily admit, they deaden the angry impulse in themselves that constitutes the second agency of the Subject. They're like iron softened by a fire of melody, and, in this way, from the unsociable, lone wolves they once were, they eventually become like angora rabbits: fluffy, soft, civilized. . . But if they keep on dissolving their lives in an ambient soundtrack, which is of course extremely melodious, the very principle of courage will disappear and the Subject within them will lose all its drive, so that when war breaks out or when they have to confront harsh repression, they'll be, as Homer says about Menelaus, no more than "feeble warriors."

–Your description of those weird MP3 player appendages is spot-on! It sounds just like my friend Penelope!

–But other friends of yours are of a completely different breed. They give up serious music, not to mention politics and philosophy, and they never leave the stadium or the weight room except to go on a special "shape up" diet. And you've got to admit that, having become strong and self-confident this way, they can display exemplary courage when they're up against invaders or the hordes of out-and-out reactionaries who hide behind the words "democracy" and "republic." However, lacking any grasp of the arts – even assuming that, as Subjects, they want to learn – and as they have no idea of what knowledge or inquiry is, nor any experience of reasoned discussion or of anything to do with culture in general, their desire for knowledge becomes fatally weakened; it's as though it were deaf and blind. Their lack of training makes them incapable of rousing and nourishing sensations that are really distinct. They almost certainly become ignorant boors and enemies of rational language, unable to use an argument when they need to win other people over or to attack their opponents. Like wild animals, they try to get hold of what they want by brute force, whatever the circumstances. They waste away in a life cut off from any knowledge and consequently extremely lacking in grace.

–That's the spitting image of my friend Cratylus, the son of the renowned Cratylus!

–If the big Other has offered the human species two basic types of exercise, physical education and the arts, I think I can conclude that it didn't do so on the basis of a stereotypical distinction between the Subject and the body but rather so that the degree of tension in the

Subject between the two crucial attributes, courage and philosophy, could be correctly adjusted according to the circumstances.

–Wow! I'm totally blown away! *cried Amantha, suddenly waking up.* You've landed back on your philosophical feet after one hell of a somersault!

–It's mere child's play! You yourself already knew beforehand that someone who adapts physical culture and poetico-musical culture, in the proper proportions, to the demands of the becoming-Subject is like the consummate musician of his own soul and a much better connoisseur of the most subtle harmonies than someone who merely tunes grand pianos.

–Yeah, sure, I knew that, *muttered Amantha,* maybe so, but you're the one who's saying it.

–At any rate, in our future communist country, anyone who exercises a position of leadership in the field of education, when it's his turn to do so, will have to see to this affective harmony if he wants our system of government to be preserved.

–But what'll we say, *continued Glaucon, ever the lover of complete lists and whole programs,* about gymnastic competitions, acrobatic dance, hunting with hounds, Formula 1 racing, betting on soccer, the Olympic games, the. . .

–Not a thing, my friend, not a thing! *Socrates interrupted him.* We'll apply our principles to all that stuff, and we'll see.

And with that, Socrates suddenly stopped like a broken clock, gave a little cough, and for a brief moment seemed overcome by the strangest, most intense distress.

— 6 —

OBJECTIVE JUSTICE (412c–434d)

Fatigue had already begun to set in. The wealth of details had a lot to do with it: the quotes from Simonides and Pindar, the challenging of Homer, the various sorts of physical exercises, musical modes, follies of desire, medicine, nutrition, and so forth. And all of this going on deep in the bowels of the night. . . Hadn't Amantha fallen back asleep? And wasn't Glaucon distracted, Polemarchus asleep, Thrasymachus recalcitrant? Socrates decided to get straight to the point.

—But who should be in charge? *he asked in a deep, powerful voice.*
They were all startled. But Socrates persisted:

—The old, the young? Intellectuals, soldiers? Professional politicians, ordinary citizens? Who should be in charge? Come on, *who*?

—Well, *said Glaucon thickly,* I have no idea. The best people, I guess.

—Oh, the best people! What does that mean, in politics, the best people? The best auto mechanic is the one who knows how to deal with the engine and fix every kind of mechanical problem, right?

Glaucon ably played the yes-man.

—Got to agree with you there, *he said.*

—So the best people, as far as our discussion is concerned, are those who move the political process forward and are able, when necessary, to overcome the difficulties or get out of any deadlocks. To do so, I suppose they have to be intelligent, capable, and, above all, to care about the public interest. But what we care about primarily is what we love. And what we love most of all is something whose interests we assume are the same as our own and whose fortunes, good or ill, we think we share. Right?

—Yeah, *said Glaucon with a sigh.*

106

–From the great mass of people who become incorporated into the political process will emerge those who, on balance, have shown exceptional dedication, throughout their lives, to promoting the process and categorically refusing to impede its progress.

–For sure, *said Glaucon*, those are the people we need.

–It's useful to observe them at every stage of their lives, to see how they remain faithful to the principles of our system of government and never betray or abandon them. Even when circumstances offer them the intoxication of vice or subject them to naked force, how do they manage to remain committed to their subjective orientation, which boils down to doing what best ensures the continuity of the political process?

–What exactly do you mean by abandoning a principle? *asked Amantha*. "Betraying" I understand. But "abandoning"?

–Good question. I think our minds abandon an opinion either willingly or unwillingly. Willingly, when we realize it's false, unwillingly, when it's true.

But Amantha, still baffled, said:

–The case of willingly abandoning a false opinion is easy enough to understand, but I don't get what unwillingly abandoning a true opinion can possibly mean.

–How come? You're well aware, aren't you, that we're unwillingly deprived of things we hold dear and that we willingly get rid of things we don't like? Now, isn't it obviously a terrible thing for us to stray far from the True, and a very precious thing to be incorporated into a truth? I'd be very surprised if you didn't think that holding opinions adequate to Being is in fact a form of immanence to the True.

–It is, *conceded Amantha*. Your argument's valid: it's only against our will that a true opinion can be lost to us.

–And we suffer such a loss as a result of fading away, bewitchment, or force.

–Wait – you've lost me! *Glaucon piped up*. What are all these distinctions you're making?

–Great gods in heaven! *roared Socrates*. Could it be that I'm starting to sound like the tragic poets? Let me be prosaic, then. I'm saying, first of all, that a true opinion fades away in people who become convinced that it's false as a result of a specious argument or, quite simply, in people who forget it. As a casualty of a fallacious argument or owing to the erosive effect of time, the opinion actually disappears all by itself. Second of all, I'm saying that a true opinion is destroyed by force when suffering, whether physical or emotional in nature, leads to an upheaval in one's beliefs. And, third of all, I'm saying that

107

a true opinion is dissolved by bewitchment when the spell of sensual pleasure or the dark torments of fear are at work.

–To judge from my own experience, *Amantha agreed*, spells and torments do in fact bewitch us.

–Why, Amantha, that's some support you're giving me! When it comes to the intensity of even the most trivial life experience, who'd dare compete with a girl? But let's draw the consequences of our temporary agreement. We'll seek out those participants in the political process who stick firmly to their basic principle, namely that what should be done is always what they think will bolster the process. The leaders could, moreover, set various kinds of tests of political subjectivation where this issue is concerned – in fact, why not right from childhood? Suppose, for instance, that we put young people in situations that are particularly conducive to forgetting or succumbing to bewitchment. We'll then be able to see who remembers the principles of action and doesn't become corrupt, and who prefers opportunities for pleasure to the continuation of the process of the True. We can also challenge these young people with difficult tasks, pain, and competitive trials and make similar observations. Finally, we can expose them to being led astray, to error, or to illusion and see how they fare.

–We can do even better, or rather worse, *exclaimed Glaucon, all fired up with enthusiasm*. I'm thinking of how young colts are thrown into a whirlwind of sound and fury to have their courage tested. Why not take our young people, girls and boys together, to some place where absolutely dreadful things are going on, and then suddenly expose them to the temptation of the most seductive sensual pleasures? We'll then be able to see if they can undergo both terrors and temptations without losing their composure. Since it's their destiny to guard the creative vitality of the political process, they should at least be good guardians of themselves and of the education in the arts that they've received since they were children. Their lives should be lived out with proper rhythm and true harmony, and there should thus be no difference between the service they render themselves and the service they render the political community. On the basis of tests like these, spread out from childhood to old age, the people most capable of creating the exciting conditions of the new system of government for everyone else will emerge by themselves, and will be hailed as such by everyone!

On hearing this, Amantha commented:

–You're so enthusiastic, dear brother! It sounds like you're devising an ideal city for us, where Good inevitably triumphs!

–Albeit at the cost of some very severe tests and arduous conflicts, *remarked Socrates.* There's a famous philosopher-emperor, Marcus Aurelius, who'd read – in the dialogue entitled *Politeia*[1] – your brother Plato's version of what we're discussing. He didn't think very much of my ideas, that Marcus Aurelius! He wrote in no uncertain terms: "Hope for nothing from Socrates' City."[2] Now that's a truly imperial ban! But, as opposed to him, we'll hold on to that hope, we sure will! What we want is a new form of government, communism. And that is, and will be, much more than a mere wish.

–That hope is wonderful, *Amantha went on.* But I'm afraid it may contain a hefty dose of lies.

–In any political conception, *said Socrates, suddenly becoming very serious,* isn't there something like a useful lie, a necessary lie, a true lie? I'm reminded of a story that was told to me by a Phoenician sailor a long time ago. "In many countries," he said, "society is strictly divided into three social classes that hardly mix with one another. First there are the financiers, the wealthy property owners, the senior judges, the military commanders, the chairmen of boards of directors, the politicians, and the big moguls of mass media, the press, radio, and television. Then there's the host of intermediate professions: white-collar workers, nurses, low-level managers, teachers, youth activity organizers, so-called intellectuals, sales reps, psychologists, literary hacks, qualified salespeople, small-firm engineers, regional union activists, florists, independent insurance agents, elementary school teachers, small-town auto mechanics, and I could go on and on. Finally, there are the direct producers: farmers, workers, and especially those newly arrived proletarians who come in droves from the Dark Continent today. Our Phoenician mythology says that this is a natural and necessary division. It's as if a god had made our country's inhabitants from a mixture of earth and metal. On the one hand, since they're all made from the same earth, they're all from the same country, they're all Phoenicians, all necessarily patriots. But, on the other hand, the metal content distinguishes them one from another. Those who have gold in their bodies are meant to be rulers, and those who have silver to be in the middle class. As for those at the bottom, the god roughly mixed scrap iron into their make-up. Except that the myth, according to some people, doesn't end there. One day, say these subversive preachers, a counter-god of sorts will appear, though we don't yet know in what form. Will it be just one man? A woman of radiant beauty? A whole team? An idea, a single spark that can set the whole prairie on fire?[3] It's impossible to know. But in any event this counter-god will melt down all the Phoenicians, or maybe even humanity as a whole, and will re-make them in such

109

a way that all without exception will henceforward be made up of an undifferentiated mixture of earth, iron, gold, and silver. They'll consequently have to live indivisibly, since they'll all share identically in the equality of fate."[4]

–That sure *is* a beautiful lie! *exclaimed Glaucon.*

–But isn't the foundation of our system of government, the education that goes along with it, like the Phoenician's counter-god? So let's let that myth make its way as it will in the evolution of ordinary life. As for us, let's ask ourselves at once what society would be like if we assume that there's no longer any gold, or silver, or scrap iron, or high or low, but only equals for whom there are no tasks that have to be reserved for this or that inferior group, but only what all must do for the good of all.

Amantha wasn't so sure, though.

–But how will we go about monitoring the people who, for a time, will hold positions of responsibility? *she asked.* It would be disgraceful for them to be like those bad shepherds who, to protect their flocks, train their dogs to be ferocious, and then the dogs, starving and vicious, ultimately turn on the sheep, changing from guard dogs into the very thing they were supposed to protect us from – wolves!

Glaucon then added:

–That's right, dear sister! We've got to do everything possible to keep those whose turn has come to hold military positions from pulling things like that on us, because, with the force they have at their disposal, they could very easily trade their position as the supposedly benevolent protectors of all the country's citizens for the much more tempting one of cruel and greedy despots.

–The best means, *remarked Socrates,* the ultimate precaution, is to give everyone the proper education. The communist Idea must command the gun.[5]

–But won't they have received such an education, in our scheme? *asked a surprised Glaucon.*

–We still don't know anything for sure, my friend. All we can say is that, in order for these temporary military leaders to demonstrate the most thoroughgoing selflessness and the most refined gentleness, both in the ranks of the army and vis-à-vis those whom said army protects, they'll have to have had the chance to receive a true education, whatever that may be.

–But don't we also have to control their wealth, *insisted Glaucon,* so that they don't own palaces, flocks, luxury cars, antique vases, gorgeous women, perfumes, and jewelry? If they have all that stuff, they'll become so enamored of it and so anxious about losing it that power will make them as suspicious as they're arrogant.

–The problem's on a much vaster scale, and the political decision about it can only be absolutely radical. Private property has to be abolished. None of the members of our political community will own his own lodgings, let alone a workshop or a storehouse. Everything will be collectivized.

–What about the women and children? *inquired Amantha.*

–Friends share everything in common.[6] The food required for workers, be they men or women, who are also militants of the community, or even soldiers called upon to defend it, will be distributed in an egalitarian manner on a weekly basis. We'll make sure that, when it comes to these people's wants, there's neither a deficit, which can exacerbate them, nor a surplus, which can sap their strength. We'll encourage meals to be taken communally, especially at midday. Overall, we'll facilitate all the projects of collective organization of that portion of time taken up by the bare necessities of survival. We'll deal in stages with the thorny problem of doing away with money. The main argument for imposing such a measure is that every Subject has the ability, which is the same in him as in the Other, to participate here on earth in the construction of a few eternal truths. We can therefore speak of a money of the Absolute that makes countable money unnecessary. Money, in the usual sense, has been shown to be the cause of most of the crimes committed both by individuals and by states, even though in every Subject there dwells an eternal light. So we'll organize material life in such a way that the circulation of capital will gradually be restricted and there will be fewer and fewer occasions to handle money, be it in the direct form of gold; in the intermediate form of coins and bills, which will in the long run be removed from circulation; or in the intangible form of drafts, orders, and other such electronic aids, whose use for speculation will be forbidden. These decisions are unavoidable for those who want to ensure the survival of our political community, since, as soon as individuals or groups gain possession of land, apartment buildings, workshops, mines, or capital, they obey nothing but their own interest, they become greedy and selfish, and they go from being militants and defenders of the community to behaving like an oligarchy that purports to wield absolute power. Hating the community and hated by its members, persecutors whose own turn will come to be persecuted, spending their whole life fearing competitors from within rather than enemies from without, they doubtless lead their own group of *nouveaux riches* to ruin, but

111

more often than not they drag the whole political community down with them as well.

Glaucon sensed that it was time for him to slip in one of those rants that were his specialty. He took off like a shot:

–What would you answer, Socrates, if someone were to say to you that the citizens of your political community, and especially those whose turn it is to exercise positions of civil or military leadership, will be as miserable as sin? And miserable through their *own* fault, at that, because they've wholeheartedly consented to a life of poverty. Really! Here are people who can be equated with the community itself, considered in its truth, and who get no advantage at all out of such a position! What a contrast with our usual leaders – the big land-owners, the builders of gorgeous mansions whose furnishings, swimming pools, flower beds, and paintings everyone gushes over – who are well connected in the business community, are bosom buddies of TV producers and control the flow of money, etc., who, in a nutshell, have a solid standing in society. Whereas *yours*, Socrates, are barely given meals and, if I understood correctly, don't get paid a cent. They have no chance of taking a cruise around the southern countries on a friend's yacht, or of hiring high-class prostitutes or throwing money down the drain just for the hell of it, or even of bribing their opponents the way all the people whose wealth, power, and happiness are envied by public opinion do. Honestly! It's as though no one in our community has any purpose in life other than just doing their duty as best they can!

–Brilliant! *Socrates complimented him.* And, to conclude, you could quote the French poet Alfred de Vigny:

> Shoulder your long and energetic task,
> The way that Destiny sees fit to ask,
> Then suffer and so die without complaint.[7]

Your description of things isn't far off the mark. And do you know how I'd answer someone who spoke to me the way you just did?

–*I*, at any rate, would keep quiet.

–Well, you'll see! I'm going to be even more long-winded than you were. First of all, I'd tell him that, if he'd followed the path of thinking *we*'ve been on since nightfall, he'd have easily found the answers to all his questions. It would certainly come as no surprise if our people, under communist rule, were ultimately very happy indeed. When we explain what we mean by this rule, however, it's not the happiness of one social class in particular that we have in mind but that of the whole community, without exception. Our approach, right from the start, amounts to thinking that it's in this type of being-together that we'll find justice, just as we'll find injustice in communities degraded by an awful system of government. Now, as Shakespeare might say, "just or unjust, that is the question." Since, for the time being, we're seeking the happy type of community, we categorically refuse to single out a select minority of privileged people in it. We want to see the big picture. We'll deal with the types of communities that have the opposite principles immediately afterwards.

Mr. Critic, I'd add, allow me to make an analogy. Imagine we're painting a statue and we're carefully applying black paint to its eyes. Some guy or other comes over and vehemently lashes out at us: "What?! You're painting the eyes, those most precious gems of the human face, *black*? It's royal purple that's required! You ought to know that the most beautiful colors are to be used for the most beautiful parts of the human being." Wouldn't we be right to reply to him calmly: "Most worthy sir! Don't expect us to paint the eyes of a statue in such a purely ornamental way that they'd end up being eyes in name only. Ditto for the other parts of the body. Our aim is the perfection of the whole, and, to that end, we must give each part of the body its proper color." And then I'd switch from the human body to the body politic: "Don't force us, dear critic, to provide the provisional leaders of our communist country with pleasures that would make anything but leaders out of them. After all, we might also imagine that when a woman goes out to work in the countryside – as everyone will regularly have to do – she'd wear a gorgeous long dress, spike-heeled shoes and a crown of gold, and that she'd only get up on her tractor to parade around the village streets when she felt like it. Or that the guys doing their week as craftsmen would stretch out in front of the fire, smoking joints, drinking Scotch, and only bothering about the clay and the wheel when their own idle chatter started to bore them. And everyone else would do likewise: boozing, snoozing, coozing, movies. For once society, from A to Z, would be only about pleasure! Well, that's certainly not what we want, because the end result would be that, with agricultural production wrecked, crafts non-existent, and industry ruined, there'd no longer be any of the activities from which our community stems, unless those involved in them did what they were supposed to do."

Just between us, let's add that, as far as those productive activities are concerned, the argument isn't as strong as it is with regard to political activity properly speaking. It is certainly very objectionable for some second-rate shoemakers, corrupt as they are to the point of being shoemakers in appearance only, to produce some very bad

113

shoes; but it doesn't yet spell disaster for the country. However, for those who, at any given time, are in charge of guarding communist imperatives and therefore the whole political community, to take on these leadership positions in appearance only and not at all in the reality of their actions is very likely to bring about the total ruin of the community, when these people, and they alone, had a unique opportunity to do an even better job of governing the collective organization with the aim of securing everyone's happiness. We are training true leaders, who come from the masses and can never undermine our system of government. So, if someone comes and says they've got to be farmers on a spree or perennial party animals, or that they've got to hold their sessions not in the heart of the country but only in some vague parliamentary committees, we'll tell him: "Hold it right there! That's not politics you're talking about!" In politics you have to examine carefully whether the choice of leaders is being made with a view toward giving them, along with power, the keenest pleasures possible, or whether what we have in mind instead is happiness on a nationwide scale. If it's the latter, then the people will have to persuade by hook or by crook those whose turn it is to be leaders, at every level, to be outstanding practitioners of that job. The same has got to be true, incidentally, for *all* the members of the political community, since in a communist country no one can claim he has no responsibility for anything. Under these conditions the country, having grown, being at peace, and possessing a first-rate collective organization, will see its various components participate, in accordance with their own desires, in the happiness of one and all.

–Well, how about that! *cried Amantha.* All's well that ends well! I detect a strong whiff of sentimentality! What are these "components" of the political community we haven't heard a thing about till now?

–Hey, young lady! *said Socrates, smiling.* You mean to tell me you've never heard of the rich and the poor?

–Precisely – what part do they play in your beautiful construction?

–I think we've got to lay the foundations of our communist society on the other side of the opposition between wealth and poverty. Both of them corrupt the citizens.

–What do you mean? *said a surprised Glaucon.*

–Suppose a construction worker suddenly becomes very rich. Do you really think he'd willingly go on supervising the cement pouring and planing the surface with his trowel for a measly salary? Assuming he's forced to do so, won't he be more likely to sabotage the work with each passing day or to stay away from the job, claiming he's got some mysterious illness or other?

114

–He'll become a bad worker, in short.

–Exactly. But, by the same token, if his salary's so low that he can't even buy himself warm clothing and proper shoes even though it's freezing cold on the construction site, his enthusiasm for work will be adversely affected and he won't have any desire to pass on to his sons a taste for this type of work, which the whole community nevertheless has the most pressing need for.

–So in that case, too, he'll become a bad worker.

–You said it. The leaders, whoever they may be – this is an important part of their egalitarian worldview – will have to prevent both of these terrible things from happening.

–What terrible things? *said Amantha, her hair all a mess.* You've really lost me there.

–Being wealthy without doing any work and being poor even though you work hard.

–All right, *said Glaucon professorially.* But there's an issue that's bothering me. If our ideal country, under a communist system of government, is prohibited from accumulating any private capital, how will it be able to defend itself against a rich, powerful state that has gangs of mercenaries armed with ultramodern weapons bankrolled by the country's wealthiest people?

–OK, here's a little story to cheer you up. Imagine a lean, agile boxer who's incredibly good at blocking his opponent's blows and throwing hard, surprise punches. Suppose this champion subjects himself to very intense daily training. Don't you think he'll be up to taking on three flabby, ignorant, poorly trained opponents?

–All three at once? That'd be hard. . .

–He can pretend to run away, then turn around and finish off the guy who's following closest to him and is already worn out, then take off again, come back quick as a flash and knock out the next guy. . .

–Hey, that's Roman history! *exclaimed Amantha.* It's the last of the Horatii killing the three Curiatii, one after the other, in a chase scene.

–That's right. Livy and Corneille remembered me:

He is one against three, but he has no injuries,
Whereas all of his opponents have suffered wounds.
He is too weak to take on three – though stronger than each –

Amantha delightedly continued:

And he sees how he can escape a mortal danger.
Yes, he runs away – but this is a clever ruse
To divide those three, and fight to better purpose.[8]

115

–Bravo! *said Socrates, grinning.* You've got a well-trained memory. In this connection, do you think the gilded youth of the affluent neighborhoods, who practice their tennis and keep in shape by running in the woods, will be prepared to go to war and get pumped full of lead for the Homeland and Virtue?

–Those dudes? No way! In the past they used to be reserve officers, but now. . .

–So I think that the youth of our communist country will have no trouble holding their ground against the mercenaries of the decadent oligarchies.

–And we could also pursue see-saw diplomacy, *said Glaucon.* Suppose we've got two potentially dangerous countries on our borders. We send a formal mission consisting of all our current leaders to the one that seems the weaker of the two. We start out by telling them something true: "In our country, amassing wealth and gold and silver is prohibited. You, on the other hand, are interested in nothing but that." Then we make a shrewd transition: "But let's put these ideological issues aside for the moment." And finally we reveal our idea: "If you sign a pact with us, all the property of our common enemy – the third party involved – will be yours; we won't ask for a thing." Our opposite numbers will certainly prefer to become allied with us, the lean, ascetic wolves, against the fat, enfeebled sheep, rather than wage by themselves a war with an uncertain outcome against wolves who are determined to fight and have nothing in their country to plunder.

–You've got to be kidding! *exclaimed Amantha.* With a little scheme like that, one of our neighbors will make a killing off the others, increase its territory inordinately, bankroll an enormous army, become a hegemonic country in the world, and attack and destroy us without the slightest hesitation.

–Dear girl, you're very naïve to call a conglomeration of wealth and violence like that a "country." From a political perspective, only the country whose organization we're attempting to define is deserving of the name of "country."

–But why? *asked Amantha, taken aback.*

–Because for ordinary states we need a name that refers to their multiplicity. A name targeting a unity, like "country," doesn't suit them, because they all contain at least two groups that are enemies of each other, the rich and the poor.

–But what about the middle class? *protested Glaucon.*

–Except during rare and short-lived revolutionary events, the so-called "middle class," especially in democracies, constitutes the mass base of the power of the rich. And that's the proof that, in actual fact, in all these "countries" there are two groups, themselves subdivided into a bunch of sub-groups. These "countries" are patchworks of ghettos. People marry within their own group, no one knows a thing about how the other groups live, and the state hovers above it all like a power seemingly unconnected to any of them but in reality in the hands of the rich and their lackeys. That's why it's important for our future diplomats not to treat the other powers as if each of them constituted a single country. With that view of things, we'd be headed for disaster. But if we conceive of these powers as multiplicities, if we insinuate ourselves into their internal conflicts, promising power to some of them, wealth to others, and freedom to others still, we'll always have lots of allies and few enemies. Our country, however small it seems to be, will be regarded by everyone as the greatest of all, because justice and the enthusiasm for thought shine forth in it. Even if it only had a standing army of a thousand soldiers, there wouldn't be any other country that could defeat it, either in its own vicinity or indeed anywhere on earth.

–All this "diplomacy" strikes me as being disgustingly cynical, *said Amantha, who in fact had a look of disgust on her face.* It reeks of the German–Soviet pact, it reeks of Stalin.

–Oh! At last! *exclaimed Socrates.* I thought you two were actually going to let me get bogged down in idiotic realism. Of course we can't reason like that! That's why the scale of our construction can actually only be the entire human world, even if we're beginning, as usual, in one specific place.

–In any case, *Glaucon remarked,* all these rules we're inventing shouldn't obscure the one great idea, the sole, or rather sufficient, idea that's behind them.

–Which is? *inquired an extremely curious Socrates.*

–Instructing and educating. If it's after a freely accepted, fully mastered educational process that the younger generation takes over from the ones who are leaving, they'll be able to easily resolve all these details – including those we haven't said a lot about, like everything having to do with family life: marriage, sex, children, inheritance, and so forth.

–You're so right. If right from the start we implement a system of government that's truly based on principles, everything will keep on expanding, like an ever-widening circle. A proper education will develop everyone's good natural character. And our country's citizens, eager to pass down to their children the education that they themselves received, will in turn improve on it while they're at it, since they'll be aware of both its minor flaws and its great value. The upshot is that each generation will be better than the ones before it.

–When they see how attractive and superior we are, the older generation will feel ripped off! *joked Amantha.*

–In summary, the leaders' primary concern must be to make sure the educational system doesn't deteriorate or collapse. When you know how vitally important the various sorts of beats, dances, and songs are for teenagers, it's patently absurd to neglect all that, without any sort of reflection on it or verbal encouragement to think about it. Such cynical indifference is tailor-made for the world of the capitalist market, whose sole concern is to inundate young people with so-called new "products" rather than to care about whether they have any subjective force and courage of thought. As far as we're concerned, "everything that moves is red"[9] isn't true in politics, nor is it true in art that "novelty" *per se* is a standard of judgment.

–And yet, *a gleeful Amantha cut in,* right at the beginning of the *Odyssey* Homer says:

A song is worthless, it really won't do
If everyone's sure that it's not brand-new.

–Well, *retorted Socrates,*

"Everyone" like that is a real yahoo.

The emergence of new styles in music is no doubt something inevitable and desirable. But we can't just accept it as our fate. Once again, I'll follow my master in music, the great Damon. . .

–. . . who was himself a student of Pythoclides of Ceos and the inventor of the relaxed Lydian mode, *said Amantha in a childlike voice, as if she were reciting a lesson.*

–Right! *cried Socrates.* The great, the very great Damon! He said the following, which you should drum into your heads: any huge change in the styles of music that are in fashion signals a change in the most fundamental laws of the state.

–How does that strange relationship come about? *asked Glaucon.*

–By "simple infiltration." We hum, we listen, we repeat. The new beat seeps into everyday life and takes root there. It then moves – quickly, casually, and suddenly – into the relationships or contracts that bind people together. In the end, it extends right into the laws and principles that, if I may put it this way, the politicians make dance to the sounds of the new music – sounds as dissolute and irresponsible as teenagers in the deafening racket of a smoke-filled club. That's why we need to insist on and to promote creative, profound kinds of music, which exemplify in their own way, owing to their beauty and to the emotion they give off, the power of the Idea as it's expressed in the fleeting visitation of the medley of sounds. These are the kinds of music to which we should entrust the always rather melancholy period of adolescence.

–But you're hardly going into any of the details, *said Glaucon, disappointed.*

–What do you mean?

–Well, all the good manners that have to be instilled in young people of both genders: to keep quiet when their elders speak, to give up their seat to them in the bus, to take care of their ailing parents, to listen to their teachers with a modicum of attention and respect, to cut their hair, clean their nails, shine their shoes, clean up their rooms, share meals with the family instead of slouching in front of the TV gorging on pizza. . .

–Legislating on such trivial things would be just plain stupid. Laws about how long a person's hair can be and what color shoe polish can be used? What nonsense! If a person acquires a crucial life orientation from his education, it will leave its stamp on his entire adulthood. An influence of that sort, whether good or bad, eventually achieves its own aim. What can nit-picking regulations and endless decrees accomplish? Not a thing. The law must ratify the real becoming of things, not assume that it can define it.

At that, Glaucon's inner lawyer and economist, which always slept with one eye open, awoke and inquired:

–But what would you say about commercial contracts, suppliers' invoices, the regulation of derivatives and the fixing of exchange rates? And in another connection, defamation suits, the scope of a court's powers, neighbor litigation? And what about taxes, the taxation on harbor operations, the assessment on pleasure-craft mooring, or the tax on a portion of the capital gains realized on real estate sales? Don't we need precise laws for all of that?

–My dear friend, if people are honest, they'll figure out the appropriate payment by themselves. And if they aren't, they'll institute large-scale fraud and bribe their elected officials to pass laws furthering their own interests. The people who spend their lives making and amending a slew of laws on such issues think they'll achieve legal perfection, which is ridiculous. They're like those invalids who are a bit depressed and are always on the look-out for some new miracle cure instead of changing their lifestyle, which is the real source of their suffering. They only make their symptoms worse, yet they go on taking all the pills that some casual "friend" or other has told them are really effective.

–Oh, yeah! I know people like that! *said Glaucon.* They think anyone who advises them not to drink so much, to stop smoking enormous smelly cigars, and not to eat big helpings of fatty beef and creamed string beans is their worst enemy.

–So, if the whole country were to behave like these "invalids," you'd hardly be thrilled. But isn't that exactly what's done by states that, although very poorly governed, nonetheless forbid their citizens, under pain of death, to change the established institutions and laws in any way, while at the same time they regard as a really great guy, a true sage on whom honors should be lavished, someone who sweetly flatters the citizens of this dreadful state, anticipates their wishes, and tries to fulfill them, all in a totally obsequious way, not with public service in mind but only the upcoming election, in which he fully intends to be a candidate?

–Yeah, *Glaucon agreed,* we're familiar with that kind of demagogue.

–What would you say about the hordes of people who are willing to take care of a state of that sort and who eagerly put themselves at its service? Aren't they brave and full of good will?

The irony, however, escaped Glaucon.

–Come on! *he protested.* We can't excuse those who let themselves be so deceived by the opinions of the crowd that they think they're great statesmen, merely because they're praised by flunkeys on TV and applauded by suckers at political rallies.

–You're really heartless! But these people may be just plain ignorant of the most elementary laws of quantity. Even if they were dwarfs, they'd think they were giants if everyone told them they were over six feet tall. Don't be so hard on them. They're more comical than anything else, with their obsession about enacting laws and constantly making new amendments, codicils, and implementation decrees, in the undying hope of limiting financial misconduct in contracts and in all the murky affairs that we were talking about a minute ago. They don't for a moment realize that they're just cutting off the Hydra's head.

–You mean that in a state, of whatever sort it may be, a real lawmaker doesn't have to bother about those sorts of regulations: if the state is governed terribly, it's pointless, it won't bring about any improvement; if it's governed wonderfully, either everyone will know what they have to do or else that will be an automatic consequence of the established laws. So now, what should our program be in terms of legislation?

–We don't have to do anything at all. Universal Reason, which Apollo symbolizes in our country, will get to work. For it's a matter of principles, which are a lot older than laws, meaning that we can say that laws may be human, but principles have something divine about them.

–So what'll this Apollo, the god of reason, talk to us about? *asked the impertinent Amantha.*

–About the inner temple that every person, as a Subject, must build in order to accommodate the truths into which he's been incorporated; about the precarious fidelity that binds us to those truths; about the honors that must be given to those who were heroes when it came to that fidelity; about the funeral ceremonies in which these heroes are spoken of fervently, even if – or especially if – it was as a messenger boy, a cleaning woman, a metal-worker, a farmhand, or a supermarket check-out girl that they showed what they were worth; about the demons and evil genies who spread the simulacra of the True, encouraging betrayal and discouraging militants. On all these issues our efforts must be guided, on a case by case basis, by the thinking of the generic or universal Reason, which we've placed at the center of our universe.

–Thus does our new country receive its founding seal, *said Amantha with rare seriousness.*

–No doubt, no doubt, *said Socrates restrainedly.* We only have one small issue left to settle now.

–We do? Which one? *asked Glaucon, surprised.*

–The only one that matters to us actually, and on which we haven't made an iota of progress: where is justice? Go get yourself a powerful searchlight, dear friend, go wake up Polemarchus, Thrasymachus, and the whole gang and ask for their help, and then, with Amantha leading the way, shine light into every corner of our endless discussion to find where justice is hiding, where injustice is concealed, how they differ from each other, and to which of the two we need to devote our lives in order to be happy, whether we're hidden in solitude or are in plain sight of both men and the gods.

–Oh, that's a load of bull! *exclaimed Amantha.* Last night you promised to get involved in the search yourself. You even said you'd be nothing but a renegade philosopher if you didn't come to the aid of justice with all your force, in every way you could.

–Yikes! *said Socrates, clapping his hands.* I forgot! It's true, what you say. Justice is like a cave explorer lost in the chasm of our argument, and it's up to me to lead the rescue operation. But you're part of the team, aren't you?

–Yeah, sure, *said Amantha with a smile.* We'll help you out.

–OK, here we go! If our system of government is consistent with the real whose concept we've laid out, it will be wise, courageous, self-disciplined, and just. Assuming we were to find one of these virtues in it, the others would have to be what we haven't yet found.

–It's like a silly card game, *Glaucon laughed.* There are four cards on the table, we know that they're the four aces, and we're looking for the ace of hearts. We turn the cards over one by one. If the ace of hearts is one of the first three cards we turn over, OK, that'll do, we can stop right there. But if it's not one of these three cards, there's no need to turn over the fourth: it's got to be the ace of hearts! The moral is, even though there are four cards, in the worst case you win in three tries.

–Wonderful! *Socrates congratulated him.* Let's treat our four virtues like your four aces. I turn over the first card, and I can see at a glance that it's judiciousness, or wisdom, or good judgment. I even see something strange about it.

–It must be a pretty weird thing for it to seem strange to you, *said a surprised Amantha.* A mystified Socrates – that'll be the day!

–That a system of government should be judicious – or wise, or possess good judgment – comes down to the fact that the assemblies it convenes deliberate in such a way that whatever they decide is really what the situation requires, isn't it?

–Well, for once, Socrates, *Glaucon said,* you're going with the flow. You're saying that, in politics, you've got to do what's necessary. . . Who'd object to a truism like that?

But Socrates pretended not to hear and continued on his way, like a stubborn mule:

–The ability to deliberate requires a form of rational knowledge, however. In the assemblies of a true system of government, ignorance and rhetoric are of no value whatsoever.

–We're with you there! *Amantha joshed.*

–But there are loads of different kinds of rational knowledge, all of them necessary for the country. Take a good computer programmer, for example. Will his ability to debug a computer or find what's on its hard drive make him a competent political militant?

–No, *replied Glaucon a little mechanically,* it will only make him a competent computer programmer.

–And what about the industrial designer who can draw a perfect blueprint of a machine, or the house painter whose knowledge of smooth, glossy colors everyone admires? Is their rational expertise what a true political assembly requires?

–No, they're just good at their own specialties.

–Oh, you said the word! Politics is not and cannot be a specialty. In politics you don't deliberate about one particular thing, but rather about *all* the situations the country's citizens are facing. And competence in these matters is automatically something that everyone, not just a handful of people, possesses. Consequently, the wisdom of deliberations and decisions is a virtue that must be found not just in a few specially trained citizens but in every person who meets the general requirements of our communist system and knows that he's actively involved in our collective destiny.[10]

– Then in our country, *said Amantha enthusiastically,* there won't be any politicians.

–No, there won't. And political knowledge will be the knowledge that, at any given time, by virtue of the large number of people who possess it, will completely subsume any other technical or specialized knowledge. This unique kind of knowledge, which deserves to be called political wisdom and governs both deliberation and the decisions resulting from it, is actually a feature of the population as a whole.

–What about courage, then?

–At first, it may seem that finding out where courage is hiding in society is not all that hard. To determine whether a state is cowardly or courageous, you just have to consider the part of it that's involved in major wars. That the men who remain behind are cowardly or corrupt isn't very important in terms of deciding whether the state is one way or the other. That, at any rate, is what everyone thinks and says: the courage of its army is the only thing that a state's courage can be gauged by.

–And, for once, everyone's right, *concluded Glaucon, beaming.*

–You fell right into the trap, young man! Everyone's wrong, and you along with them. You simply forgot two things. First, that in our political vision there's no separate army, and *everyone*'s required to take part in defending the country against unjustified aggression. Second, that, for us, courage is much more a case of seeking the end of all war and of being wholeheartedly committed to a project of perpetual peace, while still being prepared to resist should another state try to destroy us.

–As Mao said, *Amantha cut in,* "First of all, we do not like war, and second of all, we do not fear it."[11]

–Exactly. And this means that the intellectual key to courage is to be found in the body politic as a whole. It's a true opinion about what it's important to fear, but also about what it's possible to hope for, over and above a determined resistance to anything that might try to thwart such a hope. In this sense, courage must be everyone's responsibility. You might say, paradoxically, that it has a preservative function.

–Preservative? What does courage preserve? *inquired a puzzled Glaucon.*

–A proper subjective relationship – a true opinion, if you like – with regard to everything that education was able to change into a law, stipulating which things and circumstances it's permissible to fear. Courage ensures that that opinion is preserved over the long run, so that, in joy and sorrow, whether you're prey to desire or to fear, you can't escape that law.

–That's all pretty confusing, *protested Amantha.* Couldn't you clarify this business about opinion being an educational law that also happens to be indestructible? Give us one of those metaphors you have a knack for, "metaphors" that, according to you, don't imitate anything or anyone.

–Your wish is my command, young lady! Let's imagine a dyer. . .

–A dyer? What do you mean? *said a stunned Glaucon.*

–You'll see. When a dyer wants to dye a woolen fabric purple, he starts by selecting from the whole rainbow of colors a fabric that's naturally white, and only after he's painstakingly prepared it so that it can absorb the brightest color does our man steep it in purple dye. When a cloth is dyed in this way, the dye will be color-fast and the cloth can be washed thoroughly, even with detergent, and the color won't come out. But if you go about it some other way, regardless of whether the cloth is colored or is white but poorly prepared, you know what happens: the color all comes out the first time the cloth is washed, and you look like a perfect fool. Now imagine that our educational work, aimed at making all the country's citizens capable of being the guardians of our system of government, is of the same sort as the dyer's, and that well-prepared Subjects are needed for the purple of our principles. It's for just such a preparation that literature, music, and mathematics, as well as the history of revolutions or combat sports, are of use to us where the younger generation is concerned. So let's posit that the basic principles of our system of government are a kind of dye for the soul and that the aim of the educational protocol we've proposed is simply to prepare young people to take on the color of the principles so that it may be fast, in order for them to acquire, on the basis of their good natural character and their education, an unshakable opinion about what should be feared and ultimately about all the important issues: an opinion that can

124

be removed neither by that potent detergent that can wash everything out – by which I mean indiscriminate pleasure, which is more
effective at cleansing the Subject of everything that fosters its worth
than ashes or brushes are – nor by the trio of pain, fear, and selfish
desire, which, together, constitute the chemical formula of a fearful
detergent. I call "courage" that sort of power which, in any and all
circumstances, safeguards the true, lawful opinion about what must
or must not be feared, preventing life's ups and downs from fading its
brightness. Is this definition OK with you, Glaucon?

–I don't have any other one to suggest, at any rate. I guess that
animals' or mentally retarded people's instinctive knowledge about
anything threatening to them, inasmuch as it's not associated with
any educational attribute, is too limited in scope, in your opinion, to
deserve to be called courage.

–You guessed right. That's moreover why courage can be said to
be a political virtue, in the same way as Aristotle, that student of your
brother Plato's – a brilliant boy but someone I don't like very much
– says, over and over, that man is a "political animal." But to discuss
all these issues would require a separate lecture. For the time being,
let's try to get back to our fundamental concern, justice.

–But we've only turned over the "wisdom" and "courage" cards
so far in this game, *protested Glaucon.* We still have two others left,
and we don't know which of them is "justice." I'd like for you to
turn over "self-discipline" and then for it, necessarily, to be justice's
turn.

–Self-discipline – it's also called "temperance," "restraint," "moderation" – is more like a harmonious relationship, a common accord,
a sort of subjective concord, than the first two virtues (wisdom and
courage). It's an efficient organization of the Subject, which keeps the
attraction of the desire for short-lived pleasures under control. It's
what's implied in those virtually incomprehensible expressions – "to
control oneself" or "to have self-control" –and, more broadly speaking, in the traces of this particular virtue that are found in language.

–Why do you say that the expression "to control oneself" is incomprehensible? *asked Amantha. I* understand very well what it means!

–It's a ridiculous expression! Someone who controls himself is
also controlled, and, similarly, someone who's controlled controls
himself, since this type of ready-made expression refers to one and
the same individual. How could the same being, at the same time and
with respect to the same being, namely himself, be simultaneously
controlling and controlled, master and slave?

–But the expression "to have self-control," *Amantha stubbornly persisted,* doesn't really apply to one and the same being, because it assumes a split in the Subject. In the human being, regarded as a Subject, there are two parts: a better part, the one that's incorporated into a truth, and a worse part, the one whose norm is the individual's impulses. Whenever the naturally better one is in control of the worse one, we say that the Subject in question is self-controlled insofar as he controls the strictly individualistic part of himself, and that's a term of praise. But whenever the better part, under the influence of an inferior education and of associating with bad company, is weakened to such an extent that the passion for the true gives in to the death instinct, we criticize the Subject in question – occasionally we even insult him – and at any rate we say that he's not in control of himself and is lacking any real self-discipline.

–Well, *grumbled Socrates,* imagine a country shaped by our form of government and you'll see that it's worthy of praise because it's an instance of the first case you mentioned: it's self-controlled, since, according to you, everything in which the better part prevails over the worse part is worthy of that name.

–I'm trying to imagine, Socrates, I'm trying to imagine! But we can only imagine on the basis of what we've experienced. In your miracle country there will surely be desires for enjoyment, if only among children throwing tantrums, teenage girls loafing around doing nothing, puffing away on their cigarettes, and quite a lot of those pretentious, comfortably settled young couples who can talk about nothing but their vacations in Persia.

–You underestimate us, Amantha. You underestimate the incomparable happiness that comes with the full exercise of the intellect when it's performing at its peak. We'll give free rein to those desires with no specific object, those infinite desires that appear simple only because they contain within them the full measure of their creative value, since they're consistent with true opinions and pure thought. In our country, virtually everyone will supplement the hidden natural goodness of humans with everything that a discriminating education will bring out in it. At present, Capitalism's harnessing of collective energies everywhere encourages selfish impulses and their loathsome sterility. We're striving to ensure that those desires associated with thought, which in today's world are the preserve of a struggling minority under attack on all sides, become firmly established and constitute a sizeable majority.

–So it's really *our* political vision, *exclaimed Amantha, won over by enthusiasm,* that will enable the community to be in control of its impulses and the dangerous obsession with short-lived pleasures!

–And we could therefore say, *added Glaucon,* that the society we'll construct will have the calmest, surest self-discipline.

–But note, *added Socrates, who didn't want to be outdone,* that it's in this same society, where each and every person in his turn exercises governmental or military responsibilities, that the agreement between the leaders and the led is constantly guaranteed, thanks to the pure and simple elimination of the question that always and everywhere gives rise to demagoguery, if not to civil war – namely the question: "Who should be in charge?"

–But in that case, *Glaucon remarked,* we can say that self-discipline is the virtue not just of the leaders but of the led as well, and. . .

–. . . and therefore, *Socrates interrupted him,* we were right to say that self-discipline was a sort of harmony, a concord. It extends absolutely throughout the whole country, inspiring the agreement of everyone who lives there, whatever position they may hold at a given time and whatever their particular gifts, be they intellectual or physical, of attractiveness or of cleverness, of scientific precision or of creativity, poetic or mathematical, and so forth. Because it counters selfish impulses, self-discipline gives all its vitality to the common accord about the control to be exerted by what's best over what's less good, regardless of whether it's a matter of the individual or of the state.

–Great job! *said Glaucon, amazed.* We've spotted and defined three of the cardinal virtues in our future country: wisdom, courage, and self-discipline. Our fourth card, our fourth ace, is undoubtedly justice.

–So, dear friends, now's the time to blow the horn and cry "Tally-ho! Tally-ho!" Like formidable hunters, let's surround the thicket and make sure justice doesn't escape. No way can it be allowed to disappear into the fog of uncertainty. It's definitely somewhere around here, the poor little doe terrified by our concepts, which it knows have been sharpened on the grindstone of logic. You go on ahead, Glaucon. Try to flush it out. If you see it, let me know!

–I wish I could. . . For the time being, though, I don't see a thing. Maybe I'll spot it if you point it out to me – that's really all I'm capable of.

–All right, I'll head in under the trees, I'll get scratched by the brambles, and you follow in my footsteps.

–OK, go on ahead of me!

–It's a forbidding sort of place. Vines and cactus all over. Deep shadows. No path staked out. . . Let's go slowly. . . Oh, Glaucon! I found the trail! Justice won't get away from us now!

–Where? How? Is it still alive?

127

–Yes, alive and kicking; *we* were the ones who were perfect idiots.

–Well, that's hard to take! *groaned Glaucon, as if he had really, not just metaphorically, snagged his pants on the nettles.*

–But it's unfortunately true. That damned justice has been rolling around at our feet for ages, from the very beginning of our discussion, actually. We just didn't notice it. We presented the ridiculous spectacle of people looking all over for their key when it was there in their hand the whole time. We weren't looking in the direction where justice was lurking, right nearby, but toward a vague, distant horizon instead. Justice wasn't hidden, except to our gaze lost in the romantic dream of faraway places.

–I'm looking down at my feet, *objected Glaucon miserably,* but I still don't see anything.

–Think about our long conversation. I have the distinct impression that we were talking about justice, but we weren't able to figure out clearly what we were nonetheless saying about it, even if it was in the guise of what was left unsaid in what we were saying.

Amantha, who, during the last few comments, had been tugging furiously at a few strands of her tangled hair, could no longer contain herself.

–You're making it all so complicated, Socrates! *she protested.* Rather than comparing justice to a poor little doe, just say what you have to say about it. What's with this maze of what we said without knowing we were saying it, all the while saying that we knew – without always saying as much – everything that's been said, poorly said, or not said about what was said over and over?

Socrates threw up his hands and exclaimed:

–Don't get angry, you fearsome young lady! *You* tell *me* if I'm right or not. When we first began to examine the foundations of our system of government, our guiding principle was the subjective constraints that prove to be more powerful than the changing of positions. That sort of general obligation, or at least some particular form of it, I believe, is the definition of justice. Yet what we then established and have reiterated several times now – you must remember, dear Amantha – is that every person must acquire the ability to fill any position whatsoever in society, without his being discouraged for all that from pursuing the path he imagines is best suited to his own natural abilities. In essence, we said that justice is the following: everyone can improve the particular aptitudes he regards as uniquely his own while preparing, with the same eagerness, to become what Marx called a "polymorphous worker," a human animal who, from bricklayer of either sex to mathematician of either sex, from cleaning woman or man to poet, from soldier of either sex to doctor, from mechanic of either sex to architect, leaves none of the possibilities afforded them by their own times outside their scope of action.

–We said nothing of the kind, *protested Amantha*. Or, in any case, we never defined justice in those terms.

–But do you know why I think it's obvious?

–No. But I'm sure you're going to tell us.

–In the series of virtues, justice is in a way like the plus-one of the other three. To wisdom (good judgment), to courage (the knowledge of what must be feared), and to self-discipline (the control over impulses), justice provides both real power and the place of that power, the place where these virtues, once activated, can develop their subjective effectiveness. We'd naturally be hard-pressed to decide which one of the four virtues is the most important for ensuring that our communist country is as good as it can be. But we're certain that, without every person's ability to creatively and effectively replace any other person for any task whatsoever – an ability that's combined with everyone's freedom to develop their own particular talents – the other virtues will have neither a precise localization nor any universal openness. Only the dialectical relationship between localization and openness can guarantee any subjective aptitude its social or collective vigor. It's basically the actual process of this dialectical relationship that is called "justice."

–So then we can say, *a very intent Amantha, her brow furrowed, piped up,* that a person's availability for any *praxis*, paradoxically combined with the development of his *hexis*, or his own natural ability, realizes the ideal of that person's relationship with society as a whole.

–And consequently, *observed Socrates,* injustice will consist either in hindering everyone's universal competence or, in the name of that universality, in restraining or prohibiting everyone from being able to cultivate what they consider to be their unique abilities.

–A crime twice over, *concluded Glaucon:* that everyone cannot be *like* everyone else, or that everyone cannot be *different from* everyone else.

–Injustice owing to a lack of collective homogeneity, injustice owing to an excess of that same homogeneity, *said Amantha.*

Then, continuing in her somewhat pedantic vein, she remarked:

–Or to put it another way: injustice as regards equality, injustice as regards freedom.

And Socrates, carried away by the lyricism of the abstractions, added:

–The crime against the rights of the Same shouldn't blind us to the crime against the rights of the Other.

–And vice versa! *said a smiling Glaucon, who was for once the most cheerful of them all.*

— 7 —

SUBJECTIVE JUSTICE (434d–449a)

–Let's not waste any time, *said Socrates, sounding oddly on edge.* We have a long way to go. Let's just assume, without further consideration, that every country in which people's lives are governed by what we've just discussed deserves to be declared just. We've at least got a temporary form here, a sort of idea of justice, an idea suited to collective life. If this form proves to be transferrable to the individual considered in himself as a unit, and if we agree that, in this case, too, the name "justice" is the appropriate one, we'll be able to conclude that our inquiry was successful.

–The famous method of isomorphism, *remarked Amantha.*

–An isomorphism isn't something that can be observed; it has to be proved. Maybe we should settle for a similarity. What were we hoping for, at the outset of our inquiry? That by clarifying our intuition of what justice is in the larger of the frameworks containing it, it would then be easier to know what it is in the smaller of these frameworks, namely the individual. And, as it seemed to us that "the larger" one was a country, we made a concerted effort to define the best system of government the people of a country could implement, since we were sure that where everything is consistent with a political truth is where justice must necessarily be found. Let's transfer what we brought to light in the large framework, a country, into the smaller element of existence, the individual. If there's an obvious similarity, all well and good. But if something different appears in the minimal term we'll go back to the maximal term and continue our work of thought. Maybe then, if we use a back-and-forth movement between the two terms, country and individual, rubbing them together like two flintstones, we'll make the spark of justice shoot forth, and we'll be able to use its light for our own purposes.

131

–It seems to me, *said Glaucon pompously,* that you've defined the method and all we have to do now is abide by it.

–Listen carefully. If we say that two things are the same even though one is bigger and the other smaller, are they unalike in the respect in which, despite their difference in size, they're called the same, or do we instead have to say they're alike?

–Alike! *replied Glaucon, like a soldier clicking his heels together.*

–And so, for everything concerning the Idea of justice, a just person will not differ in any way from a just community but will instead be completely like it?

–Completely, *Glaucon declared, snapping to attention.*

–But we established that a system of government is just when it enables anyone to perform any of the three great functions – production, defense, and leadership – owing to which a country can go on existing, and that this requires the system of government to combine within it self-discipline, courage, and wisdom, the virtues required in a variety of ways by the three functions. No?

–Yes! *cried Glaucon.*

–So, if we find the same formal dispositions, triggered by the same affects, in the individual temporarily considered as a Subject, will it be right for us to give him the same names as those that seemed to us to apply to our communist country?

–Perfectly right! *Glaucon roared.*

–Well then, it's all easy now! We just have to find out whether or not a Subject – at the individual level – is composed, like the political place, of the three agencies that we enumerated at the collective level on the basis of the three essential functions: producing, defending, and leading.

–Easy, you say, easy. . . Well, I don't think it's easy at all. Rather, this is the time to quote Spinoza. . .

–In Latin, *Amantha interrupted him.* It's much more sublime: *Omnia praeclara tam difficilia quam rara sunt.*[1]

–I'm not so sure the things I have to say are *praeclara, said Socrates, smiling.* In fact, I think they're not. With the methods we're using for the time being in tonight's discussion we won't achieve sufficient precision. The road to the goal is longer and more circuitous. But maybe just for now we should be satisfied with our earlier discussions and initial investigations.

–That's good enough for me, *sighed Glaucon.* These convoluted arguments exhaust me.

–OK, *Socrates agreed,* let's take the shorter, more accessible route. We'll be able to tell when it's necessary to shift into higher gear. To begin with, there's an empirical argument that's pretty simple, probably too simple, in fact: each individual obviously has to have the same formal dispositions, the same character traits, if you like, as those that can be observed in the country he's a citizen of, because where can these traits come from, if not from individuals? Let's talk for a moment the way people do when they're standing around the counter in a café: "The Thracians, the Scythians, all those people from the countries up there in the north, are quick-tempered and aggressive, as everyone knows. Around here, where we live, not too far north or too far south, we like to shoot the breeze, discuss things, find out about all sorts of things. And as for the southern peoples, the Phoenicians or the Egyptians, all they care about is gold, silver, grain stocks, ships laden with amphoras of wine or olives, and carved ivory statues." All that sort of thing, my friends, really does come from peoples' temperaments and has become a national character trait.

–Yuck! *Amantha spat out.* Don't tell me we're going to start using redneck racist arguments now!

–All right, all right, *said Socrates, backing off.* Let's try to come up with something more sophisticated. The problem is whether the Phoenicians' insatiable greed, the Athenians' taste for intellectual pleasures, and the Scythians' courageous ferocity all derive from the same source or whether what we have here is an empirical proof of the existence of three distinct, particularized subjective agencies. In short, here's a first hypothesis: knowledge comes to us via a path that's different from the one taken by angry obstinacy, while the path of desire, regardless of its object – food, sex, and so forth – is equally different from the other two paths. Now a second hypothesis: each time we have an impulse to perform some action, no matter what it is, it's the Subject *as a whole* and undivided, as it were, who performs it. It's a real challenge to construct a coherent argument that would force us to choose only one of these possibilities.

–A challenge you're going to take on, of course! *said Amantha excitedly.*

–We have to back up quite a bit. So true is it that the One as such, purely self-identical, cannot simultaneously do and undergo opposite things, by means of the same thing and in relation to the same thing, that if we were to observe that sort of simultaneity we'd know that it wasn't really the One we were dealing with but rather a multiplicity.

–It would be nice to have an example, *Glaucon timidly requested.*

–Is it possible for the same thing to be at the same time and in the same respect both at rest and in motion?

–Of course not.

133

–Let's take it step by step and make sure that we agree, so as not to be at odds with each other as we proceed. If an opponent, someone who's a defender of the dialectic of appearance, were to say to us: "Look, that big, strapping guy over there on the opposite sidewalk is standing still, but he's nodding his head and twiddling his thumbs. So he's both at rest and in motion," what would you say to him, my trusty Glaucon?

–That's easy! The same thing I always say to my friends who are crazy about Heraclitus: the guy's moving some parts of his body and keeping the others still. There's nothing at all contradictory about that.

–Note that your argument moves from the motion/rest pair to the One/Multiple pair. So in that case your opponent could seek and find a better counter-example. Like a top, for instance. A top is wholly and at one and the same time at rest and in motion when it spins all around itself, with its center, which is merely an extensionless point, remaining fixed.

–No, it isn't! You have to distinguish between the axis and the circumference where a top is concerned. If the axis is not inclined, we can say that the top is motionless relative to its axis and moves in a circular motion relative to its circumference. Moreover, you can see that the closer you get to the axis, the slower the circular motion is, inasmuch as a point near the axis completes a much shorter circuit in the same time than a point located on the top's circumference does. The top can be said to combine a principle of motion and a principle of motionlessness that remain distinct from each other without the top's unity being threatened.

–Excellent, pupil Glaucon! Whatever the seeming contradictions deriving from our sensory experience may be, we won't let ourselves be unsettled by them and we'll never accept that one and the same thing can simultaneously, through the same thing and in relation to the same thing, do, be, or be acted upon by opposite things at one and the same time.

–I'm not sure that an ordinary child's top suffices to prove that version of the principle of non-contradiction, *said Amantha doubtfully.* My brother Plato's brilliant student Aristotle would find this very flimsy.

–You know I don't like that Aristotle guy. Oh, sure, he'll go places! But I don't like him. Nevertheless, you've got a point. We'd have to refute all the possible objections now to prove the principle, and, above all, clearly define all the contexts in which it's valid. We'd waste a huge amount of time. Let's just assume that the principle of non-contradiction is true and move on. If it should seem false at any time as we proceed, then we'll agree that all the consequences we drew from it are null and void.

–We'd have no choice! *said Amantha playfully.*

–Let's get back to "concrete reality," as the politicians and journalists always say as soon as you mention equality and truth to them. Saying yes and saying no, accepting and rejecting, attracting and repelling, regardless of whether it's a matter of actions or passions – those, in any case, are really pairs of opposites, aren't they?

–Of course, *said Glaucon with a shrug.* It's like desiring and not desiring. Hunger, thirst, all the desires, and also willing, or wishing, form pairs of opposites with not desiring, pushing something away, not wanting, hoping not to, and so on. If I desire something, it's because the Subject that I am moves toward what he desires, or attracts the object of his desire to him. For instance, if I want someone to supply me with drugs, I say yes to myself even before the dealer asks me the question, so impatient am I for him to satisfy my desire. But if I want to get off drugs, I'll have to say no to myself ruthlessly before I send the tempter packing. With all that kind of stuff you always find the two most important pairs of opposites: activity and passivity in action, yes and no in language.

–Be very careful! *Socrates said with his finger raised.* Take a classic desire, thirst, which you just mentioned. Might it constitute a more variable desire for the Subject than we think, a desire whose variations would have to be fixed or determined right from the start? Do we desire a drink that's cold, or one that's hot? Do we want to drink a lot or a little? In a nutshell, is thirst the thirst for a specific drink, or isn't all that sort of thing merely a set of external causes, with no essential relation to thirst as a desire? If it's hot out, the desire for coolness will be added from the outside to thirst, and if it's cold out, the same will go for heat. If I'm exhausted and covered in sweat, the desire for lots of water will be added to thirst, whereas if I'm rested a small quantity will do. But thirst as such will only be the desire for its natural correlate, the drink as such, just as hunger in itself is the desire for food, and not, in itself, the burning desire for a certain rabbit pâté.

–OK, *said Glaucon, frowning.* Every desire, in itself, is related only to the generality of its natural object and is the desire for a specific object only under the influence of external circumstances.

–But aren't you running the risk, dear friend, of seeing your beautiful certainty crumble to pieces if some friend or other of Diogenes – you know, the guy who goes around saying, in opposition to your brother Plato's so-called "theory of Ideas," that he knows what a

135

horse is but not at all what horseness is – were to whisper to you: "Hey, Glaucon, it's never Drink with a capital D that we desire but a big glass of white wine, nor is it Food that satisfies our hunger but a delicious mushroom omelet, because we naturally desire good things, not disgusting ratatouilles. If thirst is a desire, it's the desire for an exquisite liqueur, not for a mug of cat piss, and the same is true for everything deserving of the beautiful name 'desire.'"

–I admit I'd be pretty upset, *said Glaucon miserably.*

–Well, anyway, let's try and stick to the following principle: to speak of the determination of something that is as it is in relation to something else is only acceptable to the extent that that other thing is itself determinate; but something that is as it is in itself can only be related to something else to the extent that that other thing, too, is as it is in itself.

–Well, I don't get *that* at all, *protested Amantha.* It's pure Platonic gobbledygook.

–Let's see about that, young lady. Didn't you understand that an existent that we say is "greater" is said to be so only in comparison with *another* existent?

–Do you think I'm an idiot?

–Of course not. So we'd say that the other existent is smaller?

But Amantha merely nodded in dismay. Socrates took another stab at it:

–And a much greater existent is only so in relation to another that's much smaller, right?

All Amantha could say was:

–This is so pathetic.

Socrates kept at it despite the sarcasm.

–And what was greater, in the past, was only so in terms of its relationship to what was smaller than itself, just as, in the future, what will come to be greater will only be able to be so in relation to the advent, outside of itself, of something smaller?

At this, Amantha got all worked up.

–How long are you going to go on like this? *she said irritably.*

But Socrates wasn't fazed; he went on, very calmly:

–Similarly, we'd say that more is more only in relation to less, double only in relation to half, and so on for all the conceptual pairs of this sort: heavier only in relation to lighter, faster only in relation to slower. . .

–And hotter only in relation to colder, *Amantha cut in, imitating Socrates,* as well as sharper vinegar only in relation to sweeter oil, which is what gives this salad all its zest.

But Socrates, increasingly calm in the face of the storm, suddenly shifted direction slightly:

–What about knowledge, then? Doesn't the same dialectic apply? The one you call a salad? Knowledge in itself is knowledge of what's known in itself, or, if you prefer, of what we posit knowledge is knowledge of. But a *particular* form of knowledge is knowledge of what is known particularly or of what we posit is the particular object that this *particular* knowledge is knowledge of.

Amantha wondered what kind of trap she was about to fall into and replied, a bit more feebly:

–You already said all that! If I know, I know what I know – sure, I get it.

–I like to repeat myself. And this time I'll take an indisputable example. When, in the history of human groups, a real skill emerged in connection with the construction of buildings, wasn't it so as to distinguish it from the other forms of knowledge that it had to be given the name of architecture?

–Of course, *Amantha agreed.*

–That form of knowledge was determinate in its difference from the others, inasmuch as that determination defined it as the knowledge of an object that was itself determinate, to which the other forms of knowledge weren't to be referred in order to be identified. The same principle made possible the general classification of forms of knowledge and skills as they appeared throughout history.

–I see, and I think I get it, *said a suddenly intimidated Amantha.*

–Yet a little while ago you said you didn't understand a thing. Let's recapitulate for the last time. An existent that's in relation with something in general, an "object = x," as my colleague Kant[2] would say, remains exclusively, *qua* one and considered in terms of this One, self-determined, and this in no way contradicts the fact that, when it's in relation with something determinate, it is itself over-determined, provided of course that by "over-determined" we don't mean that the existent in question takes upon itself the determinations of that with which it's in relation – which would be the case if we were to say, for example, absurd things such as "knowledge of what's beneficial or harmful to health is thereby beneficial or harmful *qua* knowledge," or "the supposed knowledge of Good and Evil is itself good and evil" – and provided that we explain precisely the following: when a form of knowledge, medicine, say, is clearly the knowledge of a particular pair of opposite terms, namely health and disease, and it's impossible for that very reason to equate it with knowledge in itself, whose object – the "known" in itself or the "knowable" in itself – is something completely different, then we must absolutely give this form of knowledge, which is a determinate form of knowledge, not the simple name "knowledge" but, in relation with the determinate object that's added to pure knowledge, the over-determined and therefore compound name "medical knowledge."

Amantha mopped her brow and sighed:

–I give up. I'm sure you're right.

–That made you thirsty, didn't it! Let's get back to thirst, actually. It's undoubtedly part of that type of being in which that which is is only so by being in relation with something else. Thirst is actually thirst. . .

– . . . for a drink, *a delighted Glaucon finished for him.*

–Yes, but as we said, when thirst is thought as a relationship with a particular kind of drink, it is itself a particular kind of thirst, whereas thirst thought in itself is not thirst for a large or small drink, whether good or bad – in a word, thirst for a particular sort of drink – but, in terms of its intrinsic nature, solely Thirst for Drink as such.

–How many times are you going to repeat that to us? *said Amantha indignantly.* It sounds like the refrain of some sad song.

–The song of a concept is never sad. So, considered as a Subject, someone who's thirsty only wants to drink; that's what he yearns for, that's what his energies are directed toward.

Amantha was still resentful, though.

–Yeah, *she said,* sure, right, it's clear, we get it, we agree, we surrender. But what's your point exactly?

–It's this: if something immanently thwarts the thirsty Subject's impulse, it must necessarily be the action, internal to the Subject, of something other than the impulse that drives the thirsty Subject like an animal to drink. Indeed, we agreed that nothing can produce opposite effects in a thing at one and the same time, by the same part of itself and in relation to the same object.

–Hey! *Amantha interjected.* Heraclitus already discredited you. He denounces those who "do not understand the deep harmony of that which is at odds with itself."

–You're always throwing Heraclitus at me. Is he your darling boy or something? The example he gives of the "harmony of opposite motions," archery, is totally stupid, though. He claims the archer repels and attracts the bow in one and the same motion. No, he doesn't! One of his hands pushes the wood of the bow forward, while the other pulls the string and the arrow back. As usual, Heraclitus mistakes the combination of two separate actions for a single contradiction. There's no such thing as the unity of opposites, their fusion.

–Still, *objected Glaucon,* the archer *does* combine both motions.

–But he only does so insofar as he has two hands! The two is given, and prevails over the one. The One does not cause the opposite deployment of the Two in itself. You see, all this business about the One, the Two, and ultimately about negation is very complicated. To clarify it, let's go back to our thirsty guy.

–Oh, him! *groaned Amantha.* If he's still thirsty I'll wring his neck!

–Will you grant me, *Socrates went on imperturbably,* that there are people who are thirsty at a given moment and yet refuse to drink?

–Sure, I've seen plenty of people like that, *Glaucon agreed.*

–What should we say about such people? Both the impulse to drink and the prohibition that blocks it from being immediately gratified must coexist, subjectively, in them. The prohibition must also be different from the impulse and more powerful than it.

–Yes, *Glaucon allowed,* provided we accept the logical points you were making a moment ago, which imply the structural precedence of the Two as soon as there's any appearance of contradiction.

–Don't these prohibitions, whenever they appear, derive from a rational faculty, whereas impulses and addictions instead derive either from the body or from pathological changes in the psyche? If so, it wouldn't be unreasonable to claim that we're identifying two distinct subjective forces here. Let's call the first, which is at work in our reasoning processes, "rational," and the second – which is at work in sex, appetite, thirst, and all the other desires; is clearly different from pure thought; and is linked to the whole gamut of gratifications and pleasures – "impulse-driven." So there are really two distinct agencies in every Subject. We still need to examine the case of affects that are not impulse-driven, such as zeal, daring, indignation, and so on. Are they a third agency? Or if they aren't, with which of the other two agencies should they be equated?

–Maybe, *Glaucon ventured,* with the impulse-driven one, no?

–How would you then interpret the story of a man named Leontius, the son of Aglaion, which was told me a few years ago? This guy was returning from the Piraeus by way of the north wall, like we did last night, and, lo and behold, between that wall and the wall that goes as far as Phaleron he saw a whole pile of dead bodies: he was walking alongside the place of public executions. The sight was reminiscent of the worst gore movies. Some of the dead were in the process of decomposing, others bore the marks of torture, and still others were mutilated, their arms torn out or their throats slit and spattered with blood. Big blue flies were devouring the staring eyes of these poor wretches, left unburied out in the open like plague victims.

A terrible inner conflict then took hold of Leontius. A morbid impulse was driving him to go and look at the gruesome scene from up close. For a moment he struggled with himself and managed to cover his face with his cloak. But, overpowered by his desire, he eventually opened his eyes wide and ran over to the horrible human remains strewn over the ground, screaming: "Look at me, you poor bloody torture victims! Take a good look at me! I'm the one who's offering the most pitiful sight to you now!"[3] Isn't this anecdote a real staging of the three agencies? Desire winning out over Thought, and Affect unsure which side to take?

–Still, *remarked Glaucon,* you can see that Leontius was angry at himself for giving in to a morbid desire. In that sense, Affect is siding with Thought, even if it couldn't prevent it from being defeated.

–And that's what we often see. When his desires get the better of his rational arguments, the Subject calls himself every name in the book and rebels against what, in his own self, does violence to him like this. It's a kind of inner civil war: Affect sides with Thought against Desire. By contrast, we hardly ever observe the opposite phenomenon, either in ourselves or in other people.

–What opposite phenomenon? *asked an astonished Glaucon.*

–Getting angry at yourself because Thought successfully opposes the frenzy of a desire is something that's practically never experienced. Look at what happens when someone, who we assume is not completely immoral, is convinced he's done something wrong: he can't get angry about being hungry, cold, or having to endure great suffering because he considers that, in light of his own unworthiness, these punishments are only fitting. But if, on the contrary, *he*'s the one who's been wronged, then he gets all worked up, rebels, fights for his convictions, endures hunger, cold, torture of every sort. Yes, he's willing to face every adversity, this time not because a sense of guilt makes him think he deserves them all, but, quite the contrary, because he knows that to defeat injustice you have to be able to fail and to draw the obvious lessons from repeated failures. He can struggle heroically till victory or death but, called back to himself the way a dog is by a shepherd, he can just as easily experience the relief of a temporary retreat during which he can contemplate the rational injunctions of his thought and then take up the fight again, armed with new ideas.

–We ourselves, *agreed Glaucon,* have compared the people whose role is to guard our communist country to shepherds at times and to faithful dogs at others.

–Sure, but now we're at the opposite extreme of what we argued a

140

little while ago. We thought that Affect was an extension of Desire. But that's not at all our position anymore if it's true, as we've just said, that every time the Subject is in a state of inner revolt, Affect takes up arms for Thought.

–Yeah, you've done an about-turn, *observed Amantha.* It remains to be seen whether, as a result, Affect is an extension of Thought, which would reduce the Subject's structure to a simple opposition: Thought versus Desire. Or whether, if you pursue the rather half-assed analogy between a system of government's three functions and the Subject's internal structure, you posit that there really is a third subjective agency, that elusive Affect, which supports Thought rather than Desire, unless Thought's been completely ruined by a lousy educational system.

–I opt for the three-term structure, *said Glaucon enthusiastically.*

–But we still have to prove, *said Socrates prudently,* that Affect is distinct from Thought, the way we thought it was from Desire.

–I have a proof, *Glaucon triumphantly announced.* Little children. They scream with rage, they explode, they run all over the place, they turn red with fury, they have one hell of an affect, while thought is still totally stunted in them.

–Good point! *exclaimed Socrates.* You could also think about animals. The most ferocious ones, those whose affect is very highly developed, like bulls, roosters, or even wolves, aren't the cleverest – those would be monkeys, parrots, or foxes.

–I protest, *cried Amantha,* I solemnly protest this dogmatic old way of regarding children as animals. That's vulgar Platonism, gentlemen; it's all a bunch of garbage.

–Well, *said a conciliatory Socrates,* just to please you I'm going to quote Homer:

Beating his chest, the stalwart lionheart
Odysseus spoke to his angry heart
With words of the finest, subtlest art.

In this passage. . .

– . . . The *Odyssey,* Book 20, adapted to fit *your* context, *commented Amantha.*

Socrates kept his cool, although he was deeply annoyed by Amantha's total recall of poetry.

–In this passage, then, old Homer clearly tells us that there are two distinct agencies and that one rises up against the other: the one that subtly distinguishes between better and worse and the one that's nothing but blind rage. This time we have Thought versus Affect.

141

–Congratulations! *concluded Amantha.* You really had me going there, once again. Congratulations.

–It wasn't easy! *said Socrates, winded.* I had to work like a dog! But now we're more or less agreed: there are as many agencies in individuals, considered one by one as Subjects, as there are functions in a country, and there's a sort of similarity between these agencies and functions. Saying that a country's system of government is wise – or possessing really good judgment – will be said about an individual for the same reasons and will designate the same qualities as when it's a question of a system of government.

–And, *said Glaucon, imitating him,* saying that an individual is courageous will refer to the same causes and circumstances that make us attribute that quality to a country's system of government.

–And the parallelism, *said Amantha in conclusion,* holds for everything implied by the word "virtue," taken in its sense of "completely positive quality."

–In that case, *said Socrates delightedly,* we can say that an individual is just in the same way in which a system of government, a country, or even a state is.

–That's the goal you've been after for hours now! *said Polemarchus, suddenly waking up.*

–But we haven't forgotten, *continued Socrates,* that a system of government is just to the extent that the connection it establishes between the three main functions – producing, protecting, and leading – allows everyone to aspire to all of them.

–Of course we haven't! *exclaimed Glaucon.*

–So, at such time as each of the three agencies whose interrelationship constitutes us as Subjects makes us capable of everything that gives life meaning, we'll be just, for we'll be doing everything we should be doing, which we'll be happy to finally be able to do.

–How pleasant the feeling of being alive will be then! *said Amantha, beaming.*

–This means that the rational agency will have to be dominant, *Socrates went on,* since its particular virtue, wisdom, requires it to take care of the Subject as a whole and since, where that task is concerned, Affect can only be, and must be, a loyal lieutenant. Yet, as we've seen, a basic education, comprising literature, poetry, music, and physical training, will produce a harmonious accord between Thought and Affect, increasing the tension of the one with fine arguments and profound learning and soothing the other with the rhythm and harmony of the deepest poems and the highest works of musical art. Once these two agencies have been educated like this and know what their true role is, they'll take control, to the greatest extent possible, of Desire, which is surely the driving force behind subjective action and therefore the agency that's the most significant part of every Subject, but which, if left to its own devices in the world as it is, only sets its sights on money and possessions, conceived of as the universal means for attaining every pleasure. Thought and Affect will keep an eye on Desire, so that, obsessed as it is with repeatedly seeking immediate pleasures, it doesn't become too strong and, ignoring its own particular virtue and the organization of the Subject as a whole, it doesn't try to enslave the other two agencies and take power over the whole Subject – something that causes irreparable damage to everyone's lives, since such power is not actually within Desire's purview.

–It seems to me, *objected Glaucon,* that you've reduced everything to the Subject's internal conflicts. But there are external enemies, too. A country has to defend itself against being torn apart by senseless civil wars, of course, but also against invaders.

–You're absolutely right, *exclaimed Socrates, feeling proud of his pupil.* But isn't the alliance between Thought and Affect critical in that case, too? The former analyzes the situation and assesses the risk, while the latter enables forceful responses, or even relentless struggles. Affect accomplishes Thought's decisions. What's more, it's this alliance that justifies our calling a person courageous. Affect makes him get through situations, be they pleasant or painful, without faltering, because it obeys Thought's instructions regarding what ought or ought not to be feared. As for wisdom, it comes directly from Thought, however weak its apparent power may be, by virtue of the instructions its gives Affect and the knowledge it dispenses as to what's appropriate both for each agency considered in itself and for the overall structure composed by their threeness. And finally, there will be temperance, there will be self-discipline, as a result of the fact that Desire, which is the most significant real power, will nevertheless accept its energy to be directed by the alliance of Thought and Affect. Desire will acknowledge, as Affect does, that, in seeking to challenge Thought's leadership role, it threatens the Subject as a whole with the destruction of his inner make-up. And isn't this harmony, at once local – by virtue of the appropriateness of each agency to its own particular subjective function – and global – by virtue of the continued existence of the structure owing to which the leadership of Thought, accomplished by Affect, guides Desire – the thing that we can finally acknowledge as the definition of justice for a Subject?

143

–We've reached our goal, *said Glaucon, like someone amazed by his own victory.*

–Yes, dear friends, we've realized the dream that incited us, in the middle of the night, with the lapping of the waves in the harbor and the noise of the wind in the masts as our accompaniment, to present a sketch of what a country inspired by a true system of government could be like. We realized that the norm, on the scale of the country as a whole, was that the aptitude for the three functions required by any collective life – producing, protecting, and leading – should be systematically universalized. This allowed us to have a proper picture of justice in general: a regulated relationship among three subjective agencies representing, respectively, vital energy, Desire; intellectual leadership, Thought; and the active intermediary between them, Affect.

–A dream that's the realization of what desire, though? *asked Amantha mischievously.*

–Oh, leave Freud alone. Thought, Affect, and Desire are neither the conscious, the preconscious, and the unconscious nor the Ego, the Superego, and the Id. My own topography is better, even though it's older.

But now Socrates, in his turn, got all fired up and launched into one of those eloquent rhetorical periods of his that were all the more to be feared in that you experienced a deep sort of pleasure while getting lost in their syntax:

–True justice, my friends, has the same features regardless of whether it's a matter of a community's life or an individual's, except that, in the latter case, it's not actions observable from the outside that are concerned but rather actions that can truly be said to be internal because they have to do with the Subject and his three constitutive agencies, Thought, Affect and Desire, which means that said Subject, far from allowing any one of these agencies to do something locally that's clearly the province of another, or to upset the tripartite structure globally, instead bolsters his own inner structure by putting himself in order, by creating a subjective discipline through the practice of which he learns how to live on good terms with himself, by making the three agencies sound the way a perfect chord would on the piano, with the low C of Thought, the middle E of Affect, the dominant G of Desire, and the high C of Justice enveloping the whole; yes, the Subject as musician of himself, binding together all his individual components, and thus making the One that he's capable of being emerge from the multiplicity that he is, so that, being as self-disciplined as he is harmonious, whatever he may do – either in the

144

domain of material production or care of the body, or in one of the four generic procedures (politics, art, science, or love), or in friendly relations with individuals – he will recognize and call just and beautiful the type of action that makes the chord of that subjective music – whose other name, connected to the knowledge governing actions of this type, is "wisdom" – resound in himself again, while at the same time he will recognize and call unjust the type of action that only makes awful discordant notes be heard and whose other name, connected to the opinions that rule it, is "ignorance."

–If that sentence is saying something, what it's saying is true, *Amantha stated cryptically.*

–If, in fact, *replied Socrates in the same manner,* it was a question of declaring that we've discovered what justice is, both in the just person and in the just communist system of government, we could say that we can hardly be accused of lying.

– You can say that again! *said Amantha with a smile.*

–Well, then, by Zeus, *retorted Socrates,* let's all say so!

–I'm with you, *said the young woman,* let's all say so!

–What kind of game are you two playing? *asked an anxious Glaucon.*

–The cryptic game of shared conclusions, *said Socrates.*

But Glaucon was still in the dark. Nevertheless, he bravely ventured:

–So all we have left to do then is to define injustice.

–That issue's rather complicated in its details – for, if justice is one, injustice is multifarious – but it's also very simple once you place yourself on a sufficiently general level to be able to define injustice as a sort of rebellion within the Subject's disposition, a dispersal gone awry, a fatal confusion, the revolt of one particular agency against the structure of the Subject as a whole in order to take control of him, and in a completely reckless way at that, since we know that efficient, rightful action presupposes a strict discipline as to the separation and distribution of leadership functions, such that we speak of injustice, of dysfunction, of cowardice, of ignorance – in a nutshell, of immoral conduct – when the Subject is nothing but dark confusion and aimless wandering.

–This time, *said Amantha, though whether admiringly or critically it was impossible to tell,* we can say that if that sentence is unequivocally defining something, it must be injustice.

–If, in fact, *Socrates replied in an equally ambiguous way,* we say that we've defined the difference between just and unjust actions impeccably, that we've set out in the light of the evidence what the expressions "to be just" and "to be unjust" mean, we can hardly be accused of having ignored the concepts underlying "justice" and "injustice."

–And that's why I didn't for a moment think of accusing you of that, *said Amantha, deferring to Socrates.*

–Well, then, by Zeus, let's say so!

–Absolutely, *agreed Amantha,* let's say so!

–Don't start playing your games again, *groaned Glaucon,* let's move on, let's move on!

–An idea with high didactic value has just occurred to me, *said Socrates.* The justice/injustice pair seems to me not to differ at all from the health/disease pair, except that the former is to the Subject what the latter is to the body. Health is merely the outcome of healthy practices, just as justice is the outcome of just practices, and unjust practices produce injustice the way toxic things produce disease.

–We can be more precise, *Glaucon put in sternly.* Health is merely the maintenance in the body of a relationship of subordination among its constitutive elements, whether it's a matter of major physiological functions, of hormonal systems, or of cellular aggregates. A disease disrupts these relationships, as can be seen in the proliferation of cancer cells, hyperthyroidism, or respiratory insufficiency. Similarly, justice, as you demonstrated, is nothing but the maintenance of harmonious and efficient relationships among the three agencies of the Subject. And injustice is either a local confusion of function, which downgrades this or that agency in favor of another, or a global subversion, which destroys any possibility of Desire being led in the direction of true subjective creativity. We can therefore conclude that justice is the Subject's health, while health is the body's justice.

Everyone applauded these splendid remarks. When the clapping died down, Socrates attempted to take charge of things again.

–All we have left to do now, *he said,* is to consider whether it's more advantageous to be just, even if no one is aware that you are, than to be unjust, provided you're sure you can get away with it.

But Glaucon, buoyed by the success of his conclusion of approval, wanted to show that he was also good at resounding refutations and long rhetorical periods.

–I find it just plain comical, Socrates, that someone like you should ask such a question when you know very well that even with unrestricted access to the greatest pleasures (drink, every kind of food, boundless wealth, sexy women, absolute power, etc.) no one can tolerate living when his body is completely broken down, and when you therefore also know perfectly well, as your definitions of justice and injustice prove, that it's even more impossible to tolerate living when the natural principle by which the Subject lives is adrift and in ruin, and that this is so even if we could do anything we want, except precisely what would free us from vice and injustice.

–I had a calling to become a comic actor, *Socrates admitted,* but I preferred the theater of philosophy. Since we've finally gotten to the point where it's absolutely clear that things are as we say they are, this is not the time to give up.

–Who said anything about giving up? *said Glaucon, taking offense.*

–I see that, compared with virtue, which can only be thought in one form, there are a wide variety of vices. And this is something that has to be thought; they have to be named, classified, and put in order. At first glance, amid the infinity of possible vices, I can see four that deserve our attention.

–Four? Why four? *said a surprised Glaucon.*

–There are as many types of well-defined systems of government, with their own particular deviations, as there are Subjects who correspond to them, aren't there? Now, including our own system of government, there are five major forms of government in all, four defective ones and only one excellent one.

–So tell us the names of these systems of government.

–As regards the one that *we* want, its immortal name is communism. Whether there are only one or several rulers is unimportant in this case, since everyone can be called on to perform all its functions. In this sense, moreover, it would be like a universal aristocracy – an aristocracy, since everything is guided by the most subtle and far-reaching thought, and universal, since everyone can and must promote that thought. The French director Antoine Vitez suggested the phrase "elite for everyone."[4] I've attempted another: "popular aristocratism." In any case, this fifth system of government is good and true, as is the Subject who's constituted within it. The other four systems of government are failed forms, and the Subject resulting from them is a defective Subject.

–So what are the names of those deviations? *asked Glaucon impatiently.*

— 8 —

WOMEN AND FAMILIES (449a–471c)

It was getting darker and darker. Here and there, the oil lamps were describing little circles within which the light flickered bravely. Socrates was about to go over the four defective systems of government in the logical and historical order governing their interrelationship when Polemarchus suddenly touched Amantha's bare shoulder. The stern young woman bridled at first, then realized that he was only trying to get her attention. She leaned in closer to him, and he whispered in her ear:

–Are we going to let him get around the obstacle as though he hadn't even seen it?

–No, we definitely have to keep him from doing that, *Amantha replied.*

–Keep who from doing what? *said Socrates, turning around.*

–You, *said Amantha,* from treating us like fools.

– Oh, damn! What've I done?

–You treat us with an inexcusable lack of seriousness, if you don't mind my saying so, *replied a very irate Amantha.* You skip over a question of the utmost importance just so you don't have to get your feet wet. Do you think you can get off the hook by casually dropping into the conversation that, where women and children are concerned, it's clear that – let me quote that phrase of yours – "friends share everything in common"?

–But, my dear Amantha, isn't that true?

–Unless it's referring to something obscene, I, as a young woman, have no idea what that sentence even means. What exactly is supposed to be "shared in common"? We've been badgering you for ages now to expound your views on sexual difference, procreation, and the upbringing of young children. But every single time you've been indirect and evasive.

–She's right, *Polemarchus chimed in.* Once, you practically laughed in our faces, and I quote: "I'm like old Tolstoy. When he was asked what he thought about all this, he replied that he wouldn't say the last word on women until the lid on his coffin was closed!"

–You're not going to move on to the study of the four non-communist systems of government without first explaining inside out and upside down everything related to sex, *Amantha continued with increasing vehemence.*

–I have to say, *added Glaucon,* that *I* won't let you get around this crucial issue in this sneaky way either.

And suddenly even Thrasymachus revived, probably because he'd heard the word "sex," and spoken by a woman at that:

–You're in deep trouble now, Socrates, *he crowed.* As I've always said, whenever we finally get around to concrete issues, Socrates ducks them.

Pressed from all sides like this, our hero put on a pleading face and said:

–What are you up to, my friends? What kind of quibbling are you starting up again, at the darkest edges of collective life? I did actually think I'd cleverly avoided these questions about sex and that you'd therefore settle for my brief allusions to equality. But now you're stirring up a hornet's nest – it'll take us the next two days to deal with all this!

–So what if it does? *said Thrasymachus, who was now completely awake and completely sarcastic.* Do you think we're spending the night in this big villa just to snore away contentedly or listen to platitudes? If sex is on the agenda now, you have to explain your sexual theory to us, period.

–But with this type of subject, *said Socrates in self-defense,* the discussion always goes on for an inordinate length of time.

–When it comes to sex, dear friend, *replied Thrasymachus, who was determined to stick it to him,* there are no time limits. An entire lifetime wouldn't be enough to cover the topic adequately, everyone's so fascinated with it. So never mind about us. Just answer our questions for once and expound your doctrine on the education of women, including sex. Don't play the uptight philosopher; don't shy away from the stuff about nudity and fucking. And tell us how the awful drudgery of babies and toddlers should be handled, too. You'll see what our reaction is.

–He's right, Socrates, *Glaucon agreed.* Your listeners tonight are educated, open-minded people, prepared to accept the most revolutionary new ideas. Put your suspicions and fears aside.

–You think you're reassuring me by saying that, but you're only increasing my anxiety. If I had complete confidence in myself about the real knowledge underlying what I say, your encouraging words would be very welcome. When you're speaking before a sympathetic, well-versed audience, either you really know a few truths about important matters that are close to your most cherished concerns, in which case you can speak calmly and confidently, or else you speak without having the least bit of certainty and you formulate more questions than answers, which is my way of doing things, and then you find yourself in a situation that's not exactly ridiculous – it would be childish to feel that way – but risky and precarious, because not only might you be straying far, very far afield from the truth but you might be dragging your friends along with you to boot, on issues where that kind of straying comes with a very high price. On account of what you're trying to force me to say, I kneel trembling before the big Other, the distinguished judge of sexual matters. We're well aware that, in the Other's eyes, involuntary manslaughter is a lesser crime than misleading people about what's noble, good, and just in collective life. But if that crime has nevertheless got to be committed, as you would have me do, it would be better to be dealing with enemies than friends. That's why pushing me to my limits isn't a good thing, no, it's really not.

Glaucon greeted this speech with a loud guffaw:

–My dear Socrates, even if your speech were to exile us from the country of truth, we'd acquit you of murder, and, by the same verdict, of fraud. So you can speak without fear of having to drink the fatal hemlock.

Socrates then awed his audience with a lengthy silence, his face a frozen, inscrutable mask. At last he relaxed and said with a broad smile:

–It's true that, according to our laws, anyone acquitted of murder regains his innocence completely. So the same will hold for me if you acquit me of fraud, right?

–Of course, *Glaucon agreed.* You have no further reason for remaining silent.

–Unfortunately! I, the philosophical stage director of male roles, shall now have to deal with the female roles, so that the play can be performed. . .

–And that's a lot different, isn't it? *said Amantha ironically.*

–Not as much as all that, young lady, not as much as all that!

150

After all, our conception of the development of everyone's leadership abilities has nothing whatsoever to do with sex. On the contrary, it assumes that we attribute to women a basic nature and ways of being that are more or less the same as men's, even if this means we then have to take a look at whether this principle can really work.

–Yeah, a very close look, *groused Glaucon.*

–Honestly, you're such an idiot! *a furious Amantha protested.* Think back to the comparison that was made between the temporary leaders of our communist country and clever, faithful guard dogs guarding a peaceful flock of ordinary citizens – from which the "guardians" come, of which they're merely a detachment. Your idea wouldn't happen to be that the female dogs are only good for bearing puppies and that the protection and leadership duties have to be reserved for the males, would it?

–That's not what I said, but. . .

–Well, buddy, if you think women can do the job the same as men can, don't you have to feed them, train them, and educate them exactly the same way as men?

–Socrates, *Glaucon pleaded,* is that really what you think?

–I have no choice. . . If we expect women to provide the same services, in terms of the community's development, as men, then we have to give them the same basic education. We based the education of our "guardians," meaning all our citizens, on literature, music, and physical training, and there's no reason to change that curriculum just because we're dealing with women. The same will, moreover, hold true later on, when we talk about higher education, and about mathematics and the dialectic in particular. It'll be to everyone's benefit!

–And women'll do military training too?

–Definitely. We hope to put an end, for good, to the monstrosity of those wholesale slaughters called "wars," but if we're attacked we'll defend ourselves.

–With women at the forefront, *said Amantha approvingly.*

–That's what I've always said.

–But really! *Glaucon persisted.* What about modesty, the difference between the sexes, sexual desire? It's common practice for men to train in the nude, shower together in the locker room, and tell really dirty jokes, all that kind of stuff. Can you picture beautiful naked young women in the midst of a bunch of bozos like that?[1] Honestly, can you picture that?

In reply, Socrates adopted a half-stern, half-dreamy tone:

–Dear Glaucon, in our country there won't be – no, there'll never be – just a handful of naked women in the midst of a whole flock of

151

men. But there'll definitely be the love between a woman and a man, in the refuge of their private life. Besides which there'll be humanity as a whole: old, black, heavy, white, light, women, cross-eyed and hunchbacked, young, yellow, wan, glowing with health, every conceivable kind of body, as mixed as they are different from one another, bodies whose possible nudity will not signify anything but the simple fact that they're jointly performing the same drills requiring nudity (a very rare requirement, as I see it). Every individual will get over the particular differences involved in one or another of these joint drills whatever way he can, but with the same degree of enthusiasm.

Amantha, suddenly remembering the literature she'd read in secret, then said:

—If our dear old Aristophanes were to see one of those "very rare" nude co-ed drills he'd find plenty of material in it to beef up his male chorus leader's furious speech. Do you remember in *Lysistrata?*

> If manly you men don't stand up tall
> And for once show those damn shrews who's who,
> With just their bare hands they will all
> Spread the seeds of the blackest coup.

> They will sharpen their knives with a will.
> Nor to cut off our balls will they quail.
> Our briefs to the brim they will fill
> With shit they'll bring home by the pail.

> Riding his prick, astride him, her steed:
> This a man must have seen in his life
> To fathom what darkness can breed
> In the heart of his wanton wife.[2]

—Well, *Socrates teased her,* I see you have quite an extensive repertoire. But Aristophanes is not going to keep us from saying that women can and must – naked, if required by the oddity of the situation – pilot our fighter planes, command our assault tank divisions, and be in charge stealthily, beneath the sea, of our nuclear submarines. The truth is, hiding or exhibiting this or that part of the body is only a matter of the contingency of customs. It's stupid to hit the ceiling just because a woman shows her thighs, but it's no less so to pass laws, as the French do, prohibiting a woman from covering her hair with a headscarf. Only brainless idiots find something that's merely a custom different from their own to be ridiculous or scandalous. We ought to be wary of anyone who wants us to be outraged about trivial things like that and not about what's *truly* insane or dangerous, about having intentions completely opposed to the Good that derives from the available truths.

–That kind of blowhard is usually a fascist without knowing it, *said Amantha sharply.*

–But *our* main concern is to come to an agreement on the issue of whether our ideas are feasible or not, and, to that end, to summon an interlocutor who will discuss them – as happily as a lark or as soberly as a judge – in an attempt to find out whether the female branch of the human species is capable of sharing all the tasks of the male branch, or none of them, or only some of them, and to what category of tasks everything related to war should be assigned.

–With a method as innovative and clever as that, *snickered Amantha,* we're bound to come to a brilliant conclusion.

–Go ahead and laugh! *Socrates retorted.* Or rather, why don't you play the part of the obstinate interlocutor, the guy who's sure that, thanks to him, we're going to fall flat on our faces.

–Gladly.

So Amantha took on the suave voice of a law professor:

–Dear Socrates, dear Glaucon, there's absolutely no need for other people to challenge your conclusions: you contradict yourselves enough as it is. When you first summarized the true nature of a country and its government, you emphasized the division of labor and acknowledged that the taste for a given occupation had to do with each person's natural aptitudes.

–Of course we did, *objected Socrates,* but often, spurred on by you, we revised our analysis in a communist direction: everyone has to be able to handle everything.

–But certainly not to the point of disregarding a natural, symbolic difference as crucial as sexual difference, *Amantha continued in a very pedantic tone.* Will you deny the ontological nature, so to speak, of that difference, gentlemen?

–Not at all, *Glaucon piped up.* Women and guys have virtually nothing in common.

–So, gentlemen, the noose of contradiction tightens around your argument and strangles all the life out of it. It's absurd to argue, on the one hand, that the state must be administered in the manner best suited to its unique nature and, to that end, a highly skilled, homogeneous workforce, coming from the masses of ordinary workers, must be trained, and, on the other hand, that both the subjective and the objective difference between men and women can simply be ignored as far as all this is concerned. Can you clear up that inconsistency for us all, dear brother?

—Well, off the top of my head, I don't have an answer.

—What about you, Socrates?

—I've been saying all along that the question of the sexes is a labyrinth worse than the Minotaur's.

—And what's more, that guy Theseus needed a *woman* to get out of it.

—Ah yes, Ariadne, the eternal abandoned woman. . . Can you see why *I*'m tempted to abandon this discussion?

—But you won't, *said Amantha.*

—Oh, you know me so well. After all, whether you fall into a duck pond or the Pacific Ocean, all you can do is swim. So let's take the plunge and hope that, as with the poet Arion in the legend, a dolphin will take us on his back and set us down safe and sound on the rock on Cape Taenarum.

—What an adventure! *joked Amantha.*

—Dealing with one woman alone is already a wild and woolly adventure for a man. So all women at once. . .

—You can do it, Socrates! Confront the monsters!

—Well, if you order me to. . . Let's see now, let's recap the problem. If human beings have truly different natures, it's unlikely that they'll be suited for the same tasks in the same way. Now, men and women do have different natures. Therefore we can't conclude, as we did, that if they're educated in the same way men and women will accomplish the same leadership tasks equally effectively. Is that right?

—Absolutely, *replied Glaucon,* and I really can't see how we're going to find a way out of this.

—False dialectic, the dialectic that's no more than the skillful manipulation of counter-arguments, is sure as hell powerful.

—Huh? What are you talking about? *asked a surprised Glaucon.*

—A lot of people unwittingly rush into this kind of dispute and imagine they're really dialecticizing when all they're doing is squabbling with each other. Why? Because they're incapable of resolving a problem on the basis of the immanent multiplicity of ideas it contains. For them, the process of countering an opponent remains at a purely verbal level, and so the whole discussion is merely a matter of contentious sophistry, not dialectic.

—Fine, fine, *grumbled Amantha,* but what does that have to do with the business about sex?

—We, too, may very likely be the unwitting victims of pseudo-counter-arguments. Basing ourselves on the supposed self-evidence of the words "man" and "woman," we object to ourselves, with a suspicious sort of enthusiasm, that the same tasks can't suit natures that are so different from each other, and yet we haven't examined beforehand the idea we have about that difference and that sameness, or the type of relationship we have in mind when we assign different tasks to different natures and the same tasks to the same natures.

–Can you give some examples other than men and women? *asked Glaucon, who was really confused.*

–To begin with, ask yourself whether, among the males of the human species, the bald ones and the ones with hair are the same or whether they constitute two mutually exclusive groups. Then, once you've observed that there's a real difference between them, draw the conclusion from this that the bald men must not be allowed to fish if we see that many men with hair are good at it.

–You've got to be kidding!

–Not at all. I want to stress this. When we determine that there's a difference between people, we've got to beware right away that it's practically never a question of an *absolute* difference. The kind of difference we're talking about is relevant to the tasks that we claim it's important for. "Bald" or "with hair" surely constitutes a significant difference as regards the quality of being "a hair stylist's client," for example, but an insignificant one when it comes to fishing. When we say that someone has a natural talent for medicine and that someone else has a natural talent for archery, that doesn't mean they're different in *all* respects. It may very well be that they're equally good at mathematics. When we claim that, in humanity as a whole, the sub-group of women differs from that of men, we need to specify with respect to which skill, to which task we're conceiving that difference, in order to ultimately assign the monopoly of said task to one sex or the other. If it appears that the sexes only differ in regard to the material process of reproduction – the females bear and give birth to children, while the males just deposit their seed in the woman's womb – there's nothing about that that can convince us that men and women differ as to political skill, and so we'll stick with our point of view: the "guardians" in charge of the country's affairs at any given time can just as easily be female as male guardians.

–I'm not sure that that will suffice to shut up all the big macho males who think women are only good for sewing, cooking, cleaning, wiping kids' asses, vacuuming, and spreading their legs, *protested Amantha.*

–Well, let's once again ask our opponent, the disciple of Aristophanes and the whole reactionary clique, to tell us what the skill or task is, in the political realm, that's only suitable for men and that women have no natural talent for. I'm waiting. . .

–He'll skirt the issue, *groused Amantha*. He'll whine, like Glaucon did just now, that it's a tricky question and off the top of his head he can't come up with an answer.

–So then, *said an accommodating Socrates,* let's ask him to follow along with us in the twists and turns of the demonstration whereby we're going to prove that, as far as governing a country is concerned, there's no task that should be reserved for one sex in particular.

–Go on! I'll play the reactionary, *said Amantha gleefully.*

–When you say that someone is good in a given field and that someone else isn't, don't you mean that the former catches on easily to what it's about while the latter is at a total loss?

–Well, what else could I possibly say? *brayed Amantha.*

–And also that the one who's good at it, after studying it for only a short time, is able to come up with things well beyond anything he's been taught, while the one who's lousy at it, after studying it for ages, can't even remember what he's been taught?

–He's wacko, this Socrates dude. If the only thing a dude can say is that if someone who's lousy is lousy then the brainiac's brilliant – well, honestly, that's just too much!

–We can also say that in the one the body is at the service of the intellect, while in the other it's an obstacle to it, can't we?

–Now you're *really* mucking up the waters, Socrates! What's this "intellect" of yours? What do you do with your intellect? In the sack, you've got to get it up, not intellectualize!

–But that's just it, my dear pimp: where does sex come into anything we've been talking about?

–It's long been said: thinking's fine, but getting a hard-on's better. Hence, sex is everywhere!

–Which is tantamount to saying it's nowhere. With the criteria we're using, it's very clear that in lots of different fields many women are better than a lot of men, but it's also clear that many men are superior to a lot of women. And so nothing can be concluded except that, when it comes to governing a country, there's no task that's appropriate for women *qua* women or appropriate for men *qua* men. Natural talents have been distributed equally between the two sexes, and consequently women are naturally fit for *all* tasks, just as men are.

–And yet there are loads of chicks who are lousy at math and very few, maybe even none at all, who are, I don't know, chiefs of staff, *Amantha ventured pretty lamely, in her role as the obligatory misogynist.*

–But differences like that are obviously the result of prejudices that have affected the education of girls for centuries, to the detriment of equality between the sexes. As for us, we'll maintain that every task should be open to women as well as to men. We'll say quite simply that some women are good at medicine and others are less so, some women love music and others don't much care for it, some women are extremely attracted to the art of war and others are disgusted by it, some women are philosophers and others prefer sophistry, some women are brave and other women are fearful. . . exactly like men. Our obligatory conclusion will be that nothing should prevent any woman from filling a position of leadership when it's her turn to do so. Women and men alike can possess a nature suited to the defense of the country, and if that nature has seemed weaker in women for such a long time it's because it was deliberately atrophied in them by ruthless educational segregation and insidious propaganda about the so-called "weakness" of the female sex.

–Whereas everyone can see that we're much more resilient than men! *Amantha, who had turned back into herself, triumphantly crowed.*

–That's very true. And there's nothing better in politics than the commitment of all those women who are as resilient as they are remarkable. This excellence in women will be enhanced, from childhood on, by literature, poetry, music, and physical training, as we've outlined their use in our academic curriculum.

–Which implies that, if necessary, we'll have to strip naked, like the males, *said Amantha coyly.*

–Of course. But a woman who's forced to strip naked because one task or other in the service of the community requires it will have all the clothes she needs in her militant virtue. As for the men who might be tempted to make off-color jokes, we'll say, like Pindar:

Before it is ripe – they don't give a hoot –
They select and they pluck laughter's sweet fruit.[3]

Those males stupidly laugh at the very same thing that they themselves do, on the ridiculous pretext that a woman is doing it too. They'd be better off sticking with the saying: "What benefits us is as beautiful as what harms us is ugly."

–And with inwardly rejoicing, *said Amantha in conclusion,* that the benefit of a drill can be symbolized by female nudity, which has always been the very image of beauty.

On that point Socrates could only agree with the young woman.

–So that concludes this chapter, as I see it. The wave that arose from this old business about the role of women and their education hasn't overwhelmed us in the least. Absolute equality between men and women from this perspective is not only a question of principle for us but we're also able to prove that it's the most beneficial thing for the community as a whole.

But Glaucon, for his part, didn't feel that the communist lawmaker was out of the woods quite yet.

–There's still another wave that could drown us for good this time, *he said.*

–What wave is that?

–What becomes of that primordial unit of society, the family, in your conception of things? Who'll take care of the children? And incidentally, in this context, what becomes of equality between women – who carry the unborn child in their wombs, who nourish the fetus with their own blood, who give birth in pain, who nurse the baby – and men, who had nothing to do with the whole business other than just screwing and coming? But above all, in your conception of things, what becomes of the family? The family, as we know, is the place where all the wealth is concentrated and where, in an absolutely unjustified way, it's passed on to individual heirs and not to the community as a whole, even if it's a matter of factories, banks, artistic treasures, apartment buildings, forests, and so on. The family seems to me to be absolutely necessary for raising children, while at the same time – since it's complicit with the worst aspects of private property – it's a pillar of an inegalitarian society and, what's more, the fetish of every reactionary system of government bar none. What do you have to say about such a paradox, Socrates?

–And let's not forget, *added Amantha,* Engels' wonderful book *The Origin of the Family, Private Property and the State.* That "origin" is common to all three terms and is responsible for the most decisive victory of oppression in all of human history. We've decided to abolish the private appropriation of everything useful and valuable for the community as whole. We've decided to dissolve the state by means of a polyvalent system whereby everyone in turn fills public positions. So what could make us hesitate in the face of that reactionary idol, the family? It needs to be completely abolished. It's the family that gives substance to the truly obscene ideas of patrimony, inheritance, heredity, superiority on the basis of birth, blood, or race, necessary inequalities, and so forth. Gide was right to exclaim: "Families, I hate you!"[4] Well, Socrates, cat got your tongue?

Socrates in fact just sat there, as though he were far away. He mopped his brow. The silence persisted, and the young people, feeling uneasy, didn't dare break it. At last, Socrates said softly, almost under his breath:

–Your elder brother Plato thought he could speak in my name about this strange, almost intractable subject, the family. He took off, it's true, from a few careless remarks of mine, and he has me say roughly the following (I'm quoting from memory): "Women will be shared in common by all the men. None of them will live privately with any one man. Children will also be shared in common. Fathers won't know who their children are, nor will children know who their fathers are." Yes, but in that case, what's responsible for amorous encounters, sexual relationships, the symbolic order of inheritance? The answer Plato attributes to me is: the state, always the state, forever the state. You were right to cite Engels, dear girl. But what's happened since then? In the Soviet Union they abolished private property, but they made the state, which was supposed to wither away, stronger, and the family remained strong enough for the children of Party officials to become the beneficiaries of hereditary privilege. And, according to your brother's Socrates, private property and the family are abolished in the ever-so-famous "ideal City," but the state emerges from these abolitions with exorbitant powers. On the basis of the axiom whereby children belong to the entire community, you end up, in line with this Platonic anti-family policy, with what can only be called horrors. Marriages are decided upon by the state, which institutes a rigged lottery so that the most beautiful human animals will become couples, the way it's done with pedigree dogs or plow oxen. And it's all so as to make sure you get "beautiful children." What's more, any newborns in whom a handicap, even a minor one, is detected are discreetly murdered by the police. Brother–sister incest is legal, even recommended, since it's expected that the offspring of the inbreeding between two beautiful and intelligent adults will also be beautiful and intelligent. The number of children you can have is set by the state. If you don't reach the limit, what happens is like what used to happen with the objectives set for the five-year plans in the Soviet Union: they investigate, they find the culprits, and they punish them. And if you go above the limit you're not raised to the rank of national hero, like the coalminer Stakhanov[5] was in Stalin's day: you're punished too.

–But children aren't the same as coal, after all, *said Amantha.* Does a guy who fucks like a champion or a woman who's pregnant every ten months absolutely have to be decorated?

–That's not funny, *Socrates angrily protested, though still in a soft voice, his face expressionless.* Let's not forget that, in this ideal City, the old have the virtually limitless right to beat up on the young. Just

159

think: to train children to serve the state, Plato claims you have to take them from the time they're 5-year-olds right into battle, so they can get used to being stoic when they see people having their throats slit or being disemboweled or decapitated, and when they're wading in blood, stumbling over dismembered corpses. No, none of that's very funny.

–The brilliant French psychoanalyst Jacques Lacan, who was nonetheless a great admirer of both Plato and yourself (*and Glaucon was very proud to have this reference at his fingertips*), said that the ideal City resembled a well-kept horse-breeding stable.[6] So do you basically agree with him?

–I can understand how your brother, annoyed by the sort of resistance the family puts up to any revolutionary zeal, went to extremes and could see no solution other than virtually total state control of personal relationships and the abolition of private life. Militant fraternity in the Party being more important than family solidarities: yes, I get how you can want such a thing. But what I can't go along with are the consequences of that vision, which are well known by now. Children denouncing their fathers as "counter-revolutionaries," knowing that they'll be executed, and doing so not out of fear but in the fervor of political duty: I can see a kind of terrible esthetics of the new world in that, a convulsive vision of "the new man." But the fact remains that there's something horrific about it, and it has no chance of enduring.

–But we saw that sort of thing again in the sixties of the twentieth century, *Amantha reminded him.* Some revolutionary groups advocated a totally collective lifestyle, in communal apartments, with open, public, non-exclusive sex. Desire was legitimate in and of itself, and there was nothing more moral than giving in to it. Everyone was like brothers and sisters; they screwed indiscriminately, without caring in the least who their current partner was. That was the way it was, at least in the beginning, with the American Weathermen, some brave young people who wanted to rally Chicago's white proletarians to the cause of the revolution and who, in despair over the failure of their efforts, resorted to setting off bombs here and there, ultimately ending up in prison for the rest of their lives. Sometimes I look on those times with envy.

–Well, you're wrong to, *said Socrates.* No, that's all disastrous, it all leads nowhere. Dear friends, I, Socrates, won't pay that price for the necessary dissolution of the family, such as it is. No, absolutely not. Taking advantage of the opportunity given me here by Badiou, I solemnly protest your brother Plato's interpretation of my thinking.

160

–But what then? *Glaucon asked anxiously.* Are we at a dead-end?

–We can always begin by drastically limiting inheritances. That would already be pretty good. In only a few generations, everything that deserves to would return to the sphere of collective ownership. As for the rest, let's face it, this question of the family and the dialectics of private and public life is the cross that communism's got to bear, because love, which is truth, too, requires withdrawal, requires that a certain amount of invisibility be granted it. We can't pursue the path that would involve eliminating all distinction between public and private life simply because of the very real reactionary burden that family life represents. Nor does the threat come solely from communist ventures. Corrupt democracy – the political regime of decrepit capitalism – also loves "transparency," and the politicians expose their dalliances, or even their orgies, to public view. The desire to eradicate love's creative secrets was blatant in the countries where it was declared that politics was "in command," that it had to sweep everything away before it. But it's just as much at work in countries where money's in command: there, love's secret gratuitousness infuriates the capitalists who govern; they much prefer the lucrative public profits of pornography. In both cases they object to the fact that, where all non-political truths are concerned, withdrawal, silence, a refuge apart are necessary. This is true, after all, for artists and mathematicians, too. Yet this issue of withdrawal, of the separation between private and public life, has had family life as its dominant form right from the origins of humanity. Even the greatest lovers can't avoid the need to create that kind of refuge for their private lives. And the result of this love endowed with a refuge is that, when children are born, they're welcomed into the grace of privacy, not mercilessly exposed to the tumult of public indifference. That's why, in the final analysis, eliminating the family is something both necessary and extremely difficult. Let's bear this cross, young people, and move on. We'll have to bear it until such time as the real movement[7] has given rise to the idea that we're currently lacking where this issue is concerned.

–In short, *said Amantha ironically,* when it comes to the family, the intimate power of love leads you to Wittgenstein's maxim: "What we cannot speak about we must pass over in silence."[8]

–Let's say, instead, that we're waiting for the day when, with regard to the family and its truly problematic relationship with love and children, we'll finally be able to think: what we cannot speak about we must do.[9]

161

WHAT IS A PHILOSOPHER?
(471c–484b)

The second phase of night had begun, when the earth's silence takes on the density of a carpet. All of Cephalus' guests had gone home except for a few, who were too drunk and were sleeping right on the blue tiles of the patio. Only Socrates, Amantha, and Glaucon had survived the force of those forlorn hours that compose the vestibule of morning. Or not only them, though: Polemarchus was still there, quiet and alert. And on a leather chair, a few feet away, Thrasymachus, too, was awake, perhaps. His head was down and his eyes were closed, so it was impossible to tell whether he was really asleep or whether, like a veteran spy, he was taking in the whole conversation without appearing to. After Socrates' failure to explain what a communist conception of the family might be, nobody seemed to want to speak. Socrates himself was taking little swigs from a goblet of white wine from the islands, as if the discussion were now over. After her nostalgic digression on political and sexual collectives, Amantha had lain down on a sofa, with her hands behind her head, although her eyes were wide open. Glaucon was pacing slowly back and forth. Some words eventually emerged, haltingly, from his full, adolescent lips:

–If we keep getting bogged down in a systematic exposition of all the regulations corresponding to what you called the fifth system of government, which Amantha promptly designated with the name of communism, we'll completely lose sight of the key issue that you put off examining quite a while ago to launch into these – let's face it – rather irrelevant details about women and children, which ultimately didn't amount to much. The fact that we were unable to deal with issues like marriage, inheritance, and sex raises a much broader question, namely: Is this fifth system of government possible? And what means are there, if it *is* possible, to make it a reality? Obviously, if we assumed that a communist system of government were a reality, great benefits for the country would result. I can even think of a few you haven't mentioned. For example, the courage of soldiers fighting a battle would be boosted by their feeling certain they'd never be deserted, because political fraternity and the practice of collective action would make the word "comrade" have the same force for all of them as the old words "brother," "father," or "son" have in families. Furthermore, if women, as you suggested, were to take part in combat, either behind the shock troops, to strike terror into the enemy, or as reserves in case of some serious setback, or even on the front lines, we'd become quite simply invincible. And I can also see that, at home, provided such a system of government were in effect, all the country's citizens would enjoy a thousand wonderful things you haven't said a word about. So, Socrates, since I approve of your account of the innumerable benefits of our communism, let's not discuss it any further. Let's focus the whole argument now on the two unresolved issues. One: Is such a system of government possible? Two: If so, where, when, and how?

Socrates, caught off guard, set his glass down.

–My goodness! *he exclaimed.* That was some surprise attack you just launched on my argument! Don't you ever grant extenuating circumstances to someone who's hesitant? From the start of our discussion I just barely escaped the devastating effects of a theoretical tidal wave concerning my feminism; I drowned in another about the family; and now here you are – granted, without realizing it – unleashing the most enormous and dangerous of all tidal waves of this sort on me! Once you've witnessed it, you'll be more than willing to grant me extenuating circumstances. You'll understand my hesitations, my fear not only of putting forward such an extremely paradoxical idea, but of completely defending it as well.

–The more you try to dodge the issue, the less likely we'll be to put up with your not telling us how our fifth system of government can come about in reality. So stop wasting our time: speak!

–All right, I see. . . To begin with, we've got to remember that we arrived at this fateful moment because we were inquiring into what justice and injustice might be.

–What's that got to do with my question?

–Nothing, nothing. . . But let's suppose that we really have discovered, as we believe we have, what justice is. Do you think we'd state as an axiom that the just man must not differ in any way from this fundamental justice but must be entirely like it? Or would we settle for his coming as close as possible to it, such that he might be said to partake in the essence of justice more than other men?

–I'd go for the second position.

–That's because we conducted our inquiry into the nature of justice, into what the perfectly just man would be if he happened to exist, and also into the nature of injustice and the most unjust of men, only with a view to constructing an ideal model of all this. By carefully observing these two character types and what they actually look like in terms of happiness and its opposite, we were hoping that a rational constraint would be imposed both on and with respect to ourselves, namely having to acknowledge that the more like them we were, the more our own lot in life would be similar to theirs. Our objective wasn't to prove that these two character types could actually exist in the empirical world. Let's imagine a famous painter who has the ability to create a truly ideal model of humanity on his canvas, to conceive of and render to perfection every feature of the worthiest of men. Would this painter's artistic greatness be in any way diminished if it were impossible for him to prove that such a model human being could exist in the real world?

Glaucon, sensing a trap, said:

–Umm. . . I don't think so, but. . .

–*We*'ve proposed, in the conceptual realm, an ideal model of the true political community, *Socrates hastened to interrupt him.* Do you think this proposal would lose its validity just because we can't prove that a political order corresponding to our description of it can be established in the empirical world?

–I'm not sure. It seems to me. . .

–Well, that's the truth of the matter, period. But if, just to please you, I have to attempt to prove that our fifth system of government can be realized – by indicating the proper means and the precise degree of that feasibility – I'll ask you to grant me, as a condition of the proof, the same kind of assumptions as you did a little while ago.

–What assumptions? *asked Glaucon warily.*

–I maintain that it's impossible to do exactly what one says. I believe that nature imposes inertia and resistances of various sorts on action such that it always remains inferior to speech – provided, of course, that the chosen criterion is participation in the idea of the True. It's possible to think otherwise. But will *you* grant me this axiom?

–Of course, *said Glaucon, who was mainly concerned not to delay Socrates' argument about the possibility of communism again.*

–Then don't force me to argue that what I've made exist as a proposition in language can also fully exist in empirical reality. If we're able to discover the practical means of founding a political community that comes as close as possible to our theoretical propositions, then consider that we'll have proved, as you request, the feasibility of those propositions. I, at any rate, will be very satisfied with a demonstration of that sort.

–So will I, *said Glaucon, who found these preliminaries to be longwinded and overly cautious.*

–And then, *Socrates went on,* I think we could focus on doing some serious research in two stages. First, show what's dysfunctional in countries that aren't run according to our principles and, second, uncover, on a case by case basis, a change that's trivial in itself but would have the effect of reconfiguring the whole political community under consideration and of bringing it into line with our communist model. Ideally, this change would concern only one point or two, at a pinch. At any rate, there must be as few of these points as possible. And above all, from the standpoint of the established order in which we'll isolate them, they should have no apparent importance. I'd even go so far as to say that, in the eyes of the state that we want to radically transform, the point to which the change would apply doesn't exist, as it were. It's absolutely foreign to the state's usual concerns, and that's what will help us. What we need is a single, inexistent – albeit real – point, which, once it's been identified and spotlighted, will change everything and bring about the truth of the body politic. Yes! Let's change this one point bordering on nothingness and we'll be able to show that the whole of the state concerned will then completely change. Oh, identifying and dealing with this point won't be quick or easy! But it's possible.

–What exactly are you talking about? *asked a bewildered Glaucon.*

–Here I am, summoned to the very place where what we called the most enormous wave breaks, the wave that can shake up and capsize the boat we've rashly launched onto the ocean of rational argument. And yet I must speak, even if my awkwardness leaves me open to being thoroughly drenched by the merry wave of mockery and snorts of contempt. Pay careful attention to what I'm going to say. . .

–Will you just go ahead and say it already, *an impatient Amantha urged,* instead of wearing us down with all these aquatic metaphors that are supposed to convince us of the terrible risk you're running by speaking to us – a risk that, quite frankly, I don't think would bother a mosquito.

–OK, you beautiful, quick-tempered girl, you're forcing me to roll the dice. Well, here goes then. In every country, philosophers must be the ones to exercise leadership positions. Or, conversely, those who are responsible for exercising leadership positions. . .

–In other words, *Amantha cut in,* according to our communist principles, everyone.

–. . . they all – everyone, in effect – must become philosophers. Really and truly become philosophers, to the extent required by collective action. In short, political ability and philosophy must come together in the same Subject. Without a relentless struggle against the natural tendency to completely separate the role of the political process, which is regarded as positive, from the seemingly critical, hence negative, role of philosophy, there will be no end, dear friends, to the evils afflicting not just one nation or another but, I'm firmly convinced, humanity as a whole. What's more, the political community whose intrinsic rationality we're founding will have no chance of becoming empirically possible and of seeing the light of day in any given country so long as this relationship – which is immanent in collective action – between politics as thought-practice and philosophy as formalization of an Idea hasn't been tried out.

–So *that*'s what you've been hesitating to say for so long! *exclaimed Glaucon.*

–I knew very well that I was going against prevailing opinion to the point of making it very difficult for anyone even to believe in our political project, let alone in what it implies in terms of the notion of happiness. Because, as far as philosophy is concerned, happiness is created in every individual by the subjective process – the truth – in which he participates. And that's something that's hard to understand when you're just an ordinary citizen.

–The tricky issue, *quibbled Amantha,* doesn't seem to me to be this business about happiness. I know happiness means a lot to you – the happiness of the just man, who ought to be happier than the unjust man, and all that stuff. But I've always found it all to be a bit muddled, sorry. To associate happiness with just about anyone, all you have to do is change its definition and bingo, there you go. If you say "happiness is the Idea," then it's easy to "prove" that the Idea is happiness.

–Don't get carried away! *said an amused Socrates.* So what's the tricky issue, then?

–Since – communism requires it – any worker must be able to take part in leading the country, and since anyone who takes part in leading the country must combine political thought and the philosophical Idea, you're postulating that anyone at all can become a serious philosopher. Considering philosophy's reputation – abstract, out of touch with reality, utopian, totalitarian, incomprehensible, dogmatic, hair-splitting, antiquated, purely destructive, replacing religion with something less good, etc. – you'll be lynched in the media, or else you'll be put out to pasture as an outmoded old bore.

–But it's you two, dear friends, *Socrates protested,* who goaded me into saying what I really think.

–And it's a good thing we did, too! *Glaucon asserted.* Trust me, I won't desert you at the first chance I get, the way my dear sister's doing. I'll do everything I can for you. You'll have all my best wishes, my encouragement, my congratulations. I'll submit to your terrible Socratic interrogation with the best will in the world. With support like that, you shouldn't hesitate! Show the skeptics, and especially that damn Amantha, what you're made of.

–Well, I'll try, since you're proposing a sort of Great Alliance between us. To begin with, if I want to find a way to escape from the whole pack of media, academic, and partisan hounds, who Amantha predicts are going to tear me to shreds, I think it'll be necessary to define the predicate "philosopher," which I claim must apply to anyone who attains a leadership position. Once that point's been clarified, I'll be able to defend myself by showing how philosophy is appropriate for what a true political process requires of each and every one of us. I'll bolster this demonstration with its negative correlate: if someone objects to philosophy in the name of politics, it means that the politics he's talking about isn't real politics.

–That, at the very least, deserves to be explained, *groaned Amantha.*

–Well, follow my lead then. You'll see whether by wandering here and there I eventually find the path or not.

–Heraclitus, *said Amantha sternly,* wrote: "We must also remember the man who forgets where the path leads."

–Oh, that old windbag! *an exasperated Socrates shot back.* He should have just kept his mouth shut.

–Go on! *Glaucon cut in.* No lateral arguments! Get straight to the point!

Socrates remained silent for a few minutes. The wait was palpable; it stretched time out. Then, all of a sudden, he said:

–Need I remind you of something you should have an extremely vivid recollection of? When we speak about a love object, we claim that the lover loves the whole of the object. We don't accept that his love should choose only one part of it and reject another.

The two young people seemed flabbergasted. Amantha took it upon herself to express their confusion:

167

–Dear Socrates! What does this digression about love have to do with the definition of the philosopher?

–Oh, isn't that the typical young woman in love for you! Incapable of acknowledging that, as the great Portuguese poet Fernando Pessoa said, "Love is a thought."[1] Take my word for it, kids: anyone who doesn't begin with love will never know what philosophy is.[2]

–All right, *said Glaucon-the-sensible*. Still, this business about the object isn't easy. Didn't Lacan say that every object of desire is in fact a *part*-object, a part of the other's body, like the breast, the penis, the gaze, poop, and so forth?

–Those are objects of drive, not desire. And desire isn't love. The fact that the object's a part-object in no way precludes that it's the *whole* underpinning this partialness that desire and love are ultimately related to. But think about your own experience instead, you boys and girls who roam the world spurred on by desire. As experts in love, you ought to know everything about a young man – for instance – that moves and attracts anyone who has an erotic temperament, regardless of their gender, and convinces him that such an object as a whole is worthy of his attention and affection. Isn't that the way you behave with good-looking boys, my dear quibblers? Partial flaws in no way keep you from falling for the young man as whole. So he has a snub nose? You'll say it looks sensitive and charming. If he has a hooked nose, you'll say it looks regal, like an eagle's beak, imperial! And if his nose is neither snub nor hooked and attracts no one's attention, it means the young heartthrob is perfectly proportioned. If the young Adonis' skin is tanned by the sun, you say he's as manly as a musketeer, and if he's as pale as can be, that he's as delicate as a god. You even call a washed-out complexion a "honeyed complexion." Such verbal tricks are typical of lovers, who come up with kind words to praise someone who looks anemic as soon as they're attracted to him. Any excuse will do, and you call upon the full resources of language to make sure none of these beloved young men gets away from you.

–If you want to use me as a professional seducer, *said Glaucon,* I accept, but only for the sake of moving our discussion forward.

–You hypocrite! *exclaimed Amantha.* You know sex is all you ever think about!

–Well, *said Socrates,* let's change the subject then. Doesn't a drunk behave the same way you do, you young lovers? He'll find every excuse in the book to knock back a liter of some disgusting cheap wine. And what about someone who's in love with honors? If he can't be a general and command ten thousand men, he'll be happy to be a lieutenant and command only thirty. If he can't be a commissioned officer, he'll find untold virtues in the rank of corporal, commanding only five soldiers. And if no one wants him as a corporal, he'll still be thrilled, as a private, to look all stern and military as he reprimands some kids playing in front of the barracks. In civilian life, if no one important pays the slightest bit of attention to him, he'll be happy if his underlings in the office, some insignificant people he hardly even knows, kiss up to him. And if even *that* doesn't happen, he'll still get off on the local panhandler's humble greeting to him every morning.

–So what does philosophy have to do with any of this? *ventured Glaucon.*

–I'm getting to that. Will you grant me that to say of someone that he desires something means that he desires the whole form of the thing, not just one part, everything else being excluded from the field of desire?

–OK, I'll grant you that.

–So, if we say that a philosopher is someone who desires wisdom, it won't be a matter of a choice between different parts of that wisdom but of its whole form. Let's examine a young person, then, a girl or a boy, who doesn't yet possess the principles with which to distinguish between what's important and what's worthless. Let's assume that "he or she," as the Anglophones say, has no liking for theoretical knowledge. We wouldn't call him or her a "scientist" or a "philosopher" any more than we'd refer to someone who has no liking for food as "having a big appetite," or as "famished," or as a "food lover." "Anorexic" would be more like it. But when we see a young person who indubitably wants to taste every branch of learning, who's obviously attracted to knowledge and is insatiably devoted to it, wouldn't he or she deserve to be called a "philosopher"?

Glaucon then felt an irresistible urge to formulate an objection he considered to be irrefutable:

–There'll be lots of people who fit your definition, though. And people you wouldn't expect either. First off, the lovers of mainstream movies, to judge by their enthusiasm for seeing anything new: all the big Hollywood blockbusters and all the pretentious little French turkeys that have just opened, which, along with all the TV series, they swear provide us with real knowledge about the world today. Then there are all the people who make the rounds of festivals every summer. They, too, swear that there, at least, they learn, they become cultured, they're immersed in the delights of the Idea of music. It would be pretty odd to award all these people the rank of philosopher. They'd certainly not be up for following an argument like ours, and the very idea of spending their whole night at it would make them run for their lives. Yet they really do have a passion for new knowledge! They'll race from a Romanesque country church to a castle hidden in the hills somewhere and from a small-town concert hall to the ruins of an ancient open-air theater, provided they can hear operas, quartets, organ concerts, pianists, or even poets accompanying themselves on a guitar there. It's as though they rented their ears out to all those provincial cultural organizations! But are we going to call all these vacationing culture-vultures, these mid-summer mavens of the minor arts, philosophers?

–Don't be so scornful of people who sense obscurely that the power of art is not something to be avoided. That's a completely anti-philosophical stance.

–It's the smugness of a petit-bourgeois intellectual all right! *Amantha cried.*

–Come on, settle down, kids. That said, my dear Glaucon, we won't call your summer vacationers philosophers. There's only a vague resemblance between them.

–So how will you define true philosophers, then? *Glaucon persisted.*

–They're people whose only passion is for one kind of show alone, the one afforded them by truths coming into the world.

–That's all very well, but you ought to give us a few details.

–You're right, it's the details that count in philosophy, but they're also what make it seem so complicated and arcane. Naturally, with *you*, things will go a lot faster. Let's begin with a great classic, the theory of binary oppositions. The beautiful, for example, is the opposite of the ugly. So we've got two distinct notions there.

–For the time being, *Glaucon remarked,* that's easy enough.

–The same goes for just/unjust, good/bad, and ultimately everything that pertains to what you and your sister have learned to call the Forms. Every Form considered in and of itself, in the order of being, is one. But it's also multiple, since, in the order of *appearing*, it's always seen in combination with actions, bodies, and other Forms. Thanks to the whole apparatus of my theory of Forms, or of Ideas, or of that which of being is exposed to thought,[3] or of the essential, or of being-in-truth, or of truths, I can propose a clear distinction between the people you were talking about a moment ago – the inveterate festival-goers, the groupies who follow sopranos around, the people who make the rounds of art shows, and the ones who rush to tennis tournament finals, too – and the people we're trying to define right now, who alone deserve the name of philosophers.

–But how do you get from the metaphysical theory of Forms to the definition of the philosopher? *asked Amantha, suddenly becoming very excited.*

–The lovers of shows, concerts, paintings, and sports competitions all enjoy a soprano's pianissimo high note, a cello's vibrato, the delicacy of a sketch, the opulence of a color, a beautiful athletic body in motion, or anything that's finely wrought and appealing in whatever's offered to their sensory faculties. But this empirical experience doesn't enable their minds to understand thought's real purpose.

–But someone could object to you: what difference does it make? *said Amantha aggressively.* Since they have enjoyment. . .

–Enjoyment, perhaps. But life, dear friend? The true life that Rimbaud speaks of? The life he says is absent?[4] Do they have that true life? Imagine that someone accepts the existence of beautiful things but can't accept that the being-beautiful of these things exists as the aim and outcome of a process of thought. Suppose that this same someone is unable to follow a friend who's involved in that process and who offers in a brotherly spirit to take him with him all the way through to the end, thereby transforming his empirical opinion into rational thought. Do you think that that someone is living the true life fully awake? Rather, don't you think that his life is but a dream?

–It's not as easy as all that, *objected Amantha,* to distinguish dreams from reality, as Shakespeare saw in *Hamlet*, Calderón in – appropriately enough – *Life Is a Dream*, and Pirandello in a little of everything he wrote.

–Careful! You just mentioned three *playwrights*, three experts in life acted out, performed, illusory. What is dreaming, in your opinion, regardless of whether we're asleep or not?

Amantha thought for a few moments, then replied:

–It's thinking that something that's like something else isn't merely a likeness of it but the thing itself.

–Precisely. And therefore an anti-dreamer is someone who accepts the existence of the being-beautiful as such. Someone who's capable of contemplating that essential beauty that accounts for the fact that things that participate in it are called "beautiful." Someone who doesn't confuse either beautiful things that exist with their being-beautiful, or the being-beautiful with existing things, which, since they're beautiful, participate in that being. Wouldn't we say about such an anti-dreamer that he's living fully awake and is not lost in a dream?

–Yes, but he could just as easily be a poet as a philosopher. Doesn't Mallarmé say:

the true poet's broad and humble gesture must
Keep them from dreams, those enemies of his trust:[5]

–OK, let's accept that combination, *said Socrates with a sigh.* At any rate, I'd say that our anti-dreamer's mind, insofar as it knows the being of what exists, deserves the name of "pure thought." Whereas to the dreamer's mind, insofar as it's limited only to the existence of what appears, we'll give the name "opinion."

–Well, that about wraps things up, *said Glaucon.*

–Wraps things up, give me a break! *protested Amantha.* We still don't know what an opinion is, really. All we ourselves have about it is an opinion! "Dialecticizing": that's your motto, Socrates, isn't it? And yet we've defined opinion without any immanent discussion of any position that's different from our own. We've been analytical, not dialectical. We sound like Aristotle! If someone gets angry at us and calls us "dirty dogmatists" or "rotten totalitarians" because we've stuck the khaki-colored label of "opinion" on him and not the red label of "knowledge," will we be able to calm him down and win him over without his thinking that we automatically regard him as a lackey of American imperialism?

–Oh, *said Socrates,* it's our duty to be able to do so! Our Chinese colleague calls that "the correct handling of contradictions among the people."[6] The best course of action would be to ask this guy we've irked some questions. We'll assure him that, if he has real knowledge, no one will try to downplay that knowledge. On the contrary, we'll all be delighted to associate with someone who knows something.

–It'd be great if my brother could play the role of the angry guy, *said Amantha mischievously.* You'd put the questions to him directly and we'd have a "live" dialogue.

–Sure, why not? *Glaucon retorted valiantly.* Anything that promotes dialectical argument is fine with me. Go on, Socrates, go on.

There then ensued an intense, heated exchange all of whose twists and turns Amantha, her eyes aglow, eagerly took in. Socrates opened fire:

–So tell me, young man, you who say you have real knowledge: does a guy like you, who knows, know something or nothing?

–Something, obviously, *said a very arrogant Glaucon.*

–Something that exists or something that doesn't exist?

–That exists. How the hell could you know something that doesn't exist?

–So does it seem clear to you that, regardless of circumstances, contexts, or points of view, something whose existence is beyond doubt, or absolute, is absolutely knowable, and something that doesn't exist is entirely unknowable?

–It's perfectly clear.

–Our agreement on this point is crucial. Now, if a thing is such that it *is* and at the same time *is not*, won't it lie in a sort of middle ground between pure existence and absolute non-existence?

–The term "middle ground" is fine with me.

–Note carefully the content of our consensus at this point in our dialectical reasoning: the thing we're talking about is somewhere between minimal and maximal existence.

–I didn't agree rashly, *protested Glaucon*. Like you, I maintain that if a thing like the one we're talking about does indeed exist then it lies between the full absoluteness of being and the empty purity of nothingness.

–If pure thought has to be related to being and non-thought necessarily to nothingness, only a cognitive "middle ground" between knowledge and ignorance can be related to our ontological "middle ground." In short, we'll have to look for it somewhere between knowledge and ignorance. Assuming, of course, that such a "middle ground" exists.

–I can't see where else we could look for it.

–Is it reasonable, then, to give the name "opinion" to this cognitive "middle ground" suspended between thought and non-thought, or, by derivation, between knowledge and ignorance?

–When a definition is clear, there's no need to quibble over names, *said Glaucon, feeling quite proud of his turn of phrase.*

–Is "opinion," if it exists, the same as knowledge?

–We just said that it isn't. It's neither knowledge nor ignorance. It's in between the two.

–So the objects of knowledge and opinion are different?

–Oh, come on, Socrates! You're taking too long! Let's skip the easy questions.

–Yes, but careful! Knowledge is by nature related to the existent, so as to know the being of this existent. . . Damn it! I skipped an important link in the chain this time. With your assistance, I've got to dialecticize a distinction first.

–What distinction? *asked Glaucon, who was starting to have a hard time of it.*

–Of the things that exist, there are some of a special sort, which we call faculties. It's owing to them that I can do whatever I can do, and that anyone with the same faculties that I have can do whatever he can do. For example, let's take sight and hearing. You're perfectly familiar, I suppose, with the Form I'm referring the word "faculties" to, aren't you?

–No problem, *sighed Glaucon.* We've talked about it often enough.

–Yes, but there's still a difficulty. I can't identify a faculty by its color or its shape or by anything of the sort. Those criteria nevertheless hold for lots of other objects. All I have to do is use them in order to be able to immediately conclude, in what Sapeur Camember used to call "my deep-down insides,"[7] that these objects are different from one another. But that doesn't work for faculties, because, to distinguish one from the others, I need only take two properties into account: what they're related to and the function they enable you to carry out. It's on the basis of these two criteria that they've been called "sight," "hearing," "touch," and so forth. The faculties that are related to the same thing and are responsible for the same function I call the same, or, if the object and function aren't the same, different. What about you? How do you go about it?

–The same way as you do, *muttered Glaucon.*

–So, dear friend, let's get back to the issue at hand. Knowledge – do you say knowledge is a faculty? Or do you classify it some other way? And how about opinion? Where do you put it?

–In knowledge, *said Glaucon, perking up,* the most general term for which is "cognition," I acknowledge not just a faculty but the most important one of all. As for opinion, it's definitely a faculty: having the ability to hold an opinion is precisely what opinion is.

–You moreover agreed a moment ago that, for you, knowledge – or, if you prefer, cognition – isn't the same thing as opinion, didn't you?

Glaucon had completely revived.

–A reasonable person, *he said,* cannot maintain that the infallible and the fallible are the same thing. Absolute knowledge must necessarily differ from changeable opinion.

–These two faculties do in fact differ as to their functions and must therefore also differ as to what they're related to. Knowledge is obviously related to the existent and knows it in its being. As for opinion, all we know is that it enables one to hold an opinion. But what's its proper object? The same as that of knowledge? Can it be possible for what is known to be the same as that about which we only hold an opinion?

–No, that's impossible, *exclaimed Glaucon,* given the very thing we agreed on. If each individual faculty is naturally related to an object that's different from the object of any other faculty, and if opinion and knowledge are distinct faculties, it follows that what's known and what's held as an opinion cannot be one and the same thing.

–So, if only the existent is known, what we hold an opinion about must be something other than the existent.

–Copy that.

–In that case, *Socrates continued, scratching his chin, which, with him, was always a sign of great perplexity, whether real or feigned,* we have to conclude that the object of opinion, since it's the aspect of being of that which is subtracted from existence, is nothing other than non-being.

In an unequivocal, authoritative manner Glaucon then said:

–No, that's absolutely impossible. There's no way one could ever hold an opinion about non-being, Socrates! Think about it! When someone holds an opinion, his opinion is related to something. He couldn't hold an opinion about something while simultaneously holding an opinion about nothing. The holder of an opinion holds that opinion about a thing that's clearly counted as one. However, non-being is not *one* thing but *no*-thing.

–That's right. Besides, we ascribed non-being as an object to ignorance, not to opinion, after we ascribed being to thought. And we were able to do so only because ignorance is a purely negative faculty, whereas opinion affirms its object.

–Yet it *is* really strange! *Glaucon reflected.* We demonstrated that opinion, since it's related to neither being nor non-being, is neither knowledge nor ignorance.

–There you go! *said a delighted Socrates.* So should we then say that it transcends the opposition between pure thought and ignorance in some way? That it's clearer than thought or darker than ignorance?

–Oh, come on! *said Glaucon, shrugging his shoulders.*

–If I'm interpreting your gesture correctly, you consider it to be obvious that opinion is darker than thought and clearer than ignorance.

–Of course. We already said it's in between the two. In the middle.

–And we added that, if we were to find something that appears at once to be and not to be, this thing, occupying an intermediate position between pure being and absolute nothingness, would be neither knowledge nor ignorance but something in between the two. Well, now we know that this in-between thing is what we call "opinion."

–Well, the question's settled then, *said Glaucon exuberantly.*

–Except, *cried Amantha,* you haven't yet found this "thing" that's supposedly the object of opinion. I want to see this "thing," between being and non-being, that can't be reduced, strictly speaking, to either of the two. Show it to me.

–You're right, *said a conciliatory Socrates*. Everything's still in the conditional mood. If we do find this famous "thing," then we'll quite rightly say that it's the Form of that to which opinion is related. We'll ascribe the extremes, being and nothingness, to the extreme faculties, pure thought and total ignorance, and the intermediate term, as yet undetermined, to the intermediate faculty, opinion.

–So it's a purely formal classification, *Amantha pointed out.*

–To go further, let's have Glaucon put back on the costume of our beloved critic, the man who categorically refuses to accept the existence of the beautiful in itself, or anything that's like an Idea of the beautiful in itself. Go on, Glaucon! Play the part of the guy who denies that there can appear a truth of beauty such that it remains self-identical once it has emerged into its own eternity: the guy who only believes in changeable, multifaceted kinds of beauty, the lover of theatrical illusions, who becomes incensed as soon as you mention the unity of beauty, justice, in short, anything that a Form brings out and affirms.

–OK, here I go! *Glaucon said boastfully.*

–My good fellow, of all the many beautiful things you invoke, is there a single one that can be said to have absolutely no flaws? Same question for just decisions or commendable deeds.

–Obviously not. It's always possible to find a little flaw in beautiful works of art, and the same goes for all the rest.

–Similarly, what's double can be seen from a certain vantage point as half, or what at first glance is big can later appear tiny. Any characteristic of that sort can reverse into its opposite, can't it?

–Yes, because each thing always partakes of both opposite characteristics; it's a matter of point of view, or scale.

–Oh! *said Amantha suddenly.* That reminds me of the riddle about the man who wasn't a man, who saw and didn't see a bird that wasn't a bird sitting on a twig that wasn't a twig, and who threw and didn't throw a stone that wasn't a stone at it.

–Well, yes, *said Socrates with a smile,* these are children's games. All these sensory qualities are ambiguous. It's not possible to determine with any certainty about any of them that it is, or that it is not, or that it both is and is not, or that it neither is nor is not.

–I think, *said Glaucon in conclusion,* that we need to place these ambiguous notions between that which of being is exposed to thought and absolute nothingness. That's because they're not dark enough to be declared more non-existent than nothingness, nor are they clear enough to be more existent than being.

–Perfect! *said Socrates admiringly.* It seems we've discovered that the many ideas most people entertain about beauty and other things of the sort appear in the enormous space between non-being and what absolutely is. You and I assumed, however, that if such is the appearance of a given thing, it has to be related to opinion, not to pure thought, since it's the intermediate faculty that's responsible for apprehending everything wandering in the intermediate realm of all that exists. So we can conclude now. Let's consider those for whom beautiful things are just an obstacle beyond which there's nothing that can be called beauty-in-truth; those who are unable to follow someone who wants to show them the way to truths; those for whom many different acts are just, but who haven't the slightest idea what justice is – all those, in a nutshell, who give in to the casuistry of facts and never go back up to the principle. We'll say of such people that they have opinions about what appears in the world but no knowledge whatsoever of what they hold those opinions about.

–You're doing a great job of repeating everything that's already been said, *Amantha put in.*

With his left hand Socrates made the motion of swatting away a fly.

–Now let's consider, *he went on,* the people who love a completely different kind of show, which we'll call the essential show: things, conceived of in terms of the singularity of their being, go through the vicissitudes of appearing while constantly reaffirming this singularity. I suppose we'll say about people who take part in a show of this sort not that they hold an opinion but that they know.

–The lucky ones! *exclaimed Amantha.*

–We'll say about these "lucky ones," dear Amantha, that they love, they cherish what pure thought is related to, and about the others, that they're only concerned with opinion. We've already said about the latter people – let's call them "doxics," since the word "opinion" is the word used to translate the Greek *doxa* – that they love and cherish the mellifluous voices of sopranos, the colors of luxury wallpapers, the shimmer of opals on the fingers of stylish young women, or platinum–iridium cell phones, but that they can't bear that beauty-in-truth should be absolutely real. Would we be wrong to call these doxics "lovers of opinion" rather than "lovers of wisdom"?

–And "lovers of wisdom" is the etymology of "philosophers," *said Glaucon sententiously.*

–Let's make up a saying about these non-philosophers, *added Amantha.* "All that is merely doxic is toxic."

Socrates gave her a dirty look, then said:

177

–Will the doxics be furious that we're calling them "lovers of opinion"?

–"Philodoxers" versus "philosophers," *Glaucon summed up.* If they're furious, I'll point out to them that no one has the right to be annoyed at the True.

–But here's the main thing, *continued Socrates.* Those who cherish in each thing its own distinctive being are the ones who must be called philosophers, because they resist the temptation to remain mere philodoxers.

But Amantha wasn't satisfied. She paced up and down, fiddling with her messy hair, a worried look on her face. Finally, she burst out:

–So you guys think you've figured it all out, do you? You think we've made a lot of progress with your definition? So many convoluted arguments to distinguish philosophers from those who aren't. . . Take my word for it, we're not out of the woods yet. You still have to link this all back up with our original question: the difference between a just and an unjust life. And since, in your opinion, that question itself presupposes that we've got to make an enormous detour by way of the problem of the state and the communist system of government, we have to show that the definition of the philosopher has a rational relationship with political action.

Amantha, triumphant, stopped pacing, fixed her gray eyes on Socrates, and continued:

–Here's my request, my challenge. I've understood that, as far as you're concerned, a philosopher is able to grasp the universal nature of that which remains self-identical even as it undergoes its own changes. I've also understood that philodoxers are incapable of any such grasp and in any case regard it as unnecessary, or even harmful. How can we now prove that the collective characterization of our fifth system of government requires the masses of people to be on the side of philosophy?

–Here's what I'll say to you. Which of the two – the philosopher, the man of the universality immanent in that which is immutable beyond its own becoming, or the philodoxer, the man of endless wandering between being and nothingness – is better able to hold fast to communist principles and protect the institutions in which those principles are embodied? When it comes to standing guard over the Idea and the choice is between a blind man and a sighted one, can there be any room for doubt?

–Well, when you put things like that, *protested Amantha,* the decision's as good as made before there's been any discussion. It's a forced choice.

–Is it perhaps my analogy that's bothering you? But what difference can you possibly see between the blind and those who, by denying themselves the resources of pure thought, can never have access to the being of existents? These people, even if they're capable of becoming Subjects, from the outset have no clear model that would allow them to contemplate, like great painters, that which is perfectly True, to refer to it constantly and to have the most accurate conception possible of it, in order to lay down the founding principles of all that's beautiful, just, or good in our world as it is.

–But what if those principles have already been laid down by a few thinkers of the past? *inquired Glaucon.*

–Well, then, our sighted people will have to ensure their continued existence and safety by keeping an unfailingly rational watch over them – something that our "blind men," given over to opinion, are obviously incapable of doing. So it's those whose pure thought attains the being-true of each existent, and not the big media guns of opinion, whom we'll install as guardians, militants, leaders. . .

–Ordinary workers, too, *insisted Amantha.*

–Of course, ordinary workers, each in his turn assigned to guarding the principles and institutions. Those workers are, moreover, experienced people who, even on the level of everyday practicality, have it all over the inane TV talk show chatterboxes.

–Still, it's a real question, *said Glaucon, suddenly worried,* how an ordinary worker, once he's become the guardian of our communism, will be able to combine pure thought and practical expertise.

–You mean: how he can be both a philosopher of the Idea and an officer of collective action. To enlighten you, I think we've got to go back to the nature of the philosopher. We'll then see that it's compatible with militant expertise and that there's nothing to prevent any ordinary worker, trained in this way, from either establishing or guarding the institutions in which our principles are embodied.

–All right then, *said Amantha, grinning,* let's have the umpteenth full-length portrait of the philosopher!

–Don't laugh! It's a crucial issue for philosophy to be able to define the nature of the philosopher. That nature unquestionably involves the love of any knowledge located in the clearing[8] of that eternal aspect of being which is exposed to pure thought and, for that very reason, remains foreign to the dialectic of being born and dying. And we also know that philosophy obeys the laws of love: we love the whole of that aspect of being that's identical to the thought we form of it, because it is itself a Form. No true philosopher can give up the slightest bit of what's revealed to him this way, be it large or small, or of great or negligible worth. Which is how the philosopher differs, as we've seen, from the person obsessed with honors and from the instant gratification freak.

–But aside from this essential feature that has to do with knowledge, *Glaucon queried,* aren't there any characteristics of the philosopher that are more psychological?

–Psychology, psychology. . . That's not my thing! Nevertheless, you could say that, when it comes to what really matters to him, the philosopher is absolutely truthful and will not tolerate any duplicity or lying in anything he says.

–That seems likely enough to me.

–What do you mean, "seems," or "likely enough"? The most implacable necessity compels anyone who has a lover's nature to cherish everything that closely affects the beloved, everything around him or her and that he or she is fond of. Now, is there anything closer to philosophical wisdom and more alluring to it than the truths that glitter here and there in the dull fabric of opinion? Of course not. It is therefore strictly impossible for the philosopher's nature to take pleasure in falsehood. The conclusion that can be drawn from all this is that, thanks to the power of a true love of knowledge, the philosopher's nature develops, right from youth, as a striving after truths of any sort.

Socrates' fervor left Amantha and Glaucon utterly amazed. But their teacher kept going:

–We know that someone whose desires are intensely focused on a single object is less inclined to desire any others, the way a stream whose current has been channeled in one direction alone rushes furiously that way. So it's logical to assume that a man. . .

–. . . or a woman! *Amantha remarked.*

–. . . or a woman, *Socrates conceded,* whose desires are focused on truths and on everything connected with them will turn to the most purely subjective pleasures. For him. . .

–. . . or her! *Amantha remarked again.*

–Or her, *Socrates acquiesced,* even the pleasures of the body must have a sort of intellectual resonance. At least if this young man, or woman *(he hastened to add),* is an authentic philosopher, not an academic, armchair, or TV philosopher.

–Could you say a little more about that authenticity? *asked Amantha, a tad aggressively.*

–What I mean by that is a fundamentally disinterested character type, because the drive to get rich and to spend extravagant sums of money is the last thing that should be encouraged in a philosopher. It necessarily corrupts the very process of thought; it stands in the way of any incorporation into a truth process.

–Will you allow me, dear teacher, *interjected Amantha,* if not a criticism, then at least a minor reservation? I think the same conclusion can be reached by starting from less moralizing premises. Sure, we've got to assume there's less exposure in the philosopher's nature than in any other to anything that's incompatible with the free nature of thought. I agree that nothing could be further removed from the philosophical character than small-mindedness. But why? Quite simply, it seems to me, because philosophers seek the general logic of things, be they humbly natural or part of the most sublime constructs of the mind. A quest of that sort will be completely blocked if you're petty, jealous, envious, or a careerist.

–How true! *said an admiring Socrates.* And I'll even throw in another argument. Consider a woman or a man, dwelling now and then in the splendor of the active intellect, who's able to master the ordinary flow of time and contemplate that aspect of Being which is exposed to thought. Would it make any sense to think that a person thus transfigured by the powers of a Subject would still regard his mere animal survival as something of great consequence?

–Your example tells us that it wouldn't, *said Glaucon seriously.*

–A woman or man of that sort will therefore have overcome the fear of death. Conversely, a coward tormented by that anxiety cannot share in the true nature of a philosopher. One can add that inner harmony, disinterestedness, the love of freedom, courage, the ability to make an objective judgment about oneself, all this blocks the road to injustice as well as to the despicable spirit of competition that turns the other person, especially if he's superior to you, into a rival to be destroyed. That's why, if we want to discover what a philosophical Subject is, we'll have to pay attention, very early on in our examination of a given individual, to the conflicted relationship within him between justice and social climbing, or between reasoned argument and high-flown rhetoric.

–But not to anything having to do with knowledge? *asked Glaucon worriedly.*

–Of course, of course! We'll attempt to develop the basic character trait, the one any child is amply endowed with: ease of learning. You can hardly expect someone to be enthusiastic about an activity that bores him and in which all the effort he devotes to it is only rewarded by very little improvement.

–What about memory? *inquired Amantha.* That's my weak point, memory.

181

—Come on, *Socrates scolded her,* if you retain nothing of what you learn, or if you constantly forget the essential, you'll remain devoid of any positive knowledge. So you'll become discouraged and will ultimately come to hate the very thing you set out to do. We won't include the names of people with bad memories in the register of true philosophers.

—But what about qualities of refinement? *Amantha went on stubbornly.* Can a philosopher be a vulgar person, someone with no personal charm?

—You're touching on the key issue of proportion, *replied Socrates.* The kind of people you're talking about actually lack all sense of proportion. But take my word for it: a sense of proportion is a close relative of truth, and lack of a sense of proportion is foreign to it.

—So your philosopher, *Glaucon recapped,* is a rational person endowed with a sense of proportion and grace, willing to promote the natural becoming of an Idea befitting the real that underpins its existence. So we can see that all the qualities we required to characterize the nature of the philosopher are closely interrelated and are all necessary for a Subject defined by his full and complete participation in the process whereby being is exposed to thought.

—So, in your opinion, *asked Socrates,* would someone having that sort of philosophical nature who applied for a position that required a good memory, ease of learning, high-mindedness, a certain gracefulness, a taste for truths and justice, great courage, and ample self-discipline be virtually exempt from all criticism?

—An ideal candidate! *joked Amantha.*

—But don't we want *all* the citizens of the country whose destiny under the fifth system of government we're in the process of imagining to be like that? Don't we want them all to have all the qualities of the philosopher's nature? Because it's to them and them alone, to all of them, our friends from the vast masses of the people, that we've got to entrust the tasks required for the organization of a collective life that's finally liberated, finally worthy of the Idea that humanity can have of itself beyond the mere obligations of its survival.

—They must all be philosophers?

—All without exception, *said Socrates softly.* Yes, without a single exception.

— 10—

PHILOSOPHY AND POLITICS
(484b–502c)

Socrates' "They must all be philosophers!" had carried through the night like a muffled exhortation. But there was more of a sense of weary determination about it than any bravado. Besides, Socrates was just sitting there, mouth agape, not saying a word and idly scratching his left leg with a fork. After a couple of minutes, Glaucon couldn't stand it anymore and felt he had to gauge the extent of his teacher's uncertainty.

–Dear Socrates, *he began,* no one has anything to object to in your arguments. But haven't you sometimes wondered how those who don't dare say another word after they've been caught in some aporia or other by your amazing intellectual dexterity feel? They're sure that when it comes to your favorite game, the question-and-answer game, their lack of experience is such that, as their little slips of the tongue pile up, they're ultimately led to making huge mistakes, which are diametrically opposed to what they thought at the outset. They feel like a mediocre chess player, so surprised by his opponent's attack, long concealed in his move-by-move strategy, that he has no idea where to put his king anymore and can only lay it on its side to signal his defeat. Your listeners likewise end up feeling paralyzed and unable to say a thing at the end of the chess game that's played with arguments instead of wood pieces. But don't think that they conclude that truth is on your side. No way. They may have been defeated in the symbolic game of argument, but they're confident they can show that real facts may well prove them right. Everyone can see, they say, what happens to people who are seriously committed to philosophy, people for whom philosophy isn't just an academic subject that you drop after dabbling in it in your youth.

–What happens to them? *asked Socrates, his eyes agleam.*

–There are two possibilities, or so say your interlocutors when they talk behind your back. Most of these "philosophers" become strange, if not thoroughly immoral, people. And the only thing the tiny minority who manage to keep a sense of proportion get from this intellectual exercise you champion so vigorously is a plain inability to become involved in politics and take on leadership positions in the state.

–What about you, dear Glaucon? *said Socrates, smiling.* Do you think that they're wrong to say all that behind my back when they're brooding over their defeat in chess? Or that they're right?

–I'm totally confused. I'd like to know what *you* think about it.

–No problem! They're telling the truth, nothing but the truth. "The whole" truth, though, maybe not.

–Well, that's a bit much! *Amantha suddenly burst out.* You give us solid proof that the only way countries will escape their plight is if all their citizens become philosophers, then, with no warning, you turn around and say that philosophers are political morons! So how does your fifth system of government work, then?

–I can only answer your question, dear girl, with a metaphor.

–You pull that number on me often enough. Well, *I* say: Beware! Beware!

–Come on already, let him speak! *said Glaucon angrily.*

–Never mind! *said Socrates.* That's just like Amantha. She asks me a really tough question and on top of that makes fun of me. But first listen to my little metaphorical story, my dear girl. It'll be even easier for you to laugh at me when you see how bad a poet I am.

–Go on! Just ignore my sister, *said a furious Glaucon.*

–It's just a little sea tale. Once upon a time there was an oil tanker whose captain was a big hefty guy, a good-natured fellow, whose only flaw was that he was stone-deaf and as blind as a bat. Oh, yeah – and also his knowledge of navigation was as shaky as his eyesight was poor. Given his incompetence, the sailors were always arguing over who was going to take the helm, even though none of them knew how to steer a ship. There was a hole in the oil tank, so the ship was leaving a big trail of oil behind it. They'd been squabbling for days about what should be done to plug the leak, but they couldn't agree on anything. What's more, the general opinion aboard ship was that there was no need to know what to do in order to do it, nor to do it in order to learn what to do. The upshot was that they neither knew nor did anything. And they all kept besieging the captain, shouting out their opinions – the best one being, by unanimous consent, the opinion of whoever shouted the loudest – in order to get the poor man to let them take the helm and plug the hole. One day, one of

them managed to persuade the captain and took his place. A particularly brutal, organized band of sailors promptly pounced on the old
captain, beat him up, and threw him in the hold. As for the new guy,
they rendered him powerless by getting him to smoke opium, snort
coke, and guzzle bottles of vodka. After which they swiped everything
they could from the cabins and decided to sell the whole cargo of fuel
in the first port they came to, so that they could split the proceeds
and live the good life. They'd turn the oil tanker into an opium den, a
saloon, and a brothel for the occasion. But how could they make their
way to a port? The oil tanker, with no competent authority in charge,
zigzagged all over the place like Rimbaud's drunken boat.[1] Not that
that stopped the winning party from congratulating everyone who'd
joined it or helped it consolidate its power. "What great sailors you
are!" they said. "What sensational helmsmen!" Even when the ship
ended up running aground in a filthy bay, and its hull burst and the
viscous oil killed thousands of birds up and down the coast, they kept
on priding themselves on being first-rate navigators. They didn't have
the slightest idea that to steer a big ship's course you need to have
a certain knowledge of the seasons, the stars, the winds, maritime
maps, ocean depths, radio communications, and so on. No, they
thought that having the consent of a majority of the sailors was quite
enough. No need to have any ideas. Dangerous, even.

So that's my story, dear friends. Now let's suppose that in such a
situation there were to appear a true captain, combining the intellectual conception of navigation with extensive practical experience.
Someone who knew how to speak to the sailors in such a way as
to persuade them to get their act together so that the ship could be
repaired and then really run and steered in the direction of the destination they'd chosen for it. How do you think the anarchic gang in
power would treat him? Wouldn't they badmouth him and call him a
befuddled egghead, a behind-the-times idealist, and an outmoded old
ideologue?

–Seems likely, yes, *said Amantha,* to judge by how *you*'re treated in
the press and on television.

–So this is really a metaphor for the fate that the current state of
opinion and those who control it have in store for true philosophers.
If anyone's surprised that philosophers, as we would have everyone
become, are not highly regarded by prevailing opinion, tell them the
story of the oil tanker and they'll understand that what would be
really surprising in our situation, and I'd even say downright strange,
would be if the handful of our philosophers who weather the storm
were to be put on a pedestal!

185

–Well, *muttered Amantha,* that's one oil tanker whose purpose is not just to supply gas.

–Do you have something against oil tankers of the mind? *Socrates shot back. Then, turning to Glaucon, he said:*

–And your friend with the conventional opinions better not bug us any more with his cliché about how people well-versed in philosophy are of no use for the great masses! Because if they're of no use your friend should blame the *leaders,* who are incapable of making use of them, not the philosophers. After all, it's not for the captain to beg the sailors to please accept his authority, any more than it's reasonable, as a false poet and true liar claims, that

the wise should wait at rich men's doors.[2]

The truth is that it's for the sick man, whether rich or poor, to ring the doctor's doorbell. And it's for the person who's lost in life's labyrinth to listen to someone who knows how to find his way around in it. It's absurd to see a capable leader imploring those who need him in a dire situation to give their consent for him to take the situation in hand. In parliamentary "democracies" the people in power are like the drunken sailors on our oil tanker, and the people these sailors regard as useless, as eggheads, as people "out of touch with reality" are precisely those who could be, if people would only listen to them, real captains.

–Still, *objected Glaucon,* I think the harshest criticism directed at philosophy stems not so much from the sidelining of true philosophers by ignorant people as from the dubious impression of it given by the so-called "new philosophers," who are always holding forth on TV and having their pictures taken for magazines. *They're* the ones who make a lot of my friends say that philosophers are guys with no sense of decency, that they're all a bunch of media phonies. It's this perversion of the title "philosopher" that would need to be cleared up. And, in particular, it would have to be shown how all of this implies no responsibility on the part of *true* philosophy.

–That'll take some doing!

–Yes, but we can use what was already said about the true philosopher, *protested Amantha.* Or at any rate about the philosopher endowed, as you require, with a rigorously logical mind and a serious allergy to all forms of corruption. You related all that to the concept of truth, saying that if he doesn't adopt it as a guide to everything in life, the so-called philosopher is nothing but an impostor, forever cut off from true philosophy.

–Absolutely, *Socrates agreed.* We'll defend ourselves by arguing

186

that the true lover of knowledge, the person whose intellectual struggle is geared toward the real of being, could never be concerned with
the myriad particularities whose existence is only attested by the relationship, itself fluctuating, between the wide range of opinions and
the movement of appearances. On the contrary, he'll pursue his path
with no dimming of either his determination or his passion, until he
masters the real nature of that toward which he's turned his thought
and into which he's incorporated himself as a Subject. Indeed, in so
doing, he'll be released from labor pains, and he – and others along
with him – will give birth to a new truth and be able to take pleasure
in that point where true life and true knowledge are indistinguishable
from each other.[3]

–Oh, Socrates! *said Amantha rapturously.* It's not for nothing that
you're the son of a midwife![4]

–However, *Socrates went on,* everything else follows from this.
Can we imagine such a man putting up with hypocrisy or deceit in
important discussions? Can we imagine that, when truth leads the
way, it would be to head up a procession of evil things? Isn't truth
rather the chorus leader of all those whose integrity and self-discipline
act as a barrier to corruption? But we don't need to describe all the
attributes of the philosopher's nature again. You both remember that
we mentioned courage, high-mindedness, submitting to the disciplines of knowledge, the work of memory. . . I'd gotten to that point
when Glaucon objected that I was right, but if we turned from the
argument to reality, we could easily see that most of those who call
themselves philosophers are notorious rogues. So we need to face this
accusation, and that's why we're trotting out the portrait of the true
philosopher again: to differentiate him from dangerous imposters.

–I understood that, *said Glaucon.* But, as I explained, there are two
different cases. There are those whose philosophical nature has been
corrupted and who have become totally useless for that very reason,
especially as regards politics. But there are also those who deliberately imitate the philosophical nature in order to usurp its powers.
What's the subjective character type of those people who, by imitating a way of being and thinking that they're unworthy of and that is
quite beyond them, behave at all times in such a way that they bring
philosophy properly speaking into quasi-universal disrepute in public
opinion?

–Oh, dear friend! We have to begin with a terrible paradox.
Everyone has a philosophical nature at first. Yet it becomes corrupted
in practically all of them. Why? Because if the very qualities it requires
develop independently of each other, they prevent the philosophical

187

nature from ever reaching maturity. Yes, dear friends, courage, self-discipline, submitting to the disciplines of knowledge, all conspire to corrupt philosophy, which nevertheless requires and organizes these qualities.

–Well, now we're *really* in trouble! *groaned Amantha.*

–And to make matters worse, everything commonly considered to be good things in life – beauty, wealth, good health, a politically well-organized society – all contribute to crippling and destroying the philosophical nature. Nature itself can shed light on this paradox. Look at the seeds of plants or the young of animals. If they fail to find the food, habitat, or climate that's right for them, then the more robust they were originally, the more they'll suffer from these privations. This is a self-evident dialectical principle: the bad is more opposed to the good than to the less good. Something that was originally excellent but is treated badly will become worse than something mediocre subjected to the same conditions.

–I see where you're going with this, *said Amantha, her eyes half-closed.* To your pet subject, education.

–You can read me like a book. Of course! Let's assume that all individuals bar none start out having, virtually – as our colleague Gilles Deleuze would put it[5] – the same excellent philosophical ability, give or take a few little differences. If the ideological and educational environment provided for them by the state is terrible, that excellence will turn into its opposite, and the best among them will be the worst: that little difference in intellectual excellence will become an almost unlimited excess of depravity. After all, it's well known that a moderate temperament, even if it doesn't make sparks fly where the good is concerned, is at least still incapable of committing vile acts. Which basically means that if the philosophical nature as we've defined it encounters an appropriate educational environment, it's bound to pursue a positive path in life. But in the opposite case, if sown on arid soil and grown in defiance of good sense, it will be doomed to having all the failings caused by profound disorientation.

–Unless, *said Amantha, smiling,* it happens to encounter a teacher like you somewhere along the way.

–No, that won't suffice! It still has to be seized by some event – a passionate love, a political uprising, an artistic upheaval or what have you. For evil is all-encompassing, it stems from the situation as a whole. Don't think that young people are corrupted because they unfortunately came across bad teachers – inveterate sophists, who are merely peddlers of rhetoric, after all. No, no! The professional moralists on TV who deplore these unfortunate encounters, the politicians

188

who denounce these so-called philosophers' bad influence at their political rallies, are ultimately the greatest of sophists themselves, the ones who are constantly generating the propaganda hype responsible for confusing youth and for dooming it to the misery of nihilism.

–But where? When? How does it happen? *asked Glaucon, who was ready to take on the whole army of corrupters right then and there.*

–Quite simply through that constant, day-to-day, ubiquitous babble of voices, gently terrifying, amiably constraining, and cheerfully relentless, that's called "freedom of opinion." On TV, in the theater, in the papers, in election rallies, when the official intellectuals hold forth, and even when we just get together with friends for a drink and to shoot the breeze, what do you see? What do you hear? Everyone either criticizes or applauds statements, ideas, actions, wars, movies, in a big free-for-all with no universally valid rational principle. There's a sort of vaguely aggressive, joyful yet sinister extravagance about the booing and the applause alike. It's as though the big glass exteriors of the buildings were echoing, all throughout the city, the same seemingly conflictual but actually consensual babble of voices that's composed of all these opinions, which are so bitterly incompatible with one another that no single one prevails, except the one that decrees: "I'm free, at any rate, to say anything I want." And it's that "anything I want" that destroys the philosophical nature. What can become of a young man's or woman's thinking when it's up against the power of the incoherent babble of voices that sweeps away any idea of truth and crushes it to bits? Of what avail is an education that is itself incoherent and already caught up in the swirl of anonymous opinions? Won't young people eventually start to judge things the way the dominant babble of voices does, when it comes to what's beautiful or ugly, moral or immoral, fashionable or outdated? Won't they end up dumping their own bucket of water in the muddy stream of unverifiable information and unfounded opinions symbolized by the Internet?

–You don't have a lot of confidence in our ability to resist, *whined Amantha.*

–Oh, but resisters will be dealt with appropriately! If you're not a middle-of-the-road democrat, a diehard supporter of "freedom of opinion," you'd better watch out! You're going to have repressive legislation forbidding you to do this or that, your name will be dragged through the mud, they'll build police stations and prisons to punish the youth rebellion, and looming on the horizon, when the situation gets tense, there may even be death, as some predict will be inflicted on me.

–But can't we oppose this tyranny of opinion, *asked Glaucon,* by disseminating – clandestinely, if need be – the philosophy of truths?

–I already told you, that won't suffice. No one has ever changed or will ever change, merely through moral lessons, a character that's been set in stone by prevailing opinion. Philosophy can only be effective if the political divine has intervened first, if some event interrupts the consensual routine, if some organized action has shown what it means to be implacably opposed to prevailing "democracy." When there's real action, of the sort dictated by principles, not opinions, at a local level, then the philosophical idea can bring out its universal significance. In states corrupted by the democratic disguise that conceals the power of the rich and ruthlessly ambitious, anything that can rescue thought and justice is nothing short of a secret god.

–And who exactly is this providential hidden god? *Amantha asked brusquely.*

–The unpredictable event, the emergence of a rallying cry and of a collective organization that couldn't have been foreseen in the ordinary confused babble of opinions and their so-called freedom.

–But then, what happens to the philosophical nature that isn't lucky enough to encounter its event-god?

–Go ask the philosophers-for-hire or the media loudmouths. Their norms of action, which they're quick to call "knowledge," or even "thought," merely synthesize whatever the state of the prevailing babble of opinions is at the moment. Their "philosophy" panders to whatever exists and is dominant. Imagine a man whose job is to feed a big animal with a thick coat of fur and big, long teeth. He carefully observes its instinctive behavior and desires. He learns how to approach and handle it without taking any risks. He knows how to interpret its cries and modulate his own tone of voice so that the animal, on hearing it, will be either gentle or fierce. To this sort of empirical observation the man gives the name "life science." While he's at it, he writes a big treatise on said "science," which he teaches at the university as if it were the last word in modernity. He has absolutely no idea what, out of all the animal's desires, habits, growls, and reactions, deserves to be called "just" or "unjust." He couldn't care less about his guinea pig's inmost truth, its inner being. The only thing that matters to him is the counterpart of opinions, that is, the big animal's repetitive behaviors and stereotypical reactions. Our professor of life science calls the things the animal seems to like "good" and the things that make it angry "bad." A professor though he may be, he's unable to justify these terms, quite simply because he conflates justice and beauty with the physiological necessities of

190

survival. His "science" is nothing but sophistry because he doesn't know the basic difference between necessity and truth. Do you think a character like that can be a useful instructor for the true life that we're trying to define?

–Of course not! *exclaimed Glaucon.*

–But is this professor of "life science" really any different from those who call the empirical knowledge of the undifferentiated desires of a people under the dictatorship of volatile public opinion "political science"? You know those people who do surveys to find out what has political import, the way others, the proponents of "the science of esthetics," assess the quality of music or painting in percentages. Is a man of that ilk – a political science professor who subjects something as complex as a big public service project to the law of number – any better than a bear trainer or a sociologist who grants the right to judge a poem's value to a majority of TV viewers? In any case, since they never provide any reasoned criticism and never get to the bottom of things, these people only serve to confirm in the public's mind that a majority opinion, simply by virtue of being a majority, is beautiful and good, and that it's best to come round to it. Yet you and I can easily prove that that's a ridiculous conclusion. If the question of the movement of the planets had been submitted to the law of majority opinion, we'd still believe today that it's the sun, rising and setting, that revolves around the earth.

–That's my favorite example, *a delighted Glaucon piped up,* whenever I want to explain the difference between a truth and an opinion to one of my friends.

–But is that argument, albeit a very compelling one, able to turn all your friends away from the cult of number, from the majority-rule electoral system, and from the dogma of "freedom of opinion"?

–I admit they're often impressed for a few minutes, but then they go back to saying that "democracy, the freedom to say anything you want, is still the best thing about the modern world."

–That's because it will require a long effort and a well-nigh radical transformation of humanity for everyone to accept that the synthesis of creation and eternity is brought about by new beauty rather than by the wide variety of objects that opinion declares to be beautiful. And, more broadly speaking, that it's the mathematics of being that matters, not the existence of many different particularities.

–But what can we do, then, until such time as that whole long effort has been accomplished?

–Not be surprised, in any event, by the attacks on philosophers that will come from all sides, whether from those who only believe in

prevailing opinion or from demagogic politicians who are only interested in being re-elected.

–It must be really tough, *said Amantha, shaking her head,* to be a
philosopher as you understand the term. How can anyone resist pressure like that?

–It's even harder than you think, dear girl. Imagine a young person
who's clearly endowed with a thirst for all that's worth being thought
and experienced. He was frequently regarded as an exceptional child;
he stands out in his age group. As a result, his parents and his whole
family circle want to push him in the direction of a brilliant, lucrative career. They'll simultaneously flatter him and use him for their
own purposes. What they love about him is his future power. They'll
persuade him to put the qualities of the philosophical nature – the
thirst for learning all the disciplines of knowledge, memory, courage,
high-mindedness – to use in the sordid competition of the worlds of
business, the media, or ordinary politics. And if this young prodigy
happens to have been born in a rich, arrogant imperial state, there's
a very great danger that the corruption of his native abilities will lead
him – as was the case with young Alcibiades, who was nevertheless
my friend – to become fascinated by power. Ultimately, our well-born
young man will entertain wild hopes, even going so far as to imagine
that he can unite all the peoples of the world under his leadership and
impose the law of his own desires on the whole world.

–You've been influenced by what happened to the wonderful
Alcibiades, *said Amantha.* You loved him, I know. But so spectacular and incurable was his intoxication with power that when you
approached him to quietly tell him the truth – that he was losing his
sanity and could only get it back by devoting himself utterly and self-
lessly to it – he found it very hard to tolerate his old teacher's attempt
to help him.

–Oh, *said Socrates softly,* he actually did feel the force of my arguments, though. He was secretly in agreement with my thinking. But
the people around him were terrified at the thought of losing all
the perks stemming from his political and military victories. Those
parasites swarming around him did everything they could to turn him
away from my teaching. And where *I* was concerned, they stopped
at nothing in their efforts to destroy me. They set traps for me, they
slandered me, they plotted to have me dragged before the courts. And
that's how Alcibiades eventually gave up on becoming a philosopher!

–How sad that is! What a bummer! *commented Amantha.* You
were sure as hell right to say that the qualities that go into making a
philosopher turn into their opposite once they're hostage to a corrupt

environment. All it takes is for opinion to take over truth's place and for the power of money and influential connections to be dangled tantalizingly before the young.

–Alas, *Socrates wistfully replied,* Alcibiades is a classic example of that. The philosopher who's led astray, tainted, turned into his opposite is indeed the man who, as dynamic and talented as he is, ultimately does the most damage in public life.

–All in all, *concluded Amantha,* we'd be better off with an ordinary working man, a brave, intelligent worker who has real principles, than with a "philosopher" of that type. I've always thought as much.

–Sure, *said Glaucon.* Nevertheless, we can't do without intellectuals to promote our communist project among the masses. But where are they to be found? There's something despairing, Socrates, about how painstakingly you describe the extent to which minds are corrupted.

–Oh, despair's not my thing. We have a small minority left that will increase in size and ultimately prevail, even if it still only consists of eccentric oddballs. There are educated people who've been forced by exile or persecution to remain true to philosophy, and ordinary people, born in some small country, who, because they were free from the temptations of power, have been able to combine their independent political experience with a first-rate intellectual education. There are workers who've come from afar and have become philosophers in order to understand for themselves their own painful experience; others who've become disgusted by occupations that relied too much on conventional opinion and have rebelled, allying themselves with small militant groups and the meditation of contemporary thinkers; and still others who'd never have ventured into the labyrinth of the communist Idea if their poor health hadn't deterred them from pursuing trendy careers. In some countries, girls have very successfully rushed to embrace philosophy and politics, owing to the rage they felt about being regarded for so long as incapable of excelling in them. I myself, as you know, have only fulfilled my obligations as a critic under order from my inner daemon.[6] Together, we compose a little group that's bound to have a bright future.

–But couldn't an educational curriculum be imagined, *said Glaucon impatiently,* that would expand your odd little group to include society as a whole?

–At any rate, let's break with the prevailing view of things. Today philosophy is only something for teenagers, who give it up as soon as they get to the real problems.

Amantha, in her usual brusque manner, then asked:

–So what *are* the real problems?

–The dialectic, dear Amantha, the dialectic! All those nitwits – of both genders – either go into business, or hold forth on the radio, or specialize in purely technical fields, or run for local office, or write dissertations on the seventh-century trade in crocodile skins. . . They think they're doing so much by reading a few essays on current opinion or by attending trendy lectures. When they're old, they fade away faster than the sun in Hugo's poem "The End of Satan": "The sun was there, dying in the abyss." And, unlike our good old real sun, they never light up again. We'll do just the opposite of all that. Philosophy starting in childhood, sure, provided we get to the dialectic as soon as possible, that we devote ourselves to it in the very heart of political practice. Ultimately, life as a whole will be dedicated to the Idea in this way, and all human beings will be able to enjoy life, to a very ripe old age, as something that has allowed them to be the people they've become, which they have good reason to be proud of.

Glaucon sensed that Socrates' quasi-triumphant tone was masking some deeper anxiety, or rather a fundamental uncertainty about the real fate of philosophy and philosophers. And he deliberately rubbed salt in the wound:

–I have to admit, dear Socrates, that you're speaking with a conviction that's a pleasure to hear. But I'm sure the vast majority of those who listen to you, or even those who, over the centuries, will become acquainted with your ideas through my revered brother Plato's dialogues, or even those. . .

–Will you stop with the acting already! *said an exasperated Amantha.*

–Fine! Let's just say that most people will stand up to you with a conviction at least as unshakable as your own. They'll absolutely refuse to trust you, Thrasymachus first and foremost.

–Oh, just look at him sleeping over there! *Socrates shot back.* He looks like a big baby, our Thrasymachus. Don't try and get me into a fight with this new friend of mine, who's never been my enemy anyway. I'll do everything in my power to convince him and the rest of them. In any case, I'll try to be of some use to them for that other life, when they'll be born again and take part once more, as they're doing today, in dialectical discussions.

–*That'll* be a long time from now![7] *Amantha teased him.*

–But a long time is nothing compared with the whole of time. In any event, we shouldn't be surprised if our arguments hardly make a dent in prevailing opinion. People haven't yet seen the Idea we're discussing appear in a given material world. Under the name of "socialism" they've always just heard fine words that are used to contrive clever correspondences and ingenious verbal consonances, not the kind of risky arguments *we* venture into. As for a character type who'd correspond, for real this time, to the basic virtues of a subject-of-truth and would somehow be, in both word and deed, the kind of character type to whom we could entrust a country like the one we're trying to conceive of – well, people have never seen a single person matching that type. Still less can they imagine a world in which matching it would be the general rule. That's why I feared to elaborate on these problems. Nevertheless, constrained by truth, I eventually said that no country, no state, not even any individual will be able to do all it's capable of until the currently very small group of philosophers is enlarged to include the people as a whole. Naturally, I'm only talking about *true* philosophers, those who haven't let themselves be corrupted either by prevailing opinion or by power, whether of the financial, political, or media kind. The ones people call "old-fashioned," "useless," or even "dangerous." The group will be enlarged as a result of a necessity that will itself be put into play by a chance event and everyone will be swept up in it, like it or not. If it's objected to us that such a raising of the people's consciousness doesn't seem to have occurred in distant countries, or isn't even considered as a future possibility by those regarded as the best informed people, our answer will be that the rationality of our hypothesis doesn't depend on History or on scientific prediction, but only on the following, which is truly essential: you only have to be able to think that the chance occurrence of a variety of interwoven, and doubtless violent, circumstances opens up the possibility for a system of government in line with the communist hypothesis for that possibility to be the one that will take on the value of a principle of action for us, and ultimately for everyone.

Glaucon, still skeptical, though, said:

–You'll have a very hard time convincing a segment of public opinion that's large enough to upset the ideological balance of power in our democratic countries.

–Don't be so hard on public opinion. If workers, office workers, farmers, artists, and honest intellectuals have trouble believing in the power of our Idea, it's because of the well-established phony philosophers, who, as flunkies of the ruling order, put a whole rhetoric at its service, heaping upon the various politics of emancipation, as these are sanctioned by philosophy in the name of the Idea of communism, their same old insults: Utopia! Stale old idea! Totalitarianism! Criminal idealism! But if the passion of individuals to become the

Subjects they're capable of being is aroused by the conjunction of militants' hard work of thought, philosophers' fidelity to that work, and a few unpredictable shocks that temporarily weaken the propagandistic, repressive organization of states, people everywhere will see the future in an altogether different light. Not only will they then be easily convinced that our project is the best one, as we're in the process of demonstrating at the level of philosophy, but the masses, seizing hold of the Idea, will turn it, as Mao put it, into "a spiritual atom bomb."[8]

The expression hit home and there was a silence, a thrilling silence, as if the bomb in question was about to go off any minute. Was it intellectual terror? A dawning conviction? Profound doubt? Who could tell, in this living room overlooking the Piraeus, bathed in the clear morning light coming off the sea?

In any case, even Thrasymachus, who'd been asleep, roused himself and stared at Socrates, as if he were silently asking him a difficult question.

— 11 —

WHAT IS AN IDEA? (502c–521c)

At first, after Socrates' long, uncertain defense of philosophy and phi-
losophers and their controversial relationship with politics, everyone
had remained silent, but they eventually started drinking and eating
some fruit. Even Thrasymachus, who, as we saw, had awakened at
the mention of an "atomic bomb," good-naturedly joined in drink-
ing with the little group, though he continued to smile the smile of
someone who still has his own opinion about things.

But then Thrasymachus went back to sleep, Amantha, after a
trip to the bathroom, returned all bright-eyed and bushy-tailed, and
Glaucon rubbed his hands together impatiently. So Socrates realized
that it was time to get the ball rolling again.

–The main problem now, *he suddenly said*, is to decide on the
modalities, the mathematical illustrations, and all the intellectual
exercises that will feature in the education of the people who'll
have to fill leadership positions, which means – yes, dear Amantha
– virtually everyone, and to determine the stages of that education.
By the way, I have to confess that it was out of sheer expediency
that I said almost nothing, at the very beginning of this discussion,
about certain troublesome questions, in particular how our system of
government's militants will be installed in power. Having said that, I
realize I didn't gain much time with my expediency: we won't be able
to avoid having to justify taking a very tough stand on all the sensitive
issues. I'm sure you'll agree that as far as collective political leadership and the training of a militant humanity is concerned, we've got
to start over from scratch. But scratch, to tell the truth, is never quite
nothing. We've already discussed the people (yes, sure, as Amantha
is going to remind us, this means just about everyone) who are to
become political leaders for a certain amount of time. We've already

said that they had to demonstrate their love for public affairs in all circumstances, be they pleasant or painful, and never give way on that principle, regardless of whether the excuse for ducking their responsibilities is the difficulty of the task, a feeling of panic, or a shift in the balance of power; that unqualified people were to be educated for as long as possible; and, by the same token, that those who emerge from all these tests as pure as gold tried in the fire were to be awarded not just leadership positions but medals and public honors, both during their lifetime and after their death.

Socrates then turned to Amantha and asked:

–We did say something along those lines, didn't we, young lady?

And Amantha replied:

–As far as I can remember, after four or five hours of exhausting discussion, yeah, I think we did. But it seems to me that you'd toned down your views quite a bit, that you were walking on eggshells.

–That's the expediency I was talking about. I was afraid of getting straight to the point. But let's go for it! Let's be daring! Let's stick to our guns! Who do we need to install, as political leaders perfectly suited to our principles? Philosophers. There. I dared to say it.

–Whatever you say! *scoffed the beautiful Amantha.* But it's hardly news to us! We just talked about that for nearly two hours!

–I know, I know. We established the principle of the fundamental link between the philosophical Idea and political thought-practice. But there's still one problem. Under normal circumstances, there won't be a whole lot of these philosophers, who'll come from the masses of ordinary people, if we only rely on their native abilities. We said they'd have to have a natural character consisting of elements that rarely coexist in the same Subject and are naturally separate, as a rule.

–Huh? *grumbled Amantha.* What are you talking about?

–Don't act any more stupid than you are, young lady. You know very well that often people who are good at learning, have a good memory, are quick-witted and perceptive, who have all it takes in this regard, nonetheless lack that high-minded spirit of rational thought that enables one to live a quiet, steady life of discipline. Quite on the contrary, their liveliness leaves them at the mercy of life's ups and downs, and all steadiness fails them. By the same token, you'll see that people with steady, stable characters, the people we trust the most, the people who remain stoical or even indifferent to fear in war, are – unfortunately! – just as unresponsive and slow-witted when faced with the demands of learning. They strike us as being totally stupid when they start snoring away and yawning as soon as they have to put their little grey cells to work. But we said that the norm must be to have a share of *both* these features of the true life, liveliness and steadiness, and that the aim of a rigorous, comprehensive political education is to provide a solid basis for a Subject with that sort of balance. Because it's precisely that sort of balance in each member of our political community that we want to shower with honors and distinctions. The problem is, it's a hard balance to assess. Naturally, our candidates will have to undergo the tests we were talking about a little while ago: hard labor, pressing dangers, tempting pleasures. But now we're forced to make them tackle many different forms of knowledge, too, so that we can judge whether they can tolerate the highest forms of knowledge or whether they're afraid of thought, like people who are put off by physical effort and throw in the towel after only one lap around the track. In the latter case, their education must still go on. We won't set a fixed time limit for it, so as to give each and every individual the chance he deserves.

–That's a terrific pedagogical program! *Amantha remarked.* And we should certainly try to implement it. But what are these "highest forms of knowledge" that you speak about with such relish?

–Ah! *said Socrates.* To shed some light on that point we'll have to backtrack. When I distinguished between the three different agencies of the Subject I explained what the cardinal virtues of justice, self-discipline, courage, and wisdom were. I'd already told you that in order to have a thorough knowledge of these subjective dispositions there was another, much longer path of thought, which led to total mastery of them. It was nevertheless possible, I added, to proceed by the shorter path, drawing our demonstrations from what had just been said. You young people, as is only natural, preferred that we go fast. As a result, what I told you about these virtues was seriously lacking in precision, in my own view, even if, in *your* view, it was quite enjoyable – something you can now either confirm or deny.

–We all thought it was terrific.

–Thanks, dear Amantha. But I'm not as satisfied as you are. With an investigation of this sort, a measure that doesn't fully grasp the being of the thing in question can only ever be a poor measure. The incomplete is not a measure of anything. Sometimes, though, no sooner has the investigation gotten underway than some people find it sufficient and think that there's no need to go any further.

–You can say that again! *Glaucon agreed.* There are plenty of people who, through sheer laziness, feel just the way you said.

–So, *Socrates resumed,* let's say that it's this tendency for slackness that must be especially avoided by the principled political leader or militant. Both of them, dear friends, must therefore take the long way around and confront the difficulties and hardships associated not just with physical training but with the whole of intellectual understanding. Otherwise they'll never achieve mastery of the knowledge that I stressed is both the highest and best suited to what they are, or should be.

At this, Glaucon expressed some surprise.

–What? You mean the cardinal virtues aren't the highest virtues? There's something even higher than justice, courage, wisdom, and self-discipline? *he asked.*

–Yes, *said Socrates solemnly,* yes, much higher. But even as regards the cardinal virtues, the fact that they're not the highest concern of thought should in no way allow us either to be content with looking at a mere sketch, as we've been doing till now, or to give up trying to achieve the most finished picture. Let me repeat: the incomplete is not a measure of anything. We'd be comical characters and would deserve the fate Aristophanes inflicts on us in his play *The Clouds* – in which I appear as a ludicrous impostor – if we were to devote all our energies to dealing as clearly and precisely as possible with insignificant concerns of thought while at the same time treating the highest concerns carelessly.

But Glaucon wouldn't let him off the hook so easily.

–Great! *he exclaimed.* In a nutshell, you're saying something along the lines of "what's most important is more important than what's less important." If that's not a tautology then I don't know what is! So how am I, the disciple, the novice, supposed to react to this? Am I supposed to say "Yes, sure!" or "Certainly!"? Or maybe you'd prefer "But of course!" – or there's also "By all means!," "That's right!," "Nothing could be more certain!," "Absolutely!," and plenty of others. Have you read my brother Plato's write-ups of the dialogues? All the young people in them speak like that; they're all a bunch of yes-men. But *I'm* going to ask you a real question for once. Do you think we're going to be satisfied with these sorts of methodological clichés, Socrates? Do you think you can go on like this without telling us what that highest form of knowledge is that you talk about in veiled terms, whose object we haven't a clue about?

–Not at all, *said an angry Socrates.* All you have to do is ask me.

–But that's exactly what I'm doing!

–What you *pretend* to be doing. Because you've heard me, on numerous occasions, express my views on the subject. Now, either you've forgotten everything I said, or, as sometimes happens with you, you're trying, much to your own satisfaction, to pick a fight that can throw your old teacher off balance. But I won't fall for it, I can see right through you. All of you have heard me say many times here that the highest form of knowledge has to do with the Idea of the True. You all know perfectly well that justice and the other cardinal virtues are of use for the constitution of a Subject only to the extent that they're rationally bound up with this greatest idea of all. And right now our wily friend Glaucon knows very well what's going to happen: I'm going to repeat the same views. But this time, so as not to sound like a broken record, as you increasingly seem to think I do, I'm going to add an enigmatic contradiction. On the one hand, we only know the Idea of the True imperfectly. But on the other hand, if we *didn't* know it, even assuming we had perfect knowledge about everything else, that knowledge would be as good as useless to us. Without the Idea, we have nothing. I can't imagine that, in your opinion, there'd be any real advantage to be gained for the Subject in acquiring everything, with the exception of the True, or in having knowledge of everything, except for the True. Because in that case, for lack of the Idea of the True, the Subject would know nothing that could be said to be surely and truly beautiful or good about the world.

–A life without that Idea would sure be a dreary life, *said Amantha.*

But Socrates was off and running and wasn't listening to anyone anymore.

–As you know, most people say: "Only pleasure is true." Of course, a few snobs claim that knowledge is our true resource, or the resource of the True. What's so ridiculous is that these snobs, who define truth in terms of knowledge, are incapable of explaining what knowledge is. They end up saying that knowledge is the knowledge of. . . the True. All they do is go round in circles.

–They crack us up, *chuckled Glaucon.*

–Especially since they look down on us for not knowing what truth is, and then they turn around and give us their "definition" of knowledge, which assumes that we know all there is to know about truth! They go on and on with their pretentious dictum "all knowledge is knowledge of the true," as though they were talking to people who could instantly understand what's meant as soon as they hear the words "true" or "truth" – while only a minute before they were accusing us of not understanding a thing.

–It's hilarious!

–That said, the people in the other clique, the ones who restrict the sphere of the true and genuine to pleasure, may be in the majority, but they spout just as much nonsense as the little contingent of snobs, because they have no choice but to admit that there are false pleasures. Consequently, at the end of the day they're stuck with the paradox whereby certain specific things – some sensual pleasures, for example – are both true and false: true in that there's not a shadow of a doubt that we experience their subjective force, but false in that the devastating consequences of that force remain invisible for a long time. That's, moreover, why this business about pleasure being the true and the good of Subjects still gives rise today – long after the death of its most fervent advocate, the formidable Democritus – to endless debates.

–OK, we won't take sides with either of the two cliques, *Glaucon conceded.* That said, we haven't budged an inch with regard to our famous "Idea of the True," which, by the way, I think it would greatly simplify matters just to call "Truth."

–And yet, *said Socrates pensively.* . .

Then, after a silence and as though he were coming out of his trance, he said:

–Let's begin with what we see every day. When it comes to justice or moral elegance, most people are satisfied with appearances. The fact that such appearances are utterly worthless in no way stops them from trying to adapt their actions, desires, and ways of being to them. But as soon as it's a question of Truth, no one's content to rely on appearances anymore. They seek the reality of what is, and as a result everyone starts to disdain mere opinion. So we come back to the contradiction we encountered at the beginning: every Subject pursues Truth or makes it the guiding principle of its action, but he can barely only guess, in a very general way, what Truth is. Truth inflicts the torture of a speculative aporia on the Subject, because the Subject is unable to have a clear understanding of what it is in essence, or even to have a stable belief about it, of the sort that gives him access to all the other things. Moreover, without a clear relationship with Truth, the Subject can no longer get any proper benefit out of these other things. Indeed, without the Idea of the True, the Subject can no longer even make out, over the vast expanse of the visible, the things that have genuine value for him.

But then, as impetuous as ever, Amantha burst out:

–If this Idea of the True has all the virtues and untold beneficial effects that you attribute to it, dear Socrates, is it really fair, as you seem to have accepted that it is, for it to remain nearly invisible to the Subject, or at any rate shrouded in deep mystery, even to those Subjects who are faithful to our fifth system of government and will hold the material and spiritual destiny of the whole country in their hands?

Laying his right hand tenderly on the young woman's shoulder, Socrates said:

–Be without fear, you who love the light. You're perfectly right. If just and beautiful existents are kept apart from that owing to which they exist in Truth as well, the person responsible for guarding them, knowing nothing about the immanent relationship between the Idea of the True and justice and beauty, will be unable to ensure either their continued existence over time or their beneficial effects. Like a prophet-philosopher – if ever there could be such a character – I prophesy that all the cardinal virtues will remain largely unknown so long as their relationship with Truth hasn't been clarified. Our concept of politics – our "fifth system of government," our communism – will only achieve its definitive, organized form if people possess the knowledge afforded by such a clarification.

–That's exactly what I'm worried about, *insisted Amantha,* because I can't figure out what *you,* Socrates, think of this Idea of the True, this famous Truth, which everything is dependent on. Is it a form of knowledge? Is it the personal experience of joy? Or something I can't even imagine?

–Oh, young lady! I was sure that, when it came to a crucial issue, you wouldn't be satisfied with other people's opinions!

–Stop stalling, Socrates! This isn't about me, it's about you. I don't think it's right that you're perfectly able to explain other people's views to me but you clam up when you're asked to explain your own. What's more, you've been dealing with this Truth business for the longest time now, which makes matters even worse for you.

–But would you think it right, *Socrates shot back,* for someone to talk about what he doesn't know as if he *did* know?

–That's just another diversionary tactic. I didn't say "as if he *did* know." I asked if you'd please speak about what you believe like someone who really does believe it.

–Come on now! You know very well that beliefs, detached from knowledge, are all pathetic things! The best of them are blind. Can you see any significant difference between blind men who just happen to be walking straight and believers who just happen to believe something true? Are you stubbornly set on contemplating pathetic, blind, misshapen things rather than hearing about radiant, beautiful things from other people?

Amantha, disappointed, didn't reply but just sat there sulking. After a few moments' silence, an irritated Glaucon leapt into the fray:

–Damn it, Socrates! Don't just give up as though you were at the end of your rope! You explained the really difficult ideas of justice,

subjective harmony, and the other cardinal virtues. I'm begging you –
do the same for the Idea of the True!

–I don't think I'm up to it. When it comes to this issue, inappropriate and ineffectual enthusiasm will make people laugh. So, dear
friends, at the risk of disappointing you, I suggest that, for the time
being, we drop the question of the True, conceived of as an ontological question. What a truth is in and of itself is so difficult a problem
that even our powerful surge of intellectual energy tonight won't be
sufficient to get us to the conception I have of its solution. To be nice
to you, though, I'm willing to talk to you about the *child* of the True,
the one who most closely resembles it. If that won't do, then let's drop
the whole thing.

–I guess we'll just have to make do with that, *grumbled Glaucon.*
You can pay your debt to us some other time by talking about the
father.

–Let's hope I can repay that paternal capital to you some day, and
that you're able to make good use of it. I wouldn't want us to have
to make do forever, as we have to now, with just the interest the
child represents. But even so, take the interest, this child of the True-
in-itself. Just be very careful that I don't inadvertently cheat you by
giving you falsified accounts of the interest.

–Don't worry, we'll be keeping an eye on you! *exclaimed Glaucon.*
Now let's see those accounts.

–Not so fast! First let's agree on our method of exposition, and
remember what we claimed at the beginning of the night, as we have
so often in the past. We assert the being of many beautiful things,
many truths and many other multiplicities; we distinguish between
them all by rational thought. To that end, we also assert the being of
the beautiful in itself, of the true in itself, and likewise of everything
whose multiple-being we posited. We subsume this multiple-being
under the single idea that corresponds to it, stressing its uniqueness
and calling it "the that-which-is." And we also claim that perceptible
multiplicities are exposed to seeing but not to thinking, while we
call "idea" – which other people sometimes call "essence," a term I
dislike – that which, of these multiplicities, is exposed in its being to
thinking, not merely to seeing. Let's just add something obvious to
this brief summary: we perceive the visible through sight, the audible
through hearing, and the other perceptible multiplicities through their
corresponding senses. Let's suppose now, to cut to the chase, that a
designer designed our senses. We'll then notice that this designer lavished a lot more care on the power of seeing and being seen than he
did on the other sensory faculties.

–I haven't noticed anything of the sort, *said Glaucon.*

–Pay close attention: do hearing and sound need something additional of another kind in order for the one to hear and the other to be heard, such that, absent this third element, the one won't be able to hear and the other won't be able to be heard?

–I haven't noticed, *Glaucon repeated,* that, apart from hearing and sound, anything else is required in order to hear or be heard.

–I think that, just as with hearing, this additional something isn't required by many of the other senses either. Maybe even all can do without it. Can you think of any exception?

–No, I'm not aware of any, *ventured Glaucon, digging himself in deeper.*

–Well, you're wrong! Sight and the visible *do* require something additional.

–They do? I can't think what it would be, *groaned Glaucon.*

–Sight is located in the eyes, right? The presence of color distinguishes visible objects, right? Yet if an element of a third sort, expressly adapted for the purpose of visual perception, isn't added to them, sight won't see anything and colors will remain invisible.

–So what is this mysterious third element? *asked Glaucon in despair.*

–You call it light.

–Oh, of course! *Amantha chimed in.*

–The grandeur of the word "light" is a sign that the relationship between the sense of seeing and the ability to be seen is qualitatively superior to the relationship that yokes the other senses to their own particular spheres. Unless, of course, you don't think much of light?

–Who could ever resign himself to living in eternal darkness? *said Amantha with a smile.*

–And who is it that dispenses this extremely precious light to us? Who's the master – among all the Others hidden up there in the heavens – of this subtle mediation thanks to which sight can see and the visible can be seen as perfectly as possible?

–You wouldn't happen to be talking about the Sun, would you, the natural ruler of the visible? *asked Glaucon.*

–Of course I am! But let's be careful about the true nature of the link between sight and this sun-god. Sight in itself isn't identical to the sun, any more than is its organ, which we call the eye. However, if I may be allowed to put it this way, the eye is the most sun-like of all the sense organs. As a matter of fact, it's quite possible to think that the faculty of sight is dispensed to us by our sun-god when he infuses a sort of luminous fluid into our eyes. We also note that the sun itself is not sight, since it's one of sight's causes, but that it's nonetheless seen by sight.

–That's all indisputable. But so what?

–Well, here he is, that child of the True whose arrival I announced to you earlier! It's the sun, which Truth produces as its favorite symbol, because the place that Truth occupies in the timeless realm of the thinkable, with regard to thought and what thought thinks, is exactly the same as the place the sun occupies in the empirical realm of the visible, with regard to sight and what sight sees.

–But the problem, *said Glaucon, laughing,* is that for the time being I'm not sure I see what you're thinking.

–Listen carefully. You know that if we turn to look at things whose colors are no longer bathed in bright daylight but only in the flickering lights of nighttime our eyes see so dimly that you can almost say they're blind and our vision is lacking all clarity. But if it's at the things the sun bathes in its radiance that we turn to look, then our eyes see clearly and, even though they're the same as they were during the night, it's now evident that they're enjoying perfectly clear vision.

–Sure, sure, *muttered Amantha.* I bet you're going to suggest an analogy or an "isomorphism," as you put it, between the sun and the Idea of the True. On the one hand, there's sight, the visible, and the sun, and on the other thought, the thinkable, and Truth. But I'd really like to know, in detail, exactly how that analogy works.

–You're so impatient, young lady!

–And you – if you'll forgive my saying so – are so slow.

–Oh, *said Socrates, smiling,* you mean what your brother Plato calls my "long detours"! But you're right. Let's cut straight to the analogy, let's skip directly from the individual insofar as he sees to the Subject insofar as he thinks. When a Subject turns toward Being's and Truth's mutual illumination, he thinks and knows everything lying within that illumination, and he is himself bathed in the radiance of thought. But when, on the contrary, he turns toward what's mingled with darkness, toward what merely arises and passes away, toward the warm life of the senses rather than toward the star caught in the net of mathematics, he falls prey to unenlightened opinions to such an extent that, tossed about every which way by these shifting opinions, it seems as if the power of thinking fails him and he's less a Subject than a human animal at bay.

–How awful! *exclaimed a horrified Glaucon.*

But Socrates went on, as if in a speculative dream:

–What simultaneously imparts veridical knowledge to known beings and the power of such knowledge to knowing beings is, you can be sure, the Idea of the True. It is the basis on which scientific knowledge and exactness are possible, once it's been attained by the understanding. And yet, as sublime as this scientific knowledge and exactness may be, it's only by positing the Idea of the True as different from, and even more sublime than, they are that we can take its full measure. We already said that, although it's perfectly correct to regard light and sight as partaking in the form of the sun, it's nevertheless wrong to equate them with the sun itself. Similarly, we'll say that it's correct to regard science and veridical knowledge as partaking in Truth, but it's wrong to equate them with Truth itself, because a higher rank should be accorded to the specific nature of Truth.

At this, Amantha gushed:

–Obviously, for you, Truth's value is clearly immeasurable, if it produces knowledge and all the exact sciences and if, in addition, it must be ranked higher still!

And Glaucon added:

–I see that your supreme value is in no way, shape, or form the same as pleasure.

–You birdbrain! *Amantha snorted.* Socrates already disposed of that equivalence last night!

Did Socrates even hear them, though? He had stood up and, with his eyes closed, was speaking slowly and softly, his voice like a gentle murmur in the splendor of the morning.

–The sun doesn't merely give the visible world the passive power of being seen; it gives it active attributes as well: becoming, the rise of the sap, and nourishment. And this is the case even though the sun, the luminous exception that creates our whole daytime sky, is none of that. Likewise, only insofar as it is in truth can what is knowable be said to be known in its being. But it's also to Truth that it owes not only its being known in its being but also its being-known as such, or, in other words, that which, of its being, can only be termed "being" insofar as it is exposed to thought. Truth itself, however, is not of the order of that which is exposed to thought, for it is the sublation of that order, thus being accorded a distinct rank in terms of both its precedence and its power.[1]

Glaucon, all smiles, exclaimed:

–What divine transcendence!

On hearing this, Socrates seemed to come out of his trance:

–Transcendence? That's what you reduce. . .? Oh, never mind. It's all your fault. Why did you force me to explain my views on this subject?

207

–Go on, dear Socrates, *said Amantha soothingly,* go on. Don't pay any attention to my brother's jokes.

And since she wanted to get the Socrates machine going again by any means necessary, she added:

–You said that Sun and Truth are both rulers, the one over the visible order and sphere, the other over the thinkable order and sphere. I have no trouble at all imagining these two varieties of being, or rather these two kinds of things, the visible and the thinkable. But how are they connected, once they're placed in their generic element, light in the one case and Truth in the other?

–Well, all right, *Socrates conceded.* I'll try to enlighten us about this issue, which is the unclearest one of all. But I'm warning you – no more waxing lyrical! Only diagrams from now on, proportions: mathematics.

–OK, we've been forewarned, *sighed Glaucon.*

–Let AB be a line that's divided by a point C into two unequal segments, AC and CB. Segment AC represents that which, of being, is set out in the sphere of the visible, and segment CB, that which, of being, is exposed to thought.

–The sensible and the intelligible, in a nutshell.

–They say that's how your brother Plato sums up my doctrine. It's a lot more complicated than that, but never mind. Let's agree (this is an arbitrary but useful symbolic decision) that AC : CB = 1 : 2, in other words, with respect to the same being – any multiplicity – the dignity of that of it which is exposed to thought is twice the dignity associated with its sensible appearance.

–That's because that which of a being is exposed to thought takes in, and in a certain way doubles, what's directly given of it in the sphere of the visible, *commented Amantha.*

–Sure, why not? But let's continue. In terms of their relative clarity or obscurity, a point D divides segment AC – the sphere of the visible – into two parts, whose ratio is again 1 : 2. Segment AD represents images. By that I mean everything from shadows to our big movie screens, by way of reflections in water, mirrors, and all polished, shiny bodies.

–And of course, *Glaucon interjected,* the fact that AD is only half of DC shows how little ontological dignity those imaginary copies have. But what does DC represent?

–The visible objects in the world, what can be experienced, what is there. Everything that has to do with us human beings, but plants, too, and the whole category of tools, for instance. I'm sure you'll easily acknowledge that what's at work here is a division based on truth or the lack thereof, and its underlying principle is that the relationship between a thing that resembles another thing and the other thing it resembles is the same as the relationship, given any content whatsoever, that one's opinion of it bears to the knowledge one constructs of it.

–"Easily," *said Glaucon, grinning,* is saying a lot!

–Things will be clearer if we divide the segment of the thinkable as well. Let a point E be located between C and B such that CE : EB = 1 : 2. Section CE represents what I call analytical thought. In this section, the Subject proceeds by using real objects from the previous section as illustrations. He is therefore forced to conduct his investigation on the basis of hypotheses and to draw a conclusion without ever reaching the first principle of its conclusion. In the second section, EB, the Subject arrives at the anhypothetical principle, on the basis of a hypothesis, of course, but without needing to use any illustrations, since his method makes use of the Forms, and the Forms alone.

–I don't understand a thing, *said Glaucon.*

–OK, let's start over then. How do people who study geometry or arithmetic proceed? They assume the existence of the series of whole numbers, of plane figures, angular values, and many other things related to the problem they're dealing with. They use all this material as if it were a matter of assumptions that are well known and sufficiently obvious that, were they to adopt them as initial hypotheses, they wouldn't have to justify them, to themselves any more than to anyone else. Then, starting from these assumptions, they explain everything that follows immanently from them, and they consequently arrive at the conclusion they had in mind.

–Fine, fine, *said Amantha.* We did math, too, you know!

–So you made use of visible figures, too, and reasoned about them, even though the aim of your thinking wasn't to grasp *them* but other, purely thinkable ones instead, which the visible figures merely resemble. Indeed, mathematical demonstration has to do with the Square in itself, or the Diagonal in itself, not the diagonal line that you ineptly drew. Mathematicians use all these figures – whether modeled in space or drawn on visible surfaces, and of which there can be shadows or reflections in water – as if they were images by means of which they can arrive at the intuition of those beings that can only be grasped by analytical thought; all this is what the first section of thinkable being represents. When the Subject applies himself to investigating it, he's forced to use hypotheses and cannot arrive at the first principle, unable as he is to rise above the hypotheses.

–But why is that? *asked Amantha worriedly.*

–Because the Subject still uses, as illustrations, real objects that we classified in the second section of the sphere of the visible, the objects that have their own shadowy images in the very first section. Thus, even though the Subject is established in thought, he's still dependent on the sphere of the visible and on the relation of resemblance governing it.

–Wow, you're really giving mathematicians a bad rap!

–Bad, but only within the framework of the greatest good! But now listen and learn what I call the second section of being insofar as it's exposed to pure thought. The path of reasoning here is based on the power of dialectical reasoning[2] alone: my hypotheses aren't treated as principles but as being and remaining hypotheses that serve as aids and steps on the way up to a universal anhypothetical principle. Once that principle's been arrived at, the discursive process turns back down and goes through all the consequences of the principle right to the conclusion, never using anything from the world of the senses but moving instead from one Form to another by means of intermediate steps that are themselves formal ones, and finally it concludes with a Form.

Glaucon, as he often did, then attempted to put into logical form – so to speak – what he had understood of the Teacher's explanation:

–You're saying that it's more effective to theorize Being grasped in its exposition to thought via dialectical reasoning's means of acquiring knowledge than to rely on scientific techniques, the model of which is geometry. Of course, mathematicians, who treat hypotheses as principles, are forced to proceed discursively rather than empirically. But, since their intuiting remains dependent on hypotheses and has no means of accessing a first principle, they don't seem to you to have a true thinking of what they theorize, which, however, if reconsidered in the light of the principle, would indeed be an integral thinking of Being. It seems to me that you call the procedure used by geometers and others like them analytical thought and that you make a distinction between it and dialectical thought. You locate analytical thought somewhere between opinion (which is assigned to section AD of our diagram) and pure thought, or dialectical intellection (which is assigned to the highest section, EB). And this, moreover, explains why section EC, to which analytical thought corresponds, is as long as section CD, to which the objects of opinion correspond – a striking contrast with the difference between section AD, to which images correspond, and EB, the section of the dialectic, a difference on the order of one to four. Mathematics also demonstrates. . .

–Nice technique, an excellent summary! *Socrates cut in.* We can view things and call them as follows: *(With a piece of coal, Socrates then drew on the tablecloth of the big table the complete diagram of the different states of Being as it comes into appearing and as a Subject may be constituted within it.)*

–Make the four states that coordinate the Subject's coming-to-be correspond to the four sections. For the largest section, EB, let's speak of "pure thought," "intellection," or, better yet, "dialectical thought." For the one that comes next, CE, we'll use the phrase "discursive thought," or "understanding," or, better yet, "analytical thought." For the third one, DC, let's say "certainty," and for the fourth, AD, "assumption." We're effectively assuming that an image refers to some real referent, and we're certain that real objects exist. The existence of mathematical idealities is in turn assumed in analytical thought. But we're certain of the universality of the ideal

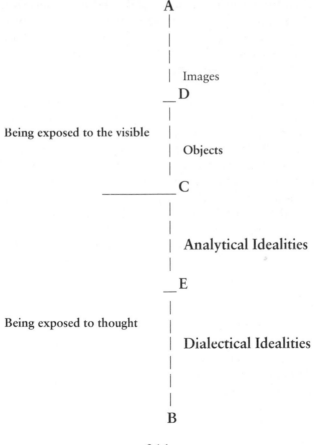

principles to which dialectical thinking leads us. This order can also be expressed thus: the more a being is given in the element of Truth, the more the Subject can think it in its own clarity.

–Which would mean that objective truth and subjective clarity, *Amantha mused aloud,* are two aspects of the same process.

–You're making me sound a little too much like Descartes! But since you mentioned light, I'll try and paint you a picture, with shadow and light intermingled.

–After the matheme, it's back to the poem! *said Glaucon playfully.*

–Well, why not? Imagine an enormous movie theater. Down front, the screen, which goes right up to the ceiling (but it's so high that everything up there gets lost in the dark) blocks anything other than itself from being seen. It's a full house. For as long as they've been around, the audience members have been chained to their seats, with their eyes staring at the screen and their heads held in place by rigid headphones covering their ears. Behind these tens of thousands of spectators shackled to their seats there's an immense wooden walkway, at head level, running parallel to the whole length of the screen. Still further back are enormous projectors flooding the screen with an almost unbearable white light.

–What a strange place! *said Glaucon.*

–Hardly any more than our Earth. . . All sorts of robots, dolls, cardboard cut-outs, puppets, operated and manipulated by invisible puppeteers or guided by remote-control, move along the walkway. Animals, stretcher-bearers, scythe-bearers, cars, storks, ordinary people, armed soldiers, gangs of youths from the *banlieues,* turtle doves, cultural coordinators, naked women, and so forth go back and forth continuously in this way. Some of them shout, others talk, others play the cornet or the concertina, while others just hurry silently along. On the screen can be seen the shadows of this chaotic parade thrown by the projectors. And through their headphones the immobilized crowd can hear sounds and words.

–My God! *Amantha burst out.* That's one weird show and an even weirder audience!

–They're just like us. Can they see anything of themselves, of the people sitting next to them, of the movie theater, and of the bizarre scenes on the walkway other than the shadows projected onto the screen by the flood of lights? Can they hear anything other than what their headsets deliver to them?

–Not a thing, for sure, *exclaimed Glaucon,* if their heads have always been prevented from looking anywhere but at the screen and their ears have been blocked by the headphones.

–And that *is* the case. So they have no perception of the visible other than through the mediation of the shadows, and none of what's being said other than through the mediation of the sound waves. Even assuming they could figure out ways of talking among themselves, they'd necessarily equate the shadow, which they *can* see, with the object, which they *can't* see, which that shadow is the shadow of.

–Not to mention, *added Amantha,* that the object on the walkway, whether it's a robot or a puppet, is already a copy itself. We could say that all they see is a shadow of a shadow.

–And that all they hear, *Glaucon completed,* is the digital copy of a physical copy of human voices.

–I'm afraid so! This captive audience has no way of deducing that the substance of the True is anything other than the shadow of a simulacrum. But what would happen if, once their chains were broken and their delusions cured, their situation changed completely? Careful now! Our fable is about to take quite a different turn. Imagine that they unchain one member of the audience, suddenly force him to stand up, turn his head right and left, walk around and look at the light streaming out of the projectors. Naturally he'll suffer from all these actions that he's not used to. Dazzled by the flood of light, he won't be able to see any of the things whose shadows he was calmly gazing at before this forced conversion. Suppose they tell him that his former situation only allowed him to see what was tantamount to idle chatter in the world of illusion, and that it's only now that he's close to things as they really are, that he can face things as they really are, so that his vision is finally likely to be correct. Wouldn't he be stunned and ill at ease? It would be even worse if they showed him the parade of robots, dolls, puppets, and marionettes on the walkway and they grilled him with lots of questions to try and get him to say what they were. Because the shadows from before would most certainly still be truer for him than anything they showed him.

–And, *Amantha remarked,* in a certain way they really *would* be. Isn't a shadow that's been validated by repeated experience more "real" than some doll you're suddenly shown that you have no idea where it came from?

His face expressionless, Socrates, perhaps as furious as he was amazed, stared in silence at Amantha, then said:

–No doubt we should go on to the end of the fable before coming to any conclusion as to what the real is. Let's suppose our guinea pig is forced to stare at the projectors. His eyes hurt horribly, he wants to run away, he wants to go back to what he can endure seeing, those shadows whose being he considers a lot more real than that of the

213

objects they're showing him. But all of a sudden a bunch of tough guys in our pay grab him and drag him roughly through the aisles of the movie theater. They make him go through a little side door that was hidden up till then. They throw him into a filthy tunnel through which you emerge into the open air, onto a sunlit mountainside in spring. Dazzled by the light, he covers his eyes with a trembling hand; our agents push him up the steep slope, for a long time, higher and higher! Still higher! They finally get to the top, in full sun, and there they release him, run back down the mountain and disappear. So there he is, all alone, with this boundless landscape stretching out all around him. All that light plays havoc with his mind. And oh, how he suffers from having been dragged, pushed around, and left out in the open like that! How he hates our mercenaries! Gradually, though, he attempts to look over toward the mountaintops and the valleys, at the whole dazzling world. At first he's blinded by the glare of everything and can see nothing of all the things about which we routinely say: "This exists, this is really here." He's hardly someone who, like Hegel standing before the Jungfrau, could say, with total disdain, "*das ist*," it just is.[3] He nevertheless tries to get used to the light. Sitting beneath a solitary tree, he's finally able, after many attempts, to make out the shadow cast by the trunk and the dark outline of the foliage, which remind him of the screen from his former world. In a pool of water at the base of a big rock he manages to see the reflection of flowers and grass. From there he eventually gets to the objects themselves. Slowly, he begins to marvel at the shrubs, the pine trees, a lone sheep. Night falls. Lifting his eyes to the sky, he sees the moon and the constellations; he sees Venus rise.[4] On. Rigid upright on an old tree stump, he watches for the radiant one. It emerges from out the last rays and sinking ever brighter is engulfed in its turn. Venus! Finally, one morning, he sees the sun, not in the ever-changing waters, or in its purely external reflection, but the sun itself, in and for itself, in its own place. He looks at it, contemplates it, ecstatic that it is the way it is.

–Oh! *cried Amantha*. What an ascension you're describing for us! What a conversion!

–Thank you, young lady. Would you do as he does? For he, our anonymous hero, by applying his thinking to what he sees, proves that the hours and seasons depend on the visible position of the sun and that the being-there of the visible is thus dependent on this heavenly body, and consequently he can say: yes, the sun is the ruler of all the objects of which my old fellow-prisoners, the audience in the big locked-down movie theater, only see the shadow of a shadow.

Recalling his first home – the screen, the projector, the artificial images, his comrades in deception – this way, our reluctant escapee is glad to have been forced to leave it and takes pity on all the others who've remained shackled to the seats they sit in as blind viewers.

–But pity, *objected Amantha*, is seldom a wise counselor.

–Oh, *replied Socrates, fixing his little beady black eyes on her,* you're a typical girl all right, fierce and heartless! Let's get back to pure thought then. In the realm of artificiality, in the cave of illusion, who had the starring role? Who could pride himself on having it all over the others? Who but someone whose sharp eye and sense memory took note of the passing shadows, recognizing the ones that came back often, the ones that were rarely seen, the ones that came in groups or always came by themselves. Someone, in short, who was the best able to guess what was going to occur next on the constraining surface of the visible. Do you think that, after contemplating the sun, our escaped prisoner would be jealous of those prophets of shadow play? That he'd envy their superiority and would care about enjoying the advantages they got out of it, however great they might be? Wouldn't he be more like Achilles in the *Odyssey*, who would have preferred a hundred times over being a serf working behind a plow to living as he was doing, in purely bogus luxury?

–Oh, Socrates! I can see that *you're* only too delighted to take refuge behind Homer too! *Amanda teased him.*

–Well, I am Greek, after all, *muttered Socrates, on the defensive.*

–What if, *Glaucon, fearing a quarrel, cut in,* we imagined that our escaped prisoner really did go back down into the cave?

–He'd have to, *said Socrates solemnly.* At any rate, if he returns to his old seat, this time it will be the darkness that suddenly blinds him after the bright light of the sun. And if, before his eyes get used to the dark again, he starts competing with his old fellow-prisoners who've never left their seats to guess what's going to be projected next onto the screen, it's a safe bet he'll be the laughing stock of the row. They'll all whisper that he went out into the light and climbed so high only to return nearsighted and stupid. The immediate consequence will be that no one will have the slightest desire to do the same. And if, obsessed with the desire to share the Idea of the sun, the visible Idea of the True, with them, he attempts to release them and lead them out so that, like him, they may know what a new day is like, I think they'd seize him and kill him.

–Oh, come on, you're overdoing it! *said Glaucon.*

–That's because one of those seedy prophets your sister was making fun of last night predicted that they're going to kill me, Socrates, because at age 70 I'll still be stubbornly asking where the exit from this dark world is, where the real day is.

A sort of melancholy mood suddenly took hold of them. Nobody said a word, and they could hear, as though from afar, the sound of the sea, or maybe it was the wind coming up. Socrates gave a little cough, drank a glass of water, and launched back into the discussion:

–What we've got to do now, dear friends, is perfectly obvious: connect the fictional presentation that we just so thoroughly enjoyed – the story about someone who escapes from the great cosmic movie theater – and the symbolic or, more precisely, geometric presentation I proposed an hour ago, namely, the line on which the four types of relationship to the real, from images to the dialectical idea by way of opinions and the analytical idea, are marked off in unequal segments.

–That won't be easy to do, *remarked Glaucon.* We've got two worlds on one side and four procedures on the other.

–But that four is divided into two: the perceptible and the thinkable. Roughly, very roughly, we'll compare what's set out visibly as appearance to the shadows that the prisoners in the movie theater see. Then we'll equate the light of the projectors with the power of the sun. Let's posit that the escaped prisoner's anabasis[5] into the mountains and his contemplation of the mountain peaks is the Subject's ascension into the realm of thought. These analogies, my young friends, correspond to what I hope is true and to what you're so eager to know about. Only from the point of view of the Other, not of the individual – that paltry thing, even were he Socrates – can it be determined whether my hopes are justified. All I can say is that everything that ever appeared to me, regardless of the time or place of the experience, was set out in accordance with a single principle governing its appearance. At the far limits of knowledge, almost beyond its scope, is what I improperly call the Idea of Truth – "improperly," since I already told you that Truth, because it underpins the ideality of every Idea, could not itself be an Idea like the others. That's incidentally why it's so hard to construct a concept of it. Nevertheless, if we do manage to do so, we'll be forced to conclude that it's in accordance with this "Idea" that everything that is, is exposed to the radiance of the exactness and beauty it possesses. And if we go on with our analogies we'll say that the lord of light's gift of light and his action as we experience them in the sphere of the visible correspond exactly to the advent, in accordance with the Idea of the True, of particular truths as well as of their corresponding thought in the realm of the intelligible.

–But that analogy is shaky, *said Amantha, frowning.*

–Oh, *retorted an oddly jubilant Socrates,* so you don't think there

216

could ever be any agreement between a geometric image and a poetic one? Well, quite apart from this incompatibility, won't you grant me that it's only by complying with Truth's injunctions that an individual can act rationally, regardless of whether the context of his action is public or private?

Glaucon answered for Amantha, who was obviously dissatisfied with this response:

–Well, *that*, at any rate, can't be denied.

–You'll also grant me, with no resistance or surprise, that the prisoners who escaped from the cosmic movie theater, the ones who made it to the top of the mountain and contemplated the sun from there, will have no desire whatsoever to be involved in messy human affairs. As they've been incorporated into a Subject-of-truth, their only desire will be to remain up there forever. Which is only natural, after all, if our movie theater allegory truly expresses the reality of this whole process, don't you think?

–Yes, *said a stunned Glaucon,* I do!

–In that case, no one should be surprised if someone who suddenly plummets down from contemplation of the Other to the petty affairs of human life should seem distraught and vaguely ridiculous. Unaccustomed to the dark into which he's once again been plunged, he's suddenly forced to defend himself in law courts or before other state institutions, places where, as far as justice is concerned, what's at stake is only its shadow, or, at best, fake objects projected by an artificial light onto the screen of the world. As regards these images, he'll be hard pressed to compete with people who are experts in them, precisely because they've never had any intuition of justice in itself.

–The mere absence of surprise doesn't constitute a proof, *said Amantha.*

–What, you're speaking in riddles now? *said Socrates caustically.* If you were to tackle our problem more sensibly, you'd remember that sight can be disturbed in two different ways, by two different causes, depending on whether one's going from the light to the dark or from the dark to the light. And maybe, if you racked your brains, you'd come to the conclusion that these remarks about sight apply equally well to the Subject. So then, my dear, if you were to see someone so confused that he can't even understand a common notion, you wouldn't laugh like a fool but would instead wonder if the aforementioned Subject, suddenly dragged from an existence that was amply exposed to its own light, weren't quite simply blinded by his lack of experience of the dark. Or whether, on the contrary, going from darkest ignorance to a little more light, he weren't blinded by the unbearable glare. In the first case, you'd know that you were dealing with someone whose affects and entire life were bound up with happiness. In the second case, you ought to feel sorry for the poor guy, but if you nonetheless felt like laughing cruelly at him, that laughter would be less ridiculous than if it had been elicited by someone who came from the radiant world above.

–I repent, dear teacher! *said Amantha, giving in with a smile.*

–May your repentance open your mind to the essential conclusions. And to this one, first and foremost: education isn't what some people claim it is. I'm thinking of all those psychologists and teachers who boast that they can introduce knowledge where it's lacking – in Subjects in whom they assume any cognitive ability to be nonexistent – exactly the way you'd transplant the faculty of sight into a blind eye. Yet what we've just understood and said is that the capacity for knowledge and the instrument that makes it possible to trigger that capacity exist in every Subject. Let's imagine an eye that could only turn from the dark to the light if the whole body were so turned. We could then imagine that it's only by turning all at once that the Subject can tear himself away from the complexities of becoming, until the indivisible intuition of being and the inherent radiance it possesses can be endured – the very thing we say is Truth.

–That's some "turning all at once!" *murmured Amantha.*

–So education isn't a matter of imposing, but rather of orienting. It's a technique of conversion, I'd say. The only thing that matters is finding the easiest, most effective way to ensure this turning around of the Subject. The point isn't to impose sight on it – it already has that. But, since its sight is turned in the wrong direction, not toward the proper things, every effort should be made to reorient it.

–But how? *asked Glaucon.* What sorts of exercises or techniques can effect a reorientation like that?

–A *conversion* like that, you mean, *said Amantha.* I love that word "conversion." I love that Socrates is attempting to extricate it from its religious usage.

–It may be, *Socrates resumed,* that most of the capacities that are called "subjective faculties" have a family resemblance with the body's capabilities: you can produce them in someone who lacks them at first by using all the resources of repetition, habit, exercise, and so on. But the faculty we call "thought" is an exception to any sort of parallelism between the Subject and his bodily medium. Since it's of the order of the Other, thought can never lose its own power. Whether it's useful and beneficial, or, on the contrary, useless and harmful therefore depends only on the direction in which that power is turned.

–You're clearing up something I've always been struck by, *Glaucon put in.* It has to do with people who are said to be bad but cunning. I've noticed that, in spite or because of their execrable character, they have very sharp eyesight and can distinguish in the minutest detail the despicable goals they're after, as well as the obstacles standing in their way. What you're telling us is that, in people like that, the Subject's eye isn't blind at all, but, because it's turned in the wrong direction, it's forced to be at the service of evil.

–I'm afraid so! *Socrates agreed.* And as a result we get the following paradox: the clearer such people see, the more wicked they are.

–But then how can a Subject's sight be reoriented in the right direction, the direction you sometimes call "incorporation into a truth?" *Glaucon worriedly asked.*

–No doubt there will have to be a kind of preparation for it, for which I can give you a metaphor. Suppose that, right from childhood, we operate on people's animal nature by removing, the way you do to release a hot air balloon and accelerate its lift-off, those lead weights that are the equivalent of everything in us that takes pleasure in ordinary passive becoming. If we turned the Subject's eye away from the seductive visions that the products of the global market tempt it with – glittery cookie packages, inflatable dolls that mimic naked women, cars loaded with chrome, computers used for moronic multi-conversations, in short, everything that turns that eye toward low and meaningless things – if, once this surgical ablation had been performed, we turned the eye toward truths instead, so that it could see them, and if we immediately urged the whole individual to incorporate himself into the Subject who orients them, then we'd see that, in these same people you're talking about, the same eye can see these truths with the same clarity that's currently turning it toward the utter worthlessness of bad things, and so we're justified in assuming that the same positive capacity for thinking exists in all people, without exception.

–That's the egalitarian foundation of our communism, *Glaucon pointed out.*

–And it's a lot more subjective than economic, *added Amantha.*

–Sure, sure, *said an annoyed Glaucon.* But some day it'll have to be both.

–Let's take it one step at a time, kids! *exclaimed Socrates.* One of the inevitable consequences of what we were just saying is that two different types of people would be – or, in the disastrous present circumstances, *are* – incapable of assuming leadership positions. First, those whose total lack of education – the neglect in which they were left – produces a sort of cynical indifference to truths. Second, those who, having jumped off the social merry-go-round, devote their entire solitary lives to intellectual pursuits. The former lack the one aim in life to which their public or private actions could be directed. As for the latter, who believe they've already been transported to the Isles of the Blessed in their own lifetime, they'll flatly refuse to be involved in politics.

–But then, won't there be anyone to run our fifth system of government? *a worried Glaucon asked.*

–Well, that will depend on our efforts. When I say "we" I mean the pioneers of the communist Idea. We've got to create the conditions – since we know that anyone's thought can be the equal of anyone else's – whereby the great masses of people will turn to that knowledge we called essential, the knowledge oriented by the vision of the True. Everyone, whether he likes it or not, must come out of the cave! Everyone must take part in the anabasis to the sunny mountain top! And if only an aristocratic minority manages to reach the top and revels in the Idea of the True up there, we won't allow what has nearly always been allowed them.

–What do you mean? *asked an agitated Glaucon.*

–Haven't you ever heard about those little elite groups within Communist parties who, after launching a victorious attack at the cost of enormous sacrifices, set themselves up at the top of the government without a further thought for the people below? Without ever turning back to the workers, peasants, or ordinary soldiers, to live among them and, as Mao said, "stay close to the masses"? We won't tolerate their enjoying any such pleasure cut off from the new world. They'll have to go back down to those who weren't able to get out, or who gave out on the climb to the top of the mountain. The transitional tasks and trivialities will have to be shared with them in the creative new context of the Idea.

–But isn't it unfair to those revolutionaries who paid such a high price for victory, for breaking out of the prison of oppression, to deprive them of a life that's a little better? *Glaucon objected.*

–Dear Glaucon, neither "victory" nor "reward" nor even "sacrifice" are really part of our vocabulary. Our guiding principle isn't to provide a particular group of people in our country, however deserving they may be, with an exceptionally good life. For us, it's a matter of that sort of life spreading throughout the whole country. We want to rally the overwhelming majority of people around that principle by giving priority to discussion and consensus, without shrinking

220

from the use of force when necessary. The main thing is for everyone to attempt to convey to everyone else what they've learned from their own experience and what can be distilled from it that's useful for common action. If an enlightened avant-garde should emerge in certain historical circumstances, its purpose won't be to gear its action toward whatever it pleases but to put itself at the service of a higher form of popular unity.

–Oh, what a beautiful picture! *said Amantha wryly.*

–I was answering Glaucon, *said Socrates curtly.* And I'm not done yet. Let's call "philosophers" everyone – and in the long run that can be, that *must* be, anyone – whose natural inclination is to be oriented by an Idea. So, take my word for it, forcing our philosophers to be concerned about those who aren't ones yet, to become attached to them, to support them in the reorientation of their lives. . .

–The conversion! *Amantha interrupted him.*

–Yes, right, in the conversion – well, that won't be the slightest bit unfair to them.

–It's as fair as can be, actually, *Glaucon agreed.*

–Absolutely. And the conclusive argument can take the following form, which you can hear as a personification of Justice speaking, my friends:

"O you who, by attempting to live by the Idea, deserve the name of philosophers, we understand why, being subject to the yoke of one of the four bad systems of government – those based not on the Idea but on military glory, wealth, freedom of opinion, and the will of a single person, respectively – you are hardly tempted to become involved in public affairs. You acquired a philosophical nature spontaneously, all on your own, not on account of a political situation that was in any event hostile to the Idea, but in spite of it. It is only fair, after all, that someone who grew up all on his own and owes his sustenance, so to speak, to no one should not want to repay anyone for it, especially not a state that couldn't care less about his pursuit of the Idea. But if you are philosophers as a result of the new political environment that we have been able to create, because the compass we used to orient collective life was the communist Idea; if, for that very reason, you have given free rein to your active subjectivity in more perfect and fitting circumstances than have those who are called philosophers elsewhere; if, in short, it is to us that you owe your ability to move much more easily between the Idea and practice, then each of you in turn is under the obligation to go back down to the communal dwelling and to get used to looking at the shadows. For, once you have reacquired that habit, your vision will be a thousand times better than that of the

221

people who have not yet been able to leave the cosmic movie theater. You will have a thorough command of the images and of what they are images of, since you will have had the intuition of artistic processes that produce beauty, scientific processes that produce exactness, and political processes that produce justice, in the element of Truth. Thus, this as yet unconstituted political community, which is nevertheless already yours and mine, will be a waking reality, not merely the stuff of dreams, as are most states today where people fight over shadows and so there are terrible civil wars fought in them only for power, as if it were something important. Truly, I say unto you, a political community whose leaders had the least desire to be leaders is the best one, and it is best protected against civil wars. Conversely, the worst of all societies are those governed by people hungry for power."

–That, *commented Amantha,* is a very forceful conclusion, as convincing as it was unexpected.

–Do you hear what your sister said, Glaucon? Are you convinced too? After hearing what I had to say, will our young philosophers go on sulking in their corner and disobeying? Will they forever refuse to share in the work of government, each in his turn, even though most of the time, like everyone else, they'll be living among pure truths?

–Certainly none of them will want or be able to get out of it, because we're demanding just things of just people. But it's just as certain that they'll only accept taking power reluctantly, like a dog being spanked – which will be a very nice change from what we see today in every single state!

–You're so right, dear friend. You're highlighting the very heart of the matter. If we can come up with a much better life for those whose turn has come to be responsible for a certain share of power than the one offered them by that power, then we'll have the potential for a true political community, because then the only people who will come to power are the ones for whom wealth isn't measured in money but rather in what's required for happiness: the true life, full of sublime thoughts. If, however, people hungry for personal advantage, people who are sure that power always favors the existence and expansion of private property, rush into public affairs, then no true political community will be possible. People like that always fight ferociously with one another for power, and a war of that sort, combining private passions and public power, destroys not only the rivals for the top positions but the country as a whole.

–What a hideous spectacle! *moaned Glaucon.*

–But tell me, do you know of any life that can inspire contempt for power and the state?

–Of course! *Amantha replied.* The life of the true philosopher, the life of Socrates!

–Let's not get carried away, *said a delighted Socrates.* Let's assume that people who are in love with power should never be in power, because if they were we'd have nothing but war between the rivals for power. That's why it's necessary for that enormous mass of people whom I unhesitatingly call philosophers to devote themselves, each in turn, to guarding the political community: selfless people, who are instinctively aware of what public service can be but who know that there are many other rewards besides the ones you can get from frequenting government offices, and that there's a life that's a lot better than the life of political leaders.

–The true life, *murmured Amantha.*

–The true life, *Socrates repeated.* Which is never absent.[6] Or never entirely.

— 12—

FROM MATHEMATICS TO THE DIALECTIC (521c–541b)

–The true life, *said Glaucon in a faint echo of what the other two had said.* Sure. But how do we get all the country's young people to understand what it is? How do we arrange for their anabasis to the light, on the model of those fallen angels who were supposedly able to escape from the depths of hell and make it up to the heavenly abode?

–It's not as simple as tossing a coin. It's a matter of enabling the individual, incorporated into a Subject, to turn away from a day as dark as night toward what is in truth and to obtain the keys to the true life. That sort of conversion is what we call philosophy. Your question is tantamount to asking what type of knowledge has the power to facilitate thought's turning away like that. Or, to put it another way: What academic subject, dear friends, can draw the individual, beyond the impermanence of all things, toward being in itself? But, come to think of it, didn't we say that our philosophers had to be genuine, well-trained soldiers when they were young?

–Yeah, but so what? *said Glaucon, dismayed at the prospect of yet another digression.*

–Anything new introduced into a curriculum has to consolidate the knowledge already acquired. It would be counter-productive if the subject we're seeking were totally useless for a soldier. Now, these soldiers, or guardians, militants, citizens, leaders, or whatever you want to call them, began their studies with the disciplines of the mind – literature and music – along with the disciplines of the body – nutrition, medicine, and physical education. We can leave the last three aside. They deal with the growth, care, and aging of the body, not at all with eternal truths. So might the subject we're seeking be literature or music?

–Absolutely not! *Amantha burst out.* Remember: we said that those disciplines were only there to counterbalance physical training. They help establish useful habits in everyone. For example, musical harmonies foster and sustain inner harmony. A graceful rhythm can promote right conduct. Poetry, whether of the mythological or more realistic type, imparts certain character traits, and so on. We're trying to train the very young, to instill ways of being in them. But as for a subject that would lead toward the True, a subject of the sort you're seeking, there's not a trace of one in this early education.

–You couldn't have reminded us more precisely: there's nothing in it that can help us go further. But in that case, my remarkable Amantha, where should we be looking? At the skills, the techniques? Now's the time, I think, to recite some tragic poetry, *said Socrates. And thereupon, marking out the feet of the alexandrines, he recited:*

In misfortune so great, what's left for us? There's a-
Rithmetic encompa-ssing all of being-there.[1]

–Oh, please, spare us! *cried Amantha.*
–That's Corneille that our teacher's adapting, *commented Glaucon, thrilled to have one-upped his sister in the practice of poetic erudition.*
–I'm thinking, resumed Socrates, a bit ashamed of his silly gag, of that really common subject – which the techniques, the analytical disciplines, and the sciences all inevitably make use of and which everyone has to learn right from the beginning of their studies – that elementary subject thanks to which we're able to count to three, and even a bit further: basic arithmetic and the counting tables, especially the multiplication table. Isn't it true that both the techniques and the sciences have to take that basic knowledge for granted?
–Well, duh! *Glaucon said with a shrug.*
–Even to fight wars you have to know how to count?
–Are you kidding?! Of course you do.
–In that regard, the Palamedes[2] presented to us by Aeschylus, Sophocles, and Euripides. . .
–. . . not to mention Gorgias, *muttered Amantha,* with his *Defense of Palamedes,* which I think is really brilliant.
–I've talked plenty about Gorgias, *Socrates interrupted her rather brusquely,* and your brother Plato devoted a whole dialogue to him. So let's leave it at that, if you don't mind. As I was saying, our three tragic authors considered Palamedes to be the inventor of arithmetic, as did a whole tradition. Very full of himself because of this stroke of genius, he claimed to have established the Greek regiments' order of battle outside Troy, counted the boats, checked the flour stocks,

assessed the bow and arrow reserves, and so on. He acted as if no one before him had ever known how to count. Which, incidentally, made Agamemnon look like a pretty pathetic commander-in-chief, who didn't even know how many feet he had!

–A comic general rather than a tragic one, *Glaucon agreed*. Clearly, even an ordinary soldier has to be able to count how many pairs of socks he's got in his knapsack.

–A soldier, of course, and ultimately any human animal. No one can live as a human and be completely ignorant about Number. But arithmetic still has to be thought in its truth.

–Which is? *asked Amantha a tad impudently.*

–I'm afraid it's one of the subjects we're seeking, those subjects whose very essence is to lead us into the realm of pure thought. Or, more precisely, to turn us toward that which, of being, is exposed to pure thought. But the fact of the matter is that, practically speaking, no one interprets arithmetic that way.

–I myself am having quite a hard time following you, *admitted Glaucon.*

–Then let me try to clarify my way of thinking. I suggest we proceed as follows. First I, by myself, will distinguish between everything in the order of discourse that leads in a positive direction and everything that turns us away from it. Once that's done, you'll step in and examine that first distinction, then you'll either agree or disagree with it. We'll then have a clearer view as to whether my conjectures are right or not.

–All right, let's do it that way, *sighed Glaucon, already feeling discouraged.*

–So here's my first distinction. Of the objects accessible to us through sense perception, some require no further inquiry by pure thought while others make serious demands on it. What principle is involved in such a difference? In the first case, understanding based solely on perception is sufficient, while in the second, perception doesn't provide anything that would allow one to make a sound judgment about what the reality is.

–I see, *said Glaucon*. You're obviously talking about objects seen from a great distance or certain illusionist paintings, like the *trompe-l'oeil* decorations on the façades of certain modern buildings.

–No, you don't get it, *said Socrates gently*. The objects that don't require pure thought are those that don't produce two opposite sensations at once. Those that do produce that sensory opposition I classify among the objects that call on pure thought. The reason for this is that, in the latter case, perception doesn't clear up the issue of whether the object falls under one predicate or its opposite. And this has nothing to do with the distance at which the object is located.

–Could you possibly give an example? *asked Glaucon, overwhelmed.*

–That's just what I was about to do. Look at the first three fingers on my right hand: the thumb, the index finger, and the middle finger. The fact that each of them appears as a finger, and therefore falls under the word "finger," doesn't depend in the least on its position, whether in the middle or on either end. Nor does it depend on its color, whether light or dark, or on its thickness, whether pudgy or bony, or on any other characteristic of the sort. Amid the dense network of these incidental differences, the Subject isn't obliged to turn to pure thought and ask it what a finger is. And why is that so? Because sight has never suggested to him that a finger can also and at the same time be the opposite of a finger.

–Furthermore, *said Amantha,* you've got to admit that thought, even pure thought, would have a hard time deciding clearly what the opposite of a finger is!

But Socrates, ignoring her clever remark, continued:

–When it comes to the *size* of the fingers, however, does sight have an adequate perception of it? At any rate, the question of whether a finger is in the middle position or at either end is no longer a matter of indifference for perception. The same is true of touch, as soon as it's a question of predicate pairs like hard/soft or thick/thin. Generally speaking, the sensory faculties – by which I mean the famous quintet of sight, hearing, smell, taste, and touch – cannot evaluate these kinds of characteristics correctly. And that's where our criterion of oppositeness comes in again, because the sensory faculty that's responsible for assessing the hardness of an object, for example, is the same one that has to assess its softness. So this faculty will report to the Subject, with respect to the same object, that "softness" and "hardness" aren't distinct predicates that a sense experience can distinguish clearly between but rather degrees along a sort of sensory continuum. And, as this continuum is a single sensory faculty, it could also be said that the same object is perceived as hard and soft simultaneously. For this reason, the Subject is faced with an aporia. Here's a sense perception telling us that an object is hard, but at the same time telling us it's soft, too. Whatever can that mean? And the same is true for heavy and light. What can the distinction between heavy and light mean if our sensory faculties tell us that heavy is light and light is heavy?

–Well, Heraclitus is sure going to be happy, *said Amantha.* I love his phrase: "Life from death and death from life."

But Socrates didn't take the provocative bait. He went on imperturbably:

–All the Subject can do is call reasoning and pure thought to the rescue to try and determine whether these reports from the sense perceptions involve two different things or only one. If it appears to thought that there are in fact two different objects, then each of them must be one and distinct from the other. Insofar as each of the objects is one and only together with the other does it make two, the Subject will think them as separate things, because if they were unseparated they wouldn't be thinkable as two but only as one. Let's apply these abstract remarks to the case of visual perception. We said that sight perceived large and small not as separate but as conjoined. To clear this all up a bit, pure thought is compelled to conceive of large and small as distinct, not as unseparated, and therefore to contradict sight. Here we have a patent contradiction between seeing and thinking. It's this contradiction that prompts us to try to find out what large and small really are, in their being. Moreover, we proceeded that way a little while ago when we made an "epistemological break," as our old friend Bachelard[3] would say, between the perceptible and the thinkable. That's what I was trying to say when I distinguished between objects that stimulate the understanding and ones that leave it undisturbed. I define as stimulants those that saturate perception with two opposite characteristics and as intellectually inert those that can be perceived unambiguously.

Glaucon seemed at once relieved and puzzled. He explained why:

–I think I finally understand your definition. But what I don't get, and I mean *really* don't get, is what it has to do with arithmetic.

–In which class of objects do you put number and the unit?

–How the heck should I know?

–You can get some idea of it from what we said about the connection between perception and contradiction. If sight or any other sensory faculty allows for the One to be apprehended adequately, as it is in its being, it's because the One isn't likely to turn our desire toward that which, of being, is exposed to thought. It's the same case as with the finger we were talking about a moment ago. It may well be, however, that the case of the One is not the same as that of the finger. To ascertain the difference, we have to ask ourselves whether perceiving the One, in the form of an object, doesn't always produce some contradiction, such that it appears no more one than multiple. The consequence of this would be, as we saw, that the Subject, faced with an aporia, would have to undertake a completely different sort of investigation in order to settle the matter. It would have to arouse the understanding within himself and ask himself what the One in itself really is. And, in light of this whole process, *we* could conclude that the study of the One is among those that turn individuals toward the vision in truth of that which is.

Having listened to this speech with a skeptical look on her face, Amantha said:

–Arithmetic so that the individual can become a Subject? That's a pretty nervy move.

–In any event, *protested Glaucon,* the sight of an object, however clearly one it may be, is certainly riddled with contradictions. It crumbles into individual parts every time. We constantly see the same thing both as one and as an infinite multiplicity.

–And let's add, *Socrates resumed,* that if that's true of the One the same will be true of any integer, which is a combination of Ones. Now, arithmetic and counting are concerned with numbers. So it follows that these subjects lead on toward a few truths.

–You see! *Glaucon said to his sister, who was sitting there silently, smiling.* Wait for the argument to be finished before you put in your two cents' worth. We've proved that higher arithmetic is one of the subjects we've been looking for. For one thing, it's necessary in almost every sphere of collective action – to be able to marshal all of an army's troops as best as possible for a surprise attack, for example. And, for another, it's necessary for philosophers who, in order to become experts in number theory, have to learn how to overcome the power of becoming so they can grasp that which of being is exposed to thought. The guardians of our communist political community – the militants, the workers, the soldiers, the leaders, everyone – are both men of action and philosophers. So I think that you practically have to say that the study of higher, or even transcendental, arithmetic must be compulsory. Everyone who really wants to take part in our community and be able to hold their own when their turn comes to exercise a position of leadership will have to commit to studying it and work at it, not superficially, merely to take away a few practical formulas from it, but until they achieve a synthetic understanding of the nature of numbers through pure thought. Yes, the more I think about it, the more I see how much this subject must be an integral part of our political project.

–Ah, the wonderful transports of youth! *cried Socrates.*

–But there are still some conditions, I think, *grumbled Amantha.* After all, loads of people today have a real fetishism of number. Just look at elections, opinion polls, and of course money: number rules all over the place.[4] I'm leery – yes, that's the word – I'm very leery of the cult of arithmetic. The most avaricious lackeys of capitalism, bank traders, are formidable arithmeticians – need I say more? It's a far cry from communism, my friends.

–You've got a point, *admitted Socrates*. We're standing on a dividing line here. On my right there's a pragmatics of number, which ranks it with business, the banks, servile opinion, and stupid numerical majorities. On my left, there's the formal science of Number, which helps the individual become incorporated into a universal Subject and whose purpose is to make that which, of being, is exposed to thought be seen in Truth. I have confidence in mathematics. It won't disappear in its enslavement to finance and business. The disinterested study of mathematics imparts a graceful upward lift to the Subject by forcing him to reason dialectically about the being of numbers without ever allowing them, in the process of this dialectic, to refer to visible or tangible bodies or to social symbols such as wealth or celebrity.

–Oh boy! *exclaimed Glaucon*. You know mathematicians all right. The "numbers" they talk about sure aren't the numbers used in business! They require delicate handling. For instance, if you claim you've found a rational way to divide the One, the mathematicians burst out laughing and flatly refuse to believe you. If you go ahead and try to divide the One anyway, they multiply it by the same amount, so that the One should never appear to be, not the One that it is, but a multiplicity of parts.

–That's a terrific description of them! *said Socrates with obvious delight*. What I recommend you do is put the following question to them: "You most worthy experts, what numbers are you discussing that are such that the One they're made up of is absolutely equal to any other One that can be conceived of and can't be distinguished from it even by the slightest little difference?" What do you think our beloved math experts would reply?

–That they're talking about numbers that we have no access to except through pure thought and that are impossible to use other than in the realm constituted by such thought.

Just this once, Socrates, clearly proud of his young disciple, patted Glaucon's shoulder and said:

–Perfect! So you see that higher arithmetic[5] is really necessary for us. It forces us, as Subjects oriented toward the True, to make use of pure thought.

–It sure does have that effect on me, *said Amantha*.

–Furthermore, *Glaucon went on*, guys with a knack for math are quick studies in other subjects too. And if the slow ones are forced to struggle over the proof of theorems and math problems, well, even if it seems to be of no use to them, you can still see that their minds become a lot sharper than they were before.

–Absolutely. The mere fact, moreover, that number theory is much more intellectually demanding than any of the other disciplines, both in terms of learning it and in terms of coming up with new solutions, is reason enough for everyone to have to get a taste of it. Without studying this subject, there's no hope of ever becoming a subtle thinker.

–Unfortunately! *said Amantha with a smile.*

–The matter's settled, then, *said Socrates, rubbing his hands together.* Number theory, compulsory for all young people! Let's go on now to the second required subject in our general education curriculum.

–It's got to be geometry, *moaned Amantha.*

–Bull's eye!

–Geometry, of course, *Glaucon said approvingly.* In warfare it's essential! When it comes to pitching camp, besieging fortresses, deploying an army or closing up its ranks, in short, when it comes to all the complex maneuvers called for in battles and on the march, you can immediately see the difference between someone who's good at geometry and someone who doesn't get it at all.

At this, Socrates made a face and said:

–Frankly, for all that sort of thing you only need a very basic knowledge of arithmetic and geometry. Geometry as a whole should be examined instead, and in particular the most recent and difficult part of it, to determine whether it can be of use in achieving our fundamental goal: an easier grasp of the Idea of the True. Because, let me remind you, to discover everything that forces an individual, once he's been incorporated into a Subject, to turn toward the place where the aspect of being that imparts essential happiness lies, the aspect to which finally having access is the only imperative that can rightly be called philosophical – that's really the true aim of our philosophy.

–So we're back to the theme of conversion, *said Amantha dreamily.*

–Yes, absolutely! If geometry forces us to confront that which of being is exposed to thought, then it suits our purposes. If it's only concerned with becoming, then it doesn't. This issue is clouded by the view of elementary geometry held by many who use it. True geometers will agree with me about this: more often than not, an interpretation of this subject that's diametrically opposed to its true nature is bandied about. It's spoken about in terms that are truly ridiculous because they're strictly dependent on empirical necessities. Important-sounding words like "duplication," "squaring," "linear construction," "addition of surfaces," and other expressions of the sort are tossed around, as though geometry were only a bunch of convenient gimmicks for skillfully manipulating figures on a plane surface. We, however, only pursue the study of mathematics for the sake of pure thought. Let's be even more precise and say: for the sake of the pure thought of what exists eternally and not of what merely arises and passes away at a given time.

–There's that phrase of Goethe's, *Amantha said softly,* "All that comes into being deserves to perish."[6]

–For once, *Socrates replied,* a poet, and a German one at that, was right, even if he attributed this beautiful maxim to the Devil. Exempt from the curse of birth and thus ordained for immortality, geometry turns the Subject toward Truth and gives form to the analytical aspect of philosophy by heralding the process whereby we turn upwards what we usually just let muddle along below.

–Conversion, as usual, *murmured Amantha.*

–In any event, we'll insist that none of the citizens of our fine communist country neglects geometry. Besides, it has some considerable incidental benefits.

–Such as? *Amantha asked a little aggressively.*

–The ones Glaucon listed – war, and all that sort of thing. But, in particular, when you look at the advancement of knowledge of any sort, you can see a world of difference between the scientists who've studied geometry in depth and those who are ignorant of it.

–So this will be the second subject, after arithmetic, that we'll require the young to study, *Glaucon said in conclusion.*

–Certainly, *agreed Socrates.* And the third one will be astronomy, right?

–Yes, *said Glaucon enthusiastically.* Because astronomy teaches us what time of the month and year it is. And that's something farmers, sailors, and generals on a military campaign absolutely need to know.

–You're so funny with all your practical justifications. You remind me of those magazines where you come across a piece of "science" news tucked away on a back page somewhere, such as: someone has discovered the solution to a problem of higher arithmetic that for 300 years had resisted all the efforts of the greatest mathematical geniuses to solve it.

–I know what you mean, *said Amantha, her eyes wide.* It's Fermat's last theorem, which was proven by the Englishman Wiles. I read all about it in *Modern Woman.*

– An excellent science magazine then! *said Socrates, smiling.* You must have noticed that, in those sorts of circumstances, the journalist invariably says two things. One: neither I nor my reader have the slightest chance of understanding anything about this. Two: unfortunately, this is completely useless "in practical life." As if creative thought weren't "practical"! It's more practical than anything else. That's why you shouldn't be afraid of your audience, dear Glaucon. If theoretical astronomy is of no use for harvesting bananas or for improving bicycle derailleur gears, we'll just have to deal with it. The subjects we're in the process of selecting for study have a kind of usefulness that's as essential as it is hard to conceive of: in every Subject they purify and revive an organ that's been ruined and blinded by our usual occupations. It's much more important to take care of that organ than it would be to keep the giant Argus' hundred eyes, if we had them, open day and night. For it's with this organ alone that we have the power to confront a truth. People who know about this subjective capacity have no need of your practical justifications. Those who know nothing about it at all are completely uninterested in subjects that no practical advantage can be gained from. You have to decide, Glaucon, my friend, who you're speaking to: the defenders of pure thought or the dyed-in-the-wool pragmatists?

–To neither of them, actually. They can all fend for themselves as to the advantages they get out of one subject or another. It's primarily for my own sake that I speak, ask questions, and answer.

–Sure, why not? Let's backtrack. We didn't choose the right subject, after geometry.

–It's not astronomy?

–Not right away. Remember, we talked about elementary geometry, the main educational illustrations of which are taken from plane geometry: triangles, circles, squares, parabolas, and so forth. All those figures are two-dimensional. But what are the heavenly bodies studied by astronomy? Three-dimensional objects in space. What's more, they're in motion, so you can say they have four dimensions: the three in space, plus time, which measures their movements. Things are actually even more complicated than that, since there are several possible types of space, which can be studied in any number of dimensions, not just two (plane), three (space), or four (space–time). To deal with these issues, mathematicians have come up with some very broad concepts, like the one – invented by the brilliant Riemann – of n-dimensional variety. Topological vector spaces, or fiber spaces, or Lie groups, and so on could also be mentioned. In the final analysis, you have objects that are much more fascinating than the planet Neptune or the constellation Cygnus, objects that combine topological, or localization, features (neighborhood, open/closed, cover, point, interior/exterior, etc.); metric or measurement features (distance, size, etc.); and algebraic or calculus features (fundamental group, decomposition, isomorphism, etc.). These are the strangest and most complex objects of algebraic topology, the queen of contemporary mathematics. There are knots, hole or *n*-fold structures, hyperspheres, the Moebius strip, the Klein bottle, and so many other amazing things to be found in it! This is the level at which every single citizen should learn mathematics. The geometry of triangles and circles won't suffice for us.

–But what will become of poor astronomy amid all these abstract constructs?

–There's something you really need to understand. The only type of knowledge that can raise an individual to the level of the Subject he's capable of becoming is the knowledge that deals with the aspect of being that remains hidden in withdrawal. Science properly speaking is unconcerned with mere sensory particularity. Of course, for the poet in each of us, the constellations shining in the heavens, albeit created out of sensible matter, are, by virtue of their very order, the epitome of beauty and sublime regularity. We'll nevertheless argue that they cannot bear comparison with the essential constellations, the true constellations underlying what appears to us of them, constellations whose speed and slowness are true and correspond to true figures, constellations that move with precision, in terms of the relationship they have both with one another and with themselves. The problem is that a rational, analytical grasp of all this exists, but no knowledge that can be directly deduced from the visible.

–But if that's the case, then what's the point of astronomers' observations, enormous refracting telescopes, radio-telescopes, or satellites sent to the edge of the solar system?

–The myriad objects in the sky should serve as models for us to attain knowledge of the invisible Idea. Suppose we found some abstract drawings made on the walls of a cave by the inspired hand of some artist from our prehistory. A modern mathematician might recognize figures of algebraic topology in them and admire how beautifully they were executed. But he wouldn't conclude that merely by gaping in amazement at these masterpieces any advance in the general theory of spaces could be made. Likewise, the true astronomer may go into raptures over the wonders of our sensible universe when he discovers new galaxies or records the background noise, the minute trace of the primordial explosion whose effects the universe has been copiously displaying for billions of years. But he won't think that this contemplative ecstasy, or making countless additional observations of the sort, can for a single moment amount to a comprehensive, consistent theory of the universe as it really is, in both its totality and its details.

–It's Rousseau – my beloved Jean-Jacques – who's right as usual, *said Amantha.* In order to think correctly, he says, "let's set all the facts aside."[7]

–Sure, we'll study astronomy by setting problems, not by noting facts, just as we do with higher arithmetic, elementary geometry, and algebraic topology. Never going beyond visible facts prevents you from usefully activating what deserves the name of thought in a Subject.

–But what you're talking about, *said Glaucon worriedly,* is quite a sublime sort of task.

–The only kind that can place these sciences at the service of a Subject-of-truth.

–You've only given us a rapid sketch of that Subject, though.

–That's because, while each of the sciences we've just singled out, taken by itself, can produce truths, they're nevertheless incapable of evaluating the *being* of these truths.

–Still, above and beyond the systematic study of all these sciences, *Glaucon replied,* we could isolate the element they have in common, the thing that makes all of them together comprise one specific type of thought. By a rigorous demonstration we could reveal the single place where all the sciences are located. If we were to do that, we'd have made some significant progress. Otherwise we'd have chattered away pointlessly.

–That would be an endless task, a very useful one actually. And yet, dear friend, even once the work was completed we'd still only be at the prelude to the music that philosophy has undertaken to play. We'd have only done epistemology, which isn't saying much. The whole problem is that, however great they may be, mathematicians and scientists are not yet true dialecticians. Although the sciences are necessary – just like the arts, political action, and transference love – they're not sufficient. Singular truths are merely the prelude to philosophy. Sure, without them our musical score wouldn't contain a single note. But the philosophical song, properly speaking, can only be sung by those who are able to carry a dialectical discussion through to its conclusion.

–I think we're back in the vicinity of our cosmic movie theater, *observed Amantha.*

–You're incredibly sensitive to all the shifts along our route. Yes, it's a question once again of what's empirical and what needs to be thought. Sight imitates thought when – first as a prisoner of the shadows of the place of bondage, of the totalitarian movie theater of images, then as an escaped prisoner under the guidance of those who return from on high – it starts out by seeing nothing at all, so dazzled is it by the outside world. It will first strive to make out the reflection of the trees in the evening, in the mirrored surface of a pond, then the stars standing out against the night sky, and then, at dawn, the big pine trees, the colorful birds taking flight, the blue of the sky, and finally the sun! Likewise, whenever we try – through the practice of dialectical reasoning, unaided by sense perception, solely by using rational arguments – to turn toward the true being of everything that exists, and we keep on going until such time as we've been able to construct a concept of Truth through pure thought, you can say that we've reached the limits of the thinkable, just as the escaped prisoner of our fable reached the limits of the visible.

–And that's what you call the dialectical approach, *said Amantha, full of enthusiasm again.*

–Of course! Why does the study of the sciences, and especially of mathematics, constitute the obligatory prelude to the dialectic? It's because it shows us, without resorting to the fallacious "obvious facts" of immediate sensory experience, that truths exist. The existence of truths is the necessary basis for constructing a concept of what they are and how they're an exception to the usual order of appearing in our world. This awareness of the true-exception is the highest point that can be attained by philosophical thought.

Unlike his sister, every time Glaucon thought they were "falling back into metaphysics" – as he put it – he started to feel the instinctive hesitation of those tempted by pragmatism.

–I wish I could see things the way you do. And yet it often seems to me that it's practically impossible to agree with your view of what is. At the same time, I think to myself that, from another point of view, it's impossible not to agree with it. So I adopt a provisional ethics[8] for myself: since we're not going to settle the matter immediately and we'll have to do a lot more talking about it, let's just assume you're right and move on from the prelude to the song itself. Let's discuss it with the same determination and precision as we did when only the prelude was concerned. Tell us about the nature of your famous "dialectical reasoning," how many different forms it's divided into, and what paths they follow, because those are the paths that will lead us to the end of all our traveling, to the journey's destination, and therefore, after twenty-four grueling hours, to rest for us at last!

– You wouldn't be able to follow me any farther, dearest Glaucon, in that direction. *I* wouldn't lack any of the requisite determination, but what about you? Keep in mind, your intuition would then no longer be dealing with an image of what we're talking about but with the True as such. . . Or at least as it seems to me to be. I'm not going to assert dogmatically at this point that the being of the True is wholly consistent with my conception of it. But I *do* contend that it's possible to have the intuition that it's not all that different from it, and I do so all the more firmly as only the power of dialectical reasoning, to the exclusion of any other approach, can convince someone of it who's an expert in the sciences we mentioned.

–OK, we'll grant you that mitigated dogmatism, dear teacher! *said Amantha with a smile.*

–There's one point, at any rate, that no one will quibble with us about. It's when we say that a thought process, not reducible to mathematics, exists that, no matter what the domain under consideration, endeavors to grasp, by the end of a methodical procedure, the true being of everything existing in that domain.

–But aside from your dialectic, *objected Glaucon,* there's still a considerable difference between the ordinary techniques and higher mathematics.

–Let's say that current techniques and disciplines are descriptive or empirical in the following way: either they deal with people's opinions and desires, as is the case with the so-called "humanities and social sciences;" or they're only concerned with the development and structure of visible things (I'm thinking of geology, botany, or zoology); or else they're about teaching people how to feed cattle or make plants grow, or even about their learning the rules for making and taking care of manufactured things, which is a matter of technology. As for the genuine sciences – physics, and especially mathematics – about which we said that they grasp something of being *qua* being, we've got to admit there, too, that at one level, since they proceed without any need for a thinking of their own process, they're a bit like the sudden appearance of Truth in a dream, rather than like Truth itself. They don't shed true light, the light of day, on their own conclusions. We can understand why this is so when we note, as we've already done, that these sciences make do with hypotheses or contingent observations that their practitioners say they'll leave untouched, given that they can't account for them rationally other than by asserting how very valuable their consequences are. Yet, if the intrinsic value of the first principle is unknown and both the conclusion and the intermediate steps leading to it are thereby compounded of ignorance, could we call "science," in the unconditional or absolute tone implied by that word, the conventional organization of all this, however logical it might be?

–And yet they *are* really sciences, *grumbled Glaucon.* They're not just descriptions or observations that depend on our sensory perception of the world.

–Certainly! But philosophy, that is, dialectical reasoning, nevertheless has a unique objective that, even though it presupposes the sciences, distinguishes it absolutely from them. It's the only discipline of thought whose method consists in destroying hypotheses one by one so that, once it has arrived at the principle itself, it can confirm – by going back down from the principle – the validity of those hypotheses. It's the only one that can really pull the Subject little by little out of the barbaric morass of individualism he's mired in and turn him upward toward his higher purpose. And naturally, in order to effect this difficult conversion, the dialectician makes use of the different sciences we spoke about as companions and aids. But the word "science," as it's commonly used, is nevertheless ambiguous if it's used for both mathematics and the dialectic. We really need another term, one that implies more clarity than "opinion" and more obscurity than "science," if that word's taken in its absolute sense. A little while ago I suggested abandoning "science" and distinguishing between "analytical (or mathematical) thought" and "dialectical (or philosophical) thought." But I don't think now's the time to argue about words, when we need to examine speculative issues that have to do with things in themselves.

–Especially if we agree with Lacan, *said Amantha, narrowing her eyes slyly,* that "the word is the murder of the thing."[9]

–Which can also be expressed, *retorted Socrates,* as: "Once brought to light, the thing is indifferent to what it's called." At any rate, I'm sticking with my classification. There are two main types of mental activity: opinion, whose objects are the changes in a given world, and thought, which is concerned with transworld being. Each of these types has two sub-types. Opinion is divided into assumption and certainty, while thought is either analytical or dialectical. I also proposed relationships among all these terms, on the basis of their ontological inscription. What being *qua* being is to the changes in a given world, thought is to opinion. What thought is to opinion, dialectical thought is to certainty and analytical thought is to assumption. As for the details, and in particular the ontological deductions underpinning this construction, we've already spoken a bit about them and we won't repeat that now; it would take too long. Let's focus on the act of dialectical reasoning itself. We call a "dialectician" someone

238

who grasps, in each existent, the rational kernel of its exposition to thought. Conversely, as regards someone who's incapable of doing as much, will you accept for us to declare him unable to truly think, dear Glaucon, precisely insofar as he can't give an account of what he claims to be thinking, either to himself or to other people?

–How could I not accept that assessment of things?

–What a yes-man! *muttered Amantha under her breath.*

But Socrates ignored her sarcasm, which he had by no means failed to pick up on. He went on:

–It's exactly the same with regard to the True. If someone is incapable of defining the idea of Truth by distinguishing it rationally from all the others and of battling his way, like a warrior of the concept, through all the so-called refutations by refuting such "refutations," not, as his opponents have done, in the sphere of appearances but in that of being-in-itself, if our man therefore can't get through these verbal traps by countering them with implacable logic, then no one could claim that a guy of that sort knows Truth in itself, or any other truth for that matter, and you'd even have to admit that, although he might be wielding a semblance of the true, it's only opinion, not thought, analytical any more than dialectical, and so the current life of someone incompetent like that is only a dreamy kind of drowsiness, and even before he awakens here on earth he'll have found himself in the realm of the dead, to sleep for eternity there.[10]

–Oh, there's another one of those sentences of our Socrates that no one can resist! *exclaimed Amantha, who was truly moved.*

–Now suppose that each of you, dear children, have children in your turn, and that you bring them up and educate them. Suppose – God forbid! – that, owing to some terrible circumstances, these children turn out to be total idiots, and that even you yourselves would say about them – with even more justification than it's said about the diagonal of a square[11] – that they're completely irrational. I don't think you'd accept for young people like that to become heads of state and the top people in charge of making the most important decisions. Would you?

–That'd be tough, having to diss them, *said Glaucon,* because we'd love them, those idiots, our kids! But all the same, I think we'd try to find a tolerable vocation for them, some sort of job that would doubtless be limited in scope but still interesting.

–That's why, before a catastrophe like that struck, you'd do your best to educate your children so that they could at least ask and answer questions, whatever the topic, according to the demands of pure thought. Which means, practically speaking, that, as parents, you'd know that the dialectic is the capstone of all the different subjects and that no other subject can be set above it. And so we've reached the end of our discussion about what the people of our communist country need to be taught if we want them all to be able to hold the highest positions of leadership when it's their turn to do so.

–Well, if that isn't a perfect pro-family conclusion! *declared Amantha.* I'm really blown away! And, what's more, it's not a bad idea, not by a long shot. Everyone I know complains about how, whenever a guy and his girlfriend get into a fight, there's never a shortage of low blows. And when it comes to children, good luck trying to talk reasonably with them. Socrates has proved that the dialectic is the secret to family harmony. Congratulations! We could. . .

–Yeah, sure, *Glaucon interrupted her,* but there's a world of difference between the abstract curriculum and practical reality. How do we spread all these different subjects, including the dialectic, among the masses?

–For people to become convinced that the Idea, in the sense we understand it, should guide the destiny of the country, we've got to take responsibility for and monitor the outcomes of the general education curriculum, as we defined its broad principles – and even a few of its details – last night and this morning. So it'll be assumed that all the virtues toward which such an education orients the masses and of which the philosophical determination is merely the synthesis have been acquired. After all, our curriculum is very simple: anybody, without exception, can and must become a philosopher. Besides, if it were otherwise, philosophy's claim to universalism would be virtually meaningless. As far as this curriculum is concerned, let me remind you, the chief virtue, the one that makes it possible to stick with it to the end, is courage.

–But that's just it, *said Glaucon worriedly.* I was wondering how differences in people's memory abilities, and also disparities in personal stamina – the sort of endurance that enables you to have a love for work in all its forms – could be overcome.

–Right, *said Amantha.* Let's not forget that we're proposing that all social differences between manual and intellectual labor be abolished.

–That's a crucial point! *Socrates agreed.* If everyone's to become a dialectician, nobody should have only one good leg! I mean: do one thing eagerly and shirk another. We all know people today who are prepared to walk twenty miles, if need be, just to see a bicycle race go by in one minute, or who are crazy about the strenuous exertions of hunting and sailing, or who can replace a table leg or grow beautiful tomatoes, who are all honest and courageous in their own way but

240

clam up when it comes to all the intellectual subjects, as they never go to the theater or read anything other than the racing results or the weather report in the paper. On the other hand, we all know experts in cellular biology or people who are unbeatable when it comes to possessive adjectives in the works of Sophocles, who talk about such things copiously with their colleagues, who have subscriptions to the opera, read the leftwing cultural journals and defend, courageously at times, the rights of foreign workers, but who are absolutely incapable of digging a ditch, fixing a motor scooter, or taking care of a rifle. Philosophy won't be able to be universalized as long as this lameness exists.

–It's the same when it comes to Truth! *exclaimed Amantha.* There sure are a lot of gimpy people! One-legged Subjects, you could even say. I know plenty of them. They claim to detest lying, but they're not in the least bothered by saying a bunch of crap and repeating opinions picked up in the gutter. They wallow in their ignorance like pigs in mud. Old Lacan was right to say that ignorance isn't a lack but a passion![12] On the whole, they'd be better off telling a few more lies and being a little less ignorant.

–That's a difficult balance, *said Socrates, smiling.* But one thing's for sure: the necessary balance between all of people's aptitudes has got to be produced as early as possible. Children love to run, jump, fight, get angry about unfairness, and so forth. They hate tattling and conceitedness – that's great! The best thing to do, then, is to go heavy on arithmetic, geometry, and astronomy so as to introduce them as soon as possible to the dialectic. As for what form education should take, it would be better. . .

–I've got an idea about that, *Amantha interrupted him.* Down with authoritarian education! All it is is following orders, boredom, and hot air. After a certain amount of time, all children, bar none, should study because they like to, as much as, or more than, they like climbing trees, watching pop stars on TV, or exchanging kisses on the sly. Otherwise, forget about it.

–You're right, after all, *admitted Socrates.* Can you be free, on the one hand, and then suddenly a slave, just because you're of school age? When someone is made to carry heavy rocks day after day they call it forced labor; it's a punishment, horrible and pointless. And yet the teaching of the sciences and the arts as a preparation for the power of the Idea would be modeled on forced labor? That's totally absurd. Lessons that are crammed into an individual's head can never mold a Subject.

–Hurrah! *cried Amantha.*

–Never use force on children, *Socrates continued,* when it comes to their studies, my friends. Education should be as free and exciting as their games. Even more so, as Amantha would have it. It's the teachers' responsibility to kindle in our human young the creative spark they all have within them. Only in an atmosphere of active freedom like this will everyone find the path to the dialectic that's most natural to him. A dialectician is someone whose thinking is able to see the big picture. But, for any given state of the world, there's an infinite number of paths to constructing the big picture of that state. Education is worthless if it doesn't give everyone the means of choosing the best path for himself so that, with the help of circumstances and as a Subject, he can become the dialectician that as an individual he was capable of becoming.

–But isn't dialectical reasoning corrupted by all those pseudo-debates on TV, the idiotic "philosophers," opinion polls, and all that stuff? *asked Amantha.* Doesn't the pervasiveness of discussion about anything whatsoever, people chatting on the Internet, that whole bit, establish a solid dictatorship of idle chatter and opinion?

–You're inciting me to make another of my famous detours. Imagine a child, adopted by some very wealthy people, who lives a peaceful life of idleness surrounded by a bunch of sycophants and freeloaders. His adoptive parents have carefully hidden from him the fact that his biological parents were poor workers whose child was virtually snatched away from them by a rich bourgeois couple who couldn't have kids, while those poor people, who were seriously ill and penniless, had all they could do just to stay alive in total poverty with the child. The whole time when he doesn't know he's being lied to, the adopted child respects, as best he can, at least when it comes to the essentials, the people he believes to be his biological parents. He doesn't put much trust in the cynical young sycophants who want to take advantage of him. But then he suddenly finds out about the lie his parents have been telling him. As a result, feeling confused, having been kept for too long in the dark about the truth of his origins to be able to chart a rational course of action, and convinced that traditional law is a lie, the adolescent he's become is very likely to be tempted, at least for a certain time, by the nihilistic principles of instant gratification and "no future" spread by his friends.

–But what does that have to do with the corruption of the dialectic? *a very surprised Amantha asked.*

–Right from childhood we have a few guiding principles where justice is concerned. These principles are like parents in the sense that they teach us what's right, and even if we're far from always applying them – any more than we always obey our parents – we still have genuine respect for them. There are, naturally, other rules of action, too, diametrically opposed to these principles and often a lot more appealing, which tempt and attract us but which we resist, for the most part, because it's still the original principles, which could be called the paternal ones, that generally carry the day. Suppose, though, that a young person is constantly asked where his or her principles of justice come from and who this famous Father is who taught them to him or her; that this "paternity" is mocked and refuted in a thousand ways; that the poor young man or the sweet young woman is harassed until they're gradually forced to think that justice, as they conceive of it, is no more just than injustice; that what they were convinced was true may well be false; that everything here on earth is in flux and relative, and so on. Then the respect they had for strong principles ever since they were children is very likely to crumble; they'll no longer be able to recognize the connection they'd felt between these principles and their own ability to become real Subjects. Their whole lives will become confused. No longer knowing which way to turn, they'll follow the seductive principles of the sycophants and freeloaders they're surrounded with and will ultimately confuse the dialectic with the chattering of opinion.

–In short, you're making excuses for today's phony dialecticians! *exclaimed Amantha*. They've been confused and corrupted, but they weren't all that bad at first.

–The communist conviction is that people are good and it's the pathologies of society, the family and the state – in a nutshell, bad systems of government – that corrupt them.

–That's Rousseau all over!

– Yes, I suppose it is. That's why our phony philosophers inspire more pity in me than terror.

–This is all just a digression, if you don't mind my saying so, *Glaucon lectured them*. I'd like to have a precise educational curriculum.

–Oh, of course! *said Socrates good-naturedly*. After the basic education we talked about – literature, music, basic arithmetic, languages, physical education, and so forth – which will take ten years, we'll have all the young people go back down into the counterpart of our famous underground movie theater, so that they can fill every possible position there, including the hardest ones – male or female unskilled laborer, lumberjack or jill, check-out woman or man, deliveryman or woman, male or female soldier, and so on – with the sole aim of rallying to our system of government all the stragglers, the ignorant, and the foreigners, so that no one, and I mean no one, languishes in the pit of images and so that they can all understand, amid life's storms, what life is like when the Idea illuminates its purpose and power. They'll remain young artisans of the visible Idea for five years. Then, for another ten years, they'll exercise their analytical thinking with higher mathematics, theoretical physics, and astronomy, until they master the most recent discoveries in those fields. Then, for five years, they'll mentally construct the dialectical synthesis of all the foregoing and they'll all be philosophers.

Amantha, however, frowned and said:

–But they won't be very young any more by then.

–They'll be about 30. They'll have completed what it takes for an individual to have the greatest chance of becoming incorporated into one or several different truth processes and thereby of becoming a Subject. They'll be able to lift their eyes upon everything that exists, toward that which, revealing as it does the being underlying this existence, is like its hidden light. When their turn comes, guided by that light, they'll tackle the difficulties imposed by positions of leadership in politics. They'll have nothing but the public welfare in mind and will regard such an activity not as an honor but as a necessary duty. They'll use their position, which is temporary anyway, only to further reinforce by their example the education of their successors, the people who, when their turn comes, will be responsible for the supreme guardianship of the communist system of government, in any and all circumstances.

–Exemplary leaders! *exclaimed Glaucon.*

–Male and female leaders, *Socrates reminded him.* Remember, once and for all, that nothing we're saying applies any more to men than to women.

–That's also because the word "leader," *added Amantha,* designates positions that each and every one of the country's citizens are to hold, and thus the word can have no gender, or color, or social class, or any predicate of the sort.

–It does have age as a predicate, though, *observed Glaucon.* People will already be 30 when they start taking their turn as guardians in the political field. Neither you nor I would be considered capable of doing so yet!

–In any event, *said Socrates in conclusion,* I think we've said enough for the time being about the education appropriate to our fifth system of government and about the character type that corresponds to it. Maybe we should take a little break?

Everyone agreed and they all began to knock back the drinks.

— 13 —

CRITIQUE OF THE FOUR PRE-COMMUNIST SYSTEMS OF GOVERNMENT

I Timocracy and Oligarchy (541b–555b)

By the time the break was over, everyone – helped along by the drinks and a bit of napping – had overcome the exhaustion brought on by the long metaphysical or scientific commentaries and the constant tension of the philosophical construction. Socrates, full of vim and vigor, a cup of milk with honey in hand, summarized the basic features of a public community dedicated to justice, that is, the features of the fifth system of government.

–If the country is governed by the standards of political perfection as we conceive it, we'll accept, for example, that children, and more generally everything connected with mental and physical education, will be the responsibility of a much larger collective than the family. All the important occupations, whether in peace or in war, will also be deprivatized and assigned to communal life. In keeping with our policies, those who are old enough to fight or promote our ideals in unfriendly countries will live – at all times, whenever war is unavoidable, but as often as possible in peacetime, too – in houses of the people where they'll own absolutely nothing of their own. For all things must belong to all the people. Unlike the professional athletes who are celebrated in our press and make astronomical salaries, our citizen-soldiers will receive from the political community only what's necessary to live comfortably and will thus devote themselves completely to developing their talents in every sphere of creative activity, and all the more purposefully in that they'll dedicate them to the growth and prestige of the communist community.

Amantha jumped at the chance to get in a dig at him.

–You've got to admit it's odd! *she said.* In a few crystal-clear sentences you summarize what your first presentation of the subject took you a whole night of arguments, and occasionally pretty muddled

245

ones, too, if you'll permit me this impertinence, to do. Shouldn't you have begun with what you just said?

–Dear Amantha, when you've managed to supervise a bunch of five kids one way or another while continuing to do your work, you'll be able to distinguish between the investigative method we used last night to construct and solve a new problem and the method of exposition I'm using this morning, whose only purpose is to convey already proven conclusions. You and Glaucon ought to remind me, instead, of the exact point in our session where we took the path that led us where we are now. I'd like to go back to that crossroads, actually, so as to go down the *other* path, the one we didn't take then, with you. And then we can all go to sleep, feeling sure that we've been absolutely thorough.

Glaucon loved summaries, classifications, and quandaries. He regarded them as a chance for him to hold forth in the somewhat obsessive way he had a knack for.

–I remember that crossroads, Socrates, *he said,* as if we were still cooling our heels there! You'd just said that if a given system of government has been determined to be an excellent one it must be so relative to other, inferior systems of government. There are four such systems of government, you said, ranging from poor to bad, so that, in all, including the one we're in the process of defining, we're conceiving of a field in which five different possibilities can be noted. I remember thinking at the time that the four systems of government you contrasted with your own were the ones we're all familiar with. The first and most famous is the one in which empires came to the fore and whose basic principle is military glory. I even dreamed of coming up with the abstract name for it that it lacks, something like "timocracy" or "timarchy." The second system of government sanctions the authority of a small group of wealthy people, and it's called "oligarchy." The third is the one based on the decisions of a majority of the assembled people; its name is "democracy." And the fourth is the erratic dictatorship of a single man, which. . .

–Or of a single woman, *Amantha cut in affably.* Don't forget that, as far as Socrates is concerned, whether it's a man or a woman, provided philosophy's involved, makes no difference.

–Whatever! *grumbled Glaucon.* Anyway, its name is "tyranny."

–Perfect! *said Socrates.* Tyranny is indeed the worst disease of the body politic. But you still haven't told me where the team of horses pulling our dialogue took one fork in the road rather than the other.

–That's because, before you could expound on the classification of

246

the systems of government, Polemarchus and my sister hit you with a really tough question. To answer it, you went on to something else having to do with women, children, and the family, which took hours. And that's why our discussion is where it is now.

–Thanks to your excellent memory, you're tossing the ball back to me at exactly the point where we changed direction during the night. OK, I've caught it now. Let's start with a commonsense remark: to each political community there corresponds a specific character type. I'm going to take cover behind the poet of poets, our national poet Homer, on this issue. You recall how they asked Odysseus:

> From where do you hail and what is your stock?
> For you are neither from oak nor from rock.

The places Subjects come from aren't trees or rocks but their homeland, their country, their political community. So, if there are five major forms of government, there must also be five major categories of subjective organization into which specific individuals fall, depending on where they come from. As regards the Subject who comes from *our* system of government – egalitarian aristocratism – we already studied his nature closely, and we set out all the arguments necessary to describe him. He's just-in-accordance-with-the-Idea.

–In accordance with the Idea. No more, *said Amantha facetiously,* but no less.

–So let's study the subjective character types that correspond to the other four systems of government. Carefully, one after the other. We'll begin with the one Glaucon dubbed "timarchy": its Subject is obsessed with honor and victory. Then there'll come the oligarchic Subject, the democratic Subject, and the tyrannical Subject. We'll see which of the four is the most unjust, the one that deserves to be identified as the absolute negation of our man-who's-just-in-accordance with-the-Idea. We'll then have a complete view of the relationship between pure justice and pure injustice, on the one hand, and happiness and unhappiness, on the other. We'll be able to bring our humongous discussion to a close because we'll have the means to decide whether we should follow the path of injustice, as Thrasymachus argued last night with his customary verve, or whether it's to the path of justice that this morning's arguments are leading us.

–That way, *Amantha remarked,* we'll be able to confirm your principle that, with a thought process, only the completion can produce a new measure.

–I'm impressed!

And Socrates was really impressed by the young woman. He paused for a moment, then said:

–To give ourselves every chance for success in the intellectual process of creating a new political measure, we'll proceed as we did before: by seeing things in the large before coming around to the small, examining the practices of political communities before judging those of individuals.

–But won't we just be going round in circles then? *asked Glaucon worriedly.*

–Of course not! We'll start with your timarchy, and then we'll describe the individual who's like it, the "timarchian," or the "timocrat." And the same for the other three: our thinking will proceed from the formal political place to the Subject that's constituted within it.

As curious, if not recalcitrant, as ever, Amantha then put in:

–But why start with timocracy? That's totally arbitrary!

–Good question, dear girl! *exclaimed Socrates.* There's a reason for doing so that's very compelling, albeit hard to grasp, namely that timocracy is the form of community that comes directly from our fifth system of government. It's the very first form of corruption of the latter. So it takes precedence over the other three.

–And then we'll go from bad to worse?

–Exactly.

–That's a very mysterious origin, though! *said Glaucon, taking his sister's side.* How can imperfection emerge from something that's consistent with the Idea? I just don't get it.

–The theory of transitions is always the hardest thing. But let's give it a try anyway. A very simple starting point is to restate what one of our group called "the primacy of internal causes": a body politic will change only if a sort of civil war pits different factions within it against each other. However large – or rather, however small – the group of real leaders may be, so long as they have the same vision of things the body politic will remain impervious to change. Consequently, dear Glaucon, if a community united by our fifth system of government can nevertheless change for the worse, it means that the spirit of civil war has infected and divided its leaders, including its military leaders, and has set them against each other.

–But how is that possible? Our rational principles virtually dictate everyone's having the same political vision!

–Yes, that's true. Our discussion has hit a snag. I think that, like old Homer at the beginning of the *Iliad*, we have no choice but to beg the Muses to share a big secret with us: the origin of civil wars, or, in other words, the origin of negation, which resides in every existent, however perfect it may be.

Amantha, who liked difficult moments, had no qualms about making the one they were going through even worse.

–To judge by how many boring poets, mendacious historians, and dancers who can't get off the ground there are, the Muses aren't easy to win over, *she remarked.*

–Well, I, for one, *Socrates shot back,* am going to invoke those melodious daughters and make them come alive in my words, as if they were playing and chatting with us, albeit with the seriousness of tragic poetry.

–What will they talk to us about? *asked a very excited Glaucon.*

–Listen carefully to them, kids: "It is difficult to bring about any change for the worse in a body politic like the one you have founded. However, as Amantha, citing Goethe, said a little while ago, everything that comes into being deserves to perish. Thus, your political order will not last indefinitely. It, too, will eventually break down. Why? For reasons having to do with both arithmetic and demographics.[1] The count of its parts, or neighborhoods, which is correlated to the fertility of couples, will gradually malfunction. Indeed, we know that, for plants as well as for animals, for men as well as the gods, the life cycle and the perpetuation of essential symbols is regulated by numbers. In the case of the gods, everything is a mirror image of a perfect infinite number. As regards the human species, in the most perfect case – the body politic you are in the process of formalizing – things are much less certain. The base number is 6. Six is actually twice 3; it is therefore the product of male perfection – the two, the emblem of separation or of symbolic abstraction – and female perfection – the three, the emblem of production or creative intuition. That is why the perfect symbol of fertility is composed of six human beings: a woman, a man, and four children. To such sets is assigned a nuptial number, which, in order to indicate the end of all solitude, is always greater than one. We call the Idea of the nuptial number not this number itself but the number that results from it, taken first according to its latent femininity, that is, repeated three times, or raised to the power of 3, and then taken according to the rest of the nuptial set, that is, the male principle and the four children, which makes five times the number."

–If I'm following you correctly, *said Glaucon, very intent,* assuming that *n* is a nuptial number, its idea is $n^3 + 5n$.

–Exactly, *Socrates remarked.* And it gets its ideational perfection from the fact that it's always divisible by 6, the base number.

–Regardless of what number n is?

–Glaucon! *said Socrates with a smile.* You've interrupted the Muses twice now! Here's what they answer: "Yes, whatever the nuptial number n is, its Idea, $n^3 + 5n$, is always divisible by 6. You can prove this, dear interrupter, by recursion on n. Nevertheless, to ensure the survival of your political community, the number of nuptial sets in any given neighborhood of the community should also be a multiple of the base number 6. And, furthermore, there should be a special nuptial number called the Iris of the neighborhood, such that its Idea is equal to the total number of nuptial sets, which, let us repeat, are units of six members: two parents and four children. For, if the law is egalitarian and communistic, any political number must also be a factor of that of which it is the number."

–I note, *said Glaucon,* that at any rate both of them – the total number of nuptial sets and the Idea of the nuptial number that's the Iris of the neighborhood – are divisible by 6.

But the Muses invoked by Socrates would not allow themselves to be interrupted by this correct observation and continued with what they were saying. They went over in silence to an enormous blackboard and chanted as they wrote the following observations in purple chalk on it:

"If N is the total number of nuptial sets of a neighborhood, and if n is the nuptial number that is the Iris – the number whose Idea is equal to the whole – then $n^3 + 5n = N$, which can also be expressed as $n (n^2 + 5) = N$. It follows that the Iris number n is a divisor of the total number N, just as is the Iris number squared plus 5. This is what the comrades in charge of the size of the neighborhoods must be unwaveringly concerned with and what, one day or other, centuries from now, they will forget: namely that the number of nuptial sets of a neighborhood and the nuptial numbers assigned to these sets must be such that an Iris number and its Idea equal to the whole can really exist. The rule of divisibility by 6 is so simple and so obviously linked to the sexual symbols 2 and 3 that the risk of forgetting is very slight. But the same cannot be said for the subtle connection between the nuptial numbers and the total number of sets they define, a connection represented by the Idea of the Iris number. Suppose, for example, that the number of nuptial sets of a neighborhood is 150. Then the Idea of the number 5, which is assumed to be nuptial, is $5^3 + (5 \times 5)$, or $125 + 25 = 150$, and 5 is indeed the Iris number of the neighborhood. But suppose that the comrades in charge haven't assigned the number 5 as the nuptial number. What will happen then? The neighborhood will not have any Iris number at all. Another example: those in charge have carelessly set the acceptable number of nuptial sets of the neighborhood at 78, which is in fact divisible by 6, because 78 = 6 x 13. Then, carried away by the dogmatic cult of the 6, they only assigned multiples of 6 as nuptial numbers. They thought they were doing the right thing, blessing nuptial fertility in this way with the fundamental number of sex! But what happens? If $n^3 + 5n = 78$, which requires n to be Iris, we get $n\,(n^2 + 5) = 78$. But if n is divisible by 6, or $n = 6q$, we'll get $6q\,(36q^2 + 5) = 78$ or, simplifying by 6, $q\,(36q^2 + 5) = 13$, which is completely impossible. Because, since 13 is a prime number, either q, the divisor of 13, is equal to 1, which gives 41 = 13, or $q = 13$, which gives 79,157 = 13, something that's even more atrocious. Which means that the neighborhood won't have any Iris at all.

These are the omissions and errors that, over the long term, will deprive your political community of the astral equilibrium that can only be guaranteed to it by the existence, neighborhood by neighborhood, of an Iris number. The first symptom of decline will be the emergence of a broad current of public opinion favoring spectacular games, the idolization of sports, the sexual misadventures of celebrities, and TV shows for ignorant viewers, to the detriment of everything that belongs to thought: deductive and experimental sciences, intense loves, egalitarian political organization, the shifting of the dividing line between the formal and the formless in art, and so forth. Future generations will acquire a taste for instant gratification, superficial trivialities and the listless cult of non-being. On this subjective breeding ground will bloom the showy, artificial flowers of proudly proclaimed dissimilarity, of minor self-centered differences, of discord, at once furtive and passionate, and ultimately of the desire for the most abject inequality to take root."

–What tragic eloquence these Muses have! *said Amantha, full of admiration.*

–Well, of course, *said Socrates in his normal bass-baritone voice.* No one expects them to chatter like magpies!

–But what will happen next? *asked a breathless Glaucon.*

–Let's listen to what the Muses have to say for another moment: "That desire for inequality, as historical experience shows, gives rise to hatred and war on all sides. The body politic tends to split into two. On the one hand, there are those who adopt profit as the norm. Taking advantage of an already ruinous state of affairs in many neighboring countries, they amass, more or less surreptitiously, money, land, *objets d'art*, stocks, bonds, drafts, and so on. In contrast to these *nouveaux riches*, there are those who continue to hold on, albeit feebly, to the idea that the only true wealth lies in what a

Subject is capable of, and who attempt to keep the communist idea and its corresponding civil organization alive. The conflict breaks out in the open and the country's political unity is shattered. This is the start of a ruthless class struggle, with much violence. But the very impetus of this struggle gradually slackens because, under the pretext of military necessities, the civil war leads to the emergence, on both sides, of ruling cliques that are seemingly pitted against each other when viewed in terms of the day-to-day situation, but that, contaminated as they both are by the intoxication of power and the worship of brute force, actually share the same belief in inequality. On that basis, since the people are weary of these endless bloody episodes, a fatal compromise is invariably reached: the divvying-up of land, houses, and money – in short, the restoration, to the advantage of both cliques, of private property. These people, who then take power and who, back in the days of the old communist order, regarded everyone as free friends and militants in the same cause, can now only think about maintaining their dominance and subjugating the people, whom they treat as if they were comprised only of clients or servants. At the same time, this new brand of leaders, maintaining a monopoly on war and weapons, split this monopoly off altogether from ordinary collective life and create a machine of state fit for combat but divorced from any control by the people. Thus is born a new type of political community, midway, as it were, between communism and oligarchy."

The Muses then fell silent, and it was in his ordinary voice that Socrates eventually broke the hush that, after such almost mystical solemnity, had for a few long minutes fallen over the room, softly illuminated as it was by the rays of the late-morning sun.

–The fifth and second systems of government! Communism and oligarchy! That's a strange mixture. And yet this is precisely what emerged toward the end of the bureaucratized Communist experiments, in Russia and China, at the end of a misguided century.

–It's this sort of hybrid regime, *asked Glaucon,* that you call "timocracy"?

–You're the one who suggested the term a moment ago. This timocracy mimics the communism it comes from and the oligarchy that follows it. After the fall of the Soviet Union, the apparatchiks of the Communist state, like their so-called enemies, became the super-rich "oligarchs" of post-Communist capitalism. "Oligarchs" – let me stress the word: that's the name they're given. That speaks volumes. The difficulty, for us, is how to define the distinctive features of the timocratic regime, the first product of a long period of decline.

–From what you've said, *Amantha remarked,* the timocratic state is built on the monopoly it has on war. That point must have far-reaching consequences.

–Yes, unfortunately it does! Because of the climate of civil war and intellectual decline, the prevailing taste will be for dynamic, impetuous, rough people born for war rather than peace – in a nutshell, those dominated by what I called in the middle of the night last night the second agency of the Subject, that enigmatic "spirit," which I prefer to call "Affect," the seat of reckless, brutal action. As for the third agency, Thought, what timocrats value above all are the ruses of war, cunning tactics, the spirit of ambush. And the most highly prized practice is to be armed at all times. At the same time, these rough and ready men, who at first were not without a kind of warrior-like integrity, become used to giving orders, to hierarchy, inequality, and the intrigues of power. As a result, they become greedy for money, just as in oligarchic states. They end up worshipping this monetary fetish, albeit on the sly. They have secret storehouses and fortunes hidden away in big villas concealed from view behind high walls and armed to the gills with surveillance cameras. Believing they're protected from rumors this way, they spend incredible amounts of money at home on banquets, booze, music, miscellaneous drugs, and especially on willing, naked women. These people actually have a conflictual relationship with their own wealth. On the one hand they're miserly, since their adoration of wealth increases due to the fact that they possess it illegally and can only make use of it in secret. But on the other hand they're spendthrifts, goaded on as they are by desire. They're like children trying to avoid the law of the father. Why? Because their upbringing was based not on persuasion but on force. They deserted the Muse of Truth, the muse of rational argumentation and philosophy. They showered honors on jogging, gymnastics, fitness training, Thai boxing, cyclo-cross racing, volleyball, ping-pong, and even sumo wrestling, rather than on the arts and sciences.

–And all that, *said Glaucon,* no doubt gives rise to governments like those of Sparta, imperial Rome, the Turkey of the Janissaries, the Mongols at the height of their power, Japan after the Meiji Era, the United States in its twilight years, or even Nazi Germany, doesn't it?

–Some of your examples are over the top. Let's not lose sight of the fact that this political paradigm is a mixture of good and evil. As a matter of fact, it owes its characteristic feature to the fact that reckless aggressiveness – the second agency of the Subject – predominates in it. I'm talking about competitive ambition, about the love of fame and glory. That feature epitomizes the origins and nature of this type of political community. This is over-simplified, I admit. But, since our only aim, as far as this matter is concerned, is to decide about the just and unjust man, it would be pointless and tedious to go over our five systems of government and their corresponding character types in minute detail.

–Yeah, this is already taking long enough as it is! *agreed Amantha-the-snide.*

–Oh, so maybe *you* could describe for us in nothing flat the character type that corresponds to the timocratic system of government? *Socrates countered.*

–That's easy! He's a blowhard, a guy on the make, and a hedonist who could be the twin of my brother Glaucon here. . .

–You've got a point, *said Socrates with a smile.* But there are nevertheless a few little differences between the timocratic man and your brother.

–Oh yeah? Like what, for instance? *Amantha retorted skeptically.*

–The timocrat's more arrogant than our friend Glaucon and far less cultured, even if it's an exaggeration to call him an ignorant boor, as the Athenians claim the Spartans are. The timocrat might enjoy conversation, but his debating ability is as mediocre as can be. He's rude to people he considers his inferiors instead of disdaining all that social status business, the way well-bred people should. On the other hand, he has a tendency to grovel before anybody who's anybody in his country, and especially before the big shots in the state apparatus. That's because he loves power and glory. His ambition can't be based on any talent as an orator or intellectual superiority, however, since the only things that matter for him are great military feats and, more broadly speaking, anything connected with war. That's no doubt why he's an inveterate athlete and a fanatic hunter.

–You haven't described his relationship with money for us. That's important, after all, for us who advocate equality, even at the price of a certain asceticism.

–When he's young, the timocrat often disdains wealth. But as he grows older he craves it more and more, for two reasons: first, his secret natural affinity, which we've already mentioned, with that extremely common character type, the Miser; and, second, on account of the fact that his moral compass comes and goes, as a consequence of his lacking a supreme Master in his life.

–What master is that? *asked the hysteric lurking within the avid Amantha.*

–Reason, once it's been supplemented by scientific, artistic, literary, historical, or even quite simply existential culture. It's the only thing

254

that can safeguard the virtues to which the whole life of the Subject is devoted.

–Well, that's a very impersonal master, *said Amantha, disappointed.*

–But you can see this young timocrat, the very image of the system of government whose name he bears, as if he were right before your eyes, can't you?

–Yeah, sure. . . But I wonder how he got to be what he is.

–Oh, let's try and imagine! Let's see. . . Maybe he's the young son of a decent man, in a country under the rule of a bad system of government. The father wants nothing to do with honors, positions of power, lawsuits, and the whole wheeler-dealer scene. He prefers anonymity to social success. He couldn't be any less of a celebrity. His favorite saying is: "The quiet life is the happy life."[2]

–I don't see the connection between a father like that and the young guy on the make we were talking about.

–Well, we need to trace things back to his mother's complaints. Throughout our timocrat's childhood, she griped about how her husband didn't have one of the top jobs in the government, which made *her* be regarded as less than nothing by the other women in polite society. She moaned that he never so much as lifted a finger to acquire apartment buildings, villas, iPods and iPhones and iTunes, horses, horsepower, horseradish, bearskin coats, stocks, coupons, bonds, masterpieces, master keys, master cylinders, or master plans, nothing! Less than nothing! She deplored her husband's weakness, his total ineptness when it came to picking a fight with an opponent and insulting him in court or in the People's Assembly. She bitterly rued the fact that *he* bore such affronts with the patience of a saint. From all this she came to the conclusion that he was wrapped up in himself and felt neither genuine respect nor any particular contempt for his wife. He was indifference personified! So she was choked with indignation, the mom was, when she told all this to her darling son, and she *had* to tell him: his father wasn't a real man, he was too easy-going, he was too this, he was too that. . . All the sorts of things that women like to say in such cases.

–Oh, right! It's *women*'s fault! *said a furious Amantha.*

–Yes, but not just theirs, *Socrates said in an attempt to placate her,* not just theirs! All the people who hover around a young man of good family tell him, sometimes on the sly, the same thing. The chauffeur, the cook, the gardener, the bodyguards – they all do it! Let's say they've seen someone who owed the young man's father money, a really big amount. Well, his father didn't do a thing about it, no lawsuit, no threats! Nothing! Less than nothing! So they all tell the young master that he shouldn't be like his dad, that he should use strong-arm tactics. "Yes, little guy," they all say in unison, "*you*'ve got to be a man, a real man, not like your old man." And if our young man, the future timocrat, leaves the house, if he goes downtown, if he hangs out in the streets, he hears the same sort of thing again: people who mind their own business are called idiots and held in low regard, while people who are trendy and involved in a million different things are flattered and showered with praise. That's the experience of the young man in the world. But, at the same time, he listens to his father, he sees from up close how he leads his life, he compares him with what the others say and do. That's why he's inwardly conflicted. On the one hand, his father feeds and waters the rational agency of the Subject, Thought, like a precious plant. But, on the other hand, his mother and public opinion encourage the opposite agency, indiscriminate Desire. As our young man is not naturally inclined to evil, he splits the difference: he entrusts the direction of his life to neither Thought nor Desire but to the agency in between the two, the one that's irascible, irritable, and unstable, which I call Affect. Since this agency, in his case, consists mainly of ambition and a hot-tempered spirit, he becomes a supremely arrogant adult who's primarily enamored of fame: a timocrat.

–He's a marvelous dialectical balancing act between the Father and the Mother, that son is! *remarked Amantha.*

–What about the others, *Glaucon added,* the democratic, oligarchic, and tyrannical teenagers? How do they manage to extricate themselves from that quagmire of the family? We need to study the other bad systems of government now. As Aeschylus says in *The Seven Against Thebes (and here Glaucon's delight in being able to prove he was as cultured as Socrates gave him credit for was only too apparent):*

Another champion before another gate.[3]

–You're really putting the screws on me, *said Socrates good-naturedly.* Well, all right, let's turn to oligarchy and the oligarchic man. Let's say that oligarchy's the system of government that's based on wealth. Voting eligibility is based on the cens. The wealthy – those who are able to pay the cens – take over leadership of the country and the poor have no part in it.

–So how do you get from timocracy to oligarchy? *asked Glaucon.*

–Silly boy! Even a blind man could see how that happens! The big banks in which they anxiously deposit enormous fortunes – that's what destroys the timocrats. First they find very expensive pleasures to enjoy, and, in order to be able to indulge in them, they get around the laws or flout them altogether. And in this regard high-society women lead the way. Then, since everyone observes everyone else and engages in mimetic competition with one another, the people as a whole become like the pioneers before them in pursuing extravagant pleasures. From then on, all they can think about is getting rich. The more powerful the cult of money becomes, the weaker that of civic virtue becomes. For wealth and virtue are so different that they invariably orient the same person's life in opposite directions.

–But what happens then? *queried Glaucon, ever the aficionado of sociology, anthropology, archeology, and positivist history.* How does the new form of the state take hold?

–When some desire holds sway over public opinion, people look all over for the things to satisfy it, and they abandon the actions and subjective dispositions whose prominence other opinions, now obsolete, used to ensure. By the end of this whole process, the citizens of a timocracy, the lovers of fame and victory, become at once greedy and stingy. They praise the rich man every chance they get and raise him to power, leaving to the poor man only despair and a wasted life.

–But what about the state, the law, the constitution? *Glaucon, as excited as could be, begged to know.*

–They pass laws defining who has a right to engage in political activity in the new oligarchic order and, as a qualification, they set a certain amount of wealth – the more powerful the oligarchy, the bigger the amount – below which you're excluded from having any share in power. These laws are often imposed by force of arms. At any rate, this type of government can only be established in a climate of fear.

–I'd like further details, *Glaucon insisted.* What's the dominant character type in this new context? And what's the main defect of a system of government like this?

–Its main defect, or just about, is that the very principle it's based on is wrong. Imagine if airplane pilots were chosen only according to how wealthy they were and no plane were ever allowed to be flown by a poor pilot, no matter how skilled he was.

–You can bet we'd see plenty of planes idling on the runway!

–As the Red Guards used to say during the Cultural Revolution in China, and they obviously had Mao in mind: "To sail the high seas, you need a helmsman." Ships, planes, systems of government, states . . . In the final analysis, it makes no difference. The only things that matter are talent and confidence. Wealth counts for nothing. But,

257

in addition, every oligarchic regime is afflicted with a fatal disease because the country where it holds sway is no longer one country but two and is always threatened by civil war. In one and the same territory there are the country of the rich and the country of the poor. Each side wears itself out plotting against the other. But that's not all. An oligarchic country can hardly wage war against an enemy country. Either the government of the wealthy has to arm the masses of poor people – and then it'll be more afraid of *them* than of the enemy – or else it will refuse to do so, and then the only thing the mere handful of soldiers on the battlefield will be able to do is take cover behind their useless sacks of gold. Actually, the oligarchic government is so stingy that it won't pay for weapons for anyone.

Amantha then seemed to take an interest in the discussion, remarking:

–They'd do what that guy from some little backwater town or other that was threatened by Rome did. There was talk of mobilization, of national defense, all that stuff. And he – a rich guy, in actual fact – suggested reducing the army to a single soldier who'd be posted on the border and who'd be able to say in Latin: "We surrender unconditionally." That way, he argued, they'd save a ton of money.

–Wealth and treason do often go hand in hand, *Socrates agreed.* But, on top of that, poverty, in an oligarchy, is often associated with trafficking, corruption, and crime. The concentration of wealth in only a few hands and the cautious restrictions placed on productive activity lead to lots of people just being there, on the outskirts of big cities, with nothing to do, since they obviously can't be the idle rich; nor can they be shopkeepers, soldiers, office employees, or even – and this is the worst of all – workers. Their designation is just "poor people." In Muslim countries they're called "the disinherited." As for Marx, he called them the *lumpenproletariat.*

–How is it, *asked Glaucon,* that the oligarchs don't take any action against such a state of affairs? Because if they did, there wouldn't be such a stark contrast between a handful of extremely wealthy people and a totally impoverished mass of people.

–Let's take a close look at your problem. The only thing the wealthy cared about back when, in the framework of timocracy, they were merely citizens, was spending their fortunes. Do you think that just because they're in power they'll have changed? That now they'll render great services to the country? They only *seem* to be rulers. They go on being neither real leaders of the state nor its true servants. Their only concern is still the wealthy and their wealth. They're "agents of capitalism," as Marx puts it. That's why they're categorically opposed to the idea of greater equality in people's material lives.

–What the oligarch primarily wants, *concluded Glaucon,* is for the oligarchic government to help him remain an oligarch.

–Exactly. And just as the drone is born among the bees in the hive to be a parasite and a blight on it, we can say that a fat cat of that sort is like a drone in the public sphere: a blight on the government and the country. But the drones in the hive – the Other saw to this – have wings but no stinger, whereas two-legged drones, the ones in oligarchic regimes, are of two different sorts. Some of them – an old man dying in poverty, a woman reduced to begging in order to raise her children, a girl forced into prostitution by her lover, a disabled man on his crutches, for example – have no stinger either. But the others, the criminals, *do* have one, and it can hurt like hell: they're hornets. It's a fact that in every country where there's a large contingent of poor people, of *déclassés,* a huge *lumpenproletariat,* you find petty thieves, drug dealers, Mafia enforcers, and bank robbers.

–So there must be loads of them in oligarchic countries, given that everyone in them is poor, except for the ruling clique.

–You said it! The drones with stingers abound there, and it's only with large numbers of police roundups and grim prisons that the government manages to cope with the situation.

–What a great description! But what's the oligarchic man, the Subject of this system of government, like?

–Take the son of an eminent timocrat. At first, owing to his Oedipus complex, he competes with his father. He follows him around like a puppy. But then one day he sees his father suddenly wrecked by the state, like a ship struck by one of Zeus' thunderbolts. His poor father! Here's a man who'd put everything he possessed, indeed his very life, at the disposal of the state, a man who'd been chief of staff of the armies, a man with enormous power, suddenly dragged before the court, slandered by informers, dishonored, forced to choose between exile and death, all his possessions auctioned off.

–I've read some incredible stories like that in the paper, *Glaucon remarked,* especially about Sparta.

–So the son sees his father's comedown; he feels it viscerally. What's more, he himself is completely bankrupt now. He panics. He who wanted to become incorporated into a Subject whose life would be ruled by honor and courage now changes completely. It's like a *coup d'état* in his soul. He feels so demeaned by poverty that money becomes his only god. Like a snake before the onset of winter, with a lot of arduous crawling and miserly frugality he accumulates enough

259

to live without worry. He then relinquishes all power over himself to insatiable desire and boundless greed. On this great king of his soul he bestows the crown, the ceremonial chains, and the holy sabre.

–Careful, dear Socrates! I'm putting up a sign: "Danger: poetry ahead," *joked Amantha.*

–As for the power of reason and the emotional, irritable, unstable, and spirited faculty, he forces them to prostrate themselves at the feet of this new king, on either side of the throne, like lowly slaves. The former he only allows to calculate his fortune and consider how to increase it. As for the latter, it may only admire and revere wealth and the wealthy and, where fame is concerned, just stick to the wealth already amassed and the means for acquiring even more.

–He plunges, *recapped Glaucon a tad pedantically,* from the loftiest ambition to the most abject avarice. He's thus formatted for an oligarchic computer.

–Let's examine in detail what you call his "formatting" – which, being less up-to-date than you, I'd translate as: his drives are suited to what the political regime demands of the individuals under its control. First of all, he values wealth above all else. His motto is "Work and Save." Second of all, he only allows himself to satisfy desires that are strictly necessary; all the rest he treats as frivolous requests, and he abstains from spending anything at all on them.

–He's really stingy, *said Amantha indignantly.*

–You can say that again! It's especially for him that money becomes, as good old Marx puts it, a "general equivalent," because the desire to accumulate wealth drives him to turn everything into money. He's incorporated alive, so to speak, into Capital. By the way, that's also the fate awaiting the budget of the state in this type of regime: society and individuals alike are mere components of the circulation of money.

–I suppose, *Glaucon then said,* that this sort of character paid no attention to the literary and philosophical teaching dispensed in the later years of high school. Had he been properly educated, he would never have allowed his desires to be dictated by the money whose stupid blindness[4] he worships.

–Right! *said Socrates admiringly.* It's because our fellow is a victim of what Marx – yes, him again – calls "the fetishism of merchandise." But careful! The fact that the oligarch is usually ignorant has a lot of other consequences. In particular, "drone"-like desires – we were talking about this a few minutes ago – crop up in the dark recesses of his soul. These desires, both beggarly and criminal, are usually kept in check in the oligarchic man by the care he devotes to his own best interests. And therefore, to see how powerful they are, you have to observe him when he's in charge of managing the fortune of a minor, an old man, or a mental patient and he thinks he can operate with impunity. It's then that we'll understand what went on when this kind of guy abided scrupulously by contracts, thanks to which he acquired a reputation as an honest and just man. Sure, he suppressed his evil desires, but the inner violence that he used to that end has nothing at all to do with his believing that that was the path of the Good, or even with the kind of self-restraint that's dictated by reason. He merely obeyed the murky necessities entailed by cynicism: he dreaded losing all the possessions he'd already heaped up through fraud and extortion. But when it comes to spending *other* people's money, well, then, sheesh, the whole swarm of his drone-like desires comes flying out with nothing to stop it!

–And so the oligarch becomes a drone through and through, *concluded Glaucon, with the sort of suspicious satisfaction that the sight of a disaster always affords.*

–Not at all, my boy! There's no way that kind of man can avoid having an inner civil war. Inwardly, he's not one but two. As Jacques Lacan would say, he's a split subject. His subjective self's motto is actually: "desire against desire." But you've got to give him credit for the fact that the good desires prevail over the evil ones in most cases. That's why he's more attractive than many other character types. But our man will always remain very far removed from unity and immanent harmony, which are the norm of the Subject once it comes into being as such in the element of Truth.

Amantha then piped up:

– Couldn't you conclude, dear Socrates, with one of those short, colorful portraits you once used to have a knack for?

Ignoring her snide remark, Socrates said:

–The oligarch's stinginess makes him incapable of publicly competing with his fellow citizens, of sharing with them a generous vision of life, which consists of victories because it is inspired by a keen sense of honor. As his greatest fear is of having to stir up a bunch of spendthrift desires in order to defeat his rivals, he refuses to spend money on any fights in which only his fame is at stake. Thus, he commits only a measly share of his resources to fighting and, like a typical oligarch, he prefers the fate of a man who, though defeated and dishonored, is nevertheless content merely because he can go on sitting on his pile of gold.

–Not bad! Not bad! *Amantha opined.*

–Anyway, *added Glaucon,* there's no doubt that a man like that is

261

strictly isomorphic with the type of government he's both the cause and the effect of, the one in which wealth alone is the measure of power.

–Maybe we've said enough about this kind of guy, *concluded Amantha with a comical look of disgust on her face.*

CRITIQUE OF THE FOUR PRE-COMMUNIST SYSTEMS OF GOVERNMENT

II Democracy and Tyranny (555b–573b)

–I think, *Glaucon went on,* that we can turn to democracy now, its origins, its nature, and its corresponding character type. First, dear Socrates, tell us, how the change from oligarchy to democracy, historically speaking, comes about.

–The impetus for that transition is none other than an infinite desire, aroused by the only object in an oligarchic regime that's identified with the Good: money. The shift from oligarchy to democracy occurs when the imperative to enjoy, along the lines of a nineteenth-century French minister's dictum "Get rich!,"[1] becomes an unlimited general imperative.

–But how does it happen in actual practice? *Glaucon's empiricist daemon queried.*

–The leaders of an oligarchic state are only in power owing to their enormous fortunes. So they don't want any harsh laws cracking down on the segment of youth called "gilded youth," who squander the family fortune on gambling, horse racing, fashion shows, cocaine, or high-class brothels. Why are they so lenient? Because the old oligarchs in power are determined to buy up, at dirt-cheap prices, the property these young people will have to sell off to pay their debts, and then, when they've practically bankrupted them, loan them money at exorbitant interest rates, which will force these young people to mortgage what little they have left. Thanks to these underhanded tactics, the rich leaders will become super-rich. But it won't be long before the effects are felt. In any state, it's impossible for people to worship money and at the same time acquire the self-discipline required for an even minimally sensible collective life. One or the other will definitely have to be sacrificed. In the case of an oligarchy, what happens is that, as a result of the oligarchs' self-serving leniency, young people who are doubtless weak but gifted, or even exceptionally brilliant minds, are eventually reduced to poverty. Excessive spending, nihilism, brothels, debts, and even prison: people of the stature of Tolstoy and Rimbaud experienced things like that in their youth, didn't they?

–Sure, *said Amantha*. But I can hardly imagine Socrates making *Rimbaud* the model for the philosophical life.

–That's because you have a stereotypical academic image of me. Rimbaud, sure, by all means! He epitomizes the burning desire for a life lived in accordance with the Idea, Rimbaud does. As he was very young, he looked in every direction, he kept at it relentlessly, he took every experience to the extreme. And at last he was saved, by work, concentration, dedication, and anonymity. He's the perfect Socratic man! But where on earth were we?

–You were observing, *said Glaucon-the-serious,* that an oligarchic regime throws scores of intelligent people out on the streets, people who've become aggressive like your so-called drones and armed to the teeth, some of them crippled with debt, others disgraced, and all of them knowing they have nothing left to lose.

–Oh, right! These people hate the regime in power that bankrupted them. They secretly plot against those who seized their property and, even beyond them, against the whole ruling class, which they consider to be complicit in that plunder. In short, these fallen *petits bourgeois* now long for a revolution. Seeing bankers, hedge fund managers, and other such multimillionaire bigwigs grandstanding on television as if they were the great benefactors of a liberal society is the last straw. Galled by the flaunting of these people's "newfound wealth" and the ubiquitous publicity showered day after day on people with fabulous fortunes, the entire middle class, its members having slowly become paupers, is ready to give in to political adventurism.

–There's nothing worse, *said Glaucon sententiously,* than devoting your whole life to the bountiful joys of the market only to end up being in constant, nagging financial difficulties.

–The evil then becomes like an invisible fire raging throughout the country, spreading far and wide. And yet the ruling class absolutely rejects every means of putting it out. They obviously won't use the method that we communists have always been suggesting: the collective ownership of all private property. But neither will they accept reforms that would nonetheless be compatible with the oligarchic system, such as passing a law that would eliminate the speculative excesses of modern finance.

–But, as you yourself said, *objected Amantha,* the appetite for gain, the lust for money, are unlimited desires. How can you expect to restrict them with a law?

–We can still conceive of laws that would introduce certain limits on the aberrations of financial circulation. That's called market "regulation." For example, you could prohibit granting loans to people who are notoriously insolvent. It would require loans having to be made at the *lenders'* risk, too, not just the borrower's. Then people would think twice about getting rich by ruining any chance of there being a sort of social harmony, even if it were inegalitarian. . .

–. . . and therefore unacceptable in our eyes, *Amantha interrupted him.* But it seems to me, *she continued,* that you're buying into the theory of a virtuous financial market. That's really like talking about the squared circle.

–I have to admit that the oligarchy won't hear of my reforms. It regards poor people, its subjects, the losers, as – pardon my French – shit. And as for itself, it just keeps on getting richer with a show of superfluous, vulgar ostentation. The spoiled rich kids live each day as it comes, incapable of making any intellectual effort, needless to say, but hardly any better off when it comes to sports either. Arrogant and lazy in equal measure, they acquire no discipline, not even the discipline of pleasure, let alone that imposed by adversity and conflicts. As for the fathers, who care about nothing but stocks, bonds, bank accounts, complex securities, take-over bids, and the current price of commodities, they're less concerned about virtue than the lousiest crook.

–I still don't see, *said Amantha, frowning,* how all that amounts to a transition from oligarchy to democracy.

–Draw the conclusions from what I just said – from class hatred, in a word. Look at the cases where the rulers and the broad masses of their subjects take part in the same collective action.

–You mean a trip? Or a migration somewhere?

–Yes, or any other situation of that sort: a mission to some distant country, a military expedition, when the officers and soldiers embark aboard the same ship or fight side by side. When they're thrown together in a dangerous situation, they observe one another, don't they? And it's never the rich who look down on the poor. It's the exact opposite. Very often, the vagaries of a battle will throw some poor, skinny, dark-skinned fellow together with a fair-complexioned rich guy with a prominent paunch. And what does the ordinary soldier see? That the other guy is completely worn out, miserable, unable to go on fighting. He then thinks to himself that such people only manage to stay in power owing to the cowardice of the dominated classes, the mental corruption that prevents the formation of a victorious organization of farmers, workers, employees, and their allies among the intellectuals. And so, when the ordinary soldiers are back together again, out of earshot of the high command, in the great twilight in which every battle ends, word goes around pretty much like this: "The people we thought were powerful are really at our mercy! They derive their existence only from our weakness. By themselves, they're nothing!"

–And then, *said Glaucon,* revolution's in the making.

–You bet! All it takes is a slight outside influence for a living organism, if it's weak, to become critically ill. It can sometimes even come into mortal conflict with itself without any outside action at all. A state like the one we've just described can similarly fall ill and unleash a civil war within itself on the flimsiest of pretexts. Each side calls in help from foreign powers – the oligarchs from oligarchies and the democrats from democracies. The rebellion sometimes even plunges the whole country into a bloodbath without the slightest outside intervention.

–If I understand correctly, *said Amantha,* democracy arises when the lower classes, led by the political leaders of the middle classes that are becoming paupers, are ultimately victorious. They kill some of the oligarchs, they exile others, and they share the responsibilities of power and governing with the people who are left. Moreover, as we know, these responsibilities are eventually assigned by lottery. But don't the poor end up being duped by the quasi-rich in this process?

–That's another story. . . At any rate, this is really how democracy is established, through originary violence, and then through a sort of secret terror that makes the former rulers, even those who rallied to the cause at first, take flight.

–What we need to do now, *said Glaucon a tad pedantically,* is to take a close look at how these democrats govern themselves and at what the true nature of this much-vaunted democratic system of government is. As for the character type corresponding to it, I think, dear Socrates, that you'd call it purely and simply "the democratic man."

– Of course I would, *said an amused Socrates.* You know, there's practically only one word that matters on the lips of our democrats, the word "freedom." In a democratic country, they claim, you're free to say and do whatever you like.

–All they do is peddle what the propaganda of the "democratic" countries, our beloved Western powers, is always drumming into us, *Amantha remarked scathingly.* We're "free" at any rate to make money and become billionaires on the backs of poor people the world over. But that really needs to be examined a bit more closely.

–That's just what we intend to do, *Glaucon announced in a self-important tone.*

–Oh, so now you talk about yourself in the plural? *said Amantha sarcastically.*

–Quiet, kids, *Socrates cut in.* Let's note, to begin with, that wherever people have the right – at least theoretically – to do pretty much whatever they please, each person chooses the model of life he likes and tries to make his own life match it. So in a country with a democratic government there'll be people with remarkably varied outward appearances.

–Which doesn't stop them, *grumbled Amantha,* from being oddly alike and repeating things like parrots as soon as you broach real issues.

–Let's not get ahead of ourselves. It's nonetheless true that this type of state has all sorts of charms. The big cities, bursting with goods, are like a multi-colored garment, dazzling the eyes of amazed foreigners with every possible and conceivable shade and hue. So they have a tendency to exclaim: "Isn't democracy wonderful!" And it may well be that most people – beginning with the ones who are like children or the fashion-conscious, inasmuch as their desire is aroused by variety – consider the democratic state to be the most attractive and desirable one of all. What's more, the freedom that democrats pride themselves on extends to many aspects of the state's constitutional structure as well. It may be federal or centralized, consist of two, or even three, legislative chambers, or only one, and either have or not have a Constitutional Council that judges the laws without consulting anyone else. In addition to the head of government and his ministers, there may even be kings and queens: "democracy" and "republic" are not synonymous. There are an extraordinary number of methods used to organize the basic rite of this type of system of government: the election of representatives. Voting can be either direct or indirect, by majority or proportional, by the largest remainder or the highest average method, by one round of voting or by two, by a list of candidates or by individual candidates, held at a national level or narrowed down to tiny constituencies, etc. It's all very simple: it's perfectly possible to demonstrate that, with one type of voting, a given party will win, and with another type the opposing party will win, while the number of votes obtained by one or the other of them remains unchanged. You can also have "popular" referendums on the Constitution, on international treaties, on secular schools, and on climate change, but also on the right to carry a revolver on one's belt or on the odor of pig excrements given off on the plains. In short, there's something a bit like a "constitutional supermarket" about democratic countries.

—But how does it work? Who makes the decisions, with all these overlapping methods?

—Most of the important decisions, the ones regarding the police, war, alliances, and the big financial and industrial groups, are secret decisions, made in meetings that are not provided for in the Constitution and that the public doesn't know about. Meanwhile, only for show, there are heated "debates" on minor issues, like the marriage of gay priests or the protection of blue whales. But don't worry, they've still got their so-called freedom! If someone has real leadership ability, he's not in the least obliged to exercise authority, nor to submit to it either, for that matter, if he doesn't want to. War is fought only by volunteers, mercenaries of sorts; no one else can be bothered. If some small, powerful group thinks war is in its own interest, and even if the majority of people might want peace, there's a good chance that war will occur. If the law bars you from being a representative or a senator, you can become one anyway, provided you're determined, patient, rich, and well-connected with the majority in power. That's because justice is variable. Criminal defendants, provided they're part of the political establishment or the financial or media elite, have nothing to worry about. You see people who are likely to cop the maximum sentence, especially for corruption, and who normally could only avoid prison by going into exile, walking around without a care in the world on the streets of their provincial hometowns, or even appearing on the benches of the National Assembly or the Senate, as if they'd become invisible heroes. Naturally, if you're poor and your skin's the least bit dark, it's a whole other story! You're constantly stopped by the police and you get three years in prison for some trifling offenses. When it comes to knowledge and pure thought, people are perfectly free, too. We argued, you remember, that to become an enlightened citizen, a "guardian," as we call it, of our communist country, it was necessary to be immersed in high culture right from the games of childhood and for kids' minds to be taken over, as it were, by what really matters. Well, in our democracies, they couldn't care less about any of that; they don't even wonder what a leader does or doesn't know, what his experience of the world and of truths is. He just has to say he's everyone's friend, which is no sweat off his back, and he's a shoo-in in the elections.

–You've got to admit that's a pretty enjoyable way to live, *said Glaucon*. The democrat's like a little god.

–For someone who's only concerned with the passing moment, or for someone who's got money, it can be pretty good. In the long run, though, if you want to live by an Idea and, even more, if you're at the bottom of the social ladder, it's another kettle of fish. Anyway, those are the advantages of this kind of state. You've got a government with an anarchic, many-splendored appearance. In addition to this freedom, so dizzying that it boggles the mind, there's a sort of purely formal equality that actually lumps equality and inequality together.

–All I have to do now, *said Glaucon,* is ask my eternal question. How will you describe the man who corresponds to this paradoxical system of government? And, to begin with, how on earth does he emerge, if I can put it this way, from the belly of the oligarch?

– It's a long and fascinating story. Let's take an oligarch's son. His dad, a man who's very tight with his money, raised him in line with the principles we're familiar with: get rich and save. Like his dad, the son makes a tremendous effort to control his fondness for the pleasure afforded by the cities, pleasures that are all the more expensive in that they're less natural. By the way, so as not to neglect a whole part of the explanation, do you want us to distinguish between desires that are necessary and those that aren't?

–Yes, *said Amantha*. And since it's going to be about desires, don't be prudish just because a young woman is participating in the discussion for once.

–Fine, fine, *replied Socrates with a suspicious little laugh*. Let's start with the obvious. We'll say a desire is necessary if it has to be satisfied simply in order for us to go on living.

–But can't we expand the definition? *Glaucon put in*. We could argue, for example, that a desire is necessary if it's really beneficial for human beings to satisfy it, without it necessarily being obligatory.

–OK. Let's say a desire is unnecessary, or artificial, if satisfying it, however pleasant that may be, is neither obligatory nor even beneficial for what my colleague Spinoza calls the *conatus*.

–Huh? What the hell does that mean? *asked a startled Amantha*.

–The inclination of every living individual to strive to continue to exist.

–So, *said Amantha*, a desire is artificial if it's not directly entailed by the life force? If, in short, it belongs to the symbolic order?

–Oh, that Lacan! A lot of women love Lacan, I really wonder why. OK, the symbolic order it is! But let's take an example closer to Freud. The desire to copulate is certainly a desire that's necessary for the continuation of the species in question, even if it's the noble human species. The desire for a few little peripheral turn-ons – kissing on the mouth, stroking the breasts, touching the genitals, and other such caresses – to the extent that satisfying it helps get the two copulation partners in gear, could also still be said to be necessary by proxy, if we adopt our dear Glaucon's broader definition. Right?

– I think so, *said Glaucon, blushing.*

–But if, for example, I ask a woman to put on a black corset and boots, to whip me mercilessly then give me a blow job and, when I come in her mouth, to swallow my sperm, I doubt that that desire can be qualified as necessary, even by proxy.

–Oh! *exclaimed a shocked Glaucon.*

–A certain lady, who I see is not saying a word, ordered me not to be prudish. I always obey the ladies. Anyway, this type of desire probably belongs to what the lady in question calls the symbolic order. If you go to professional women, paid experts of the "symbolic order," to satisfy it, it can be quite expensive. It's the taste for that sort of thing, or even for far more complicated – far more "symbolic" things – that the son of the oligarchic dad has been trying to repress in himself ever since he was a child, because the tight-with-his-money dad told him that all that stuff was harmful to the body, bad for the soul, and, on top of that, prohibitively expensive. However, the dad's not the only one giving advice. Remember the "drones" we were talking about? In an oligarchic world, they're actually the people who adore the symbolic order! The more sophisticated, artificial, unrelated to any necessity a pleasure is, the more they love it.

–Aren't we getting off the track of how the democratic character type is created?

–Not at all. Let's get back to our kid who was raised by his dad to love making money and not to know anything about expensive vices. Now, as a teenager, he starts hanging out with gangs of young "drones," those hot-blooded, venomous insects who can introduce him to every variety of pleasure, everything from snorting coke to orgies by way of psychedelic music, costume parties, Orangina mixed with vodka, joyrides in a Ford Mustang and what have you. This is when his oligarchic superego starts turning into a democratic one. Just as in a long civil war the balance of power can suddenly shift if one of the factions gets assistance from outside allies who share its political ideology, the young man's character can change when powerful unconscious desires, counterbalanced up till then by family pressure, get assistance from kindred desires outside him. Naturally, there may be a counter-attack from the oligarchic habits, if outside allies of that party come to the aid of what, in our young man, still remains attached to them. These might be the bitter reproaches and high-handed lectures given him by his father or other family members. The upshot is that a war with himself will be declared within him, and, with regard to the family values, he'll be torn by a terrible inner conflict between rebellion and conservatism. In some cases the counter-revolution is victorious. The conservative principles will restrict, or even eliminate, the democratic rebellion. Some of the unconscious desires that had come to light will be repressed, others will disappear, and a sort of guilt will haunt the young hero's conscience, enabling the old order to regain its hold over him.

–What a disgraceful victory! *Amantha exclaimed disapprovingly.*

–But a precarious one. Because it frequently happens that, after this initial defeat of the artificial desires, other desires of the same kind, multifarious and powerful, take advantage of a kind of helplessness of the Name of the Father and suddenly surge forth from the inexhaustible reserves of the unconscious. These new desires dragoon him into a sort of acceptance of everything the rich city has to offer: beautiful, superfluous objects, scrumptious food, high-tech gadgets, trips to the other side of the world, fancy scarves and striped dresses, drugs and cars, roofs and bulldogs, and so forth. Life becomes an – often clandestine – expedition of sorts through the infinite variety of little pleasures. In the end, these materialistic impulses storm the citadel of principles that made the young man or woman a Subject. That's because all resistance was impossible. Up against the temptations of capitalism, what can Subjects devoid of any knowledge or useful practices, Subjects for whom the road to truths is now blocked, do, except disintegrate and dissolve into the individuals who are their live supports? In such circumstances, it's clear that fallacious arguments and false opinions have invaded the stronghold. As a result, it's as if these young people were living in a world of criminals whose only principle was to be able to afford consuming whatever they like. Of course, there are occasionally subjective counter-offensives from their families or some of their friends. The thrifty, respectable party that ruled the oligarchic world makes its voice heard in their inner deliberations. But the fraudulent rhetoric within them shuts the gates of the royal citadel of their souls, and neither the rescue forces of thought that might come from outside to defend the failing principles nor the wise counsel, the fruit of long experience, dispensed by their elders can gain entry any longer. The discourse of "personal fulfillment," as the resident sophists put it, wins the battle. Modesty is regarded as the height of stupidity; women who cover their hair

or aren't inclined to wear skirts that come up to their ass are persecuted. Reserve, a reflective temperament, rational argumentation are
considered by the trendy loudmouths as forms of cowardice and by
the big shots on TV as being about as worthy of media attention as
a burned-out candle. And as for spending moderately and refusing
to live on credit, well, that's just a load of backwoods bullshit. The
violence behind all this is basically that of the swarm of unnecessary
desires aroused by the inexhaustible supply of objects dumped on the
market, even though they're as ugly, destructive, and strident as a
swarm of locusts.

–Oh, Socrates! You raging poet! *said Amantha, full of emotion.*

–The temptations of consumerism and money can drain the Subject
of its virtues and leave it naked and utterly alone. It's the Eleusinian
mysteries in reverse: the Subject thus "purified" is then filled to the
brim with pointless insolence, authoritarian anarchy, miserly extravagance, and meek shamelessness. With crowns on their heads, all these
splendid attitudes march forward amid a fiendish procession where
the latest radio hits blare out over the bass going boom-boom-boom,
as though the earth were quaking from such a racket. Names change
things. Disregard for everything that's not your own little self is called
"the autonomy of the human subject." Being rid of every principle
connected with collective life is called "personal freedom." The most
ruthless careerism adopts the sweet name of "social success." Being
even the least bit concerned about workers, lower-level employees, or
small farmers is denounced as "populism." Advocating outrageous
inequalities, the competition of all against all, and police repression of
the poorest people in society is called "the courage to start from reali-
ties." Obviously, with lessons like these, a young person will quickly
progress from the – no doubt too narrow – world of necessary desires
in which he was raised to the heady world of unnecessary desires, to
satisfy which he'll be prepared to sacrifice every universal truth won
by human thought since the dawn of time.

–I can practically continue for you, *said Amantha excitedly.* And
what's more, I can do it in a contemporary style. The girls in countries
like those will invest as much money, time, and trouble in the trivia
of looks and luxury as in all the serious things in life. Some of them
will eventually fall into nihilism. They'll end up dead on a sidewalk
somewhere, with their straight purple hair, surrounded by a bunch of
wasted companions and stray dogs. Most of them, though, when they
get older, will give up the craziest of the risks they'd been taking and
settle into a humdrum routine of little indulgences. Taking refuge in
their precious female "self," they'll clear out the clutter in their heads.

A little old-fashioned concern with security and a little promiscuity; a little career–family balancing act and a little vacationing-in-the-nude in Spain; a big dollop of careerism and a pinch of social discontent; a reliable husband and a few hook-ups on the sly; lots of idiotic celebrity magazines and a smidgeon of the latest novels; a theoretical love of "others" and a practical hatred of women wearing headscarves or burkas. It's all about being for the equality of everything galore, except for whatever you don't happen to like. These gals surrender their subjective selves to the first stupid thing that comes along, worry about whether it will affect their "emotional stability," then give it up and enthusiastically move on to the next stupid thing.

–Not bad, not bad, *said Socrates appreciatively.* Let's also mention all these young people's relationship to truths and rational arguments. Those sorts of things put them off, and they won't allow them into the citadel of their soul. Suppose we tell them: "Dear friends, there are joys that draw their force from universally valid desires, and pleasures that correspond only to our selfish desires. On the level of conscious choices, at any rate, we should give priority to the former and at the very least acknowledge their superiority. The latter we need to beware of, and there are many situations where it's necessary to give them up." Do you know what they'd reply?

–They're going to give you hell! I can already hear them.

And so saying, Amantha put on her aggressive tough-girl act:

–"Socrates! You're just an old stick-in-the-mud! All our desires are great. They're all good, because they're *my* desires, not yours. And what's really awesome is enjoying everything at the same time. Long live the equality of everything in myself!"

–There you go!

–That *is* in fact the life led by someone for whom everything's equal to everything else, *observed Glaucon.*

–I'm afraid so! The man of the worldwide exchange and instant communication of everything. In what he calls his incomparable, his irreplaceable self, a man like that combines a hundred different, ever-changing personalities. He's so attractive and versatile, this democratic individual! He's so like the state with the same name! It's easy to understand how loads of people, men and women alike, all of them like eternal adolescents, can't imagine any better system of government than this illustrious democracy.

–All you have to do now, if I understand correctly, is present tyranny and the corresponding character type to us.

–The tyrant. . ., *Socrates began.*

–The fascist, no? *Amantha interrupted him.*

–The fascist tyrant, if you like. What a great subject for a talented portrait painter!

–But how is it that we go from democracy to this kind of tyranny? *Glaucon inquired.* Didn't Mussolini, Hitler and Salazar all come to power in a democratic context? After being elected?

–And so did Pétain, *Amantha remarked.*

–Isn't the overthrow of freedom – even corrupt, enslaved freedom – even when it's assented to, paradoxical? *asked Glaucon.*

–To get around that problem we can perhaps recall the means by which the transition from oligarchy to democracy takes place. When carried to extremes, the norm of oligarchy is a relentless concentration of wealth. The indifference to anything but wealth, the absence of any real principles lead to the destruction of that regime. But what's the norm of democracy – in the ordinary sense of the word, that is?

–Freedom, *suggested Glaucon.*

–No, it's not! *protested Amantha.* Not freedom like that, crude freedom, "freedom" reduced to the compulsory gratification of personal desires through the objects available on the market. The norm is in fact normless "freedom," meaning sheer animality, because the essence of such normless personal freedom is, quite simply, private interest.

–OK, *said Socrates.* And the competitive fury of private interest, the indifference to anything else, including any principle, or even any truth – that's what destroys our third system of government, democracy, from within and replaces it with one version or another of the fourth: a fascist-like tyranny.

–How so? *said Glaucon, who was a bit lost.*

–The leaders of "democratic" countries gradually become run-of-the-mill demagogues who, under cover of "freedom," destroy all reference to any norm other than the ruthlessness of private appetites. Anyone who wants to curb the expansion of these appetites and the absolute "value" of satisfying them is called a communist, a totalitarian, and an enemy of freedoms. Those who call for the collectivization of everything in the public interest – medicine, education, means of transportation, energy sources, drinkable water, banks – are deemed to be old-fashioned, people stupidly opposed to modern methods of production and exchange. For the political leaders to be ruled by their own self-interest – to remain at all costs in power, be re-elected indefinitely, profit from the ambient corruption – and for the people they govern to have no relationship with the leaders other than one of envy and curiosity – photos in celebrity magazines, absurd opinion polls, gossip, and anecdotes – is all it takes to destroy public spirit and to transform politics, which is a thought, into mere shadow play.

–But they still have freedom! *said Glaucon stubbornly.* Even in families. With the old symbolic authority of the father gone, the son is naturally anxious, but he's free, he can do whatever he wants.

–Except there's nothing he wants to do, *Amantha cut in.*

–Oh, come on! You're exaggerating. Fathers, who were once real dictators, often end up being afraid of their sons. Isn't *that* a kind of liberation? And look at foreigners, too – aren't they free? If they've got money, at any rate, they're just as free as other citizens. And if they're poor, they're no more nor less free than the bum down the street. But in a democracy, it's not like in hereditary oligarchies. Poor people are still free to become rich some day.

–You can't really believe that! *said Amantha with supreme contempt.*

–In any case, *Socrates resumed,* the truth is that, in this sort of democracy, as our good old Marx said, all the relations of authority have been dissolved "in the icy waters of egotistical calculation."[2] Even in places that are theoretically safe from corruption by money – schools, for example – some teachers. . .

–Oh, I know a thing or two about that, *cried Amantha.* A lot of teachers are scared of the students, so they play up to them and only make them read or study the latest trendy bullshit. The students, moreover, don't give a damn about anything. They're on a first-name basis with the teachers, who joke around ridiculously to avoid being heckled in class. I've even seen some of them sing rock or rap songs and shimmy to the music on their desks!

–You're such a pessimist! *protested Glaucon.* There are some really great teachers.

–Yeah, but they're few and far between. A really firm grip is required, or else older guys who have an incredible aura of authority about them. I happen to have my own theory about all this, incidentally. Fathers, teachers, even policemen, even judges or presidents are worthless now, and respect for them is gone, because, in democracy, they've become merely the equals of us girls.

–What do you mean? *said a shocked Glaucon.* How can you, a woman, say such a thing? After all these decades of feminism?

–Precisely because I know women, today's women in particular. They're not worth a damn. All they think about is getting ahead by stepping on men and their girlfriends. And on top of that they make everyone feel sorry for them, the poor dears! If the world were run by women it would be like a beehive, a nest of ants, termites! What an awful thought!

–I have a feeling Amantha's trying to provoke us with this, *said Socrates, attempting to arbitrate.* But let's put this burning issue aside, at least for the time being.

–But, *persisted Glaucon,* we agreed that under communism men and women are the same.

–Obviously, *said Amantha with a shrug.* Did I say anything different?

–Well, I don't get you, *confessed a frustrated Glaucon.*

–At any rate, *said Socrates, smiling,* men, who've already got their hands full with women, are no better off when it comes to animals. In a democracy, a pet is as free as its owners. And, what's more, it eats better than an African; its food is top quality! Horses and donkeys, if there were any left, would walk proudly through the streets with their heads held high, jostling anyone who got in their way.

–In a democracy, the horses neigh that they're free, *Amantha snickered,* and the donkeys bray the same thing.

–Oh, that's idiotic, *said a disheartened Glaucon.*

Socrates thought they should really be a bit more serious and said:
–The truth is that the war of private interests makes everyone become irritable and overworked. At the slightest obstacle, the slightest hindrance, people protest, they cry, they accuse, they sue. Everyone's a victim of everyone else. General "victim protection" laws are passed, on the basis of isolated incidents that TV has transformed into public scandals. These arbitrary laws that keep piling up, detached from any principle, are only of use to the police, so that they can persecute the weakest in society. All this legal and law enforcement chaos, like the lack of any strong political conviction among the people, creates an environment in which the fascists will thrive.

–So how do they gain strength? *Glaucon asked worriedly.* How is it that in certain circumstances they manage to take power?

–We saw that a disease intrinsic to oligarchy inevitably leads to its destruction. Similarly, the obsession with individual free will, once it has spread like a disease to all spheres of the public interest, leads, virulently and insidiously, to democracy's enslavement. Dialectics, in the ordinary sense of the term, teaches us that an extreme action in one direction causes a violent reaction in the opposite direction. This phenomenon has been observed with respect to climate, plant life, and all living organisms. It seems that the same thing has also been proven true as regards a country's political organization. If personal

276

freedom, in large quantities, remains foreign to any truth, it can only turn into slavery.

–It seems to me, *remarked Amantha*, that that same dialectical reversal affects individuals as well as communities.

–Absolutely. And, as a result, tyrannies and fascisms – exemplifying the fact that freedom, albeit sophisticated but lacking either principle or concept, reverses into brute slavery – always arise in circumstances that are claimed to be democratic or republican.

–That's a historical fact, *agreed Glaucon*. Think about Caesar and Augustus, Mussolini, Salazar, Hitler, and so on. But I had a different question in mind: what's the disease, common to both democracy and oligarchy, that ultimately puts everyone in chains?

–I think it's the group of people who are both extravagant and lazy, the parasites, in a word. A few loudmouths among them march in the lead, and the troop of cowards follows behind them. We called them the drones of a political community, remember?

– But only the leaders, the caudillos, the führers have stingers, *Glaucon reminded him.*

–Yet it's still the case that they behave in the collective body the way an infectious microbe does in the individual body. Good leaders, on the model of good doctors, need to monitor this parasitic social group very carefully. You can also think of a savvy beekeeper: he prevents drones like these from arising in the hive. If he sees any, he destroys them mercilessly and throws the honeycombs they live in into the fire.

–Wow, you've turned into a man of Terror now! *exclaimed Amantha.*

–I'm getting carried away, you're right; it's an easy way out. Let's get back to analytical methods. A country of our liberal West can be divided into three classes. The first of these is the class of evil drones, those parasites who, owing to the combination of economic liberalism and their own laziness, proliferate in "democratic" countries at least as much as they did in the old feudal oligarchies. What's more, this group of parasites is a lot more active in the new environment than it was in the oligarchic one.

–And why is that? *grumbled Amantha.*

–Because the oligarchic regime, set in its ways, looks down on upstarts like them and won't give them any positions of power, whereas in a democracy their scope of action is, so to speak, unlimited. In the assemblies and during electoral campaigns, ruthless ringleaders and shrewd orators hold forth, while the backbenchers and provincial VIPs sit on the benches and merely applaud. Under these circumstances, almost all business falls into the hands of a few cliques of wheeler-dealers.

–So what are the other two classes? *asked the impatient Glaucon.*

–The capitalists, first of all, whose determination to hold on to and increase their assets keeps them away from the turmoil and risks of getting involved in politics. It's from them that the drones, who secretly promise them that they'll protect their established fortunes, get most of their honey. . .

–They're obviously not going to try to get it from people who have nothing! *Amantha joked.* And what about the third class?

–It's the working people, the great mass of workers, farmers, employees, minor civil servants, and so on. They'd be the most powerful group if they united under the banner of an Idea.

–But they only rarely do, *observed Glaucon.* They don't constitute an organized political force.

–They're kept from doing so in every way possible. And, to begin with, they're divided by bribery. The self-proclaimed "popular" leaders distribute to a segment of the working people – whom they call the "middle class" – what they've managed to screw the rich out of, keeping a big share of it for themselves while they're at it. That way, said "middle classes," whose chief concern is to hold on to their ill-gotten standard of living, will flat-out refuse to be aligned with the poorest and most vulnerable workers, who also happen to be, always and everywhere, the ones most eager to unite under the banner of a new egalitarian politics.

–Not to mention that the capitalists, too, will defend themselves, *Glaucon said.* They'll establish political parties, buy up newspapers, engage in large-scale corruption.

–Of course! And even though they have neither the means, nor the intention moreover, of overthrowing the established order, the rumor will be spread that it's them, not the drones, who are plotting against the people. They'll be made to appear like raging oligarchs.

–And they'll inevitably become ones! *Glaucon added.* When they see the corrupt middle class, the populist demagogues, and the most ignorant segment of the working people turning against them, their old oligarchic, feudal reflexes will return and, with the help – they hope – of the army, the police, the clergy, and the courts, they'll set their sights on a conservative revolution. There'll then be a period of social unrest, with trials, factional struggles, shock troops, the army divided, enormous demonstrations, conspiracies of every kind, and so forth.

–And it's then, I think, that a charismatic leader will make his appearance, right?

–He's the man of the hour. The motley conglomeration of the corrupt middle classes and the deluded people will install as its leader some guy who was created out of nothing and whose power only comes from this alliance, against a backdrop of social unrest and fears. This creature of circumstance will declare himself to be "the nation's savior" and will combat conservative moderation, of course, but he will especially combat any independent popular organization whose aim is to unleash the people's political power and bring its scattered masses back together.

–So is it this "savior," *asked Amantha,* who'll become a tyrant or a fascist leader?

–Every time. His transformation reminds me of a story told by Pausanias. If you sample human entrails cut up in pieces and mixed with bull, calf, and goat innards, you'll be instantly changed into a wolf. When the "nation's savior" sees the crowds mesmerized by his speeches, he won't be able to keep from sampling the bloody entrails of his own people. Look at how, only a year after taking power, Hitler had the whole wing of his party that believed in a true fascist popular "revolution" murdered, the SA stormtroopers of his old buddy Röhm, whom he went to insult and humiliate in prison before they executed him. That's how it always is. While claiming to be reducing the debt, bringing the bankers under control, making the nation stronger and getting rid of unemployment, the fascist leader turns over to the police torturers everyone in his own camp whom he doesn't like or who's stealing his thunder. He appoints special courts, where paid informers get innocent people sentenced to death. With his big voracious wolf's tongue he greedily laps up the blood of his parents, whom he sends into exile or murders. It's an inexorable law that such a man will either die from the blows dealt him by his innumerable enemies or else build up absolute tyrannical power, a ruthless fascist dictatorship.

–For that, *remarked Amantha,* he'll need an enormous, loyal personal bodyguard, a ubiquitous secret police.

–I think he'll always be able to find enough thugs, *replied Glaucon,* if he gives them permission to loot one category or other of the population: Chinese merchants, Armenians, Jews, Arabs, Gypsies, communists, and so on.

–And even a lot of middle-class types who are hostile to that kind of regime, *Socrates added.* If someone who's fairly well-off is suspected of being an enemy of the fascists, he'd be well advised to obey what the Delphic oracle, according to Herodotus, revealed to Croesus: "Since a mule has become the king of the Medes, my friend, may your tender feet not prevent you from fleeing along Hermus' pebbled shore, without for a second fearing that you'll be regarded as a coward."

–It's a safe bet that if the fascists catch him they'll hang him, after methodically torturing him.

–No doubt about it. And, unlike our old Homer, we won't say about the "nation's savior" that

his greatness was lying there in repose, like a great recumbent effigy.

On the contrary, after turning lots of his enemies into recumbent effigies, he'll stand alone in the chariot of the state and, with his "savior" disguise tossed aside, he'll appear in his true guise as a fascist dictator.

–Not right away, though! *objected Amantha.* The build-up of his power and the display of his blood-soaked happiness come about more slowly, in my opinion. In the early days, at the beginning of his reign, he's all smiles with everyone, he kowtows to everyone he meets. He loudly proclaims how much he hates dictatorship and makes a lot of promises, both to his entourage and in his public declarations. He announces a moratorium on debts, he nationalizes a few factories and turns their management over to his friends, he confiscates a few abandoned estates and gives the land to the farmers who supported him. He's all sweetness and light.

Socrates was amazed.

–You took the words right out of my mouth, *he said.* And then what happens?

–Once he has disposed of his sworn enemies by bribing some and destroying the others and he thinks he's got nothing more to worry about on that front, he immediately stirs up wars, because he knows that if there's a war the people will accept to obey a leader. He also knows that, since war requires very high taxes, the citizens, reduced to poverty, will be preoccupied with daily survival and will have neither the time nor the will to plot against him.

–Brilliant! *commented an ecstatic Socrates.* And what then?

–If he suspects any people of having too free a spirit to tolerate his absolute power, war is a good pretext for eliminating them: you send them off to the front where there's next to no chance of getting out alive, or you simply hand them over to the enemy. For all these reasons dictatorships of this sort need war.

–But all these underhand tactics, *objected Socrates,* won't make him very popular. How will he be able to go on?

–He'll have to crack down even harder, over and over again.

Inevitably, in his immediate entourage, among the people who gave him a boost in his march to power, there will be a few who say what they think amongst themselves, or even in his presence. The bravest ones will openly criticize his policies. So he'll have to get rid of those people if he wants to preserve his monopoly on making all the important decisions. As a result, there will be no strong personalities left in the end, either in his own camp or in his enemies'. It will be the universal reign of the mediocre and the losers.

But Socrates had admired the beautiful Amantha's eloquence long enough and wanted to regain control now.

–That means the dictator and his cronies will have to keep a sharp eye out for any people who have even so much as an ounce of courage, intelligence, or high-mindedness, *he said.* The "happiness" promised by the fascists, whether they like it or not, inevitably involves declaring war on all these people of merit, setting traps for them until the country is totally purged of them.

–That's the kind of purge that'll kill the patient, *said Glaucon sardonically.*

–I'm afraid so! *said Socrates with a smile.* The fascist dictator is the opposite of the doctor. The doctor removes the worst from the individual body in order to save the best. The fascist works the other way around as far as the collective body is concerned: he eradicates the best to save the worst, which he rules over.

But Amantha wasn't about to give up trying to outdo Socrates.

–In short, the fascist is hostage to a beautiful necessity, *she said.* Either he spends his life among a bunch of despicable people who hate him or he ends up being murdered.

Socrates, however, determined to take charge again, replied:

–Given these circumstances, the more he's despised by his fellow citizens, the more he'll need a large, loyal police force under his orders. And I don't think there'll be a shortage of candidates from the social classes destabilized by the crisis of democracy. All the drones we were talking about will see it as a great opportunity for them to live the good life at the expense of the masses.

Amantha didn't consider herself to be out of the running quite yet, though, and added:

–Let alone the foreign mercenaries attracted by the pay. And even some workers, yanked out of the factory and relocated to the führer's palaces, so bedazzled that they can't imagine ever going back to work. That's what the great leader's new buddies, his crowd, are like, surrounded by the hatred of all those who haven't given up on a modicum of integrity. At one extreme, there's the corruption and heinous practices of the mercenaries and, at the other, the total, absolute refusal of any compromise with the regime.

Socrates, amazed by such a precise description, now turned to one of his favorite subjects:

–If what you say is true, this might make us doubt the wisdom of the poets, even Sophocles, because in *Ajax the Locrian* he writes:

> Wise the tyrants who from tyrants more wise
> Have chosen their friends and seek their advice.[3]

Amantha then returned to the charge, saying:

–Euripides, dear Socrates, is not to be outdone either. In *The Trojan Women* he praises tyranny as making one "godlike."

Socrates, though, wouldn't let her overtake him.

–Well, what about in *The Phoenician Women*, then? *he said.* Do you remember?

> For laws to be broken and crime succeed,
> The tyrant, in whom ferocious joys breed,
> Seeks the unjust as the man he will need.[4]

But Amantha wasn't defeated yet. She said:

–I know, I know. . . You're going to tell me that as soon as the poets have a chance to take advantage of the rulers' benevolence, they rush in, gather the people together, and, making use of their beautiful, sonorous, persuasive voices, sway them over to seemingly democratic but actually despotic forms of government. You're of course going to point out that they're paid a lot of money by tyrants as well as by parliamentary leaders, and that it's only when they're in the vicinity of truly popular governments incorporating an Idea that they suddenly run out of breath. Trust me, though: our great poets are charitable enough to forgive you for your speculative fury toward their artistic innocence.

–Are you done yet? *asked Socrates, irritated.*

–*This is all just a digression, after all, said Amantha, backing off.* Let's get back to the issue at hand: how will the fascist leader come up with enough money to maintain a secret police force, his personal bodyguard, his underground residences and his conquering army?

–If the state has reserves, particularly in the form of gold or foreign currency, he'll sell all of that off. Nor will he have any compunction about selling to the top bidder national treasures like paintings or sculptures from the museums or the vast quantity of sacred objects found in churches. Every little bit will help the police budget, and taxes won't even have to be raised!

–That's all very well, *objected Amantha,* but once he's sold everything off, he'll be flat broke. The bitter, hard-up cops will start plotting behind the scenes.

–No problem, *Glaucon, throwing up his hands, replied to his sister.* The Great Leader, the Guide, will then sponge off the people who put him on the throne. They'll have to pay for his entourage, his minions, his secret advisers, his mistresses, his cops, his executioners, and his court jesters.

–Do you mean, *Socrates shot back,* that the people who, owing to their confusion and passivity, enabled the fascist gangs to take over the state will now have to support this whole crew as well?

–They won't have any choice.

–But come on, the people will rebel! A lot of people will say that once a political creature of the people – a son of the people, in short – has grown up and been elevated to a position of absolute power, his people-father can't go on supporting him, his lackeys, his snitches, his whores, and the whole bunch of thugs around him indefinitely! For a father to become the slave of his son's slaves – perish the thought! The people wanted to be rid of the oppressive domination of the rich, of the self-proclaimed "democrats," or "civilized people." They didn't want to be plundered by a bloodthirsty mafia. So they'll order the usurper – him and his whole coterie – to leave the country, the way a father kicks out of his house an ungrateful son and all the disreputable freeloaders the son has invited into it.

–Just let the people-father try to kick out the dictator born from their own womb! They'll soon realize how great their misfortune is. They'll rue the day they fathered, cuddled, and raised such a baby. It's too late now, though. He's stronger than they are.

–Good God! *exclaimed Socrates.* According to you, the tyrant is a parricide! He slits his old parents' throats and tramples on their dead bodies!

–That's precisely *(and Glaucon was thrilled to be steering the discussion)* what everyone calls fascist tyranny. The people have fallen from the frying pan into the fire. They tried to avoid the suffocating smoke of the upper middle class's secret despotism but ended up in the boiling pot of the rabid lower middle class's despotism. Before, they had all the deadlocks and illusions of confused freedom, but now they've had to don the uniform of the harshest and bitterest kind of slavery, that of those who are slaves of other slaves.

Amantha, not wanting to be left out, commented:

–That's what the colonized people of African countries are like, too, when the poor Whites from the mainland look down on them and abuse them, calling them "Camel Jockeys," "Ay-rabs," "jungle bunnies," and other lovely things of the sort.

–Yes, *said Glaucon pedantically,* as Hannah Arendt correctly observed, there's a historical continuity between the imperial savagery of the "democrats" and the cruelty of the fascists.

–Great job, dear friends! *Socrates congratulated them.* Thanks to you two, I think that we can take pride in having brilliantly described the transition from democracy to fascist tyranny and, while we were at it, the overall form of that type of system of government. But we still need to examine the corresponding character type.

–The prototype of the tyrant, *Amantha agreed.*

–Only here's the thing: we're missing a conceptual tool.

–After so many hours of discussion, *Glaucon moaned,* we're still missing a tool? Which one?

–A rigorous analysis of the different kinds of desires. Tyranny is the point where political violence and libidinal violence become impossible to tell apart.

Glaucon, anticipating an enormous digression, felt depressed and said glumly:

– Well, go on then, if you must.

–We've already distinguished between pleasures that are necessary and those that aren't. Let's take it one step further. Of the pleasures and desires that aren't necessary, there are some that seem to be positively exempt from any law. They exist in every person right from the start, lurking in the depths of the unconscious. But they're partly repressed by the law, itself driven by the desires, with which it has a dialectical relationship. In some individuals, with the help of rational thought, these rogue desires can be rendered harmless for the most part. In other people, though, they remain plentiful and strong.

–Could you be more precise about these "rogue desires"? *asked a wary Amantha.*

–You, like everyone else, know what they are, since they're the ones that wake up when you're asleep. The agency of the Subject that's associated with the supreme calmness of rational thought is precisely the one whose rest is ensured by sleep. However, that's when the wild, animal-like agency, the one that ferociously demands its daily ration of food and drink, rears up. It fights off sleep and tries to give free rein to its own inclinations. This is what are called the drives. In this drive state, the agency of the Subject called desire will stop at nothing! It breaks all bonds, whether of morality or thought. As Freud correctly observed, the Subject's liberated desire is then the desire to have sex with the mother and, through object transference, with all sorts of things: men, garter belts, prostitutes, goats, panties, gods, or children. By the same token, this desire is also the desire to murder the father, and, through transference, it becomes an aggressive drive that nothing can stop. In a nutshell, in the middle of night the drive combines a free-floating object with unlimited transgression.

In response to this colorful description Amantha struck an ironic pose. Glaucon was pensive for a moment, then asked:

–But what can we do when sleep, that irresistible force, delivers us over to our drives?

–How about a good psychoanalysis? *said Amantha facetiously.*

–Hey! *Socrates retorted.* Didn't your great French thinker Jacques Lacan say that I, Socrates, was the forerunner of all psychoanalysts?[5] After all, even if we hadn't discovered the ideal political constitution, since we'd have become, by virtue of speaking, intellectually nimbler, more capable of being positive and creative and less focused on brief, destructive pleasures, we'd fall asleep, after practicing mental concentration this way, armed with a rational agency full of beautiful proofs illustrated by conclusive examples, and meanwhile we'd have taken care not to subject the desiring agency either to pure abstinence or to the vain, all-consuming quest for total gratification, so that it might settle down and not disturb the Thought agency with either its sorrows or joys, thereby helping that agency preserve its ability to attempt on its own, with only its own resources, the difficult investigation of what it does not yet know about what the past erases, the present dissipates, or the future obscures; and all this we'd have done at the same time as, on the verge of sleep, we'd have soothed the agency of Affect enough for us not to be angry at anyone, so that, having kept in check the drive aspect to which Desire and Affect are exposed and having given a strong impetus to the third agency, Thought, we'd be able to give in to true rest, when dreams have finally stopped communicating only forbidden desires disguised as enigmatic images, and we'd then have a chance to make it through the night to our truth.

–Well, *we* at any rate have made it through one hell of a sentence! *exclaimed Amantha.* At the "even if" at the beginning I held my breath, and I was sure that by the time you got to the "so that" at the end I'd die of suffocation!

–I was trying to say things the way I see them – in the totality of their immanent relationships. Let's just keep in mind what's going to be of use to us: deep within each of us there lie astonishing, wild, rogue desires. Those of us who consider ourselves to be in the small minority of sensible people are no safer than anyone else, as our dreams prove.

285

–All right, all right, *said Glaucon impatiently.* But where does politics come into all this?

–Remember what we said about the democratic man now. Brought up by a rather tight-fisted oligarchic father who hated unnecessary desires like parties, luxury, gambling, prostitutes, etc., he was given a counter-upbringing by the gang of kids he hung out with once he became a teenager. His friends, who were already corrupt, loved the desires that are considered sophisticated and subversive at that age. Under their influence, our young man, motivated in fact by a very understandable hatred of his father's stinginess, gave in to every excess. Since he was endowed with a sounder character than that of his corrupters, however, a fierce struggle raged within him. Pulled in opposite directions, he chose a middle way between two fundamentally incompatible lifestyles. Making use of both of them – stinginess and extravagance, respect and insolence, family discipline and debauch, and so forth – he believed he was behaving sensibly. And in fact his life was neither completely dissolute nor completely law-abiding. That's how he went from being an oligarch, like his father was, to being a democrat.

–Yeah, right, *grumbled Amantha.* The middle ground, the happy medium, not this but not that either. . . That's what democracy's all about, neither fish nor fowl.

–No doubt, no doubt, *admitted Socrates.* If we've got the communist Idea in mind, that sort of democracy is certainly not the best thing there is. But remember that it's not the worst thing either.

–And so it's back to tyranny, fascism. . .

–. . . which are democracy's offspring. Suppose our young democrat has grown older, faithful as ever to his fragile existential compromise. He has children and he naturally brings them up in accordance with his "happy medium" principle. As they grow up, these children will rebel, as usual, against the paternal principle. But their inner defenses will be a lot weaker than those of an oligarch's son. Boys and girls alike will indulge in a chaotic lifestyle that's vehemently defended by their corrupters as "freedom," "rebellion," or "nihilism." Try as the old democrat might to come to the aid of the "happy-medium" desires, to preach the ordinary democrat's noble eclectic "wisdom," the faction of boundless, lethal desires will win out. This time, the corrupters will resort to a sort of unrecognizable erotic passion with increasingly repulsive objects, so that this desire, as the lead drone, will bring along with it a taste for looting, brutality, and ultimately racial hatred, torture, and murder. Hewing as closely as possible to the mindset of the fascist gangs' future members, the corrupters will naturally begin with the ordinary forms of corruption. Although it's only an accomplice of the other desires at first, the eroticism I'm talking about will buzz around among the clouds of incense, the mind-numbing music, the hashish smoke, the gambling for money boozed up with beer and vodka, the ridiculous, drunken choruses, the impromptu hook-ups, and so on. But little by little the stinger of boundless desire and its demand for absolute power over the others and for readily available means for its instant gratification will be implanted deep within the young democrats' flesh. Propelled by a sort of fatal dark drive, their self will then fall prey to true madness, pushed to the point where, if they detect any opinions or desires in themselves that are ordinarily regarded as respectable and requiring a vestige of modesty or personal restraint, they'll kill them all off and expel them from their psyche, to such an extent that, having now become Subjects devoted to the cult of death, they'll end up purged of every acceptable standard of behavior, and this will leave the place wide open for a madness that has come from somewhere else.

–That's some vivid portrait of the young fascist! *said Amantha, full of admiration.*

–The literally pornographic drive whose effects I'm trying to describe can be called the Subject's tyrant. But this same sort of insanity can also be found in intoxication – alcohol and drugs – or in pathological rage, when people think they can order the gods around.

–So, *said Glaucon in conclusion,* a young adult like me will be prone to joining the ranks of a tyrant or a fascist leader when, with his own natural disposition and incidental corruption reinforcing each other, he becomes drive-ridden, an addict, and aggressive.

–Ultimately, *remarked Amantha,* aren't you talking about what Freud calls the death drive? Isn't that what prevails in the fascist subjectivity?

–Absolutely. And that's why we can now describe the inner life of the tyrannical or fascistic character type, so as to gradually get to the portrait of the Great Leader, of the Führer, who always rules a state given over to this type of government.

–Can I try?

The question had come from Amantha, who immediately launched into the description without waiting to be asked.

–He feasts, he fucks, he smokes, he drinks. Where money's in abundance, hookers, mafiosi and informers are superabundant. He sends his servants packing, abuses his cronies, humiliates his acquaintances, holds women in contempt, gets blow jobs in the corridors, struts around in his underwear in the early morning in the dining room of a luxury hotel. But immediately thereafter he dons a military uniform covered with medals and clicks the heels of his big shiny black boots on the parquet floor. He wants to have power over everyone, men and women alike, since he doesn't have any over himself. At this rate, he goes through all his money. He borrows, he sells. But one fine day he's really and truly broke. And then the aggressive bitterness of the bankrupt *petit bourgeois* hits him. The host of desires within him, under the sway of the great drone Thanatos, drive him here and there like a maniac, looking all over for anyone he can squeeze money out of. He gets used to things like blackmail, mugging the elderly and the disabled, and the most sordid shenanigans as though they were self-evident. Money! He's got to have money! And power! Or else all his anxiety and suffering will come back, with the voice of death. Nor are his parents spared. So he squandered his share of the family estate? Big deal. The rest of it will be his, too, one way or another. Destroy his mother and father? Why not, if it means he can go on enjoying other people's fear, their obedience, the look of simultaneous complicity and fear in their eyes? If it means he can screw willing bimbos and be wiped out at roulette at the casino one evening, surrounded by all the low-cut dresses and tuxedos? If his old mom and pop should put up a struggle, why not scream, hit them, threaten to throw himself out of the window right before their eyes? What's a shriveled, tearful old mother next to an alluring top model with naked thighs, discreetly siliconed boobs, and a juicy pussy? What's a bald father bent over by arthritis next to a pretty boy with his shirt open to his navel, a wiggly little ass, and a big dick? Only, at this rate, the father and the mother will have no money left either, while the swarm of drone-desires, the Death horde, buzzes louder than ever. Won't our young hero be tempted, for lack of anything better, to break into an ATM, snatch an old lady's purse in the street, or sell some impure heroin on dark street corners? As a result, the old ideas he used to think were right, even if he didn't comply with them, the ideas that enable you to distinguish between what's honorable and what's despicable, will die a definitive death within him. The new ideas, the ones accompanying the death instinct, will win a decisive victory. . .

–Yes, *an enthusiastic Socrates cut in,* yes! Previously, those new ideas only appeared in his dreams, when, for a few hours, sleep lifted the censorship imposed on his conscious mind by the Law of the father; when democracy, despite its mediocrity, its worship of the happy medium, prevented the death drive from entering the paths of the conscious mind. This is – this is precisely – what the tyrannical man, the convinced fascist, is like: in his waking state and all the time now, he's what he only occasionally was as a young democrat in his nightmares in the middle of the night. Now he doesn't shrink from any horrific crime and seeks out every sort of pleasure, even the most loathsome ones. The drive he harbors within him, which fosters an oppressive state of inner lawlessness, controls the poor guy the way a tyrant rules the state. He'll stop at nothing to gratify his corrupt self's obscene desires, both the desires that were put there by the group mentality of his teenage years and those that were lying dormant in his unconscious, whose chains have gradually been broken by his life choices and their criminal energy set free.

–The question is how all that's connected, overall, with the origins of a fascist state, *Glaucon mused.*

–If, in a given country, people whose subjectivity is of the fascist type – the type we've just described – are few in number and average opinion has no liking for their machinations, they'll probably join a foreign tyrant's praetorian guard or lend their assistance, as mercenaries, to some imperial power in dirty wars. If they can't find a fascist country prepared to take them in or a war in which they can give free rein to their death drive, all they can do is remain in their own country and commit a bunch of loathsome minor crimes.

–Of what sort?

–Spraying walls with anti-Semitic graffiti, attacking Blacks or Arabs with iron bars on dark street corners, desecrating graves, insulting women, forming commando units in the service of the state or the bosses in order to break strikes, and so forth. They also love informing on people, like writing to the police that their neighbor is an undocumented African worker. They're born snitches, who commit perjury with a straight face in exchange for an envelope stuffed full of dollars.

–And that's what you call "*minor*" crimes?

–Well, it's because all these crimes can seem almost petty compared with the disaster that the fascists' coming to power represents. And, in order for that disaster to come to pass, the tyrannical character type has to have proliferated, and all these people together, realizing how many of them there are and aided by the popular masses' inertia and the so-called "leftwing" parties' stupid conservatism, have to bring to power the one person among them who expresses the most complete conviction in his speeches. They make a tyrant of him. From then on, either a popular revolt led, if possible, by some supporters of a new system of government sympathetic to the communist Idea will sweep out the tyrant and his henchmen, or else the tyrant, bringing in, if need be, foreign mercenaries as corrupt as he is, will drown the rebellion in blood and mercilessly punish his fatherland – or his "motherland," as the Cretans, perhaps more correctly, put it – in the same way as he once abused his parents without a qualm.

– Unfortunately, there are more instances of the second possibility than of the first, *said Glaucon gloomily.*

–Note that these people were exactly the same in their private lives as they are when they exercise power. Either they surrounded themselves with sycophants who were prepared to go all out to assist them in their vile deeds or, if they needed a favor from someone, *they* were the ones who groveled like an obedient dog, ingratiating themselves with the person on whom the favor depended and playing all the roles of the loyal lackey, only to disappear and behave like perfect strangers, or even ruthless enemies, once they got what they wanted. That's why these people, throughout their lives, neither love nor are loved, since they're always either tyrants or slaves. A fascist will never be able to taste either freedom or friendship.

–In short, *Amantha, who was finding all this a bit long, summed up,* it's a dog's life, ferocious and/or obedient.

But Socrates, for the time being, didn't care about the young woman's gloomy reaction. He had, moreover, turned toward Glaucon and seemed to be speaking only for him:

–Can't we say that it's absolutely impossible to trust these people about anything?

–*Absolutely*'s the word all right.

–And that they take injustice to its extreme?

–Given our agreement on the definition of justice, there's no doubt about it.

–So let's sum up. The worst of men is the one who, in his waking state and all the time, is what the good man is only in his dreams, and only rarely even then. In order to fall to such a sorry state, this sort of man, being a fascist character type from early on, has to have succeeded, through intrigues and violence, in wielding power all alone. And the longer that solitude lasts and grows, the more the Subject will be devoured by the tyrannical corruption harbored within him. Tyranny is the solitude of the person who has lost the power to love and thus can only wield the sterile power to doom both himself and others to death.

— 15 —

JUSTICE AND HAPPINESS
(573b–592b)

Socrates seemed troubled by his own words. He sat there silently, with his eyes closed, in that strange light that, in brightest day, hints by a sort of clear paleness at the still distant evening. Was he perhaps thinking that what he'd just said about the tyrant – that a long period of solitude shackles him to his self – applied equally well to the philosopher? Doesn't philosophy issue from skepticism, the way tyranny issues from democracy? But then Amantha got things underway again, saying:

–Here's your chance, dear Socrates, if you still have the strength, to return to the difficult problem of happiness. Your vivid description of the tyrant's life would seem to suggest that his solitary ferocity leads to a sort of inexpressible misery in the depths of his soul, and that the more time goes on, the more the exercise of absolute power exacerbates this secret misery. Can that relationship between objective injustice and subjective dereliction be generalized? I mean, if the relationship is examined in the element of Truth, since I'm well aware that public opinion, when it comes to how happy the rich and powerful are, is very volatile. Just look at the celebrity magazines!

Socrates looked at the girl inquisitively, as if he had awoken to find her standing at his bedside.

–What you're suggesting, *he said,* is that I climb a huge mountain on crutches, with no beaten path to follow! Well, I'm going to put questions to *you*. You asked for it!

–OK, dear teacher. I'm all ears.

–We agreed that there was a sort of isomorphism between the form of political regime and the type of individual who lives in it, right?

–Absolutely.

–It can also be argued that what one political regime is to another,

291

the individual corresponding to the former is to the individual corresponding to the latter.

–In essence, *said Amantha,* this diagram *(she drew it right on the table),* and this is only an example, shows a structural parallelism.

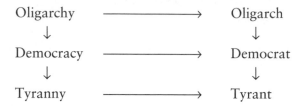

Oligarchy	⟶	Oligarch
Democracy	⟶	Democrat
Tyranny	⟶	Tyrant

And, *she added,* the diagram is commutative.

–I can't compete with that! At any rate, I'm sure you can answer the following question. From the point of view of Virtue, and therefore, ultimately, of immanence to the Idea of the True, what is the relationship between the tyrannical system of government and the communist system of government as we've briefly described it?

–It's a relation of opposition. One is the worst of systems of governments, the other is the best.

–Right, but you've got to admit, dear girl, that the question was too easy! The relation you're talking about is self-evident, since we defined our communism precisely in terms of the norm of the True. As soon as it's a question of happiness and unhappiness, though, things become much more complicated.

–I see the problem, dear teacher. As regards happiness and unhappiness, principles won't suffice. We'll have to conduct an empirical investigation.

–Exactly. And not let ourselves be dazzled by the sight of the tyrant, who's only one solitude among others, or by the sight of the little clique around him. We need to penetrate into the interior of the country, examine it as a whole, and, like spies of the Idea, burrow our way right into its heart of hearts before we can draw any conclusions.

–I'm sure a spy like that would come to the conclusion that no country is more forlorn and wretched than the country ruled by a tyrant and that, in terms of collective happiness, none could compete with a country that was run by a true communist system of government.

–Well, you said so, not me. . . I have something a little different in mind. I think we'd need to resort to the same type of intellectual espionage when it's a matter not of systems of government but individuals. Now, who is able to judge who someone is? In my opinion, it's a person who can penetrate, solely by deductive reasoning, into the structure governing someone's psychology. A true spy in the service of the Idea won't be fooled, like a child who only sees things from the outside, by all the deceptive trappings tyrants intentionally put on display for suckers. Our spy can see what's behind the scenes. He's the one we should all pay attention to. He's never a dupe of the deliberate confusions between being and appearing. He's shared the tyrant's life, he's witnessed what goes on in his private life, he's observed his behavior in the tight little circle of his close friends and family, when he takes off his stage mask for a moment. Like Shakespeare devoting his theater to kings' fears, our spy has studied the tyrant's reactions when a threat is developing, when fatal conspiracies are taking shape. Sultry nights, invisible daggers, poisons, and nightmares! The person who's seen all this can tell us about the bliss or misery of the tyrant, as compared with other figures of individuality.

–Sure. But do you have a spy of that caliber among your friends and acquaintances?

–Yes, I do, and you know him well: your brother Plato. He saw Dionysius I and Dionysius II, successive tyrants of Syracuse, up close. Even too close. But your brother's away on a trip at the moment.

–So let's pretend to be those spies ourselves! *said Amantha enthusiastically.* Let's imagine that we've feasted and slept with tyrants.

–Oh, really, Amantha! *said Glaucon indignantly.*

–Yes, yes! And let's answer our own questions this way.

–Fine, *said Socrates, smiling.* Just remember that the state and the individual are alike. As you move freely from one to the other, tell me what each of them experiences, in historical time as well as in private space.

–Well, to begin with, *said Amantha hesitantly,* it seems to me that if we accept that a country ruled by a tyrant is a country that's enslaved, then an individual who tolerates or, worse yet, supports, tyranny must himself be – subjectively, inwardly – reduced to slavery.

–Bravo, well done! *exclaimed Socrates.* But try to be more precise. Even in a country with a despotic government you can find people who claim to be free in that they have the outward appearance of the figure of the master, right?

–Yeah, but they're very few and far between. Virtually all the people – and especially those whose convictions obey the dictates of reason, of moderation – are plunged into the most abject slavery, and they're fully aware of it.

–Your remark about reason is very helpful. What can you deduce from it in light of the relation of isomorphism between state and individual?

–Well, if we begin with the similarity between state and individual, we should be able to show that the inner being of both of them has the same structure. Which means that, instead of the potential greatness of a Subject, there are only abjection and a lack of freedom in both the individual and the state.

–And, to complete the analogy, *Socrates stressed,* we should refer to the three agencies of the Subject – Thought, Affect, and Desire – that we identified late last night. In the individual who corresponds to tyranny, the agency of Thought is subservient to that little part of the "Desire" agency that's ordinarily kept in check but that in this case runs rampant: the vilest desires, envy, informing on people, the outrageously exaggerated satisfaction of trampling on the weak. We can say about an individual whose subjective form has been affected in this way that he's not in the least free but has instead fallen into the paradoxical figure of someone who's the slave of himself.

–That's some diabolical dialectic! *exclaimed Amantha enthusiastically.* At last – the portrait of the fascist! It's really the spitting image of him. In fact, no fascist state ever achieves its stated objectives: the thousand-year Reich, the Italian Empire, and all that millenarian rhetoric. The sputtering war machines the fascist serves sink into material and intellectual poverty and merely rust away after the defeat. And it's the same for the individual tyrannized by his basest desires: he always has the feeling he's failed. The fascist secretly regards himself as a failure and spends his whole life trying unsuccessfully to overcome the lethal duo of resentment and guilt.

–Because you equate "tyranny" with "fascism," you're forced to tilt things in favor of Nietzsche. But that actually works pretty well. It seems to me, especially if we're talking about fascism, that the fear devastating the country and its citizens has to be emphasized. Under no other political regime do you find as many stifled wails, repressed moans, and cries of the tortured that secret prison cells keep from being heard. It's an accumulation of suffering that fear alone conceals.

–So, if the individual is prey to the same ills as the country, *said Glaucon, who couldn't stand keeping quiet any longer,* we can already conclude that he's the most miserable of men.

–You're jumping the gun! *protested Socrates.* There's something even worse than a person who's subject to the rule of tyranny, or fascism, if you prefer. There's the person born under such a rule who has the misfortune to be torn by the convulsive circumstances of the fascist system of government from an undeniably wretched, yet anonymous, life and propelled to the top of the state.

–I guess you can consider that that's worse, *said Glaucon lamely.*

–Guess, guess. . . We shouldn't be guessing anything. We're not propping up beliefs here. We have to deal with this issue by purely rational means, because it's the most important issue of all: how to distinguish between a life lived in accordance with the True and a life doomed to failure.

–Oh, of course, said Glaucon, *embarrassed to have blown it.*

–And, to shed some light on the extent of the problem, I'll use an analogy. Take one of those wealthy landowners who own a very large number of slaves – let's say fifty, or even more. On the scale of the Family and Property, they're like what tyrants are on the scale of the state, at least in one respect: they wield absolute power over a lot of people. Qualitatively, it's the same thing. It's only quantitatively that the tyrant has it over them. Yet, what we observe is that these landowners live in complete security on their estates as a rule and aren't obsessed with the fear of a slave revolt. Do you know why that is?

–I think, *replied Glaucon, ever the sociology buff,* it's because they know that in case of trouble they can count on all the other landowners in the area, who are armed and organized in militias, and, if that's not sufficient, on the military might of the central state.

–There you go! Now suppose an evil genie whisks one of these wealthy landowners – one who has fifty or more slaves – away from his country and its government. He deposits him, along with his family, all his belongings, and all his servants and slaves, in a deserted place where he can't hope for assistance from any other "free" man – and by "free" man we naturally mean a slave-owner. Can you imagine how enormous and intense his terror would be at the thought of himself, his wife, and his children being quite simply massacred by the slaves?

–He'd shudder in fear night and day, *Glaucon agreed.* The only way he could escape his plight would be to curry favor with some of those slaves, promising them a thousand different things and summarily decreeing that he'll free a small number of them. In order to divide his class enemies, he'd be forced to kiss up to those of his slaves who were prepared to cooperate.

–It would be even worse if the evil genie settled a bunch of neighbors, all staunch democrats, around his estate. In the name of "human rights," these people wouldn't tolerate one person setting himself above the others and claiming to rule over them. If such were the case, they'd organize a devastating military expedition against the "dictator," and they'd bomb his house and kill all the women, children, servants, and pets. And if they captured him they'd have him tortured and murdered in secret prisons.

–Our man would in that case be imprisoned, as it were, by his neighbors.

–But doesn't the tyrant live in just such a prison? We described his distinctive psychological make-up, dominated by the merry-go-round of fears and drives. Though endowed with a greedy nature and curious about every new and unfamiliar sensation, he's the only one in his country who can't travel abroad and – as is every *petit bourgeois*'s desire – see the sights with a flavor of mystery about them that are on offer in foreign countries. Shut away in his palace like a woman in the gynaeceum, he envies ordinary people, who can go out whenever they feel like it and see colorful or unusual things.

–Nice! *conceded Amantha.* The terrible tyrant as a housewife – that's really something!

Socrates, unsure whether she was admiring or making fun of him, shrugged his shoulders and went on:

–Those are the evils to which the character type with a deviant subjective orientation is exposed, the character type to whom Glaucon gave the title of the most miserable of human beings a little while ago: the tyrannical man. For all these terrible things to befall him, he just has to be compelled by fate to take power and become a tyrant himself rather than remain a private citizen. Although he's incapable of mastering his own drives, he's now the master of everyone else. He's like someone who's constantly sick, whose body is very weak, and who, instead of remaining quietly at home sipping herbal tea, is forced to spend his life taking on gangs of burly youths in the street and fighting well-trained gladiators in the arena. This man's suffering is then unutterable. Since he has effectively become a tyrant, his life is even worse than the one you considered to be the worst of all, the life of an ordinary private citizen plagued by fascist drives. Thus it's absolutely true – even if prevailing opinion maintains the contrary – that the real tyrant is nothing but a real slave. His life is an abyss of abjection and servility. He spends his time buttering up thugs. Unable to satisfy his desires, he forgoes anything of real worth and, to anyone who observes the appearances as a Subject-in-Truth, it's clear that the tyrant's a loser whose life is engulfed in the fear of what's going to happen and who, like Macbeth or Boris Godunov, rolls around on the ground beset by horrifying visions.

–Basically, *said Glaucon,* his psychic reality is like the state he rules: it's a mixture of poverty, informing, stupidity, and terror.

–You said it. And we can also ascribe to him the evils we mentioned earlier, those of the tyrannical character type. They were already in him virtually, but once he comes to power they spring into action: jealousy, treacherousness, injustice, bitter solitude, vulgarity, and all the different kinds of inner corruption he harbors and nurses. As a result, his fate is the most horrible one of all, and he turns everyone who comes near him into a wretch like himself.

–Enough already! *said Amantha ironically.*

Socrates, like a priest, then raised his hands heavenward, turned toward Glaucon, and in a solemn, perhaps slightly ironic tone, said:

–Now, my friend, like the final judge in a prestigious music competition, reveal to our audience who, in your opinion, should be awarded first prize for happiness and who second. Then, in the same category, rank in order the five character types corresponding to the five different systems of government: the communist, the timocratic, the oligarchic, the democratic, and the tyrannical.

–Oh, I'm not going to rack my brains. In terms of happiness I declare them to be in descending order in the very order we examined them, which is the one you just mentioned.

–You're right, you didn't exactly put a lot of effort into it, *protested Amantha.* A more appropriate ranking might be: first, the communist, and then the democratic, the timocratic, the oligarchic and, in very last place, the fascist.

–Except that modern democracies, *Glaucon shot back,* may well be merely oligarchies in disguise.

–Let's focus on the extreme cases only, *suggested a conciliatory Socrates.* Without any help from a herald blowing his horn,[1] I proclaim what the three of us are all agreed on: the best and most just of men is also the happiest, and we equate him with the one whose country is ruled by our fifth system of government, the communist system. He's the one who's sovereign over situations, just as he's sovereign over himself. By the same token, the worst and most unjust man is also the unhappiest, and we equate him with the fascist tyrant, who reduces his people to slavery and is himself only the slave of the despicable means used to establish and maintain that slavery. I further add to this proclamation that our judgment is based on what really exists, and therefore the equation between justice and happiness is absolute and not contingent on the point of view – changeable as it is, and dependent on what they know or don't know – not only of men but even of the gods.

–Yay! *exclaimed Amantha, overjoyed especially because of that last point.*

–This is just a first skirmish. Dear Amantha! Time and again you've mocked my fervor in defending that paradoxical conviction of mine, namely that only the just man is happy. Well, I'm going to give you another chance to do so: I've been holding in reserve two additional proofs concerning this point.

–You have? What proofs? *asked Glaucon eagerly.*

–You'll tell me whether they're good or not. The first one is based on what we established ages ago: just as a state is defined by three distinct functions, the Subject is split into three different agencies.

–I really don't see how you can get from the three-part division of the Subject to the just man's happiness.

–That's precisely what I'm going to show you. Since there are three agencies of the Subject, we can assume that there are three types of pleasure particular to each of them, just as there are three types of desires and three types of imperatives. Let me remind you what the three agencies are. The first is the one that allows people to have access to knowledge, and we call it "Thought." The second is the one that triggers anger, indignation, enthusiasm, that whole spirited component of the Subject I suggested we call Affect. The third is so multifarious that we weren't able to find one name to designate it. We did agree, though, that the word "Desire" was a good match for what's most salient, most unchanging in this third agency, as can be seen in the experience of everything involving food, drink, or sex. We also retained the phrase "love of money," because the desires we're talking about can hardly be satisfied without money. I want to stress that point, since it's essential to the argument that follows. It can be argued that Desire, considered abstractly, is the desire for profit, which is the universal means of its gratification. In everything that follows, it will be both justifiable and convenient to associate this third agency with the phrase "love of profit."

–The modern word to designate a guy who's controlled by that agency would just be "capitalist," *observed Amantha.*

–OK, sure, but where does the just man's happiness come into all this? *said Glaucon irritably.*

–Patience, my friend, patience! As far as the irritable and touchy agency – that energy we call Affect – is concerned, its characteristic desire is for power, victory, and fame. It's the passion for being the winner and for being showered with honors.

–Are we to understand that happiness is of the stuff of which greatness is made?

– Patience, I told you. Finally, the agency of knowing, Thought, always and entirely leads on to the knowledge of truth as it is in itself, and, consequently, of the three agencies, it's the only one that, being essentially disinterested, is not in the least concerned about profit or conspicuous social success. Wouldn't it be appropriate to call it "the passion for knowledge" or "the passion for wisdom"?

–You already taught us that quite a while ago, *said Amantha.* The right phrase, if by "wisdom" is meant the condition we're put in by the process of a truth within us, is "the love of wisdom," or. . .

–. . . or, in Greek, *philosophos,* philosopher! *a jubilant Glaucon cut in.*

–A word, I dare say, destined for a great future, *agreed Socrates.* Anyway, now we're able to distinguish between three different categories of human beings: the philosophers, whose object cause of desire is a truth; the ambitious people, whose object is fame; and the capitalists, whose object is profit.

–But what about the communist? *asked a disappointed Amantha.*

–I'd say he's the one whose glorious political energy is in the service of the passion for the True. We'll get back to him later, don't worry. For the time being, let's ask ourselves what the three sorts of pleasures particular to each of these three character types are. What do you think, Glaucon?

–It's clear for the last two: each will claim that his is the most enjoyable life. The capitalist will say that, compared to making profits, the pleasure of being talked about on TV, not to mention the pleasure of learning, is just a bunch of malarkey. The ambitious man will say that the pleasure of amassing money is vulgar and that the pleasure you get from knowledge, inasmuch it doesn't attract anyone's attention, is just idle nonsense.

–So what about the philosopher, then?

–That position strikes me as the hardest one to formalize.

–But we can assume that, in comparison with the joy you feel when you recognize the True as it is in itself and you construct a sort of eternal life for that joy through the process of thought, all other pleasures fade. The philosopher will consider them to be a far cry from true pleasure. He'll regard them only as strict necessity, for he'd have nothing at all to do with such pleasures if they weren't required by the pure obligation imposed on human beings to strive to continue to exist.

–I'm not sure, *objected Amantha,* whether you're giving a demonstration here or merely begging the question.

–True, all we're doing is repeating the natural position of our three human specimens. And the further difficulty is that we're judging

299

their lives in relation to the different types of pleasure, so that our question doesn't have to do with which life is the most admirable or shameful, or even, more broadly speaking, which is the best or worst life. Our problem has to do with which life is the happiest, or at any rate which is the one least vulnerable to sadness. This is the point about which we need to determine which of our three guys – the capitalist, the ambitious man, or the philosopher – comes closest to the truth when he boasts about his own kind of life. Amantha! How would you proceed?

–I think we could start with one of your pet topics. You often ask: "To whom should we give the task of judging what ought to be subjected to the most critical of judgments?" And when no one says anything, you answer your own question, as usual: "There are three possible judges: experience, wisdom, and reasoning." So we could measure the value of our three guys in terms of experience, wisdom, and reasoning capacity. But I can't say any more about it.

–Excellent! Wonderful! *said Socrates enthusiastically.* Which of our three fellows has the most experience when it comes to the pleasures we just mentioned? Suppose – and this is absurd, but never mind – that the capitalist stumbles upon the knowledge of a truth as it is in itself. Would we say that his experience of the pleasure afforded by such knowledge is greater than the experience a philosopher might have of the joys of profit and consumption?

–To tell the truth, Socrates, *Amantha hesitantly began,* your. . .

–It's totally different! *Glaucon, as excited as could be, interrupted her.* The philosopher has had the same sort of childhood as everyone else, so, way back then, he'd necessarily have acquired, even if only unconsciously, some experience of the other two kinds of pleasure: possession and pride. On the other hand, the capitalist, should he happen to stumble upon a knowledge of what truly is, is under no necessity to have a genuine experience of the pleasures associated with that type of knowledge. It'll leave him cold as ice and, what's more, that indifference will block any desire in him to become involved in a truth process.

–On the other hand, *remarked Amantha, you*'re under an obvious necessity to interrupt me.

–Take it easy, kids. We agree on a first point: the philosopher has it over the capitalist when it comes to his experience of the two sorts of pleasure that are not specifically his own. Let's turn to the ambitious man, the lover of power and glory. Would we say, dear Amantha, that the experience the philosopher may have of pleasures that are contingent on honors and success is lesser than the experience the

300

ambitious man may have of the pleasures to be derived from a life lived by the Idea?

–I pass, *said Amantha sulkily.* Go ahead, Glaucon, go ahead!

–Honors, media hype! *Glaucon took off.* All three of our character types get to have them, provided they're successful. The rich man, the hero, and the wise man are all applauded by the crowd. So all three of them experience the pleasure of being recognized and admired. But when it comes to the pleasure of contemplation, it's impossible for anyone but the philosopher to enjoy it.

–As far as empirical knowledge, lived experience, goes, the philosopher is therefore the one who has the finest judgment.

–You bet he does!

–Besides, he's the only one who adds a healthy dose of pure thought to empirical knowledge. As a matter of fact, the instrument that's required to arrive at sound judgments is not at either the capitalist's or the ambitious man's disposal. Only the philosopher has it.

–What instrument are you talking about?

–Proofs, and, more broadly speaking, rational argumentation. That's the philosopher's tool par excellence. So we can now conclude. If wealth and profit were genuine criteria of judgment, whatever the capitalist declared to be good or bad would be immediately judged to be such by everyone.

–That's precisely the case in our Western democratic countries, *grumbled Amantha.* Whatever the capitalist says is right!

–But we don't think so! *Socrates corrected her.* Not any more than we think that the man on the make, the man of the social spectacle, can turn success and honors into the infallible criterion of the good, the true, and the beautiful.

–Anyway, capitalists and media personalities are six of one and half a dozen of the other! *Amantha added.*

–Since the sole criterion of judgment is a combination of experience, pure thought, and rational argumentation, what the rationalist philosopher declares to be true is in fact most likely to be true.

–You never cease to amaze us, *said Amantha, all smiles.*

–And I've got more where that came from, *Socrates gleefully replied.* Of the three pleasures we've distinguished between, the one that's inherent in the agency of the Subject on which our ability to think depends is the most enjoyable. As a result, those of us in whom this agency is prevalent have the most enjoyable lives.

–And so here we are back at the true life, *murmured Amantha.* I'm right to say "the true life" rather than just "the most enjoyable life," because someone who's willing to think is a qualified judge when it comes to evaluating his own life's eligibility for the Excellence Award for the happy life.

Amazed by this remark, Socrates looked affectionately at Amantha.

–But who'll get second prize? *said Glaucon anxiously.* I think it should be the careerist, the scrappy guy on the make. He's closer to the true life, at least in terms of his courage, than the trust fund kid sitting on his pile of gold.

–And so, *said Socrates in conclusion,* in last place as far as the pleasures of life are concerned will be the capitalist. Those are two demonstrations that prove the just man's victory over the unjust man when it comes to happiness. There's a third one, so crucial that it could occupy the place of the Holy Spirit in the Christians' Trinitarian mythology. The Holy Spirit, as you know, speaks after the Father, who tells us about the superiority of the desire for truth to all the others, and after the Son, who tells us that the philosopher knows better than anyone else what a true pleasure is.

–So what does this fictitious third person tell us? *asked a suspicious Amantha.*

–He says that only the pleasure of the person who gives himself up to thinking is pure and fully real. The other two sorts of pleasure, derived from wealth or media hype, are merely the nebulous sketch of a shadow. That's at any rate how I interpret the cryptic maxims of one of our ancient philosophers, who, we may surmise, transcribed the Holy Spirit's declarations. Anyway, if the Holy Spirit is right, it may well signal the final, irreversible defeat of the unjust man.

–But the Holy Spirit's just a convenient excuse! *exclaimed Amantha.* You announced you were going to give us a third proof, and here you are foisting hermetic poetry on us again!

–Help! *cried Socrates.* Glaucon, back me up! Your sister's maligning me! Answer my next few questions right away and as briefly as possible. Question 1: Is pain the opposite of pleasure?

–Yes.

–Question 2: Is there a subjective state in which we feel neither of the terms of this opposition, neither pain nor pleasure?

–Yes.

–Question 3: When the subject is in that neutral subjective state, equally distant from pleasure and pain, does he enjoy a sort of respite, or rest – yes or no?

–Yes.

At this, Amantha burst out in anger:

–We promised, we swore we wouldn't play the role of the young yes-men that are in my brother Plato's so-called "dialogues"!

–I answered "yes" because I think the answer's yes, not because of any yes-manism on my part, *Glaucon replied sharply.* Go on, dear Socrates!

–Question 4: Is it true or false that in many circumstances, illness in particular, what suffering people praise as most pleasurable is not pleasure but the cessation of suffering and the ensuing rest from it?

–That's true. But, *added Glaucon with a cautious glance at his sister,* maybe that's because the rest is no longer connected to a neutral intermediate state. It becomes a positive pleasure.

–And so you'd also say, I assume, that the cessation of pleasure and the ensuing rest constitute pain?

Glaucon sensed that something was amiss.

–I'm not sure this symmetry between pain and pleasure really works.

–Yet you do seem to be arguing, aren't you, that the rest that's midway between pleasure and pain becomes pain when pleasure stops, and pleasure when pain stops?

–That *is* in fact my impression.

–Do you think it's possible for something that's neither a term nor its opposite, like the subjective rest relative to pleasure and pain, to become now one, now the other? I'd add that when pain and pleasure occur in a Subject, they stir up violent internal motions in it. Yet the state in which we feel neither pleasure nor pain is rest, not motion. So we can easily see that the idea that the absence of pain, as rest, is pleasure, while the rest resulting from the cessation of pleasure is pain, is contrary to reason and groundless. The neutral state, as compared with pain, can *seem* like pleasure, but it isn't. And the appearance of pain that the cessation of pleasure brings about in relation to the neutral state has no true being-pain. These similarities merely trick the Subject.

–Your demonstration, I must say, is completely convincing.

–It can be bolstered by empirical observations. If you take, for example, pleasures that don't come after any pain, you'll immediately stop thinking that pleasure and pain are the inherent negation of each other.

But Amantha remained skeptical.

–You still need to convince me, *she said,* that these pleasures that have no connection with any pain really exist.

–Oh, there are loads of them! Just think of sweet smells, for instance. Think about when the mimosa bursts into bloom, in February, on the shores of the seas in the south. Without our having felt any pain beforehand, their fragrance overwhelms us with an extraordinary intensity, and when we walk away from the tree all that's left in us is joy; we're not afflicted by any pain.

–Glory be to spring! *said Amantha with a smile.*

–OK, let's not get carried away, though. The pleasures that come solely from the body's activity – intense, varied pleasures – are often akin to the cessation of a sort of gloomy apathy or painful tension.

–And there are also the pleasures and pains associated with future expectation, *Amantha added,* and with the anticipations that attempt to assuage that expectation.

–I propose a geometric image. Assume that on a given surface we can define three distinct areas such that only one of the three borders on the other two, and let's call them simply the Top, the Bottom, and the Middle.

–Which requires, *said Glaucon-the-pedant,* that our surface be oriented in space, and that "Middle" be the name of the one that borders on the other two.

–Let's not go into the topological details.

–It's the tricolor French flag, *grumbled Amantha,* with the white in the middle, that damn center where all the stupid sheep graze.[2]

Socrates, attempting to evade the young woman's sarcasm, went on:

–If someone – a point on the surface that has a few little flashes of insight – moves from the bottom to the middle, won't he quite naturally think he's at the top? Then, if he's blown by the wind toward the bottom, so that he lands back in it, he'll obviously have the feeling that he's fallen from the top to the bottom. And all this will be the case because he has no true knowledge of the spatial order governing the Bottom, the Middle, and the Top. He's on the surface, but his way of being on it is confused. We shouldn't be surprised that so many people, kept at a distance from the True and conducting themselves with respect to virtually everything only by confused opinions, are unsure about pleasure, pain, and what lies in between the two. When they're in the pain zone, they really *do* suffer. But when they go from pain to the zone in between, they're instantly convinced they're experiencing pleasure at its peak. Just as if, knowing nothing about white, they were to regard grey as the opposite of black, they contrast the lessening of pain with pain, since they're ignorant about pleasure. That's what their mistake is.

–Top and Bottom. Black and White. . . Those are pains, *remarked Amantha,* that are duly situated in space and colored.

Socrates nodded but seemed eager, all of a sudden, to change the subject.

–Aren't hunger and thirst, things of that sort, voids prescribed by a certain condition of the body?

–By that standard, *said Glaucon,* ignorance and nonsense are voids prescribed by a certain condition of the Subject.

–And, *added Amantha,* these voids can be filled either by stuffing yourself and drinking like a fish, or by learning a thousand different things and marshaling thought.

–Excellent! But when there's a void, of any sort, what fills it best?

Sensing a possible shift in the direction of the discussion, the two young people reflected. Amantha finally said:

–Whatever, with respect to a given void, has the most reality.

Socrates then launched into an impassioned interrogation.

–If we take the whole sphere of being-there into account, which existential modalities can we say participate unconditionally in that which, of being, is exposed to thought? Should we mention in this regard the way of existing that includes champagne, lobster *à l'américaine,* and, more generally, three-star restaurants? Or should we instead emphasize the way of existing that features true opinion, rational knowledge, pure thought and, more generally, the intellectual capacities?

Socrates paused, then, in rather solemn tones, continued:

–The question is at once simple and fundamental. Can we say – about that which, participating in universality, the self-identical, the immortal, and the true, belongs to the category prescribed by these attributes and which requires a Subject incorporated into it to be in the same category – well, can we say, about it, "it *is*" in a more essential way than can be said about that which, in the ordinary sphere of being-there, is never self-identical, arises only in order to pass away, and therefore belongs to the category prescribed by these negative attributes, as does any individual participating in it?

–As usual, *protested Amantha,* your question prescribes – I'm using your jargon – its own answer.

–But still?

–What my dear sister means, *Glaucon piped up,* is that, as we've known for ages, self-identity is a sign of pure being for you. And therefore constant change is a sign of something that, inasmuch as it falls short of rational knowledge, is ultimately only a sham being-true.

–To please Amantha, let's use a different kind of language then, *concluded Socrates.* Let's say that, in a given world, what's limited to the repetitive care of bodies participates less in that which of being is exposed to thought, and is consequently less true, than what's incorporated into a Subject.

–Can't we simplify all that even further, *Glaucon suggested,* by saying: bodies belong less to the Idea of the True than Subjects do?

–We'd still have to ask ourselves what, in a given world, a body of the True might be. But that's another story.[3] What we can say at any rate is this: the filling of a void whose being is more real and that is filled by beings whose being is also more real is more real than is the filling, by beings whose being is less real, of a void whose being is also less real.

–You betcha! It's perfectly self-evident, that sentence! *exclaimed Amantha mockingly.*

But Socrates took no notice of her remark and went on:

–If we call "pleasure" the fact of being filled with what belongs to our nature, then a filling whose being is more real by things whose being is also more real will define a pleasure that's more real and truer than the pleasure afforded by participating in something whose being is less real, and therefore by being filled in a less true and real way, such that the pleasure will be more doubtful and its participation in the true very inferior.

–Now *there*'s a high-flown sentence for you! *said Amantha, mocking him again.*

–And I'm going to attempt another that's even worse! *said an amused Socrates.* Listen carefully: Those who have had no access either to pure thought or to virtue and who can think about nothing but eating a good meal, frequenting child prostitutes in Thailand, or cheering wildly at some rigged soccer game are assigned, as it were, to the Bottom; then they sometimes come up to the Middle and spend their whole life wandering from one to the other without ever crossing the border between the Middle and the Top, without ever being able to orient themselves by the latter, or even managing to look up to that true Top, as a result of which, unable as they are to drink from the springs of Being as it is in itself and thereby to taste an intense, pure pleasure, they go around with their heads down, looking at the ground like cattle, grazing at one table after another, trying to outdo one another stuffing themselves and fornicating, which is why, competing fiercely over who'll get to have the most enjoyment, always greedy for more, they stamp the ground, butt one another, fight one another with horns and iron hooves, and kill one another with ever more sophisticated weapons, all because they haven't filled with any real beings either their own being or the place where that being dwells.

–Fabulous! *commented Glaucon.* I'm going to attempt one that's just as long now. Listen carefully, I'm continuing: Therefore these people necessarily only have pleasures mixed with pain, poor copies of the true pleasures, sketches of sorts that always overlap and whose apparent intensity is only due to contrasts with the outside, such that the lack of true thought precipitates them into violent erotic drives, on behalf of which they fight like dogs over a bone – or the way the warriors who were ignorant of the truth fought over a mere image of Helen under the walls of Troy, if we're to believe Stesichorus, who wrote:

> The Greeks and Trojans, to stir up war,
> Had Helen's image and nothing more.

–Not only do you invent two miserable lines of poetry that Stesichorus wouldn't have dared write, *cried Amantha,* but, what's more, your sentence isn't really long or really useful.

–Well, try and do better yourself! *said Glaucon, whose feelings were really hurt.*

–When I feel like it, I'll let you know.

–Settle down, kids! *said Socrates, attempting to arbitrate.* Let's move on. Isn't what happens with individuals as regards Affect necessarily similar to what happens to them with Desire? Once the Affect agency is set in motion, it will make them envious owing to ambition, aggressive out of vanity, and angry, so unstable is their temperament. And then all there will be is a desperate craving for honors and victory, and fury, devoid of all reason and foreign to all thought. So I'll say that desires, including those arising from private interest or motivated by the spirit of competition, may – provided they yield to the authority of rational knowledge and logical argumentation – aid in tasting the pleasures a thoughtful mind can lead them to. I claim that these originally dubious desires will then have access to the truest pleasures, simply because a truth is now guiding their existence. And I'll even add that these will be the pleasures best suited to their particular being, if it's true that what's best for a Subject is none other than what defines its existence as being appropriate to a specific truth, not to an empty generality.

Amantha could no longer contain herself; she just had to get in the long sentence of her own that would show her brother up:

–When the Subject as a whole, without any neurotic inner split, places himself under the authority of what philosophy calls a "truth," which is related to the agency of "Thought," what happens is that each of his three agencies becomes an active element of the truth process, thus an aide to justice, and each therefore enjoys the pleasures suited to its own particular function, hence the best

307

pleasures, the truest among all the ones it can aspire to; and this is the exact opposite of what happens when Desire or Affect takes over and forces the other two agencies to pursue a pleasure foreign to their nature and detached from any truth, without, however, the dominant agency's achieving its own pleasure; and so we can safely say that what's furthest removed in an individual from what philosophers and rational argumentation designate as that individual's becoming-Subject by virtue of being incorporated into the becoming of a truth is at the same time what's most likely to produce effects of abandonment and devaluation of pleasure – a certainty from which it may be inferred that, since what's furthest removed from rational argumentation is what's foreign to any universal principle and order; since, for their part, fascinating, tyrannical desires are the things most indifferent to universal principles; and finally, since, by contrast, the desires of a communist Subject as we've defined him inspire such principles, the necessary consequence of all this is that the person furthest removed from the true pleasure proper to human beings is the fascist tyrant, and the people the least far removed from that pleasure are those men or women who participate in the process of a system of government corresponding to the communist Idea; or, to put it more simply, we know for a fact that the bleakest life is that of the fascist tyrant and the most joyful life that of the communist citizen, as we've produced its concept, obviously, although we don't yet know if it can find its real in the tormented history of countries and governments.

Amantha was out of breath. Socrates applauded enthusiastically, as if a beautiful actress had just set one of Sophocles' speeches on fire. Glaucon, being a good sport, joined in the clapping with the others, then gave his sister, who blushed with pleasure, a hug. After this emotional moment, Socrates, with a somewhat Mephistophelian smile on his face, took over the dialogue again.

–Do you know, dear friends, exactly how much better the best life is than the worst?

–I can't even see how to make sense out of your question, *said Glaucon brusquely.*

–The basic arithmetical facts are seemingly very simple. There are only three agencies of the Subject and there are only three types of pleasure: that of the Top, that of the Middle, and that of the Bottom. Now, three times three equals nine.

–OK, but so what?

–So nothing – that's the whole problem.

–What do you mean, nothing? *Glaucon, bewildered, continued.*

–The fascist tyrant crossed the border between the Middle and the Bottom and lives as far as possible from the Top. But he resides in his realm with such a retinue of degrading pleasures that to say he's nine times unhappier than the communist citizen seems way too easy. The problem needs to be approached some other way.

Under the wrathful eye of his sister, Glaucon, too intrigued to react, agreed to play the part of the uncritical interlocutor again. There then began a long dialogue between Socrates and Glaucon during which Amantha almost fell asleep.

–So how should we go about it?

–There are five different systems of government, *said Socrates.* In descending order: communism, timocracy, oligarchy, democracy, and tyranny, also known as fascism.

–Right.

–Each of them can be said to be removed from the first one by as many degrees as is implied by its distance from it.

–That makes sense.

–So the tyrannico-fascist system of government is at a remove of five degrees from the communist system of government.

–OK.

–But that tells us nothing if we don't know anything about the specific intensity of the pleasures inherent in communism.

–Nothing, it's true.

–As a matter of fact we know that that intensity is measured by a factor of 6.

–I believe you, but I have no idea why.

–Because 6 is the first perfect number, that is, a number that's equal to the sum of its divisors other than itself, as is shown by $6=3+2+1$.

–That *is* in fact a sign of perfection.

–Now we can say that the pleasure associated with a given system of government is less than the communist system of government's pleasure by as many degrees as the number measuring that same inferiority to communist pleasure of the system of government just above the one being considered, multiplied by the latter's rank.

–I confess I don't understand a thing.

–Well, for example, timocracy comes right after communism. The degree of inferiority of its own specific pleasure to the pleasure of communism, located just above it, will thus be $1\times2=2$.

–Why 1? Why 2?

–Because the degree of inferiority of the communist system of government to itself is the number that measures identity, or 1. And because timocracy is in second place.

–OK, now I get it! The degree of inferiority of tyranny is then $1\times5=5$.

–No, not at all, Glaucon, not at all. You have to multiply a system of government's rank by the degree of inferiority to communism of the system of government just *above* it, not directly by the number 1 assigned to communism. The formula's simple. Let r_i be the rank of a system of government, and, since there are five systems of government, $1\leq i\leq5$. Let $D(r_i)$ be the degree of inferiority of the pleasure associated with the system of government of rank i relative to the pleasure associated with the communist system of government, which ranks in first place. We then have two rules defining the recursive computation of the number $D(r_i)$:

(1) $D(r_1)=1$
(2) $D(r_{i+1})=D(r_i)\times i$

So you can see that in the case of timocracy, which is in second place, we get:

$$D(r_2)=D(r_1)\times2=1\times2=2$$

–Oh, please! Give me another example!

–Let's take democracy, which is in fourth place. The rules require that in order to compute $D(r_4)$, you have to know what $D(r_3)$ is. We know that $D(r_2)=2$. We apply the second rule and get:

$$D(r_3)=D(r_2)\times3=2\times3=6$$

So oligarchic pleasure is six times less than communist pleasure.

–I agree with that calculation.

–Since we've got $D(r_3)$, rule 2 will give us $D(r_4)$. We. . .

–I can do it, *cried Glaucon delightedly.* The formula is:

$$D(r_4)=D(r_3)\times4=6\times4=24$$

Democratic pleasure is twenty-four times less than communist pleasure!

–Good job, my boy! So now we can easily get to fascist tyranny. We have:

$$D(r_5)=D(r_4)\times5=24\times5=120$$

The pleasure associated with fascist life is thus 120 times less than the pleasure that will one day be associated with communist life.

–The pleasure you get from living in a tyrannized country sure isn't great.

–We know the exact measure of its intensity.

–How is that possible?

–We said that the perfection of the pleasure associated with future communist life equaled 6. If the pleasure of fascist life is 120 times less than that, it equals 6 divided by 120, or 0.05.

–What an amazing number!

–It's no more than a little prick of satisfaction. In fact, the only great pleasure you can feel that, in a sense, a despotic regime would be the cause of is the one you get from the collapse of that regime, when the boundless sufferings it has caused finally end.

–But you taught us that the essence of pleasure can't be the cessation of pain. The Top is not the negation of the Bottom.

–You've got a good memory, my dear Glaucon. In that case, and in that case alone, there's often the pleasure of a liberation. But that pleasure, however great it may be, is fragile, sometimes uncertain or non-existent. Because liberations of that sort, especially if they come from outside, herald periods of unrest. Think about the liberation of France by the Anglo-American troops in 1944–5 or, even worse, the "liberation" of Iraq by the Anglo-American troops in 2002. The Iraqi people's "pleasure" was zero, whereas the tyranny exercised by Saddam Hussein was fierce.

–At any rate, that's one question settled.

–That's actually why we have to go back to the strategic stakes of our discussion, namely the definition of justice and the question of the just life. If I remember correctly, our interlocutor, brilliantly played by Glaucon, argued the following thesis: injustice brings great advantages to a person who pushes it to the extreme of perfection, provided he's able to persuade prevailing opinion that he's someone who's perfectly just. Right?

–Yes, *agreed Glaucon*, that's right.

–Now that we've clarified the matter and that you and I agree, let's turn to that defender of the unjust life's advantages and try to find some new ways to convince him of his error.

–What "new" ways? We already knocked ourselves out trying to take him down a peg or two.

–To recapitulate our arguments, we need a beautiful, powerful metaphor.

–The lover of Ideas, *said Amantha suddenly waking up*, always resorts to a metaphor when he's in trouble.[4]

–But not just any one, *an unruffled Socrates replied.* An integral metaphor of the Subject. A metaphor as powerful as those of the gorgeous monsters told of in myth: the Minotaur, the Sphinx, Medusa, Cerberus, and so forth.

–Well, let's see then, *said Amantha, whose curiosity always got the better of her sarcasm, calming down.*

–Let's first imagine that a skilled sculptor of the contemporary school models, in a variety of materials – cardboard, clay, wood, or scrap metal – a form that can be regarded, depending on the viewer's point of view or the lighting, as representing one existing animal or another, from the most monstrous or ferocious, such as the giant squid, the shark, or the vulture, to the most ordinary and docile, such as the sheep or the domestic rabbit. Then an excellent sculptor of the baroque period creates a magnificent lion in bronze. And then the greatest virtuoso of classical sculptors carves, out of black marble streaked with white and yellow, a human form so indeterminate that you can't tell if it's a man or a woman. Finally, an anonymous artist from no particular period and who isn't the least bit concerned about imitation – I like him for that – wraps the composite animal, the lion, and the human being in a big tarpaulin to which he, too, gives a human form, but one that's even more stylized, vague, undecidable than the one that's under the tarpaulin.

–What a weird kind of work, *said Amantha, intrigued.*

–From the outside you can't see any of the forms that are inside. Someone who has no way of making a hole in the tarpaulin thinks that there's only one form inside, that of a human being.

–Whatever kind of comment can we possibly make about a wrapping like this for our bosom enemy, the defender of injustice? *asked Glaucon, scratching his head.*

–Here's what we'll say to him: "Dear defender of injustice, your position amounts to saying that it's advantageous for the human form, of which the big tarpaulin is the model, to fatten the composite animal and the mighty lion inside it while starving and weakening the human figure that's the third component of what's inside. You consider it good for human nature, as it appears in the world, that animalistic chaos and the wild beast's ferocity should run the show within, doing whatever they like to the man inside. Instead of their seeing to the harmony of the three components, you'd like them to shake up the human tarpaulin, biting and devouring one another in a bloody free-for-all. Our own thesis is obviously more reasonable.

312

To submit to a principle of justice is tantamount to thinking that you ought to say and do only what will give the inner human form the means to guide the overall human form, the one that can be seen from the outside – means by which the man inside will, for one thing, be able to look after the composite animal form, as a farmer does when he feeds and tames the docile species while keeping the wild, bad ones from increasing – and, for another, make an ally of the lion's nobility, so that, by sharing his responsibilities with all the inhabitants of the human tarpaulin, he's able to get them to be on good terms both with each other, inside, and with the "himself" that is merely the total exterior of that multifaceted inner being.

–That's at least a metaphor whose didactic function alone explains what can be understood about it. Because in itself, just as a metaphor, you've got to admit it's goddamn enigmatic. Well done, dear teacher! *Amantha congratulated him.*

–Metaphor or no metaphor, *Socrates calmly went on,* and however we approach the problem, it's certain, in any case, that someone who praises justice speaks truthfully, while someone who praises injustice is totally wrong. Regardless of whether you adopt as your criterion pleasure, the reputation one enjoys, or advantage, it turns out that a person who's on the side of justice is also on the side of truth, while someone who disparages justice not only speaks in a hateful way but also knows nothing about the very thing he's disparaging.

–That's you all over, dear Socrates, *said Amantha fondly.* If someone were to slit his own son's throat, you'd patiently explain that he only did so because he didn't know where Truth was. . .

–I've given proofs many times about the correctness of that point of view, *said Socrates a little testily.* And I'll continue to do so. Gently and patiently is how we'll disabuse someone who's all for injustice, because he's not getting it wrong on purpose. We'll say to him: "Dear friend, don't custom and law agree on the distinction between what's shameful and what's honorable? We act honorably when the strictly animal part of our nature is under the control of what attests to the properly human aspect in us. We could almost say: under the control of the divine spark, or the share of eternity implied by our acts. We act shamefully when our serene inner being falls under the yoke of our latent savagery." Won't he have to agree?

–Of course, *Glaucon hastened to agree.*

–Anyway, once he's swallowed that, all the rest will have to follow, *muttered Amantha.*

Socrates, who was perhaps aware of this subtle warning, attempted to beef up his position:

313

−If the commonest opinion has always and everywhere condemned total existential anarchy, it's because the person who indulges in it gives a lot more power than he should to the great, terrible beast of protean Desire. Similarly, we rebuke the arrogance and bad temper of someone who has let the lion of Affect grow and get stronger within him to an unnatural degree. If we come down hard on the extravagant spending and sterile ostentation of the idle rich, it's because they actually weaken the lion so much that it results in intolerable cowardice. If flattery and servility are frowned upon, it's because they enslave that same lion of Affect to the protean beast of Desire, which, due to its overweening love of wealth, eventually turns the lion into an ape. And, finally, why do the rich scorn poor workers and have no qualms about calling them "barbarians" or "poorly integrated into society," or about passing criminal legislation against them, parking them in filthy housing projects and checking their documents, beating them, arresting them, even executing them, as soon as they act as though they might rebel? It's because the rich and their parliamentary parties are terribly afraid that the lion of worker Affect, once inspired by the sheer humanity of the Idea, will subjugate the beast's cowardly acts, and the result of this will be a political force and courage all the more threatening to the power of the rich in that the latter are in reality corrupt and cowardly.

−I still don't see how the danger that all these vices represent can be avoided, *said Glaucon, rather upset.*

−The empirical individual must submit to the man within him, the man who's capable of truth and is thus inhabited by a flame that can be allegorically described as divine. This sort of obedience doesn't work to the detriment of the individual, as Thrasymachus – who, by the way, is peacefully snoring away without listening to us – thinks. On the contrary, nothing is more beneficial to him, to such an extent that the rule also applies to the external form of power, the communist community, which must be, like the man within, that which in the political order – and unlike any social group pursuing nothing but its own interest – is capable of truth.

−So, regardless of whether we are dealing with his political commitment or his private life, is your thesis, *asked Amantha,* that a human being will be said to truly think only if he devotes all his energy to the discipline that must be consented to, since it establishes the power of a super-human ability in people?

−That's a bit of a stretch, young lady, secretly in love as you are with transcendence. But overall you're right.

−So what becomes of the body in all this business? *inquired Glaucon.*

−As far as the physical condition of the body – food, gymnastics,

314

all that sort of thing – is concerned, we won't accept as the only rule for our lives the irrational, animal instinct that requires survival, gratification, and enjoyment. The best thing would be to worry about health and place a high value on being strong and attractive only to the extent that those things are potential means of acquiring sound good sense. Physical equilibrium should only be sought after if it serves to interpret the Subject's immanent symphony brilliantly.

–You want us to be the musicians of our subjective harmony, *concluded Amantha.*

–That's a nice phrase. Let's also keep a sense of harmony when it comes to the extremely pressing, difficult question of money and spending. Let's not let ourselves be dazzled by what opinion, in this capitalist world that is the world of corruption, regards as happiness: never stop increasing your wealth and buy all that glitters on the great global marketplace. If we turn toward our *inner* government, we'll find in it what we need in order to make these money matters subordinate to the development of our capacity for creating something that has universal meaning beyond our immediate desires. We'll do the same with regard to public recognition, willingly accepting the kind we think will bolster what's best in us and avoiding, in our private lives as in our obligations on the world stage, the people who might disturb our becoming-Subject.

–Then it's likely, *noted Glaucon, not without a certain melancholy,* that we'll have to refuse to be involved in any political activity.

–No, by the Dog![5] We'll be very involved in politics among the people of our country. But not at the level of official positions, not in the state – on the contrary, at a distance from the state. Except in unpredictable revolutionary circumstances.

–Circumstances that would establish a political order like the one we've been talking about since yesterday? *Glaucon asked.* Is that what you mean? Because for the time being that order only exists in our theories. I don't think a single example of it exists anywhere in reality.

–And yet it's likely that many very real political movements, in many different countries, are sympathetic to our Idea, since the scope of the idea is universal. However, regardless of whether those movements are powerful or have only recently gotten off the ground, are numerous, or are few and far between, that's not what determines us as Subjects. Naturally, we hope that someday there will be systems of government that will provide the Idea with the real it's based on. But, even if that's not yet the case, it's nevertheless this Idea and none other that we'll attempt to remain faithful to in everything we undertake.

315

— 16 —

POETRY AND THOUGHT
(592b–608b)

Socrates gloated:
–This political order we're founding is the best! The best, not in itself, which is meaningless, but the best of all the ones that we can extract by thought from the field of possibilities. The arguments in its favor are legion, but none is more compelling than the one that hinges on our considered relationship with poetry, since we've required that its mimetic aspect must never be tolerated. That requirement is imperative – let's even say that it acquires the status of self-evidence – now that we've distinguished between the various agencies of the Subject and conceived of each one's distinct nature. Dear Amantha and Glaucon! You're the brother and sister of my friend Plato, the inspired and rather concise stenographer of our freewheeling speech. So you can't be dirty informers in the pay of tragic poets and other such mimeticians, can you? I can speak to you with complete confidence, can't I? Let me risk my all. Without further ado, I contend that poetry that's excessively characterized by imitation causes extensive damage to the formal intelligence of its audience if they don't have the antidote, namely the knowledge of what that poetry really is, in its being.
Glaucon, finding these statements to be very muddled or overly cautious, took the risk of making an unsolicited remark:
–It seems to me, dear teacher, that you're getting all worked up over very little.
–It's because I still have a sort of respectful fondness for Homer going back to childhood when I first studied him, and because Homer really does seem to have been the original teacher, the guide, of all our fine tragic poets. But it's inappropriate to respect a man more than the truth. Whence it can be inferred that I need to speak. . .

–Hey! *Amantha interrupted him.* Stop beating around the bush!

–All right, all right, I'll get to it. But let me at least, in such sensitive circumstances, use the famous Socratic dialogue, in which getting to the answer requires taking a roundabout way from the question.

–OK, I'm waiting for your questions, *said Glaucon with a sigh.*

–Can you two give me a general definition of mimesis? I don't quite understand what the point of it is.

–What kind of question is that?! *exclaimed Amantha in her soft, high-pitched voice. You* don't understand, and you think *I* can?

–There'd be nothing so strange about that. Very often, people with poor eyesight understand what's going on better than people with sharp eyes.

–That does happen, it's true, *said Glaucon.* But, even if I have an idea that I think is brilliant, all it takes is for you to be here, and my eagerness to express it fizzles out. You go first, dear teacher!

–Well, pay careful attention then, *Socrates continued, quite pleased with himself.* Do both of you want us begin our philosophical inquiry in accordance with our usual method? Usually, for any multiplicity made up of elements to which we give the same name, we posit the unity of a Form. This time as well, if it's OK with you, let's choose from among any of the multiples in this room. We can see that there are loads of beds and tables. But, so far as all these pieces of furniture are concerned, there are only two ideas, the bed-idea and the table-idea. Still in line with our usual conceptual procedure, we posit that a craftsman can only make these pieces of furniture, which we'll later use, by looking toward their particular ideas, toward the bed-idea for a bed and toward the table-idea for a table. As for the idea itself, no craftsman has the ability to make it. How on earth would he go about it? Yet there actually is a kind of universal craftsman, who's able to make all the objects that each of the specialized craftsmen manufacture on the basis of one given idea.

–What a man he must be, that specialist of all things! *said Amantha, full of admiration.*

–How right you are! *continued Socrates.* Not only can he make every kind of furniture, but he makes everything that grows from the earth, too. And he makes all living organisms, himself as well as the others. Everything, to tell the truth, is within his creative purview: the earth, the heavens, the gods, all the stars that shine at night, everything in the subterranean gloom of the underworld – he can make all of that.

–Who are you trying to kid, Socrates? *protested Amantha.*

–You don't believe me? What exactly do you doubt, dearest friend?

Do you think there's no way a universal craftsman of this sort could ever exist? Or is your idea, more specifically, that there's one kind of existence such that, in it, it's possible to be the creator of everything, and another in which that's in fact impossible? Let me tell you something. You yourself, from a certain point of view, could be that all-powerful craftsman, a creator of universes.

–That'll be the day!

–It's quick and easy. Very quick and easy, even. Take your mirror – women all have one – and turn it around night and day in every direction. In no time at all you'll make the sun and the stars of the sky in it, in no time at all the earth, in no time at all yourself and other living creatures, and plants, and furniture. . . And, finally, you'll make beds and tables too.

–Sure, *said Glaucon,* but I'd only be producing the *appearance* of objects, not what they are in truth.

– Now we're getting somewhere! *said Socrates gleefully.* You hit on my point exactly. Because the painter is one of the craftsmen we were talking about, isn't he? So you'll tell me that what the painter creates has no truth to it. Yet one can say that if he paints a bed on the wall of this house of Cephalus' where we've spent a night of passionate philosophizing and an entire day of interminable discussions, he is *really* creating a bed on the wall.

–A bed that's only an appearance of a bed.

–Well, what about the carpenter, then? You were saying a moment ago that, when he makes a particular bed, he isn't making the bed-form that we maintain is what a Bed really is. If he doesn't make the Bed that really *is,* he doesn't make a being-bed, but a bed that's *like* the being-bed, although not actually being it. In that case, anyone who says that the work of a carpenter or, more broadly speaking, the work of a craftsman is in the perfect order of being is very likely not telling the Truth. We shouldn't be surprised that material products of this sort are complicated, in terms of their relationship with truth.

–Then let's not be surprised, *muttered Glaucon, looking bewildered.*

–Now let's try to understand, on the basis of these examples, what that famous mimesis might be. Aren't there ultimately three beds, as far as thought's concerned, rather than just one? The first is the one whose being lies naturally in itself and about which we'd say, I think, that it's the work of the big Other. Otherwise, where would its eternal life come from?

–I haven't got a clue, *confessed a beleaguered Glaucon.*

–The second bed is the woodworker's.

–I guess so.

–The third is the painter's. Right?

–All right. And what next?

–There's no next. There are only three beds! The painter, the carpenter, and the Other: that's the Holy Trinity that reigns over the threeness of the instances of the bed.

–What elegance there is, *Amantha exclaimed,* in that Trinitarian scheme!

–Provided, however, that it's connected with the other essential numbers, like the One and the Two. Take the big Other. Regardless of whether it was a free choice or whether some higher necessity required that more than one Bed – of the sort whose being lies naturally in themselves – should not be made, the fact remains that it made only one copy of this Bed-that-is. Bringing two, or even more, of them into existence is something the big Other didn't do, and will never do.

Amantha was now passionately involved in the argument.

–How can you be so sure? *she asked.*

–Well, if it made two and no more, we'd still already have a multiplicity. And, since any multiplicity requires an additional term that supports the unity of that multiplicity, there would have to be a third Bed, which would possess the formal unity of the other two. But then *it*, not the other two, would be the Bed-that-is.

Amantha was full of admiration for him.

–You're really outdoing yourself, Socrates, *she said.* That's a truly amazing argument!

–Some day they'll call it "the Third-Man Argument"[1] and they'll use it against my own doctrine! At any rate, we can be sure that the Other was aware of this when it dealt with the Bed and the beds; and, as it absolutely wanted to be the one who makes the Bed-that-absolutely-is, not the particular maker of a particular bed, it created the true Bed's natural uniqueness. So would you agree to our calling the Other the father of the Bed, or some such thing?

–That would be fitting, *said Glaucon,* since it created both that Form and all the others in the natural order.

–We could also call the carpenter "the manufacturer of the bed."

Amantha put in:

–That way we'd have the Father and the Manufacturer. But what name should we give the third guy of the Trinity, the Painter?

–Neither manufacturer nor maker, in any case.

–Obviously not.

319

–But what's his share in the being of the bed, if it's neither the universality of the idea nor the particularity of the object?

–I think, *said Amantha hesitantly,* that the most fitting solution would be to call him the imitator of the real that the others are the manufacturers of.

–So you're deciding to call the person who's at two degrees of separation from the nature of the True an "imitator," or, to sound erudite, a "mimetician." Let's apply your definition to the tragic poets. Suppose that when they're describing a king their language, which aims at conveying verisimilitude, is basically mimetic. So first we'll distinguish the universal form of royal power; then, putting that form to the test in the real world, a king who has really existed – Agamemnon, for example; and, finally, the imitation of the latter by the poet. And there we find our three terms and our two degrees of separation again.

–But is "two" really appropriate? *objected Amantha.* What the painter attempts to imitate – at least if he's reduced to the mimetic aspect of his art – is of course not the One-truth of what he wants to reproduce. But it's not the multiple objects that the manufacturers make from that form, either. It's those objects not as they *are* but as they *appear*; and so I wonder if there aren't actually four terms, like when you presented the dialectical process to us in the guise of a divided line: the universal Form, the particular object, the appearance of that object, and the imitation of that appearance. There would then be three degrees of separation between the artist and the big Other, not two.

An amazed Socrates applauded. But Glaucon wasn't following anymore and said as much:

–I can't follow you.

So Socrates said:

–Dear Glaucon, think about our famous bed. You look at it sideways, or head on, or from underneath: each time you'd say it's different from itself. But isn't it really the case that, without differing at all from itself, it *appears* to be doing so? Now think about the painter. What's his aim, with respect to the objects he depicts? Is it their being as it actually is that he's imitating? Or their appearance as it appears instead? Is the imitation the imitation of an image or of a truth?

–Of an image, I think, *Glaucon ventured.*

–The mimetic therefore operates at a great remove from the truth, and if it seems able to reproduce everything, it's only to the extent that the share of each thing it grasps is exceedingly small. It's actually only a simulacrum. Let's say the painter, without knowing a thing about woodworking, is going to paint a carpenter. It's clear that he'll then be operating completely from the outside of what characterizes a carpenter. If he's a skillful painter – in terms of the mimetic – his carpenter will fool children and naïve people; it just needs to be seen from a distance and to have the superficial characteristics of a real carpenter. The lesson in all this, dear friends, is clear: if someone tells us he's met a great guy who knows all the craftsmen's skills without exception better than the craftsmen themselves, we'll instantly reply that that's sheer gullibility. Our interlocutor has come across a charlatan, an imitator whom he was taken in by. If he thought the guy knew absolutely everything, it's a safe bet that he can't tell knowledge from ignorance and imitation.

Glaucon exclaimed:

–Yeah, absolutely, that's for sure! We'll shut his trap for him.

–Unless it's the tragic poets or our old Homer, the father of all poets, whose "traps," as you put it, we have to "shut"! That's another kettle of fish. Lots of people actually say that the poets, Homer first and foremost, are masters of all the skills, of all things human that are connected with vice and virtue, if not of all things divine. Their argument is brief and to the point: a good poet, they say, motivated by the desire to express to perfection what he puts into poetry, can only write a poem about what he knows or he'll show himself to be incapable of putting his subject matter into poetry. What should we think about this "demonstration"? One possibility is that our interlocutors have run into some crafty mimeticians who've snowed them with a lot of fine words. Mentally conditioned like this, even when they came into direct contact with these mimeticians' works, they couldn't sense at what an enormous remove – three degrees – these works were from real being. They didn't realize that, for people with no knowledge of the truth, putting things into poetry is easy: they put imitations, not real beings, into poetry. The other possibility is of course that our interlocutors are right: good poets actually do have genuine knowledge about everything that all their readers say they speak so admirably about.

–But how can we decide? *Glaucon wondered.*

–Imagine someone who can do both: the real and its imitation. Do you think he'd devote all his energy to becoming exclusively a manufacturer of images? That such craftsmanship would constitute the entire glorious meaning of his life, as if he'd never had anything better to do?

–Well, why not? *muttered Amantha rather ironically.*

–Oh, come on! If he really knew the truth of what he's imitating, or

321

representing, he'd devote himself to producing that truth rather than imitating something that's merely its support. He'd leave behind him, as monuments to his memory, as many sublime works as he could. He'd want to be someone who's praised himself rather than someone who sings the praises of others.

–Assuming, *said Amantha who still had reservations,* that personal prestige and social utility are in actual fact something that the former can lay claim to. That's debatable. . .

–Let's not split hairs! *said Socrates, annoyed.* Let's simplify things. We won't hold Homer or any other poet accountable for everything they write about. Take the art of medicine. We could ask: Was that famous poet who writes poetry about diseases and their cures ever a real doctor, or did he just settle for a pastiche of medical talk? And what about that other poet, whether ancient or modern, with his verses on the Great Health? Would we say he really cured real patients, the way Fleming or even Claude Bernard[2] did? Or what about that other one, who uses charming cadences to teach the merits of a healthy life? Did he, like Pasteur, establish a whole school dedicated to the study of severe infections and the defenses that vaccination combats them with? We could go on like this, but I suggest we drop this line of questioning. We'll spare the poets and won't torture them anymore about anything having to do with technique. We'll concentrate instead on the most important and difficult subjects about which Homer chose to express himself: war, strategy, government, education, and so on. As far as those are concerned, we do perhaps have the right to say to him: "Dear Homer, if, as regards the truth of a virtue, you're not idling at three degrees of separation from it; if you're not what we call a mimetician, that is to say, a manufacturer of images; if you've managed to be at only two degrees of separation from the True; and if, finally, you're able to distinguish between the Forms that constitute a model for bettering men's lives, both public and private, and all the ones that make it worse, then tell us, dear poet, what political community owes its radical transformation to you, the way Russia owed its to Lenin, and the way many others, big or small, owed theirs to many others, both in the past and today, from Robespierre to Mandela, by way of Toussaint Louverture and Mao Zedong? What country regards you as an outstanding legislator? Sparta had Lycurgus and Athens had Solon. But what about you? Where is that country?"

–I don't think he'd be able to answer, *said Glaucon.* Even his disciples and descendants, the Homerids, are silent on that subject.

–Does anyone remember a war from which Homer emerged victorious, either as chief of staff or as the main adviser and strategist of the general staff? Is Homer ranked among those distinguished by their practical achievements? Can anyone cite Homer's many ingenious technical inventions, in any field of activity, the way people do for Sostratus of Cnidus, the builder of the lighthouse of Alexandria, or for Papin of France, who made a steam-activated engine run? And if he didn't accomplish anything on behalf of the state, did Homer at least work for the benefit of private individuals? Have the memories of a single person whose education he directed during his lifetime come down to us? A single one who appreciated seeing Homer on a daily basis and who bequeathed to subsequent generations a life orientation that could be called "Homeric"? That's what Pythagoras, who's beloved precisely for teaching of that sort, is credited with. Even today, the master's remote disciples call "Pythagorean" a way of life that, according to them, is different from any other. But what about Homer?

–Tradition, *said Glaucon,* is very silent about that as well. Of course, people do talk about one of Homer's disciples, who was allegedly his son-in-law, according to the countless gossipy stories that have gone around about the life of the tremendous blind poet. Some guy named Boosphilus. But when it comes to this cow-lover[3] it's hard to decide which is funnier, his name or the outcome of his education, because they say that throughout his life Boosphilus regarded Homer, his father-in-law and Greece's greatest poet, as a complete nobody.

–Those stories are well known. But let's get serious. Suppose Homer were really capable of being humanity's mentor along the road to its progressive betterment. Suppose that, as far as these matters go, he weren't a mere imitator but a truly learned man. Wouldn't he then have had countless acolytes who loved and honored him? Inveterate sophists like Protagoras, Prodicus, and so many others are always persuading all sorts of respectable people, in private sessions, that they won't be able to manage – as Engels would say – "private property, the family or the state" if they don't knuckle under to the educational authority of the aforementioned sophists. The disciples of these peculiar teachers worship their talent so fervently that they all but carry them around triumphantly on their shoulders. So, would the people of Homer's time, knowing that such a man could help them learn true virtue, have allowed him – like Hesiod, I might add – to travel far and wide, all on his own, declaiming his poems in dusty village squares in order to earn his living? That's completely implausible! Wouldn't they have preferred the company of mentors like them to all the gold in the world? Wouldn't they have gone to great lengths to keep them at home with them for good? And if they'd failed in their efforts to entice – or bribe – them wouldn't they have followed these phenomenal professors to the ends of the earth to avail themselves of their lessons, until they'd gotten all they could out of them?

Amantha then said:

–When it comes to Homer, dear Socrates, you speak in such eloquent tones! Prose versus poetry, huh?

Socrates replied rather testily:

–All I'm trying to do is establish that none of the poets from Homer on, whether it's virtue they write poetry about or anything else, have any grasp of the truth. Let's go back to our comparison between painting and poetry. A painter who's absolutely incapable of mending a shoe will nevertheless be able to produce a completely convincing shoemaker on his canvas, at least as far as those who are as ignorant as he is are concerned. Why? Because for these ignoramuses looking at the painting, a "shoemaker" is only an assemblage of shapes and colors. Similarly, a poet covers all the crafts with the colors given them by words and phrases, without being a master of any of them, except for imitation. And so those who enjoy the enchanting show of words imagine that when a poet speaks about shoes with holes in them, or military tactics, or maritime crossings, or whatever it may be, he speaks extremely well about them, since that poet will have imparted an irresistible charm to language by using intonation, rhythm, and melody. But if poets' works are stripped of everything connected with their musical coloration you know what happens: nude, the poem is crude.

Amantha said snarkily:

– Nice turn of phrase, Socrates! Totally musical and colorful! But you still need to explain what intellectual processes are needed to strip a poem.

But Socrates, pretending he hadn't heard her, went on:

–Let's get back to the broader question of the difference between being and appearing. The poet of imitations, the mimetician, has no grasp whatsoever of what is. He settles for what appears. So let's not stop mid-stream, let's deal with the problem thoroughly. Let's use the painter once more.

–Once too often, perhaps, *Amantha interjected.* Is language a painting?

–Let's take it point by point, *said Socrates good-naturedly.* At every step of the way, young lady, tell me whether you agree or not. The painter depicts a hunting rifle or a violin, say. But when it comes to *making* one of those things, you've got to go to a gunsmith or a violin-maker. Right?

324

–Of course you do, *said Amantha.*

–But is the person who truly understands the construction of these objects, whether a rifle or a violin, the painter? Or is it the person who makes them: the gunsmith, or the violin-maker? Or is it only the person who knows how to *use* them: the hunter, or the violinist?

–Probably the user, but only provided that by "construction" you meant. . .

–Let's generalize then, *Socrates interrupted her.* For each object of this sort, there are three different skills involved: using it, making it, and representing it. Do you agree?

–It'd be hard not to.

–Nevertheless, the virtue, beauty, and aptness of singular things, whether we are talking about a musical instrument, an animal, or an action, lie in the use for which each of the things is intended – when it's manufactured, if it's something man-made; when the decision about it is made, if it's a matter of something practical; or when it's born, if it's something natural. It therefore follows necessarily that the person who has the most experience of a given object is its user and that he's the one who should inform the maker about the positive or negative features he finds in the object he uses when he uses it. The user – the violinist, say – can discern the qualities and defects of an object, a violin, because he knows from experience what he's talking about. By relying on him, the maker – the violin-maker – can do his job. As a result, when it comes to this instrument, we can see that the maker has an informed belief about the qualities and defects of what he produces, because he associates with someone who knows, because he's forced to listen to someone who knows. But the user alone possesses the knowledge. Right, Amantha?

–You said I was to give my opinion after each point, but you're making a long, complicated argument. So why don't you just go right through to the end, and then we'll see. It's poetry we're interested in, after all, not any business about shoes with holes in them, Viennese waltzes, or duck hunting.

–Precisely! I'm going to go back to the imitator, hence the poet. Since he's satisfied with merely representing an object, he doesn't acquire any knowledge of its beauty or its aptness, which only the object's use can provide, nor does he acquire the informed opinion about these matters that you get by being around someone who knows and tells you how to depict the object properly. In a nutshell, the mimetician will have neither true knowledge nor an informed opinion about the beauty or defects of the object he's copying. His mimetic competence is reduced to this double lack. He'll nonetheless go on copying objects in spite of his not being able to discern their qualities and defects at all. In imitating, his guide, for sure, will be that purely apparent – and I'd even say commercial – "beauty" that servile public opinion and those who have no knowledge whatsoever chase after.

–If you say so. . .

–In any case, I think I'm justified in saying that we agree about two points. First of all, the imitator hasn't the slightest rational knowledge about the objects he imitates, and mimesis as a whole is merely a kind of entertainment devoid of all seriousness. Second of all, those who dabble in tragic poetry with lots of alexandrines, epic or iambic verses, and dactylic hexameters, are all as mimetic as can be. What do you think, Amantha?

–I think that, when you're being crushed by your opponent, you have no choice but to consent to sign whatever agreement he's offering you.

Socrates looked at her, nonplussed, then slowly turned to Glaucon and asked:

–Glaucon! Faithful friend! Will you grant me that the imitative process is at three degrees of separation from everything under the authority of the Idea of the True?

–Yes, *said a startled Glaucon*, it's at three degrees. . .

–. . . below zero! *snorted Amantha*. The imitative process is shivering in its boots, its balls are shriveling. Just like yours, brother dear![4]

Socrates burst out laughing at the shocked expression on Glaucon's face and said:

–Now, now, you uncouth young lady! Let's look at the problem from another angle. You've many times observed, dear Glaucon, that something of invariant size can nevertheless seem different from itself depending on whether it's seen from up close or from a distance. The same stick can seem bent or straight depending on whether it's seen in water or out of it. The same object can seem to be concave or convex owing to an optical illusion caused by how the colors are distributed. Experiences like these are obviously very disturbing for the Subject. *Trompe l'oeil* painting, magic tricks, and all the other similar sorts of trickery can only cast their spell on us because of this unfortunate feature of our nature or, if you like, this limitation of our perceptual capacities.

–So are we doomed to error then?

–Not at all! We've discovered a wonderful source of help in measuring, counting, and weighing. Thanks to those rational actions, the Subject is no longer inwardly ruled by the unreliability of appearance, the elusive obsession with variations in size, number, or mass. His guiding principle is henceforth the ability to calculate, measure, and weigh. Now, it can be argued that these abilities are ultimately dependent on reason, which is itself inherent in the Subject.

–And therefore, *concluded an elated Glaucon,* the Subject can eradicate imitative illusions from his life.

–Oh, my! Not so fast! Very often, this Subject who can measure and says that there exist quantitative relations of superiority, inferiority, or strict equality between two terms simultaneously declares that the terms in question are contradictory. Now, we agreed that it was impossible for a Subject to entertain two opposite opinions about the same things at the same time if he used the same subjective disposition to do so.

–You mean the same agency of the Subject, in the sense that we distinguished three of them? *asked Amantha.*

–Exactly. So the conclusion is clear: the agency of the Subject that judges contrary to measurement and number cannot be the same agency that judges in accordance with them. The former has to do with the animal, or ordinary, aspect of the Subject, while the latter, with the aspect that overcomes those limitations.

–Are you trying to make us think that poets are animals? *Amantha asked.*

–You're the one who's saying so! Anyway, I've proved that painting, and ultimately all the arts ruled by mimesis, create their works at a great remove from the Truth, and even at a remove from any incorporation of the individual into the process of a singular truth. These so-called artistic practices only associate, in a relationship of complicity and corrupt friendship, with those aspects of an individual that are completely foreign to exactness and logic. Vacuity coupled with void, the mimetic produces only vacuity twice voided.

–How vehement you are! *Amantha cut in.* But you're making things too easy for yourself, as I already told you, by taking it for granted that poetry and painting are one and the same thing. You weaken your case further by limiting yourself to purely imitative painting, which we'd be hard put to distinguish from photography, and the worst kind of photography at that. You pompously declared: "I've proved that. . .," but let me tell you something, you haven't proved a thing.

–It's obvious that girls should be appointed as defense counsel for poets, *Socrates commented.* They'd win the trial!

–Don't be misogynistic on top of everything, please. Can't you give up the painting model and just describe the agency of the Subject that poetry, you say, has affinities with? Then we'd be able to see whether the subjective effects of poetry are merely, to borrow your phrase, "vacuity twice voided" or whether they have real value.

–You're throwing a challenge at me! *said an admiring Socrates.* OK. Let's try and go about things differently. Hmmm, let's see now. . . Mimetic poetry imitates the actions peculiar to the human species in their two main guises: compulsory action and voluntary action. In both cases, poetry depicts the way in which individuals, when involved in such actions and depending on whether their state of mind is happy or unhappy, experience them as either mournful depression or blissful exhilaration. Do you agree, dear Amantha?

–Many poems are indeed focused on the emotions of sadness and joy. But lyricism isn't the whole of poetry, not by a long shot.

–But it's the most significant part, at any rate as far as the public at large is concerned.

–You're surely not going to support your argument with sales statistics for poetry sold in airports or with audience ratings for poets who appear on TV, are you?

–Heaven forbid! On the contrary, my question is this: when a person is considered in a situation that's conducive to the controlling of his emotions, is he under the sign of the One or under the sign of the Two? What I mean is, is he in a state of inner peace or is he in revolt against himself? At the cognitive level, there's the person who's disturbed by visual perceptions that, although occurring simultaneously and having to do with the same object, are nonetheless contradictory. Can't he be compared, at the practical level, with someone whom joy and sadness place in a situation of revolt and war against himself?

–But we already covered all that! *said Amantha.* Remember: at midnight last night, or around then, we settled our score with Thrasymachus, and we said that every Subject is full to the brim with thousands of contradictions of that sort.

Socrates slapped his forehead and exclaimed:

–Oh, right, of course! But we need to add one more point that, in the exhaustion of the night, we dropped.

–What point? *Amantha asked warily.*

– Basically, we proved that a person who deals with the blows of fate by obeying an active principle of moderation – let's imagine the worst, the death of a child for instance, or of a love relationship – will be able to bear such blows a lot more easily than just any old person. Now we've got to examine whether this attitude comes from the fact that he doesn't feel anything at all, that he's truly indifferent, or whether, given that it's impossible to be indifferent, his strength of character comes from the fact that he's able to keep his despair in check.

–The second hypothesis is obviously the right one! *crowed Glaucon.*

–But in what context, *Socrates went on,* does a given individual make use of this rational power that allows him to withstand grief, or in any case to put up a fierce struggle against it? When other people are watching him? Or when he's dealing only with himself alone in solitude?

–It's especially when he's being observed that he has to display a certain mastery of his emotions. In solitude, I think that someone – a man or a woman, it makes no difference – whose child has been murdered will have no qualms about screaming out their pain, rolling on the floor tearing their clothes, crying for hours, or just sitting there stupidly, not moving, all of which things he or she would be ashamed to do in public.

–That's a very striking description, dear Glaucon. You're a terrific psychologist. But now we've got to go beyond the phenomenology of pain and sorrow. In an individual, whoever he may be, the subjective ability to resist giving in to emotions falls under the immanent law of reason, whereas it's the contingency of our misfortunes that makes us give in to grief.

Amantha, growing impatient, complained:

–I really don't see what your point is. What do these observations have to do with the status of poetry?

–Be patient, dear girl! I'm going to move from the psychological to the logical, then from the logical to the poetic.

–Well, hurry up and take the first step already!

–We described the individual we're discussing – someone, for example, who has lost his favorite child – as torn, in the same situation and at the same time, between two conflicting tendencies. So let's agree to posit that the necessity of the Two predominates in him, or that he's intrinsically split.

–Into two parts? *Amantha muttered.*

–Why, yes, almost! On the one hand, there's that part of himself that's prepared to obey the law of reason, whatever that law might dictate. Now, reason says that, in life's painful circumstances, it's best to remain calm, as far as possible, and not to burden the people around you with shrill cries of despair. It's actually a matter of episodes in which the distribution of good and evil – in terms of the Subject's fate – is never entirely clear. The future, which lasts a long time,[5] is rarely kind to someone who claims to have been mortally

329

wounded by what's befallen him. In reality, nothing of what occurs within the bounds of a person's life is worth wallowing in excessively. Even if you're only concerned about efficiency, like the person who said "it doesn't matter what color the cat is so long as he can catch mice," you can see that excessive grief stands in the way of what could help us most quickly.

–Well, I don't see the why or the wherefore of that, *said Glaucon*.

–Suppose you're playing dice, for big stakes. Five times in a row you get terrible totals: threes, fours, and even a two. You detect a gleam of malicious joy in your opponent's eye. Will you give in to depressive rage and throw the dice in his face? Or will you inwardly tell yourself that a throw of the dice will never abolish chance[6] and consequently maintain your steely composure? We should react to the harsh blows of fate in accordance with the dictates of reason. It's childish to do nothing but whine and rub your bumps and bruises. Instead, to accustom the pathetic individual that each of us usually is to healing whatever's ill and to raising back up whatever has fallen as quickly as possible, the rule should be to rely on the Subject he's capable of becoming. True resolve will always abolish complaint.

–Your eloquence, *said Amantha with real admiration*, would revive the immortal part of any suffering person. But, in your attempt to repudiate poems, aren't you actually in the process of writing one for us?

– I'm going to take cover from your mockery again in the thick-walled bunker of logic. Answer me point by point. Isn't it the highest subjective agency in us, Thought, that tries to abide by the rule of reason?

–That's *your* view of things at any rate.

–And what do you think of the agency that revives distressing memories in the individual, the agency for which complaining is a pleasure that never gets old?

–I can easily imagine that you're going to say it's irrational, sterile, and maybe even – if you're on top form – very similar to cowardice.

–You took the words right out of my mouth! But in that case we can see that it's the touchy, irritable, irascible, unstable subjective agency – the one I called Affect – that's susceptible to imitations as plentiful as they are varied. The calm, rational agency, that guardian of personal persistence,[7] on the other hand, is not easy to imitate. Even supposing one tried to imitate it, it wouldn't be easy, either, for the motley crowds of people gathered together by theatrical festivities to identify with that agency. So we can understand why the mimetic poet has no connection with the rational agency of the Subject and

330

why his skill can't satisfy it: as the general public is his target, he's complicit with the irascible, irritable, unstable, touchy subjective agency, since that's the one that's most easily imitated. Do you agree, dear Amantha?

–You told us there'd be a dense network of questions, but, just as you criticized Thrasymachus for last night, you've actually dumped the enormous bucket of your argument over my head. I'm drenched with dazzling signifiers! All I can say is this, in the manner of a football cheer: "Go Socrates, go, go, go!"

–OK, here I go! I declare that my argument is irrefutable, that it's right for us to attack the poets since they're nothing but imitators, and that it's legitimate to lump them together with the painters. They're like the latter in that their works are of scant importance where Truth is concerned. This comparison can be further substantiated by the fact that it's with the heteronomous part of the Subject that they're associated, not with the part that steers it in the direction of the universality of the True. So it's perfectly right for us to refuse these kinds of poets admittance to our community ruled by communist dictates, because they arouse the purely empirical part of the Subject, encouraging it with imaginary forms, reinvigorating it, and thereby weakening the rational part, the only one that's dedicated to the dialectic of truths. It's exactly like when you let a country fall into the hands of the crudest reactionaries, allowing them to gain strength without doing a thing about it while you turn a blind eye to the persecutions suffered by the partisans of true politics, egalitarian politics, emancipatory politics. It must be said that poetry at the service of mimesis implants a hateful orientation of thought in the individual who is to participate in becoming a Subject. Poetry of that sort actually celebrates the unthinkable and the unthought and revels in the confusion, in the indiscernibility between grandeur and abjection, as it weaves its melodies about one and the same thing, now with epic exaggeration, now with melancholy disparagement. In this way the poet only creates imaginary forms, at a remove from the Truth that could be regarded as infinite.

–Wow! *said a jubilant Amantha.* There's a first-rate anti-rhetorical rhetoric for you!

–You ain't seen nothing yet! I've only touched on the petty crimes of poetry. There are ones that are a lot worse.

–My God! *exclaimed Glaucon, amazed.* What could be worse than being compared to a cross between a mere dauber of walls and a horrible reactionary?

–The worst thing is poetry's ability to wreak havoc on the minds of

331

the most decent people. Very few can avoid it, and probably neither you nor I could.

—Not even you? I can scarcely believe that.

—Try it yourself on the best of us. When we hear Homer or one of the great tragic poets imitate one of our favorite heroes, prostrate with grief – he declaims a long speech full of wailing, he sings and tears his hair out, beating his breast with his enormous hands the way a Buddhist monk strikes a gong – you're well aware that we then experience a deep pleasure in identifying with a grief-stricken character like that. With the utmost seriousness we praise the poet whose talent was able to affect us so powerfully.

—I have to admit that that's what happens to me when I hear Euripides.

—I'd say Aeschylus. A generational difference, I guess. In any case, you've no doubt also noticed that when it's we, in our private lives, who are afflicted by terrible grief, we don't behave anything like the hero from a moment ago. We even pride ourselves on the opposite: suffering concentrated in a sort of numb composure, restrained courage, no show of emotion. We're convinced that moderation like this, which is a relief to other people, is appropriate to a Subject, while whining, even of the tragic sort, is only a kind of personal breakdown inflicted on everyone who witnesses it.

—When my father Ariston died, I thought the exact same thing. And yet I felt like crying something awful!

—I myself, when my dear wife Xanthippe had cancer, forgot about our terrible quarrels and the fact that she often waited up for me at night with a broom in her hand, and couldn't hold back my sobbing or my tears. . . But let's get back to the argument. Here's a man – the one the poet conjures up – whom we'd consider it unacceptable and shameful to be like in ordinary life. So do you think it's natural that when we see him on stage, or when we are only under the spell of poetry imitating his grief, we not only don't feel anything negative, but we actually enjoy it and applaud wildly?

—It *is* actually pretty strange.

—Let's probe deeper into the problem. First let's consider that impulse that we were trying to repress a moment ago in our domestic tribulations, the impulse that demands its share of tears, sighs, and wailing because it's in its nature to desire them. Then let's consider that it's precisely because they trigger this impulse, Affect, and arrange for it to be gratified that the poets give us pleasure. And, finally, let's consider that the opposite impulse, Thought, which is the best part of ourselves, since it lacks the kind of education that ought

332

to combine knowledge and discipline, has a very hard time restraining the impulse to grieve, given that that impulse is fueled by the theatrical display of someone else's suffering. Everyone in fact imagines that, as long as it's only a play, there's nothing shameful about pitying and praising a person who, although he claims to be a good man, grieves and weeps at every opportunity, and that they can derive a pleasure from the public expression of his grief that it would be out of the question to deprive themselves of by rejecting the poem as a whole. Very few people are capable of understanding the harsh law of the drives: the causes of enjoyment are transferred indiscriminately from other people to ourselves. Anyone who encourages the pity he feels when watching someone else and lets it grow too strong will find it very difficult to keep his own propensity for pathos in check.

–I can only agree with you about that, *said an awestruck Glaucon.*

Pleased to have met with such approval, Socrates kept going:

–Can't the same be said about laughter as about pity? We often enjoy listening to vulgar, stupid jokes in a comedy, or even in our private lives, and what happens? We laugh as hard as we can, without feeling the slightest guilt, whereas we'd be ashamed to tell the same sort of idiotic things ourselves. We're in the exact same situation then as someone watching a grim melodrama. Just as we identify with the obvious tricks of pity, all it takes is for someone else to give in to the desire to provoke laughter at all costs – something that, aided by reason's seriousness, we repress in ourselves for fear of being taken for a clown – and we laugh right along with them! We gradually let down our defenses this way and, without even realizing it, we end up becoming a buffoon pure and simple, even among our close friends.

–The parallel between comedy and tragedy is very striking, *commented Glaucon, still spellbound.*

Socrates, in ever more brilliant form, then went on:

–The remark can be extended to all the affects of an individual who is in the process of becoming incorporated into a Subject: affects in the order of desire, pain, or pleasure (such as the pleasures of love or political anger, for example), which we claim are inseparable from our actions. Poetry's imitation of them makes them thrive; it waters what should be left to wither, it puts in charge the part of ourselves that ought to obey. In so doing, poetry, be it comic or tragic, negates our most cherished rational desire, which is to become better, and thereby happier, rather than worse, and thereby unhappier.

–Well, I think the case is closed, *said Glaucon.*

So Socrates felt he could conclude with a majestic sentence. He took a deep breath and said:

333

–And so, dear friends, when you come across admirers of Homer who say that this is the poet who educated Greece and that, in the administration of human affairs and education, he's the one to look to and learn from so as to be able to live by giving meaning, with his poems as a guide, to the whole scheme of life, you should on the one hand welcome these lovers of poetry joyfully, embrace them, regard them as people who are as decent as can be, and agree with them that Homer is the greatest poet of all, the inventor of tragic poetry, while on the other hand you should hold fast to our conviction, whose positive aspect is that the only poems expressly suited to our fifth system of government are hymns dedicated to our ideas and paeans to those embodying them, and whose negative aspect is that, if you put the purely sweet lyric or epic Muse on a par with them, pleasure and pain will hold sway over the masses instead of collective discipline and the principle that we tirelessly declare, in common and in accordance with the common, to be the best for everyone.

Socrates caught his breath. Outside, the sun had almost disappeared over the sea and the shadow of the columns was making stripes on the tiles, an abstract painting that imitated nothing but itself. But Amantha suddenly roused herself and trained her beautiful opaque eyes on Socrates, saying:

–Dear teacher, may I make an inappropriate remark?

–Isn't that the role you often play, you indomitable young woman? *replied Socrates, in a tone that was more weary than good-natured.*

–It's just that you haven't convinced me, either about poetry or the theater. Your target – an art that's assumed to be the mere reproduction of external objects and primitive emotions – is very narrow, whereas you act as if it represented practically the whole field. Neither Pindar, nor Mallarmé, nor Aeschylus, nor Schiller, nor Sappho, nor Emily Dickinson, nor Sophocles, nor Pirandello, nor Aesop, nor Federico García Lorca fit into your scheme.

Socrates, a tense look on his face, said nothing. Glaucon was wide-eyed with astonishment. Amantha, suddenly feeling hesitant, nevertheless went on:

–It seems to me. . . I'd say part of your argument is a justification of sorts, as though you wanted to apologize, maybe to yourself first of all, for having banished the poets and their art from our political community.

Socrates hesitated for quite a while, too, then realized that he couldn't refuse to give an answer.

–That's not entirely wrong, *he said.* Pure reason, however, forced me to pronounce that sentence. But just so you don't accuse me of

334

boorishness and backwoods populism, I'd like to remind you that I wasn't the one who started all this. The quarrel between poetry and philosophy is a very longstanding one, as evidenced by these old poetic descriptions of philosophy and the philosopher:

- Philosophy: A dog barking at its master.
- Great is the empty eloquence of fools.
- The mob of wise men who think they can master God.
- Subtle thinkers, beggars all.

And thousands of others that bear witness, on the poets' side, to this ancient antagonism.

–But why should those old idiotic things keep being repeated? *Amantha stubbornly persisted.* Why not lay the foundations for a new peace between philosophy and poetry?

–Look, I don't mind saying that if mimetic poetry in the service of pleasure has any valid argument to make regarding the place it deserves to hold in a communist political community we'd be happy to offer it that place, because we're perfectly well aware that poetry of that sort continues to appeal to us. The fact remains that we're not allowed to betray what for us is the self-evidence of the True.

–Well, *said Amantha with a smile,* try and get my dear brother to agree to that compromise.

–Gladly! *said Socrates, perking up.*

So he turned to Glaucon and said:

–My dear friend, aren't you, in spite of everything, captivated by epic poetry, especially when it's Homer who's revealing its charms?

–Yes, unfortunately, I am, *Glaucon confessed pathetically.*

–So isn't it fair, in that case, to allow it into our community, if it can manage to justify itself with a superb song? Let's go even further. Let's give its defenders, who, like us, aren't poets but only poetry lovers, a chance to defend it in prose and try to prove to us that it's not only pleasant but beneficial for a communist system of government and for ordinary people's lives. Let's give them a sympathetic ear: how advantageous it would be for us if they could prove that it's both pleasant and helpful!

–Then what will become of your implacable demonstration? *asked Glaucon, who was baffled by what he interpreted as a 180-degree turn.*

–The truth, *said Amantha,* is that Socrates doesn't believe for a minute that poetry's lawyers' arguments can lead to its acquittal.

–Oh, *said Socrates eagerly,* how I wish they could! But if they can't, we'll have to do as those passionate lovers do who realize that their passion is causing them serious harm: they renounce it and split up, broken-hearted. It's terribly wrenching, but they do it. And we, too, conditioned as we are by the culture our beautiful cities afford us, harbor a great love for epic, lyric, or tragic poetry. We'd be thrilled if it were revealed to be excellent, to be the more than true! But, so long as it remains incapable of justifying itself, whenever we listen to it we'll repeat to ourselves like a charm the "implacable demonstrations" that Glaucon mentioned. Because we refuse to slip back into that childish love of ours, which the majority of people share. We sense only too well that we shouldn't get seriously attached to this kind of poetry, as though it were part of a truth process. Instead, whenever we listen to or read it, we should beware of its charms, like someone who's exposing his innermost subjective equilibrium to the greatest danger. And it would be best to make a rule for ourselves out of everything we've said about poetry.

–Those are very small concessions, *remarked a disappointed Amantha.*

–The truth of the matter is that it's a great struggle, my dear young friends, yes, a great struggle – much greater than you realize – in which the stakes are every Subject: Good or Evil, the creation of a truth or the triumph of conservatism. In such a struggle we must beware of fame, wealth, and power, which lead us to neglect the queen of subjective qualities, justice. But, alas, we must also beware of poetry.

–Amen! *quipped Amantha.*

But Socrates pretended, and would go on pretending, not to hear.

336

EPILOGUE

The Mobile Eternity of Subjects (608b–621d)

Beyond the colonnade, the sky, visible in patches, was drained of color. As night came on, the sticky heat enveloped everything. Amantha, in her black summer dress, sitting up very straight with her eyes closed, looked like an armchair oracle. Glaucon had stretched out on a carpet and was lying with his hands clasped behind his head. Socrates, looking exhausted, was pacing back and forth. Thrasymachus had disappeared, as if by magic.

It was Amantha who got things going again with a question:

– Are there any awards, sort of like outstanding achievement prizes, for individuals who become Subjects by being incorporated into a truth process?

Without budging an inch from his comfortable position on the floor, Glaucon replied:

–Given how hard that type of conversion is, the prizes would have to be really luxurious!

To which Socrates grumpily responded:

–What sort of luxury can you expect a life limited to the span of time between childhood and old age to have? Compared with eternity – if it exists, at least – it's a ridiculously short period of time.

–What are your thoughts about such a great disparity? *murmured Amantha, as erect, somber, and inscrutable as ever.*

–Well, do you think an Immortal can take temporal affairs of that sort seriously rather than be concerned about eternity?

–That would be odd. But what's your point?

–This, which you must certainly have noticed: the Subject that an individual can become is immortal, imperishable.

–Wow! *exclaimed Glaucon, a stunned look on his face.* I hadn't

337

noticed anything of the sort! Could you prove that the Subject never dies?

–You can do it yourself; it's really easy.

–I wouldn't even know where to begin. But if you'll explain this "really easy" proof to us, I'll try, at any rate, to follow you.

–Open your big ears, dear Glaucon. We begin with the obvious fact that good and evil, in the most ordinary sense, exist. Evil is everything that has the power of killing and destroying; good, everything that has the power of invigorating and preserving. A particular form of evil is associated with every singular thing. For example, the specific evil associated with the eyes is called "ophthalmia," with the whole body, "disease," with wheat, "blight," with wood, "rot," with iron, "rust," and so on. Truth be told, to nearly every singularity there corresponds an inherent evil that's particular to it, an innate disease of sorts. It's this inherent evil particular to each singular thing, this structural defect, that causes it to die. If that evil can't destroy it, however, then nothing else can. Actually, we just need to remember our definition of good and evil to see that neither what's neutral about a thing – what's neither good nor evil in it – nor, *a fortiori*, what's good in it can cause it to die. So, if we observe that a certain type of real being has an evil that of course afflicts and corrupts it but is never able to completely destroy it *qua* singularity – to dissolve it in the indifference of being – we can then be sure that a being so constituted cannot die.

–The argument's formal structure makes it irrefutable, *said Glaucon*. But it still has to be proven that such a being exists.

–You'll see, *said Amantha in a husky voice,* that it's none other than the Subject. With our Socrates, all good things come to those who wait.

Socrates retorted:

–We were discussing the Subject – in fact, you were even the one who raised the question of his becoming. Isn't it only natural, then, that an argument should be tailored to the conclusion it seeks to reach? Follow me step by step, young lady.

–Sir, yes, sir!

–Do there or do there not exist immanent dispositions that threaten the Subject's integrity?

–Of course there do! Blind fury, cowardice, ignorance. . .

–Can we say that any one of these states of the Subject causes him to come undone or cease to be? Careful now! We don't want to make the fatal mistake of thinking, just because injustice is the inherent evil particular to the Subject, that when the unjust, foolish individual is caught in wrongdoing he dies of injustice!

338

–But why not? *Amantha interjected.*

–Because that would be to confuse "individual" and "Subject." Let's take it from the beginning again. Disease, the manifestation of the body's structural defects, wears the body down, wastes it, and brings it to the point of not even being a body anymore in the full sense of the term. Likewise, all the objective singularities we mentioned a moment ago, under the influence of the evil inherent in them – the evil that, having taken root in them as though they were its natural habitat, corrupts them through and through – move toward the point of non-being. Let's look at the question of the Subject from the same angle. Should we conclude that injustice, his inherent evil, having taken root in him as though he were its natural habitat, corrupts this famous Subject and withers him away to such an extent that, by separating him from the body, his material support, it forces him to die?

–It seems to me, *Amantha replied,* that that would be to confuse the individual incorporated into the Subject from which a truth proceeds and the Subject himself. You're talking about "objective singularities," but the point is, a Subject isn't an object.

–Bull's eye, clever Amantha! Besides, it would be quite illogical to maintain that something can be destroyed by the particular evil of something else while its *own* evil can't destroy it. But here's where it's necessary to go into detail, my young friends. For example, we wouldn't say that the evil particular to food *qua* food – whether it was fished weeks before or left for too long in a beat-up old refrigerator, or had rotted in the sun, or other disgusting things of the sort – can be the direct cause of the body's death. Rather, we'd say that the serious defects of these foods can activate the body's own particular evil, disease, and that this inherent evil alone causes death. It's only indirectly, through disease, that the food's deterioration is involved in the death of a living body. We'd never claim that the body, whose singularity is completely different from that of food, perished because it was subjected to the food's particular evil, unless the external evil had activated in the body the evil that's naturally the body's own.

–I get it, dear teacher! There's no need to go on! But what about the Subject, then?

–I'm getting to that! It's a simple consequence. When have we ever seen that the body's particular evil, disease, could produce in a Subject his own particular evil, injustice? Do you rape your neighbor because you have measles? Or murder your mother-in-law because you're dying of yellow fever? The Subject can't be destroyed by an external evil in the absence of his own particular evil. From the fact

339

that one singularity is different from another it follows that none, insofar as it's different, can die from another one's particular evil.

–That sounds like a theorem in metaphysics, *remarked Amantha.*

–It is! Either it must be proven false or – at least until someone comes up with a proof of this sort – we'll laugh at anyone who claims that measles or yellow fever can cause the destruction of the Subject. Nor for that matter will slitting someone's throat or carving up his dead body into thin slices of flesh succeed in destroying the Subject into which that someone has been incorporated. In order to think that diseases and murders can have such an effect, you'd first have to prove that these incidental modifications of the individuated body make the Subject unjust and wicked. For we know, I repeat, that when a given singularity's particular evil is introduced into a singularity that's ontologically different from it, if the evil particular to the latter singularity isn't active, then it won't be destroyed, regardless of whether it's a subjective or an objective singularity, or both.

–But it's inconceivable that anyone will ever be able to prove that a dying Subject becomes more unjust simply because he's dying! *exclaimed Glaucon.*

–It's not as simple as that, dear Glaucon. Imagine a determined opponent of the doctrine of the Subject's immortality. So as not to be forced to admit he's wrong, he'll have to find a way around our demonstration. So he'll argue, contrary to your position, that, as a matter of fact, someone who's dying *does* become worse than he was, that his injustice wastes him away. You'll therefore have to make him state explicitly that if he's right, it must be because injustice is fatal to the unjust man, just as yellow fever can be to the body, and that it's under the influence of injustice, which is deadly by its very nature, that those infected with it die. And so those who are more unjust will die sooner, while those who are less so will die later.

–But exactly the opposite is true! *protested Glaucon.* First of all, if some of the unjust die sooner, it's because, as we see happening all the time, they've been punished for their crimes. And, second of all, if injustice were really fatal to the unjust man, it wouldn't seem like a dreadful punishment; it would instead be a sort of release. But the opposite, unfortunately, is only too obvious: wherever it can, injustice slaughters the just, while the unjust man thrives with brazen vitality and with a sort of constant lucid alertness, to boot. Oh, that damn injustice is a far cry from being fatal to the person who harbors it within him!

–Well said, dear Glaucon! *Socrates commended him.* If in fact the Subject's structural defect and his own particular evil can't kill or destroy him, then it's even more difficult to imagine how an evil assigned to the destruction of something else can do so.

–That's exactly what I was saying, *crowed Glaucon.*

–So we can conclude, then. If a given singularity cannot be destroyed by the action of any evil, whether its own or another singularity's, we declare its necessary, continuous existence to be self-evident. But if it cannot cease to be, then it is immortal.

–That's totally amazing! *was all Amantha could say.*

–Let's add, *the flattered Socrates continued,* that, as a result, the number of real Subjects cannot be fixed in advance, nor even determined, however such a determination may be understood. The only thing we can know for certain is that that number can't decrease, since nothing can ever destroy a Subject. The number can obviously increase, however, since a Subject emerges into the world as that into which individuals can be incorporated. Now, we know that a blind life force constantly renews the stock of individuals without caring about how many of them there are. Yet this increase in numbers is by no means a necessary one. Let's say, since the immortal Subject is composed of mortal multiplicities of which he's the algebraic formula or the Idea, that the life force alone ensures that this Subject can never lack for any existing thing.

–But just because it can never lack for any existing thing doesn't prove that the Subject himself must exist as a symbol or Idea of everything that exists in him, *Amantha pointed out.*

–You put it exactly right: the Subject is eternal, but his emergence into existence is contingent. Hence the fact that, in order to know what a Subject is, it won't suffice to consider him from the point of view of his material composition. He must be apprehended in Truth, in the purity of his formula. And, to that end, we need to gain access to the Subject through a sufficient use of our powers of reason. Only then will we discover his true beauty and will we be able to draw a true line of demarcation between justice and injustice.

Socrates paused to catch his breath. Glaucon considered saying something then, but his teacher didn't leave him time to do so.

–Often the truth of a Subject, *said Socrates,* resembles the namesake of our dear Glaucon here, Glaucus-the-sailor, the little god of the warm seas, whom the incomparable Ovid, the born singer of our Roman rivals, has speak in the following way after his metamorphosis:

Again at length my thought reviving came,
When I no longer found myself the same;

Then first this sea-green beard I felt to grow,
And these large honours on my spreading brow;
My long-descending locks the billows sweep,
And my broad shoulders cleave the yielding deep;
My fishy tail, my arms of azure hue,
And ev'ry part divinely chang'd, I view.[1]

When they caught sight of this Glaucus, it wasn't easy to make out what he'd been like originally. The old parts of his body had been broken off, worn away, and ravaged by the ceaseless action of the waves. And new parts made of shells, seaweed, and pebbles had accreted onto his original appearance, so that he resembled a sea monster much more than his own imperishable nature. The Subject likewise appears to us concealed by countless transformations. But we know what must be seen in him. We really do know.

Socrates was silent then, for quite a while. Outside, the sun was gone and night was already mingling with the sea. At last Glaucon, unable to contain himself any longer, asked:

–So? What is it that we must apprehend in the Subject?

–Truth. Philosophy. We must think about what the subjective process grasps, what sorts of things it associates with. We must conceive of the Subject in terms of his kinship with his immanent Other, which is immortal and addressed to everyone for all time. We must follow his impulse and regard him as if, repeatedly pulling himself by this very impulse out of the waves in which he's now partly submerged and shaking off his crust of shells and stones, he were ridding himself of the coarse accretions of stony earth in which he's inevitably covered, since he finds the food for his eternal creation in the mud of the worlds he evolves in. Stripped in this way, he will disclose his true nature, which is also the nature of the True.

The excitement was then at fever pitch. Here were our three heroes, on the brink of night as on the brink of true life. An exhausted Socrates took several big swigs of ice-cold water right from the pitcher. When he resumed, it was as though he were invigorated by a fresh burst of energy, as though he'd overcome another bout of weariness.

–That will do for the time being. We accomplished our task by using solely rational means. To defend justice – contrary to what Homer and Hesiod constantly do – we never mentioned its rewards or its reputation in popular opinion. As a result, we made a fundamental discovery: it's justice in itself that's the hallmark of a Subject, and it's to justice that the Subject must refer his action, whether or not he possesses Gyges' ring, the story of which Glaucon told us last

342

night, or even, on top of that, the cap of Hades, which, as Homer tells us in Book 5 of the *Iliad*, also makes its wearer invisible.

–So we needn't talk about all those stories of reward and punishment, *concluded Glaucon, visibly relieved.*

–Well, why shouldn't we? *said Socrates with a wry smile.* Since we're beyond reproach when it comes to being disinterested, why not render unto our beloved justice and the other virtues all that should rightfully come back to them?

–What comes *back, remarked Amantha,* must therefore first be what *comes.* But where does what comes back to a just life originally come from?

–From human beings during their lives, from the Others after death, *replied a suddenly rather solemn Socrates.*

–You're assuming a universal doctrine of judgment that you vigorously contested last night. You told us that the just man could seem unjust to others and the unjust man just, so that it was only from the point of view of the Subject himself that his genuine nature could be revealed. Have you forgotten that?

–*You,* dear girl, *muttered Socrates,* are the one with the short memory. We granted that opposition between being and appearing only for the sake of pure rational argument. Indeed, we wanted to establish the difference between justice in itself and injustice in itself without interference from anything external to them. But now, at the end of our journey, it's time to say that when it comes to justice, the truth cannot be concealed from either men or the gods.

–Well! *exclaimed Amantha.* That's quite a dramatic turn of events!

–Granted, *said Socrates, suddenly as humble as he'd been self-assured.* That being the case, though, allow me to present you with a plea on behalf of justice. Let's all three of us, as united as can be, accept the opinion that both men and the gods have of it, which, I repeat, is justice rendered to justice. Let's ensure that justice always wins the prize for appearing, which those imbued with its secret radiance are entitled to. Let it be clear for the three of us that what justice deserves comes from its very being, and that it can never deceive those who practice it as it really is.

–You're asking a lot of us, *protested Amantha.*

–He who persuades always ends up asking. So first grant me that the Other, at least, can't be mistaken about the true nature of either the just or the unjust man.

–Otherwise it wouldn't be the big Other, only the little one, *Amantha joked.*

–If it can't be mistaken about the difference between them, then, inspired by its love for the one and aversion toward the other, it will grant each of them, for everything that's within its power, his just deserts. The only obstacle will be that the world order, imposed by a disastrous system of government rather than by our communist one, will distort its action. If, on the other hand, we assume that people's lives are governed by the rational vision that we've been endeavoring to set out for so many hours now, then nothing will stand in the way of the Other's power to grant the just man the full measure of what's due him. If a Subject imbued with justice is faced with poverty, illness, persecution, or slander, there are only two possibilities. The first possibility is that the world is enjoying the peace brought about by communism. In that case these ordeals are only temporary; they're part of the dialectical construction of the Subject and, even during his lifetime, the Subject will attain well-being, the Great Health, and creative freedom, just as his true worth will be recognized by his contemporaries. The second possibility is that the world is devastated by one of the four bad systems of government: timocracy, oligarchy, democracy, or tyranny. It is they that must be held solely responsible for the just man's sufferings. The Other will in that case make sure that the just man is rewarded after his empirical lifetime, especially since he stood firm in such terrible circumstances. Indeed, the Other cannot forsake the man whose burning desire is to become just; he cannot neglect him for whom practicing active virtue is the sole means of becoming the Other that he is as far as the human animal is able to.

–It would be hard to imagine the Other abandoning the man whose desire is to be the same as the Other, *Amantha remarked.*

–That, at any rate, is the prize the Other awards the just man. But what do mere mortals do? Isn't it essentially the same thing, if we confine ourselves to the ordinary experience of the way things are? Shrewd but unjust people are like those runners who run a good race at the beginning but then collapse during the last leg of the race. They're very quick off the mark, but they finish with their tail between their legs, jeered by the crowd, and they run off into the locker room without even having qualified, while the true runners who make it to the finish line win the prize and are awarded the crown. Isn't that exactly what happens with the just? Conducting their endeavors, their relationships with others, and their entire life well, they're held in high regard by everyone and win from their fellow men the prize for the most important victory of all: the victory of the Idea, at the very heart of life, over what would deny it.

–Well, aren't you in fine fettle! *exclaimed Amantha, her eyes sparkling.*

–I'm happy to mention all the wonderful gifts that ordinary life bestows on the just, gifts that are actually nothing next to that Truth with which justice expressly illuminates their subjective selves. And nothing, either, next to what they're rewarded after death.

–What are those incredible rewards? *inquired Glaucon.*

–I can only tell you what legend holds them to be.

–Go ahead! *Amantha teased him.* Seize the chance! Be a poet in spite of yourself, as you're encouraged to be by your eternal youthfulness!

–Unless it's the beginning of senility. . . At any rate, I have neither the talent nor the inclination for retelling the marvelous, diabolical stories told by Homer, Virgil, Dante, or Samuel Beckett. I'll settle for the tale told by a good fellow by the name of Er, from Pamphylia, an ordinary soldier who died in the trenches during a stupid war. Ten days after the artillery assault that had killed everyone, or just about, the corpses, which were already stinking up the countryside, could finally be collected. Oddly enough, only our poor Pamphylian's body had been spared from putrefaction. He was brought back home for the funeral rites. Twelve days later, as he was lying on the funeral pyre, he suddenly came back to life! And instantly this guy who'd come back to life, sitting there on the woodpile on which he was supposed to have gone up in smoke, told his dumbfounded family what he'd seen in the world beyond. So here's his story, which I'm going to tell as if I were he.

And Socrates, with his famous talent for comic impersonations, then launched into the story:

–No sooner had the subjective principle in myself been separated from my body than it took to the road with a host of others. We came to an unearthly place. On the ground there were two gaping chasms in the earth, adjacent to each other, and, opposite and above them, two openings in the sky. Halfway between heaven and earth judges were holding court. Once they'd returned their verdict, they fastened to the justs' chests the text explaining the grounds for the decision and ordered them to take the road leading to the opening in the sky on the left.[2] On the backs of the unjust they pinned the entire account of their evil deeds and commanded them to take the road leading to the chasm in the earth on the right. When my turn came, the judges told me that I'd been chosen to take a message to the human world about what happens in the world beyond. They advised me to listen and observe carefully and to make a complete and accurate report. I saw those who'd been judged either going down, on the right, into the chasm in the earth, or going up, on the left, into the opening in the sky. From the other chasm in the earth, the one on the left, bedraggled individuals covered in ash were coming back up. From the other heavenly opening, the one on the right, those coming down were clean and pure. And all these people constantly arriving seemed to be returning from some long journey. They joyfully set up camp in the enormous, enchanting meadow, as though to take part in some public festival. Old acquaintances were delighted to meet up again and talked at length with one another about the experiences they'd had, some in the bowels of the earth, others in the opening in the sky. The former couldn't relate their sufferings without moaning and weeping, so diverse and terrible were the torments they'd undergone or seen others undergo during their endless journey below the earth: a thousand years of darkness and horror! The others, who'd come from heaven, were still all aglow with the ineffable sensations they'd experienced there and with visions so sublime that no account of them could do them justice.

After we'd spent seven days of fruitful discussions and patient waiting in the enormous meadow, we were to leave at dawn on the eighth day, for four days of walking in indeterminate places. "Here," said one of my companions, a German called Gurnemanz, "time becomes space."[3] I didn't quite get what he meant. Be that as it may, we then came to a place from which we could see a straight line, sometimes dazzling, sometimes contracted into the dark gust of a storm, stretching across the sky. After another day of walking we arrived right at that line where light and energy were swapping identities. A synthetic voice, emanating from dark space, explained to us that what we were looking at was the axis of an image of the Universe that was now going to be projected for us onto the sky.[4] It was a spectacular film, on the scale of its heavenly screen! It was very long, so I'll spare you the details. At the very beginning, all you could see – but "see" isn't the right word for it – was the tiny point of pure energy out of whose explosion space–time–matter was created. The idea of becoming took over the sky and its trace was precisely that line – luminous matter or active void, it makes no difference – which was for us the distant sign of the spectacle. Then, the vaporous layers of the atomic explosion expanded and spread apart, and their nebulous cohesiveness seemed to disappear into the inner emergence of their spatiality. We, the spectators, then had the strange experience of a time that we instantly knew was immense, whose immensity we could feel intimately – billions of years! – even though, on the scale

346

of time today, it was only a matter of a few hours. Very slowly, in this space expanding before our very eyes, there appeared ovoids, whorls, conglomerations of little points of light that gradually separated from one another. This, said the invisible official spokesperson, was the birth of the galaxies. A rapid plunge of the camera into this boundless jumble of shapes – a kind of zoom from infinity to close up – took us to the huge local cluster of Virgo, then, within that cluster, to a whorl, then, within the mid-section of that whorl, to a star that, though belching its millions of degrees of nuclear combustion all over the place, was nevertheless only a medium-sized star: the Sun! Around it was the machinery of the planets, from Mercury to Pluto, which was shown us in all the perfection of its ellipses, and all the various satellites, one by one, which made sorts of ellipses embedded in the main ellipses. I admit I have to give up here – too much geometry for me! One more zoom flushed out our planet Earth, on which, thanks to the special glasses that were handed out to us, everyone could see his own country of origin in 3-D: the Greek, his Greece, the Gaul, his Gaul, the Russian, his Russia, the Uzbek, his Uzbekistan, the Panamanian, his Panama, and I, Er, by Zeus, my unassuming little Pamphylia! What a joy it was to go so easily from the inaugural Big Bang and the expansion of the All to my beloved homeland! What a relief my native land, with nothing either especially glorious or off-putting about it, was to me after all those monsters of black light!

But now the gigantic diorama, which all of us walkers had gaped at in utter amazement, came to an end with a crashing C-minor chord. All that remained was the axis of energy–matter, and only a reduced model of it at that, since it was being held in the lap of a beautiful, poker-faced woman who, we were told, was Nadia Necessity. The official spokesperson introduced Nadia's three daughters to us, Lucia Liberty, Dora Destiny, and Delia Dreamy, though we couldn't decide whether they were incorporeal digital mirages or real. Sitting on either side of their mother, they seemed to be weaving the silk thread to which the epic of the universe had been reduced. Just as in pre-Raphaelite paintings, these women were dressed in white tunics, with garlands of purple flowers in their hair. A melancholy trio, they sang of the ecstasies of time, Dora of the past, Lucia of the present, and Delia of the future. Perched on a platform, a herald with a long trumpet suddenly made a sound so dreadful that a deathly silence fell over all the travelers of the world beyond. He ordered us to line up, while onto the platform were brought two huge barrels that only later would we learn were filled to the brim, one with models of lives and

347

the other with numbered tickets. Then, in a booming voice, the herald made the following proclamation:

"This is the word of Dora Destiny, the daughter who is nothing at all like her mother, Nadia Necessity:

'O you whose subjective incorporation was short-lived, you are now at the beginning of another cycle of life, hence of death, for you are naturally part of both. No guardian angel shall choose your future life for you; on the contrary, *you* shall choose your angel. He who draws the first lot shall choose the life to which he will be bound by necessity. Virtue alone shall remain a free attribute: each shall have a greater or lesser share of it depending on the value he sets on it. As regards this choice of one's own life, only the one doing the choosing is responsible for it. No Other is to be held responsible.'"

And so saying (Er resumed), the herald threw the numbered bits of paper from one of the barrels up into the air above our heads, and everyone grabbed the one that fell closest to him, except for me, who wasn't allowed to touch them. In this way, the crowd of the dead were put in order, from one to just over 400 million. Then all the possible models of lives from the other barrel were spread out right on the ground. There were a lot more of them, of all sorts, than there were dead people who were to choose them. There were many different life models of tyranny, some long-lasting, others abruptly cut short and ending up in the figure of a destitute exile forced to go begging along the roads. There were also models of lives of men who, in some cases, were renowned for their personal appearance, their good looks, or their military prowess, and in other cases for their lineage, in particular for the outstanding caliber of their ancestors. There were also lives that were perfectly ordinary in all of these respects. In this regard, there was no difference at all between the choices available to women and to men. There was actually no ranking of Subjects at all because, inasmuch as each person was choosing a new life, he would inevitably become different from what he was. . .

When Socrates came to this sentence in Er's account – which he rattled off like a ventriloquist, with a heavy Pamphylian accent in a higher-pitched voice than his own – he couldn't resist speaking in his own name:

–It's precisely at this moment, dear friends, that a person faces the greatest danger of all. That's why each of us must give up all other studies and devote himself to this one alone: the scientific capacity to recognize – even beneath its unassuming veneer – a life worthy of the name, and no longer confuse it with a life with a brilliant veneer but only paltry actual substance. The only teacher worth finding is the one who can teach this capacity. Let us learn from him, for example, how to discern what effects, good or ill, beauty has when it's mixed with wealth or poverty or other traits that make up an individual. Or what happens when subjective characteristics, whether innate or acquired, such as being a bourgeois or a proletarian, an ordinary citizen or a ruler, a strong guy or a weakling, an ignoramus or a learned person, and so on, are blended together. On the basis of these analyses, let us learn above all how to become a Subject, and, consequently, how to choose an admirable life rather than a degraded one. For then we will have learned that a life, regardless of how lowly it may seem, is admirable when it's oriented toward justice and that being oriented toward injustice, no matter how brilliant and famous one may be, is tantamount to ensuring one's own degradation. That's the only criterion. We must hold this conviction in ourselves, even into the world beyond, with as firm a grip as what Lenin, the revolutionary, called the "iron discipline" of the communist project. Otherwise, when the time comes to choose our new lives, we'll let ourselves be corrupted by the prestige of wealth and the other forms of private or family interest. And in that case we'll choose the lives of tyrants, or of corporate executives, or of stock-market mathematicians, or of media blowhards, or of Mafiosi in three-piece suits with mansions on the Riviera, or of fawning politicians, or even of sexy teenage pop stars performing on nauseating TV variety shows. Such choices will lead to perpetrating unbearable evil all around us and will make us suffer even more ourselves. If we're well educated by a teacher, though, we'll want to choose an ordinary-seeming life, a life neither corrupted by social prestige nor crushed by the demands of mere survival, a life open to the universal adventures of a just Subject. That's where every-one's chance for real happiness lies.

–That's really incredibly interesting, *remarked Amantha,* the rela-tionship between what's "ordinary" in someone's life and the chance to be involved in the "extraordinary" process of creating Truth and the Subject that's its body.

–Sure, *said Glaucon,* but where were we with what happened to Er, the witness of the dead?

Socrates then resumed in his Pamphylian voice:

–At the moment when the herald had thrown into the air the lottery numbers that determined the order in which the dead would choose their new lives, he'd solemnly declared: "Even he who is the last to choose can acquire a good, pleasant life if he gives his choice serious thought and matches it with vital intensity. Let the one who goes first be careful and the one who goes last not be discouraged."

349

He'd barely finished speaking when the person who'd drawn number 1 came forward and chose the life of the CEO of the biggest retail conglomerate in his country, the one whose well-known chain of giant box stores, located on the outskirts of every town, bore the names *More Is Better*, *Load Your Cart*, and *Gimme more!*. Carried away by his insane greed, he'd chosen this life without having bothered to look into all the details. He hadn't realized that this existential fate included, among other horrors, the fact that the CEO, though of course in command of a huge fortune, married to a supermodel and the father of four sons, would only be truly sexually attracted to little girls under the age of seven. He'd bribe gangsters to procure them for him or, all in one day, he'd make round trips in his private jet to far-off Asian countries just to get a blow job on the sly from a little girl in disgusting public restrooms. Caught in the act during one of these sprees, he'd be arrested, repeatedly beaten, and handed over in prison to thugs who would turn him into a bedraggled sex slave. Once released from prison and deported, he'd return home, where he'd have been deserted by everyone and, as listless as a jellyfish adrift on the water, he'd glom on to a bunch of Russian bums who'd adopt him as their whipping-boy, get him forcibly drunk, and send him into fancy restaurants to clown around, until the bouncers would eventually throw him out. In the end he'd be found dead, with his hands and feet frozen, under a bench in a public square. When the lottery winner took a closer look at the kind of life he'd picked, he began to howl, to insist that there'd been a mistake, to beseech the unyielding Fates, and to beat his head on the ground. He wanted to die again on the spot, properly done away with this time, rather than forty years hence, frozen and with his face in his own vomit. Forgetting the warnings of Dora Destiny – "No Other is to be held responsible" – he lashed out at fate, the daemons, and his other dead companions, but never blamed his own blindness. And yet he wasn't a bad guy, far from it. He'd lived in a country that was governed in an orderly fashion, where he'd been a post office clerk. He'd never done anything out of the ordinary, not even been in charge of the local branch of his union, played the trombone in a marching band, biked up a mountain, or read *The Brothers Karamazov*. But still, he'd died without having done anything out of the ordinary in the sphere of Evil either. Moreover, he'd arrived in the enchanting meadow by the easy road that came down from heaven, not by the hard road up from the chasms. In the little town where he lived, the only thing he knew, in terms of wealth, fame, symbols of power, or objects of everyone's envy, was the *Load Your Cart* supermarket, where he and his wife did their shopping. Which was perhaps the cause of his absurd decision.

–Of course! *Glaucon cut in.* When it came time for the crucial decision to be made, we've seen the effects that this poor guy's having been virtuous only through habit and prudence, not philosophy, had on him.

–Unless, *Amantha added, in an attempt to qualify things a bit,* throughout his whole mundane life he'd been tormented, without wanting to admit it, by an uncontrollable desire for little girls! So maybe he *did* make the right choice!

–But how could we know for sure? *said Socrates in his normal voice.* Our friend Er made an interesting observation on this point. The majority of those who choose in this rash way come from heaven. They haven't been schooled in suffering. Those who come from the bowels of the earth have suffered and seen others suffer, and they don't take the choice of a life lightly. If we add to this the chaos created by the lottery, the result is that, generally speaking, the dead trade their previous good lives for bad ones, and vice versa. If, every time life brought them to this world, human beings were imbued with rational philosophy and if, moreover, they weren't forced by chance to be among the last to choose in the world beyond, it would seem, from what Er reports, that they'd all stand a good chance of living happily on our earth, and even of traveling back and forth between this world and the next, by the level road from the openings in the sky rather than by the steep road from the underground chasms.

–But how did Er himself finish his story? *Glaucon asked impatiently.*

Socrates resumed the story in his Pamphylian tenor voice:

–The way the dead made their choices was an enlightening, pathetic, and occasionally riveting sight. Most of the choices made were in fact dictated by the habits of their previous lives.

I saw the French poet Mallarmé choose the life of a swan because he'd devoted many magnificent poems to that bird and was particularly obsessed by it:

A swan of old remembers it is he.[5]

I saw the Italian tenor Pavarotti choose – foolishly, in my opinion – the life of a nightingale.

The person who'd drawn number 700,627 was none other than our famous Emperor Alexander the Great. Unaccustomed to having such a humble rank, he chose the life of a lion to compensate for it:

351

"Since the goddesses of the world beyond have seen fit to grant me only a humiliating position," he said arrogantly, "at least on earth I will be the indisputable king of beasts."

I saw a female textile worker gleefully snap up the life of a machine-tool repairer. "The machine really took it all out of me, so now I'm going to take it all out of the machine."

A little farther along came Agamemnon. As is common knowledge, he'd had to sacrifice his daughter so that ten years of a war as bloody as it was unjustified might begin. No sooner had he returned home than his own wife, with the help of her lover, had slit his throat while he was in his bath. That had inspired in him a profound disgust of war and a holy horror of the female sex. Consequently, he chose the life of a puny homosexual, unfit for military service.

I saw a soccer player from a very minor provincial team, barely out of childhood, who'd died from an overdose of performance-enhancing drugs. To my great surprise, he chose the life of a star of that sport, world-famous, of course, but who would die at around 35 under suspicious circumstances. I was about to warn him, but he clapped his hand over my mouth: "Quiet! I'll be an incredible player, and that's all I care about."

I saw Thomas Jefferson, the famous president of the United States, racked with guilt for having used – he, the man of the Enlightenment – a stock of slaves for his own benefit, choose the life of a fugitive Negro living in dire poverty in the snows of Canada.

I saw a clown choose the life of an ape.

I saw Hypatia, the great mathematician of Alexandria, who was murdered by fanatic Christians in the fifth century, choose the life of Emmy Noether, the great German mathematician of the twentieth century. "Unlike the false God," she said, "mathematics has the infinite power to allow us to think beyond the boundaries of what it has become at any given time."

It was Odysseus to whom chance had allotted the last place. The memory of his arduous wanderings had cured him of all ambition. He spent ages trying to find the life of some ordinary person who'd been completely uninvolved in public affairs. With difficulty he managed to ferret out, off in a corner, the hard-working, never-changing life of a poor, industrious check-out woman at *More Is Better*, who, as she was the single mother of four children, got up every day at 5 a.m., did the housework, mended the clothes, washed the sheets, counted her pennies out one by one, and had nothing but the routine of domestic life to fill up her existence. Needless to say, none of the other dead had wanted that life. Odysseus immediately took it and said that even if chance had given him first dibs, he would have made the exact same choice.

When all the dead had finished choosing their lives, they went over to Dora Destiny in the order established by the initial lottery. The Fate allotted to each of them the incorporeal angel befitting the life he'd chosen and who would be its invisible guardian. This angel instantly sparked in its appointed human being the desire to go over to Lucia Liberty and to take in his hands the silk thread, the symbol of the Universe. Thus his life choice was regarded as having been made freely. He would then go over to where Delia Dreamy was weaving, and this time the choice was regarded as irreversible. Never able to go back, each of them next proceeded to the foot of Nadia Necessity's throne, paused for a while there – respectfully or ironically, depending on their personality – then ended up, behind the throne, in the desolate, stifling, pitiless plain through which the River of Forgetfulness flows. After a whole day of walking and feeling intensely thirsty, we all camped out together in the evening on the banks of that strange river whose water cannot be held by any vessel. You were then allowed to drink right from the river a given amount of water that was determined by your angel. Those not held back by any sense of caution and whose lungs were parched by the long crossing of the desert drank without restraint. In any case, once you'd drunk you'd forget everything. Nevertheless, those who'd obeyed the angel and drunk circumspectly would some day be able to remember a few bits and pieces of their experience in the world beyond, while the others would never be able to do so.

–That's amazing! *Amantha interrupted him.* That's the whole secret of the famous doctrine of reminiscence!

But Socrates, ignoring her comment, went on, with the requisite accent:

–We were sleeping on the shores of the intangible waters when all of a sudden, in the middle of the night, there was a clap of thunder and an earthquake, and all the dead were sent flying every which way. They sped away like shooting stars to the places of their new births. As for me, I'd been forbidden to drink the water of the River of Forgetfulness. Obviously! Or I wouldn't be here telling you this story. But where I got my earthly body back from, and how, I have no idea. I suddenly saw myself lying on the funeral pyre from which I'm speaking to you right now, and from which, as well – now that I've finished telling my story – I'll shut up.

A long silence ensued in the balmy night that had now fallen over their exhaustion and emotion. They knew that it was the end of this

353

tremendous adventure in words, thoughts, and dreams. Here, in this harborside villa, something for the ages had taken place. And they'd been observers far more than participants in it, so this "having taken place" moved them deeply, as would a long declaration of love inseparable from a kind of ultimate abandonment. For they had the responsibility of telling and retelling, on their own, the immense arc of their dialogue.

Socrates, as he knew, still had to tell the end, which had come just as night had fallen. He did so concisely:

–It's with this myth that we can conclude. It can be a source of salvation for us, if we trust in what it teaches us. We have the ability to cross the River of Forgetfulness easily and to raise the individuals that we are to the level of Subjects. And then we can be sure – capable as we doubtless are of the greatest Evil, selfishness, but also of the greatest Good, truths – that the upward-leading path that allows us, in accordance with the rules of justice and true thought, to participate in a certain kind of eternity, is open to us. We'll be on good terms with ourselves and the Other then, in the circumstances of this world as in the worlds unknown to us. We'll find in ourselves the prizes that the winners of the Olympics are awarded by their friends, families, and countries. And, in doing the work from which eternal truths proceed, we'll learn what happiness is.

NOTES

Alain Badiou's 1989–90 seminar on Plato's *Republic* and his more recent seminar *"Pour aujourd'hui: Platon!"* (2007–11) constitute an invaluable source of commentary on Plato and on this text in particular. I have translated some of these comments here, but notes such as these obviously cannot do justice to them. The seminars can be accessed at http://www.entretemps.asso.fr/Badiou/seminaire.htm.

NOTES TO THE PROLOGUE

1 Badiou adapted these lines from Pindar's Fragment 214 in classical French alexandrine verses. Almost every single citation from ancient Greek authors in Badiou's text comes in for similar treatment. I have attempted to render the poetry in rhymed verse, though not in alexandrines – a verse form particularly unsuited to English. The sources of most of the classical literary citations will not be given here. They can easily be found in any critical edition of Plato's *Republic*.

2 A famous lyric poet of his time, Simonides (556–468 BC) will be mentioned again, albeit allusively, in Chapter 10, where Socrates speaks of a certain "false poet and true liar."

3 As Badiou explains in his Preface, the (Lacanian) big Other, sometimes simply referred to as "the Other" in his text, replaces God.

4 This is the first use of the expression *savoir-faire* ("know-how") in the French text – a phrase that, as a translation of the Greek *techne*, has been rendered variously as "art," "craft" and "skill" in English. As a sort of umbrella term for such diverse activities as the fine arts, cooking, skilled craftsmanship, navigation, medicine, and other sciences, it is "a very elusive word to translate," as the distinguished translator of the *Republic* Desmond Lee explains (London: Penguin, 1987, p. 15). Although *savoir-faire* is translated in this instance as "art" (since medicine is usually so called), elsewhere and for the most part I have translated it as "skill," bearing in mind that Badiou's Socrates is very dissatisfied with the phrase and even attempts, in Chapter 1, to replace it with the term *technique* – although that, too, strikes him as inadequate.

355

5 I retained Badiou's idiosyncratic usage of "beautiful soul" (*une belle âme*) here in preference to the usual modern English translations ("good person," "good, honest person," for the Greek *chrestous*). A beautiful soul, for Plato, is a well-ordered and virtuous soul with all that connotes of purity, nobility and generosity.

NOTES TO CHAPTER 1

1 In his Plato seminars Badiou has spoken at length about the stakes of Socrates' combat with the sophist. Some of these comments were encapsulated in the introduction he provided for the publication of an excerpt of this chapter in the journal *Lacanian Ink*, which it is perhaps worth quoting at length: "It is as if, for Plato (or rather his textual stand-in, Socrates), it were impossible to begin to think affirmatively without having first refuted the sophist. The word 'refute,' moreover, is not really accurate. Rather, it is a question of defeating him, which means: reducing him to silence. The violence of that moment, which also involves a dark comedy of sorts, derives from the fact that all means are fair, once it's not so much a matter of being right as it is of winning. What is involved here, in a way, is a sort of struggle to the death, in the sense it takes on in Hegel, when the Master and the Slave confront each another in order to determine how thinking will continue. Here, too, the issue is one of determining how philosophy can become established, and in order for that to happen, the sophist – the man who places language at the service of personal interest and the established powers – must leave the public stage. The fact that this moment is a negative one is also owing to one key point: rhetoric, of which the sophist is the master, accompanies a thinking in which negation holds sway. Why should this be so? Because the sophist defends a thesis (an opinion) only insofar as he knows that he could *also* defend the opposite thesis. This is the inevitable consequence of a thinking – actually an intellectual and verbal dexterity – that is made to serve not the invariance of a principle but rather the variability of opinions, which reflect power relations, localized desires and interests. The battle between Socrates and Thrasymachus is ultimately a battle between philosophy, the handmaiden of the eternity of truths, and rhetoric, the handmaiden of the opportunism of interests. Ontologically, it affords a potent version of the battle between two orientations in thought. One of them gives credit to Being for being thinkable as being what it is. The paradigm is therefore mathematics. The other makes Being no more than the momentary display of language's ability to orchestrate the cutting up of Being and, as the need arises, to induce its negation. Therefore what counts is linguistic flexibility, which also exploits non-sense or contradiction. Poetry, we sense, is not far off. As far as Socrates is concerned, Thrasymachus is diabolical, albeit with no grandeur other than his sheer brutality. He is diabolical in Goethe's sense: the Spirit that always negates" (Badiou, 2010, pp. 85–6).

2 Thrasymachus, unlike Socrates' young interlocutors, uses the familiar *tu* form of address with Socrates, who, for his part, addresses everyone individually as *tu*. The distinction is lost in English.

3 The phrase "Socratic irony" refers to Socrates' strategy of pretending to

know less than an interlocutor when he in fact knows more and of feigning agreement with him so as to trip him up later.

4 In the *Critique of Pure Reason* Kant used this simple equation to distinguish between analytic and synthetic propositions.

5 What Socrates says in French – "*Bizarre, bizarre, et je dirais même plus: bizarre*" – is a humorous allusion to well-known lines spoken by the bumbling twin detectives Dupont and Dupond (Thomson and Thompson in English) in *L'Île noire* (*The Black Island*), a story in *The Adventures of Tintin* series by Hergé.

6 This is the first instance of Thrasymachus' catch phrase "in my opinion," which, along with "to be precise" (another of the *Tintin*'s detectives' linguistic tics), Badiou will turn to comic effect as the dialogue progresses.

7 The wrong done to victims and the impossibility of testifying to it are themes of Lyotard's *The Differend* and *The Postmodern Condition*.

8 The Athenians under Alcibiades' command were defeated by the Spartans at the Battle of Notion in 407 BC. In the *Symposium* the handsome, gifted Alcibiades, who was in love with Socrates, relates his failure to seduce him. Socrates later suffered from his pupil's rejection of philosophy, as he explains in Chapter 10, where Alcibiades is cited as the classic example of a brilliant young man corrupted by the people around him.

9 This is an abbreviated version of Mao's statement on "meeting the masses," made to the crowd on August 10, 1966: "You should pay attention to state affairs and carry the Great Proletarian Cultural Revolution through to the end!" (Mao Zedong, 1961–77, vol. 9).

10 This vocabulary of the Subject derives from Badiou 2011b, pp. 91–104, where there is a full description of the faithful, reactive, and obscure Subjects.

11 "The true life," a life oriented by the Idea, will feature more prominently later on, in Chapter 9 in particular. For an individual, the true life "is the acceptance of his or her incorporation into the process of a truth. A life has meaning when it is immanently polarized in the real by the Idea" (October 28, 2009; this seminar can be found at http://www.entretemps.asso.fr/Badiou/09-10.htm).

NOTES TO CHAPTER 2

1 In Plato's *Republic* Gyges is a shepherd in the service of the King of Lydia. The King of Thule, as Badiou has it here, is the subject of a ballad in Goethe's *Faust* that was later set to music by a number of composers, including Gounod, whose opera *Faust* includes the well-known aria "Il était un roi de Thulé."

2 Badiou often expands Plato's allusions and indirect references to poetry – such as this one, to line 592 of Aeschylus' *The Seven against Thebes*, into rhyming verses. The rest of the original line, a description of the wise seer Amphiaraus, who chooses to put no blazon on his shield because he prefers to be rather than merely appear to be the best, is quoted by Glaucon a moment later.

3 Not giving way on one's desire (*ne pas céder sur son désir*) is the ethical injunction formulated by Lacan at the end of his Seminar VII (Lacan, 1992, p. 321).

4 In the *Odyssey* (16.97–8), Odysseus and Telemachus acknowledge that, in the case of a quarrel, brothers ought to support each other.
5 The legendary poet Musaeus was associated with mystic rites and with the Eleusinian mysteries.
6 Amantha has altered the passage (*Iliad* 9.497–501) by substituting some words for others and by leaving out a line.
7 In Plato, the verses cited at this point are the opening lines of a poem that Glaucon's lover supposedly wrote to praise him and his brother Adeimantus, both of whom distinguished themselves at the Battle of Megara. In Desmond Lee's translation the lines read: "Sons of Ariston, pair divine/Sprung from a famous sire" (Plato, 1987, p. 116).

NOTES TO CHAPTER 3

1 The French anthropologist and sociologist Marcel Mauss (1872–1950) wrote the classic work *The Gift* (Mauss, 2000), in which he argued that gifts give rise to reciprocal exchange in cultures around the world.
2 As used here and elsewhere in the text, Nietzsche's concept of "the Great Health" from his *Gay Science* (Nietzsche, 1974) implies health in a more moral sense than the mere absence of illness or disease.
3 The French writer and orator Jean Jaurès (1859–1914), a committed anti-militarist and ardent defender of Dreyfus, co-founded the socialist newspaper *L'Humanité*, for which he wrote numerous articles. He was assassinated in 1914 by a fanatical French nationalist.
4 These famous tactics of Mao Zedong have been said to derive from Sun Tsu's classic book *The Art of War* (Sun Tsu, 1971).

NOTES TO CHAPTER 4

1 When the popular French cyclist Richard Virenque was asked at trial in 2000 about his use of performance-enhancing drugs during the Tour de France, he replied that he had taken them *à mon insu de mon plein gré* (literally, "unwittingly willingly"), an amusing phrase that was quickly adopted by the French.
2 Kant's famous 1797 essay "On the Supposed Right to Tell a Lie from Altruistic Motives" (Kant, 1949) is a counter-attack against the French liberal thinker Benjamin Constant, who, in his essay "On Political Reactions," had rebuked Kant's unconditional prohibition against lying, even to save a friend from murder (Constant, 1988). For Constant, telling the truth in all circumstances would make society impossible.
3 Lines 383–4 of Book 17 of the *Odyssey* read: "whether he be craftsman, prophet, physician or shipwright" – as quoted in Lee's translation of the *Republic* (Plato, 1987, pp. 144–5).
4 The irascibility of Colonel Blimp, the stereotypical British cartoon character from the 1930s, is reminiscent of that of the eponymous character of *Les Aventures du Colonel Ronchonot*, to whom Amantha is referring in the French text when she says: "*Un peu colonel-ronchonno, cette description!*" Written by Gustave Frison, the weekly illustrated series was published in

Paris from 1884 onwards. The name derives from the verb *ronchonner*, meaning "to grouse," "to gripe." Here the emphasis is on forcing soldiers to obey orders.

5 With a sly wink, Badiou alludes here to *le roi barbu qui s'avance* ("the bearded king who comes forward"), a refrain from *La Belle Hèlene*, the 1864 operetta by Jacques Offenbach with lyrics by Henri Meilhac and Ludovic Halévy. In the operetta, which is a parody of the origins of the Trojan War, Agamemnon introduces himself by singing "*Le roi barbu qui s'avance, –bu qui s'avance, –bu qui s'avance, c'est Agamemnon!*" and the chorus takes up his boast, ending with a rapturous "*C'est Aga, Aga, Aga-mem-non!*"

6 A great Russian director whose acting method combined psychological and physiological processes, Vsevolod Meyerhold (1873–1940) inspired a number of revolutionary artists and filmmakers, including Sergei Eisenstein. As a fierce opponent of socialist realism, he ran afoul of Stalin in the late 1930s and was tortured and later executed.

7 The proverb "Opportunity makes the thief" is perhaps less widely known in English than its counterpart, "*L'occasion fait le larron*," is in French. The implication is that, given the opportunity, we would commit crimes we might otherwise have refrained from committing.

8 The poet in question is René Char (1907–1988), and the line comes from the title of his collection, *Dehors la nuit est gouvernée*.

NOTES TO CHAPTER 5

1 Badiou is riffing on Plato's text here, exaggerating the foibles of a man of this sort and indulging in a series of playful alliterations.

2 In the *Republic*, the example Socrates cites is accepted as such by his interlocutors. Here, in Amantha's reproach, Badiou has delightfully incorporated what is usually found only in a translator's note to the text.

3 Plato says only that Herodicus invented a regimen of physical training and medicine to cure his own illness. Badiou's Herodicus, morally more than physically ill, it would seem, has become the target for criticism of modern-day health fanaticism used as a means of avoiding truths.

4 As Badiou notes in his Preface, one of the key Platonic concepts, the Idea of the Good, is designated "the Idea of the True" in this book. Explaining his reasons for this decision in his May 19, 2010 seminar, he noted that the concept had long been saturated with a moralistic neo-Platonic and ultimately theological interpretation, whereas the Idea of the Good has no moral connotation. (This seminar can be found at http://www.entretemps.asso.fr/Badiou/09-10.2.htm.)

5 The original line from Phocylides, a sixth-century BC lyric poet, appears thus in Reeve's translation of the *Republic*: "once one has the means of life, one must practice virtue" (Plato, 2004, p. 90).

6 This line – *Iliad* 4.218 – was already adapted by Plato, who changed the subject and the predicate from singular to plural, which is precisely what Amantha accuses Socrates of doing a moment later. The line "he sucked the blood and in skill laid healing medicines on it" (in Lattimore's translation; see Homer, 2011, p. 119) is expanded considerably by Badiou.

7 In a major departure from the *Republic*, where it is considered acceptable for the unhealthy to be left to die and for those whose psychological constitution is incurably corrupt to be put to death, Socrates advocates here the rehabilitation or re-education of such people. Eliminating some of Plato's passages that deal with what is now regarded as reprehensible eugenics is one of the strategies mentioned by Badiou in his discussion of his own text in his May 19, 2010 seminar.

NOTES TO CHAPTER 6

1 *Politeia*, the Greek title of the *Republic*, is a word that has been translated variously as "state," "city," "city-state," "form of government," etc. Badiou's preferred term in French is *politique*, for which "system of government" seems to be the closest translation in English.

2 Farquharson's translation reads: "Don't hope for Plato's Utopia, but be content to make a very small step forward and reflect that even the result of this is no trifle" (Marcus Aurelius, 1998, p. 85).

3 This is an allusion to Mao Zedong's 1930 essay entitled "A Single Spark Can Start a Prairie Fire" (Mao Zedong, 1961–77, vol. 9, pp. 65–76).

4 In explicating this passage (seminar, January 13, 2010, available at http://www.entretemps.asso.fr/Badiou/09-10.htm), Badiou pointed out that contemporary ideology, minus the gods, is no different from the myth, which is based on the idea that the division of society into classes is something *natural*. The role of the counter-myth is precisely to undermine that foundation by de-naturalizing it and by introducing the notion of egalitarianism. The counter-myth would contain "an element of *destruction* (of classes), an element of collective *fusion* (in the sense of Sartre's 'group-in-fusion,' i.e. a moment of indistinguishability between each individual and all of them), and an element of strict *equality*."

5 In "Problems of War and Strategy" (originally published in 1938), Mao wrote: "Every Communist must grasp the truth, 'Political power grows out of the barrel of a gun.' Our principle is that the Party commands the gun, and the gun must never be allowed to command the Party" (Mao Zedong, 1961–77, vol. 2, p. 224.)

6 Although this sentence amounts almost to a throw-away remark here, it will become the focus of Chapter 8.

7 These lines (translated here by Stan Solomons) are from "La Mort du loup" ("The Death of the Wolf"), written in 1838.

8 Corneille, 1996 (*Horace*, Act IV, Scene 2, p. 65).

9 "Everything that moves is red" doesn't quite capture the May '68 slogan "*Tout ce qui bouge est rouge*," which rhymes in French.

10 Plato reserves this wisdom for the elite class of guardians only.

11 In his speech "On the Correct Handling of Contradictions among the People" (February 27, 1957), Mao stated: "We stand firmly for peace and against war. But if the imperialists insist on unleashing another war, we should not be afraid of it. Our attitude on this question is the same as our attitude towards any disturbance: first, we are against it; second, we are not afraid of it" (available at http://www.marxists.org/reference/archive/mao/selected-works/volume-5/mswv5_58.htm).

NOTES TO CHAPTER 7

1 "All things excellent are as difficult as they are rare" (Spinoza, 2005, p. 181).
2 In *The Critique of Pure Reason* Kant posited, in relation to appearances, the transcendental object, which is non-empirical and can be represented only by the placeholder X (see Kant, 1999).
3 In the *Republic*, Leontius addresses his own eyes, rather than the dead bodies, when he says (in Lee's translation): "There you are, curse you – a lovely sight! Have a real good look!" (Plato, 1987, p. 216).
4 Antoine Vitez (1930–90), one of the great directors of the twentieth century, headed the National Theater of Chaillot and later the Comédie-Française. He sought to create an "elite theatre for everyone," often staging ancient Greek and Russian plays that he translated himself. In 1984 he produced *L'Écharpe rouge* (*The Red Scarf*), Badiou's *roman-opéra,* at the Festival d'Avignon and the Lyon Opéra.

NOTES TO CHAPTER 8

1 Badiou remarked about this passage: "Naked boys working out together, there's nothing unusual about that. But will they tolerate doing so around girls who are naked, too? There's no problem here for Plato, whose feminism is exceptional for his time and who cannot conceive that the difference between the sexes might interfere with the guardians' education" (seminar, May 19, 2010, at http://www.entretemps.asso.fr/Badiou/09-10.2.htm).
2 I wish to thank Joe Litvak for his assistance with the translation of the first stanza of Badiou's extended, witty adaptation of a few lines from *Lysistrata.*
3 It is thought that the line Plato adapted from Pindar (Fragment 209) was originally intended to ridicule philosophers, since the unripe fruit it refers to was that of wisdom.
4 André Gide's *Les Nourritures terrestres*, from which this line comes, was originally published in 1897. The book's attack on the family, or what Badiou has elsewhere called "the primordial nucleus of egoism, of rooted particularity, of tradition and origin" ("One Divides into Two," in Badiou, 2007a, p. 66), influenced many French intellectuals, including Camus, Sartre, and Derrida. See Gide, 1949.
5 Alexei Stakhanov, a celebrity in the Soviet Union for setting records in coal mining, was held up as an example for others to follow.
6 "Lacan didn't care much for the *Republic*," Badiou commented in his 1994–5 seminar on Lacan's anti-philosophy. "He said it was like a well-kept horse-breeding stable. But Lacan didn't conclude from this that Plato was appalling, totalitarian, or what have you. He concluded that Plato is pulling our leg from start to finish. In other words, it's absolutely inconceivable that someone like Plato (because, for Lacan, Plato is not just anyone) could believe such a horrible, depressing thing. So Lacan thought that the *Republic* was a fundamentally ironic dialogue" (at http://www.entretemps.asso.fr/Badiou/94-95.htm).
7 "Communism," Marx and Engels wrote in *The German Ideology*, "is for us not a *state of affairs* which is to be established, an *ideal* to which reality will

have to adjust itself. We call communism the *real* movement which abolishes the present state of things" (Marx and Engels, 1998, p. 57).

8 This famous aphorism, given here in the Pears–McGuinness translation, is the last line of Proposition 7 of Wittgenstein's *Tractatus Logico-Philosophicus* (1999, p. 74). Badiou takes strong exception to it: "It is thus quite simply false that whereof one cannot speak (in the sense of 'there is nothing to say about it that specifies it and grants it separating properties'), thereof one must be silent. It must on the contrary be named" (Badiou, 1999b, p. 95).

9 The French contains a play on words involving the verbs *faire* and *taire*. "What we cannot speak about we must pass over in silence" is "*Ce dont on ne peut parler, il faut le* taire," while "What we cannot speak about we must do" is "*Ce dont on ne peut parler, il faut le faire.*"

NOTES TO CHAPTER 9

1 "Love is an idea," or "to love is to think," as it has been translated elsewhere, comes from a poem in "O pastor amoroso" ("The Shepherd in Love") by Alberto Caeiro, one of Fernando Pessoa's heteronyms (see Pessoa, 1998).

2 Badiou, for whom love is one of the four conditions of philosophy, fully endorses this notion from Plato's *Symposium*, citing it in his *Éloge de l'Amour* (Badiou, 2009a, p. 11).

3 This is the first instance in the text of the key phrase "that which of being is exposed to thought" (*ce qui de l'être s'expose à la pensée*), with which Badiou translates the Greek term *ousia*. In his May 19, 2010 seminar (available at http://www.entretemps.asso.fr/Badiou/09-10.2.htm) he explained: "*Ousia* designates what it means for being to be identical to thought. 'We are, as a result, at the point where the being of the object is indiscernible from what, of this being, is thinkable. This point of indiscernibility between the particularity of the object and the universality of the thought of the object is exactly what Plato names the Idea' [Badiou, 2011b, p. 107]. No greater error can be committed with respect to Plato than to maintain that his thinking is dualistic. The opposition between the sensible world and the intelligible world is fallacious. As far as Plato is concerned, there is only one world; the sensible one 'participates' by degrees in the intelligible one in a *dialectical* process. The dialectic designates precisely the possibility of a process of thought whereby the object of thought is indiscernible from the thought of the object. As I told you earlier, the dialectic is a process that is its own result. That's why I propose the following translation for *ousia*: that which of being is exposed to thought. In short, I translate the term with its signification unpacked. But the word that truly translates *ousia* has yet to be invented."

4 *La vraie vie est absente* is a well known line from Rimbaud's "Une saison en Enfer" ("A Season in Hell"), in Rimbaud, 1998.

5 "Toast funèbre" ("Funerary Toast"), in Mallarmé, 2006, p. 48.

6 See Ch. 6, n. 11.

7 *Sapeur* (Combat engineer) Camember was the dimwitted soldier-hero of one of the first French comic books, *Les Facéties du sapeur Camember*, written by Georges Colomb (alias Christophe). The *feuilleton* episodes appeared from 1890 to 1896 before being published as a volume in 1899. The phrase

that Badiou's Socrates cites here – *dans le fort de mon intérieur* – is typical of Camember's mangled yet poetic speech in that it humorously transforms the common expression *dans mon fort intérieur*, which means "deep down" or "in my heart of hearts."

8 "The clearing of being" in Heidegger refers to the open region in which beings can emerge in "unconcealment" before withdrawing again.

NOTES TO CHAPTER 10

1 "Le Bateau ivre" ("The Drunken Boat") is one of Rimbaud's best known poems. See Rimbaud, 2009.

2 The "false poet and true liar" was Simonides.

3 Badiou expanded on this point in his seminar of October 29, 2009: "The true life is indistinguishable from the life of the true, which means that the individual, by incorporating himself into the subjectivizable body, *brings the true to life*. The true would not be alive if there had not been such an incorporation. At the same time, from the perspective of the individual, it can be said that the individual brings to life something of which he is not the measure (something that is incommensurably greater than himself)."

4 In the *Theaetetus* Socrates says that he is "the son of a midwife, brave and burly, whose name was Phaenarete" (Plato, 2009, p. 95).

5 "The virtual" is a key concept of the "transcendental empiricism" of Gilles Deleuze (1925–95).

6 Socrates claimed to have a daemon, a sort of inner voice or "divine sign" that told him what to do or not do, usually the latter. He attributed to his daemon his decision not to defend himself at his last trial.

7 In the French text there is a *jeu d'esprit* that can't quite be captured in translation. Amantha playfully reproaches Socrates by saying "*Vous les renvoyez aux fameuses calendes grecques!*" According to *The Routledge Dictionary of Cultural References in Modern French* (p. 177), "The word *calends* corresponded to the first day of each month in the Roman calendar. [. . .] Accounts were traditionally settled on the first of the month. The Greeks did not have *calendes* and consequently *renvoyer aux calendes grecques* means to put off indefinitely."

8 In 1964 Defense Minister Lin Biao called Mao Zedong's ideas "a spiritual atomic bomb of infinite power" against which even the nuclear weapons of the US could not avail.

NOTES TO CHAPTER 11

1 This passage is discussed in greater detail in Badiou 2011b (p. 107), where, with respect to the distinctive status of the Idea of the True, he writes: "Finally, as for the Idea itself, given that it only exists in its power to bring forth the object 'in truth' and, hence, to uphold that there is something universal, it is not itself presentable because it *is* the presentation-to-the-true. In a word: there is no Idea of the Idea. This absence, moreover, can be named 'Truth.' Exposing the thing in truth, the Idea is true and is, therefore, always the idea of the True, but the True is not an idea."

2 Badiou told me that he intentionally used the noun form of the infinitive here, *le dialectiser*, rather than the simple noun *la dialectique*, in order to convey the sense of the *process* involved in dialectical reasoning.

3 In a diary entry recounting a trip through the Swiss Alps in July 1796, Hegel noted his skepticism regarding the sublimity of nature: the mountain peaks had failed to inspire awe in him.

4 Badiou here adapts almost verbatim lines from Samuel Beckett's *Mal vu mal dit / Ill Seen Ill Said*: "From where she lies she sees Venus rise. On. [. . .] Rigid upright on her old chair she watches for the radiant one. [. . .] It emerges from out the last rays and sinking ever brighter is engulfed in its turn. On" (Beckett, 1981, p. 49). He included this excerpt, he explained, because he wanted to give more weight to the passage to the outside world, the better to balance it against the cosmic movie theater (Seminar, January 21, 2009).

5 *Anabasis*, the title of Xenophon's account of 10,000 Greek mercenaries stranded on foreign soil fighting their way back home, is also an important trope, in poems by Saint-John Perse and Paul Celan in particular, which Badiou has written about in *The Century* and elsewhere.

6 See Chapter 9, n. 4. Citing this line elsewhere, Badiou comments: "Ever since Rimbaud everyone repeats that 'the true life is absent.' Philosophy is not worth an hour's effort if it is not based on the idea that the true life is present" (Badiou, 2009d, p. 14).

Notes to chapter 12

1 The comical enjambment on the word "arithmetic" here reproduces that in the French: *Dans un si grand malheur, que nous reste-t-il? L'a-/Rithmétique qui s'é-tend à tout l'être-là.* As Glaucon is quick to point out, Socrates is (farcically) adapting Corneille, specifically lines from his early tragedy *Médée*, Act I, scene 5: *Dans un si grand revers, que vous reste-t-il?* asks Medea's confidante, to which Medea, in the first instance of "Cornelian self-assertion" in his theater, replies: *Moi./Moi, dis-je. Et c'est assez. Moi* (Corneille, 2007).

2 In the tragedies Socrates evokes, Palamedes, considered to be the inventor of counting, was condemned to death by Odysseus, among others, on false charges of being a Trojan spy.

3 Louis Althusser's reading of Marx in the 1960s made famous the notion of the epistemological break, first introduced by Gaston Bachelard in his *Formation of the Scientific Mind*. The phrase designates a break with previous ideological conceptions.

4 Amantha's reservations about the pervasiveness of number echo one of Badiou's chief preoccupations. For example, "What is the nature of the link between freedom of opinion and the law of number?" he asked in his February 17, 2010 seminar, then answered: "Opinions are governed by a principle of equivalence – one opinion is the same as another. They circulate in the same way as money (which is their actual paradigm), in a space of general substitutability where what is in reality affirmed is the sovereignty of merchandise. What ensures the triumph of an opinion is its number, the fact that it has numbers behind it."

5 The phrase "higher arithmetic," which Socrates, echoing Glaucon's earlier remarks, uses here, is synonymous with what he calls, a moment later, number theory, the science that considers numbers in themselves. Basic arithmetic, on the other hand, is appropriate for business and war.

6 A translation of the Anaximander fragment, this line from Goethe's *Faust* was notably cited by Hegel (in *The Dialectics of Nature*) and discussed by Engels, Nietzsche, Freud, and Heidegger, among others. Badiou seems to be fond of the line, as is evidenced by his referring to it at least a couple of other times, in his play *The Incident at Antioch* (Badiou, in press) and in an interview with Daniel Bensaïd (Badiou, 2006a).

7 Rousseau argued in the *Discourse on Inequality* that it was necessary to lay facts aside in favor of conditional and hypothetical reasoning.

8 Cf. Descartes' *morale par provision* in the *Discourse on Method*.

9 Amantha is actually citing Hegel, who did indeed call the *word* the murder of the thing; Lacan, in borrowing from Hegel, makes the *symbol* the culprit: "Thus the symbol manifests itself first of all as the murder of the thing, and this death constitutes in the subject the eternalization of his desire" (Lacan, 1977, p. 104).

10 This complicated sentence is the adaptation of a similarly long one in the *Republic*.

11 The incommensurability between the diagonal and a side of a square was often used by the Ancient Greeks as an illustration of "irrational" numbers.

12 What Lacan called "the passion of ignorance" is the analysand's resistance to knowledge, the *jouissance* derived from his or her symptom (Lacan, 1988, p. 271).

NOTES TO CHAPTER 13

1 In the passage that follows, Badiou replaces Plato's mathematics, which he considered to be too obscure and archaic for readers today, with his own, modern mathematics. As he explained elsewhere: "Essentially, it is as if communism were the original state and, with its transformation, the cycle of ordinary political regimes began. Plato explains this process by referring to an obscure, complex mathematics of populations, including a key number that ends up being forgotten. [. . .] [W]hat Plato is putting forward, with the help of a semantically archaic mathematics, is in reality a profound idea, namely that repetition necessarily means erosion; it is always paid for by a loss (anticipating Kierkegaard), in particular when it concerns processes that claim to have achieved a kind of permanence. My solution was to keep the fable-like character of the passage but replace the obsolete math on which it depends with modern mathematics" (seminar, May 19, 2010).

2 This is a well-known French aphorism: *Pour vivre heureux, vivons cachés* (literally, "To live happily, let us live hidden away").

3 Glaucon is alluding here to the other failed systems of government and their corresponding character types, to which he has just suggested the discussion move on.

4 Plutus, the god of money, was represented as being blind.

NOTES TO CHAPTER 14

1 French Prime Minister François Guizot (1787–1874) famously advised those who complained of being disenfranchised under the regime of Louis-Philippe to "get rich" (*Enrichissez-vous!*).
2 It was the bourgeoisie that had "drowned the most heavenly ecstasies of religious fervour, of chivalrous enthusiasm, of philistine sentimentalism, in the icy water of egotistical calculation" (Marx and Engels, 2002, p. 222). This sentence is also cited in Badiou, 1999b and 2008b.
3 *Ajax the Locrian* is a play that has only survived in fragments. At *Republic* 569a–b Plato attributes to Euripides the line quoted there, but Badiou, following most modern commentators, has Socrates give credit to its rightful author, Sophocles.
4 Plato only refers vaguely to "other poets" who sing the praises of tyranny; he does not cite these lines, which Badiou has adapted in any case.
5 In Lacan's Seminar VIII there is a lengthy discussion of Socrates and transference love.

NOTES TO CHAPTER 15

1 Plays were judged at dramatic festivals in ancient Athens, and a herald announced the results.
2 There is a play on words here. In French, the line reads: *Avec le blanc au milieu, ce maudit centre où broutent tous les veaux.* The literal meaning of *veaux* is "calves," but the word can also mean morons, people who blindly follow the crowd, or political centrists, as Amantha implies here. (De Gaulle famously called the French *"des veaux."*) The herd mentality is perhaps better indicated in English by sheep than by cows, but of course the joke does not come across in either case.
3 What Socrates chooses not to discuss here, Badiou expounds on in his seminar of October 28, 2009: "Every truth has a body. The notion of a 'body of truth' here designates the fact that a truth isn't a transcendent ideality but *appears in a world*. And I call 'subject' that which is constituted as incorporated in the process of a truth. The body of a truth is consequently a *subjectivizable* body." See *Logics of Worlds* (Badiou 2009c) for a detailed exposition of these concepts.
4 There is always a moment in philosophy, Badiou has said, when resorting to metaphor becomes necessary; in Plato, this is the moment when the philosophical discourse "confirms its own law by tipping over into *muthos*." This is because philosophy is a discourse that "begins in mathematics but ends by stretching deductive argumentation to such a point that it eventually becomes poetry, that is, it ends up in a metaphor" (seminar, October 28, 2009).
5 As opposed to Plato's Socrates, who uses this oath several times in the *Republic* (as elsewhere), Badiou's Socrates swears only this once "by the dog."

NOTES TO CHAPTER 16

1 The Third-Man Argument, introduced in the late dialogue *Parmenides*, is Plato's own philosophical critique of the earlier version of his theory of

Forms. Aristotle, in explaining the objection, posited that if a man is a man because he partakes in the Form of man, then a third Form would be required to explain how man and the Form of man are both man, and so on *ad infinitum*.

2 Sir Alexander Fleming was awarded the Nobel Prize for his discovery of penicillin in 1928. The great French physiologist Claude Bernard (1813–78) was one of the founders of experimental medicine.

3 Boosphilus seems to be a name of Badiou's own invention, since the character is called Creophylus in the *Republic*. The bovine overtones of the name render Glaucon's epithet, "cow-lover" (or perhaps "beefeater," as Desmond Lee suggests), that much clearer.

4 No doubt these lines are funnier in French, where the notions of freezing cold and fear are neatly combined in the familiar expression *les avoir à zéro* (with the direct object "*les*" referring to "balls").

5 *The Future Lasts A Long Time* is the English title of Louis Althusser's autobiography, *L'Avenir dure longtemps*, published in the US as *The Future Lasts Forever*.

6 Here Badiou is alluding to the title of the famous poem by Mallarmé "Un coup de dés jamais n'abolira le hasard" ("A Throw of the Dice Will Never Abolish Chance"), a favorite reference of his, to which he has devoted much thought. See in particular Badiou 2009e, 1999a, 2005a, 2005b. An echo of the poem occurs again at the end of Socrates' speech, in the line "True resolve will always abolish complaint" (*Toujours la décision vraie abolira la plainte*).

7 Personal persistence, in psychology, refers to the ongoing connection between one's life and personality, by means of which the self avoids discontinuities over time.

NOTES TO EPILOGUE

1 These lovely lines from Ovid's *Metamorphoses* are here translated by Nicholas Rowe (1674–1718).

2 Badiou reverses Plato's "left" and "right." When I queried him about this, he replied that it was an intentional decision and suggested a connection with the political symbolism of left and right.

3 In Richard Wagner's opera *Parsifal*, the eponymous hero, walking with the old knight Gurnemanz to Monsalvat castle to observe the Grail Ritual, remarks that he is hardly moving yet seems to be traveling far. Gurnemanz tells him that in this realm "time becomes space" ("*zum Raum wird hier die Zeit*").

4 The poetic description of the Big Bang that follows differs significantly from Plato's account of the structure of the universe, the "spindle of Necessity" that underpins it consisting of an outer wheel, the Zodiac, seven inner wheels, the Sun, and the five planets known at the time.

5 This fragment is from a famous Mallarmé poem, "Le vierge, le vivace et le bel aujoud'hui," ("This virginal long-living lovely day"), translated here by A. M. and E. H. Blackmore (Blackmore, 2000, p. 287).

BIBLIOGRAPHY

Badiou, Alain 1989–90. Seminars on Plato's *Republic*. Available at http://www. entretemps.asso.fr/Badiou/seminaire.htm

Badiou, Alain 1995. "Platon et/ou Aristote–Leibniz," in M. Panza and Jean-Michel Salanskis (eds.), *L'Objectivité mathématique*. Paris: Masson.

Badiou, Alain 1999a. *Deleuze: The Clamor of Being*, trans. Louise Burchill. Minneapolis, MN: University of Minnesota Press.

Badiou, Alain 1999b. *Manifesto for Philosophy*, trans. Norman Madarasz. Albany: State University of New York Press.

Badiou, Alain 2005a. *Being and Event*, trans. Oliver Feltham. London: Continuum.

Badiou, Alain 2005b. *Handbook of Inaesthetics*, trans. Alberto Toscano. Stanford, CA: Stanford University Press.

Badiou, Alain 2006a. *Briefings on Existence: A Short Treatise on Transitory Ontology*, trans. Norman Madarasz. Buffalo: State University of New York Press.

Badiou, Alain 2006b. "Politique et vérité" (interview with Daniel Bensaïd). *Contretemps*, 15, 47–56.

Alain Badiou 2007a. *The Century*, trans. Alberto Toscano. Cambridge: Polity.

Badiou, Alain 2007b. *The Concept of Model*, ed. and trans. Zachary Luke Frasier and Tzuchien Tho. Melbourne, Australia: re.press.

Badiou, Alain 2007–11. *Pour aujourd'hui: Platon!* (Seminar). Available at http://www.entretemps.asso.fr/Badiou/seminaire.htm

Badiou, Alain 2008a. *Conditions* [1992], trans. Steven Corcoran. New York: Continuum.

Badiou, Alain 2008b. *Number and Numbers*, trans. Robin Mackay. Cambridge: Polity.

Badiou, Alain 2009a. *Éloge de l'Amour*. Paris: Flammarion.

Badiou, Alain 2009b. "For Today: Plato! Prologue – Epilogue," trans. Susan Spitzer. *Lacanian Ink*, 34: 53–93.

Badiou, Alain 2009c. *Logics of Worlds* [2006], trans. Alberto Toscano. London and New York: Continuum.

Badiou, Alain 2009d. *Philosophy in the Present*, ed. Peter Englemann, trans. Peter Thomas and Alberto Toscano. Cambridge: Polity.

Badiou, Alain 2009e. *Theory of the Subject*, trans. Bruno Bosteels. London: Continuum.

Badiou, Alain 2010. "Reducing the Sophist to Silence," trans. Susan Spitzer. *Lacanian Ink*, 35: 84–97.

Badiou, Alain. 2011a. *Entretiens 1: 1981–1996*. Paris: Nous.

Badiou, Alain 2011b. *Second Manifesto for Philosophy* [2009], trans. Louise Burchill. Cambridge: Polity.

Badiou, Alain in press. *The Incident at Antioch*, trans. Susan Spitzer. New York: Columbia University Press.

Bartlett, A. J. 2010. "Plato," in A. J. Bartlett and Justin Clemens (eds.), *Alain Badiou: Key Concepts*. Durham: Acumen.

Bartlett, A. J. 2011. *Badiou and Plato: An Education by Truths*. Edinburgh: Edinburgh University Press.

Beckett, Samuel 1981. *Mal vu mal dit / Ill Seen Ill Said*, trans. Samuel Beckett. Paris: Les Éditions de Minuit.

Blackmore, A. M. and E. H. Blackmore (trans.) 2000. *Six French Poets of the Nineteenth Century: Lamartine, Hugo, Baudelaire, Verlaine, Rimbaud, Mallarmé*. Oxford: Oxford University Press.

Clemens, Justin 2001. "Platonic Meditations: The Work of Alain Badiou," *Pli*, 11: 200–29.

Constant, Benjamin 1988. "Des réactions politiques," in Benjamin Constant, *De la Force du gouvernement actuel de la France*. Paris: Flammarion.

Corneille, Pierre 1996. *Horace*, trans. Alan Brownjohn. London: Angle Books.

Corneille, Pierre 2007. *Oeuvres complètes*. Paris: Gallimard.

Gide, André 1949. *The Fruits of the Earth* [*Les Nourritures terrestres*, 1897], trans. Dorothy Bussy. New York: Knopf.

Hallward, Peter 2003. *Badiou: A Subject to Truth*. Minneapolis, MN: University of Minnesota Press.

Heidegger, Martin 1976. Interview taken by Rudolf Augstein and Georg Wolff, September 23, 1966. *Der Spiegel*. (Also available at http://lacan.com/heidespie.html).

Homer 2011. *The Iliad*, trans. Richmond Lattimore. Chicago, IL: University of Chicago Press.

Kant, Immanuel 1949. *Critique of Practical Reason and Other Writings in Moral Philosophy*, trans. and ed. Lewis White Beck. Chicago, IL: University of Chicago Press.

Kant, Immanuel 1999. *The Critique of Pure Reason*, trans. Paul Guyer and Allen Wood. Cambridge: Cambridge University Press.

Lacan, Jacques 1977. *Écrits: A Selection*, trans. Alan Sheridan. New York: Norton.

Lacan, Jacques 1988. *The Seminar of Jacques Lacan. Book I: Freud's Papers on Technique 1953–1954* [1975], ed. Jacques-Alain Miller, trans. John Forrester. Cambridge: Cambridge University Press.

Lacan, Jacques 1992. *The Seminar of Jacques Lacan, Book VII: The Ethics of Psychoanalysis 1959–1960* [1986], ed. Jacques-Alain Miller, trans. Dennis Porter. New York: Norton.

Mallarmé, Stéphane 2006. *Collected Poems and Other Verse*, trans. E. H. and A. M. Blackmore. Oxford: Oxford University Press.

Mao Zedong 1957. "On the Correct Handling of Contradictions among the

People." Available at http://www.marxists.org/reference/archive/mao/selected-works/volume-5/mswv5_58.htm

Mao Zedong 1961–77. *Selected Works*. Beijing: Foreign Languages Press, vols. 2 and 9.

Marcus Aurelius 1998. *The Meditations of Marcus Aurelius Antoninus*, trans. A. S. L. Farquharson. Oxford: Oxford University Press.

Marx, Karl, and Friedrich Engels 1998. *The German Ideology*. Amherst, MA: Prometheus Books.

Marx, Karl, and Friedrich Engels 2002. *The Communist Manifesto*, trans. Samuel Moore. London: Penguin.

Mauss, Marcel 2000. *The Gift: The Form and Reason for Exchange in Archaic Societies*, trans. W. D. Halls. New York: Norton.

Nietzsche, Friedrich 1974. *The Gay Science: With a Prelude in Rhymes and an Appendix of Songs*, trans. Walter Kaufmann. New York: Vintage Books.

Pessoa, Fernando 1998. *Fernando Pessoa and Co: Selected Poems*, trans. Richard Zenith. New York: Grove.

Plato 1968. *Republic*, trans. Allan Bloom. New York: Basic Books.

Plato 1987. *The Republic*, trans. and ed. Desmond Lee. London: Penguin.

Plato 2004. *The Republic*, trans. C. D. C. Reeve. Indianapolis, IN: Hackett Publishing Company.

Plato 2009. *Theaetetus*, trans. Benjamin Jowett. Rockville, MD: Serenity Press.

Rimbaud, Arthur 1998. *Poésies*. Paris: Gallimard.

Rimbaud, Arthur 2009. *Oeuvres complètes*. Paris: Gallimard.

Spinoza, Baruch 2005. *Ethics,* trans. Edwin Curley. London: Penguin.

Sun Tsu 1971. *The Art of War*, trans. Samuel B. Griffith. Oxford: Oxford University Press.

Wittgenstein, Ludwig 1999. *Tractatus Logico-Philosophicus*, trans. David Pears and Brian McGuiness. New York: Routledge.

INDEX